POSITIVE
PSYCHOLOGY

Sara Miller McCune founded SAGE Publishing in 1965 to support the dissemination of usable knowledge and educate a global community. SAGE publishes more than 1000 journals and over 800 new books each year, spanning a wide range of subject areas. Our growing selection of library products includes archives, data, case studies and video. SAGE remains majority owned by our founder and after her lifetime will become owned by a charitable trust that secures the company's continued independence.

Los Angeles | London | New Delhi | Singapore | Washington DC | Melbourne

POSITIVE PSYCHOLOGY

THE SCIENCE OF WELL-BEING

JOHN M. ZELENSKI

Los Angeles | London | New Delhi
Singapore | Washington DC | Melbourne

Los Angeles | London | New Delhi
Singapore | Washington DC | Melbourne

SAGE Publications Ltd
1 Oliver's Yard
55 City Road
London EC1Y 1SP

SAGE Publications Inc.
2455 Teller Road
Thousand Oaks, California 91320

SAGE Publications India Pvt Ltd
B 1/I 1 Mohan Cooperative Industrial Area
Mathura Road
New Delhi 110 044

SAGE Publications Asia-Pacific Pte Ltd
3 Church Street
#10-04 Samsung Hub
Singapore 049483

Editor: Robert Patterson
Assistant editor: Katie Rabot
Production editor: Imogen Roome
Copyeditor: Neil Dowden
Proofreader: Leigh C. Smithson
Indexer: Silvia Benvenuto
Marketing manager: Tamara Navaratnam
Cover design: Wendy Scott
Typeset by: C&M Digitals (P) Ltd, Chennai, India
Printed in the UK

Library of Congress Control Number: 2019943574

British Library Cataloguing in Publication data

A catalogue record for this book is available from the British Library

ISBN 978-1-4739-0214-5
ISBN 978-1-4739-0215-2 (pbk)

At SAGE we take sustainability seriously. Most of our products are printed in the UK using responsibly sourced papers and boards. When we print overseas we ensure sustainable papers are used as measured by the PREPS grading system. We undertake an annual audit to monitor our sustainability.

To Michael Zelenski, my father and first writing teacher

Contents

CONTENTS

CONTENTS

About the Author

John Zelenski is a Professor of Psychology at Carleton University in Ottawa, Canada. As a researcher and director of the Carleton University Happiness Laboratory, he studies individual differences in happiness, and how personality manifests itself 'in the moment' as emotional, behavioural, and cognitive processes. His recent work has focused on two areas: the causes and consequences of social behaviour (e.g. in relation to the personality trait of introversion–extraversion), and the links among nature, people's sense of connection to nature (nature relatedness), happiness, and environmentally sustainable behaviour. He has also taught a range of personality, methods, and positive psychology courses at Carleton and around the world with Semester at Sea.

Acknowledgements

I am grateful to many: my teachers, mentors, colleagues, and students, to the team at SAGE, and to family and friends who have provided encouragement for this book and shaped my thinking about positive psychology. In particular, Cheryl Harasymchuk, Katie Gunnell, Chris Davis, Zack van Allen, and Eve-Marie Blouin-Hudon have generously and skilfully provided assistance and feedback on this project.

How to Use This Book

CHAPTER INTRODUCTIONS
AND CONCLUSIONS

Each chapter contains an introduction to introduce you to the area under discussion and a conclusion that summarizes the key information to take away.

IN FOCUS

The 'In Focus' sections highlight cutting-edge and interesting research developments to provide you with emerging insights and controversies that arise from constantly evolving areas of research.

RESEARCH CASE

The 'Research Case' sections look at a specific piece of research, key studies, or theory in closer detail to help you understand the links between study methods and conclusions.

TRY IT

The 'Try It' sections have various questionnairres or exercises for you to try out theories and practices for yourself!

TEST YOURSELF

The 'Test Yourself' sections contain questions that are designed to test your understanding as you progress through each chapter.

WEB LINKS

There are 'Web Links' at the end of each chapter to point you in the right direction when you would like to know more about a given topic.

FURTHER READING

Each chapter has collated a range of articles and books for you to read if you wish to explore this area further.

ONLINE RESOURCES

A newly introduced key phrase or piece of terminology will be emboldened throughout the text. For a more detailed definition of these phrases please visit https://study.sagepub.com/positivepsychology to view the glossary. You will also find instructor questions and student MCQs for further learning.

Part I

Introduction

1

Describing the Science of Positive Psychology

INTRODUCTION

Imagine you wake up to a new day, have a small breakfast, and then open your web browser to see the headline "Government begins adjusting tax policy to maximize happiness". How would you react? Whether it's along the lines of "Impossible – they'll have no money" or more "It's about time!", that headline is becoming increasingly likely. Leaving aside the specifics of tax policy, many countries' governments now want to measure citizens' happiness. They are working with social scientists to develop national indicators of well-being, and a core component of these measurements will involve asking people how happy they feel.

For example, in 2010 UK Prime Minister David Cameron announced that government would begin measuring the happiness of its citizens (Stratton, 2010). The idea is that this would provide a useful tool in developing government policy. With these data, the UK Office for National Statistics noted a small increase in happiness over 2013, and some suggested that hosting the Olympics in London might have contributed to this (BBC News, 2013). The UK's happiness index is similar to Bhutan's long popularized measure of gross national happiness (see Musikanski, 2014). Such measures are often justified by contrasting them with economic indicators. Governments have long relied on economic data to make decisions. As one example of an economic indicator, *gross domestic product* is the full sum of a country's economic activity. It is carefully assessed, and its changes are frequently reported in the media. However, as American Robert Kennedy (1968) articulated in a moving speech at the University of Kansas, "it measures everything … except that which makes life worth living". It does not allow for the health of our children, the quality of their education, or the joy of their play. It does not include the beauty of our poetry or the strength of our marriages, the intelligence of our public debate or the integrity of our public officials. It measures neither our wit nor our courage, neither our wisdom nor our learning, neither our compassion nor our devotion to our country …

Kennedy was describing a limitation of economic indicators. Although they are meant to measure (at least proxies of) progress and quality of life, they do it in a way that leaves important gaps because they focus on money. There may always be ineffable aspects of human nature that resist quantification, but governments are now assessing 'the things that matter' more broadly by asking people how happy they are. The idea is that by measuring well-being more directly, societies can adjust policies to increase it. This argument has rapidly gained popularity over the last few years.

Kennedy's speech is over 50 years old, and its sentiments can be traced back even further. Then why do we see countries beginning to take national happiness indicators seriously now? The answer to that question takes us to a beach in Hawaii, a fitting setting for the beginnings of the positive psychology movement. On this beach, two influential psychologists had a chance meeting while on holiday with their families: Martin Seligman, who was well known for research on learned helplessness in dogs and then learned optimism with people, and Mihaly Csikszentmihalyi, whose distinctive name is nearly synonymous with work on the state of total absorption known as **flow**. As he later recounted (Csikszentmihalyi & Nakamura, 2011), the two began talking about the future of psychology, and found common ground in thinking that it could become broader or, specifically, more positive. They noted that mainstream psychology seemed to focus on mental illness, maladaptive behaviour, irrationality, prejudice, aggression, and so on, but that much less work focused on happiness, optimal performance, and exceptional abilities.

Professors often have lofty conversations like this, and most of them achieve few tangible results. This conversation was an exception. Seligman was about to become president of the American Psychological Association, a large and powerful organization of researchers, teachers, practitioners, and students in the USA. With the prominence of the APA presidency, the resources of that organization, and a tremendous amount of skill and effort, musings on a Hawaiian beach became a force for change in psychology; they hatched the positive psychology movement.

A detailed history of how this was accomplished is probably not the best way to tempt students into this fascinating area of psychology, so I will keep it brief. In a nutshell, Seligman and Csiksenztmihalyi began by contacting prominent psychologists and asking them to nominate young 'rising stars' who might be interested in the movement. They selected a group of promising scholars and, at a luxurious resort in Akumal, Mexico, together developed a manifesto that provided an initial definition of positive psychology. It described positive psychology as being about optimal human functioning, and it created a roadmap for implementing the new movement (see www.ppc.sas.upenn.edu/opportunities/conference-archives). This involved putting the 'political' machinery of psychology into action, for example with special issues of journals, research funding, lucrative research prizes, networks of scholars who promoted each other's work, and so on. The early days of the positive psychology movement are represented by special issues of the prominent journal *American Psychologist*, first with a series of articles by senior researchers in January 2000, and then by more junior researchers in March 2001.

Undergraduate and graduate courses in positive psychology began to appear, along with webpages, handbooks, and textbooks. (For a more critical history, see also Yen, 2010.) Undoubtedly, the current popularity and scope of positive psychology owe much to the US movement that took shape at the turn of the millennium. Yet the content of positive psychology has a much longer, broader, and more international history. The movement collected and highlighted previous research on positive topics, while also generating a burst of new studies and applications (Rusk & Waters, 2013). But we are getting ahead of ourselves. What is this positive psychology anyway?

DEFINING POSITIVE PSYCHOLOGY

Cramming a comprehensive description of an entire sub-discipline into a single sentence is unlikely to succeed, and this is certainly true with positive psychology. Many definitions have been proposed; after searching publications on positive psychology, Hart and Sasso (2011) assembled a collection 53 definitions! For our purposes, **positive psychology** *is the parts of psychology that deal with (positive) experiences, dispositions, contexts, and processes, in individuals and groups, that facilitate well-being, achievement, and harmony.* To unpack this a bit, psychology is the science (i.e. research) of mental life and behaviour, and the application of that knowledge (e.g. in therapy, personnel selection, policy recommendations). Psychology is about people's thoughts, feeling, social interactions, habits, dispositions, responses to environments, and so on, and understanding how these develop and change over time, their physiological correlates, and their associations with health or lack thereof. Positive psychology is the positive parts (topics or perspectives) within this enterprise. This sounds simple enough, but things become more complex when we take time to consider what we mean by 'positive' – it can be understood in many different ways. Our working definition uses the terms 'well-being' (health and happiness broadly), 'achievement' (success, fulfilment), and 'harmony' (considering individuals, groups, and environments) as shorthand clarifications, but there is much more to consider.

It is probably impossible to come up with a set of 'necessary and sufficient' criteria that provide an ironclad definition of positive psychology. We will explore the strengths and weaknesses of various approaches, and some seem clearly better than others. Nonetheless, it is probably best to view positive psychology as made up of things that have a 'family resemblance' (cf. Mervis & Rosch, 1981). With some thought and practice, you will be able to identify topics that are part of the positive psychology family, even if you cannot come up with a single rule that is distinctive and applies to each. This is not uncommon. For example, think of the category 'bird'. We might think of defining birds as creatures that fly, but penguins and kiwis do not fit. We might think that only birds have feathers, but then so did some dinosaurs, so the feathers rule seems overly inclusive. It is not essential that we define positive psychology with one reducible criterion for it to be useful (Diener, 2003).

WAYS OF UNDERSTANDING 'POSITIVE'

When we speak of a positive psychology, to what should the 'positive' apply? One way to understand the scope of positive psychology is to decide which parts should be positive. There are at least four possibilities, which are considered below: positive intentions of psychologists; positive ideology about human nature; a similar but less rigid appreciative stance on human nature; and positive topics (see Sheldon, 2011).

Positive as Good Intentions

The first way we could understand positive psychology is by including the psychologists who wish to make others' lives more positive, through either research or applications. I believe most positive psychologists have this worthy goal. When we study the personality characteristics of happy people or which psychological exercises can improve moods, the hope is that this information might someday be usefully applied. When a life coach helps people refine their goals, the intention is to improve those lives. However, 'good intentions' does not seem like the best way to define positive psychology. Many psychologists whose work does not seem to fit under the positive psychology umbrella still care deeply about improving the lives of others. For example, the psychologists who study the links between traumatic brain injury and mental illness do not wish either of these on people; rather, they hope to generate knowledge that will eventually help alleviate suffering. This is laudable and filled with good intentions, but probably does not fit within the field of positive psychology (though it may, depending on the perspective they take – read on!). As a comparison, we do not speak of 'positive biology' when medical doctors help heal their patients. Good intentions are found throughout science; they do not distinguish positive psychologists uniquely.

Positive as an Ideological Perspective

Another way we could define positive psychology is with an ideological assumption or stance. For example, like the humanistic psychological tradition, we might assume that people are naturally good or growth oriented (unless thwarted by disruptive experiences). This sounds very positive indeed, but it can be problematic from a scientific perspective (Held, 2004), something that is also very important to positive psychology. For example, psychologist Dan Batson has vigorously argued that people often help one another for altruistic reasons, that is without regard for compensation or reciprocation (Batson, 2014). This can be contrasted with more selfish motivations; for example, perhaps the helper is actually motivated by the small favours, reputation, or mood boosts that can follow. There is certainly nothing wrong with taking the position that people are altruistic, but we must also put that assumption to the test. Indeed, Batson has engaged the altruism debate with both logic and psychological experiments. Psychologists continue to debate this issue, and both sides have provided research findings that argue for their positions. Large questions about human nature are not conclusively answered with a couple experiments; those issues are larger.

With this in mind, it seems problematic to define an entire branch of psychology with an assumption about human nature. Our *theories* can make these assumptions, but we must then put them to the test. When results contradict a theory it is falsified and we must develop a new theory that can account for those discrepant results. This is ultimately how we increase our knowledge about (positive) psychology. Thus, to make progress in understanding positive psychology, we must be willing to reject some early assumptions. We do not want these rejections to falsify the entire area! If we define positive psychology as positive assumptions about human nature, we risk having positive psychology 'disproven'. Analogies to other fields help underscore the issue; is it possible to falsify biology, chemistry, or economics in their entirety? No, even though prominent ideas in those fields have been revised over time. In economics, the central assumption that people act in purely rational, self-interested ways now seems implausible, yet the field continues to produce important social science because it can revise this assumption. In positive psychology, our knowledge and theories will evolve, and we can identify what is positive about positive psychology in ways that do not put its existence to the test.

All that said, there is another, more immediate and pragmatic reason to avoid taking a rigid or strong ideological position: scientific integrity. You may not care about saving positive psychology from existential threat, particularly if the easily ascribed assumptions about the goodness of people turn out to be wrong. It is also true that positive psychology could exist for a long time before broad assumptions were convincingly refuted. Nonetheless, a willingness to test and disprove core ideas is essential to science, and it is essential to its credibility. If positive psychology is defined by rigid assumptions about human nature, it is difficult for credible science to come from it. We do not want to produce easily dismissed or agenda-driven 'evidence' like that coming from the tobacco industry or Holocaust deniers. Thankfully, there are better ways to define positive psychology.

Positive as an Appreciative Stance

An alternative is to align positive psychology with an appreciative stance about human beings. At first glance, this view of positive psychology may seem similar to a positive ideology, but it is different in an important way. Rather than assuming that people are good, a researcher with an appreciative stance is able to collect information objectively (or at least as objectively as humans are capable of), yet look at this information from a positive, or appreciative, perspective. Even while recognizing that humans sometimes make errors, get sad, and do silly or destructive things, a positive psychologist might think that, on balance, people are pretty neat. One can have a sense of appreciation for human accomplishments or quirks, and see individual failings in a larger context of wonder.

For example, writing on the blog Data Colada, Nelson (2014) described a study that revealed the classic 'false consensus effect' (Ross, Greene, & House, 1977); that is, people sometimes draw on their own behaviour when judging the behaviour of others, often leading to biased answers. We perceive 'false consensus' between ourselves and others. In Nelson's study, this bias was evident when shoppers were asked how many other people bought various products on their last trip to the grocery store. For example, those who had purchased laundry detergent on their last trip estimated that 69 per cent of others did too, whereas those who did not buy detergent thought that a mere 29 per cent of others did on their last trip. (The actual number was 42 per cent.) This pattern emerged across all 18 products the researchers asked about – a classic judgement error now found in the domain of shopping. What is noteworthy about Nelson's blog post is that he took an additional step and looked at the data in another way. When he averaged the estimates across people (regardless of whether or not they purchased the items), he found a very strong correlation ($r = .95$) between the actual percentage of people who purchased a given item and the research participants' average estimates of that percentage. As a group, participants identified which were common and which were uncommon purchases very well. This can be seen as an example of another robust phenomenon: the wisdom of crowds. Even when individuals have difficulty knowing or guessing something accurately (Sir Francis Galton's classic example is the weight of an ox at a fair), the average of many people's ratings is often surprisingly accurate. To bring this long example to a close, Nelson's blog post clearly demonstrates how psychologists can have a sense of appreciation for human psychology. This is a potentially useful way to think of the 'positive' in positive psychology. In Nelson's own words, "As a judgment and decision making researcher, one of my tasks is to identify idiosyncratic shortcomings in human thinking (e.g., the false consensus effect). Nevertheless, under the right circumstances, I can be entranced by accuracy. In this case, I marvel at the wisdom of crowds." (It may be worth noting that Nelson probably does not consider himself a positive psychologist.)

As useful and uplifting as an appreciative stance can be, we should remain cautious of a slippery slope towards ideology or more problematic positive biases if the appreciation goes too far. We must consider the broader context. I believe the greatest strength of positive psychology has been its ability to *rebalance* psychology. In the early 2000s, the movement probably had such rapid influence because psychology had become overly concerned with the unpleasant and destructive aspects of human nature. One might say psychology had slipped down the slope on the other side of the hill. (In the early 2000s when reporters discussed national measures of happiness with me, they often suggested suicide rates as a good proxy – thank goodness we are setting the bar a bit higher these days!) Adding some appreciation for what goes right seemed to put psychology on a more balanced, accurate, and objective footing. Thus, it seems healthy and useful that (positive) psychologists cultivate a sense of appreciation for human nature, but do so with some flexibility, open-mindedness, and lucidity. This need not make them different from all other psychologists, but it does seem a reasonable feature of positive psychology.

Positive as a Set of Topics

If you told friends that you were taking a course on 'positive psychology', what kinds of things would they assume you are learning about? Happiness? Love? Gratitude? Achievement? These seem like good candidates (and they are things we will get to). In this vein, one way we can define the 'positive' in positive psychology is via its topics; positive psychology is about positive things. For example, positive psychology is about forgiveness rather than revenge, joy rather than sadness, cooperation rather than competition, resilience rather than defeat. Positive psychology seems to be about the positive poles in dichotomies such as these. Positive topics may describe positive psychology reasonably well, but there is more to consider.

First, this might just seem like a word game. Is there really anything different about positive psychology if we merely focus on new terms to study the same old issues? No. But there can be more to this approach, and in potentially useful ways. For example, consider the two statements "I want to eliminate James's depression" versus "I want to make James happier". The second version might be understood as merely restating the first, but it can also mean more. When we focus, as much of psychology did in the twentieth century, on merely alleviating distress, we neglect the possibility of going further. After alleviating his depression, why not help James flourish and thrive? Is there a way his wife Maxine, who has never been depressed, might become lastingly happier or more fulfilled than she is today? Consider this simple diagram:

$$-10\ -9\ -8\ -7\ -6\ -5\ -4\ -3\ -2\ -1\ \mathbf{0}\ +1\ +2\ +3\ +4\ +5\ +6\ +7\ +8\ +9\ +10$$

Positive psychology is not about bringing people from negative to 0, but rather about focusing on what lies in the positive territory of this metaphorical number line (or literally interpreted as a scale of happiness). When we focus on terms or topics in the positive zone, it goes beyond word games, instead prompting new domains of study and application. Freud's goals were modest in this regard; for example, as he is frequently quoted, "much will be gained if we succeed in transforming your hysterical misery into common unhappiness" (Breuer & Freud, 1957, p. 305). Whereas Freud seemed more focused on the negative side of 0, we now know that most people are happy (Diener & Diener, 1996) most of the time (Zelenski & Larsen, 2000). Thus, a positive approach is not simply unrealistically 'Pollyannaish'; it is necessary for psychology to develop a full understanding of typical human experience and behaviour.

In this vein, consider the intriguing definition of positive psychology as "nothing more than the scientific study of ordinary human strengths and virtues. Positive psychology revisits 'the average person,' with an interest in finding out what works, what is right, and what is improving" (Sheldon & King, 2001, p. 216). Implicit in this definition is the idea that positive psychology need not be only about the +10s. Ordinary and typical behaviour is often positive; we do not need to seek out genius, fame, or euphoria to find positive psychology.

We can apply the *greater than zero* analogy beyond happiness, for example to personal strengths, intergroup relations, optimal performance, and so on. Still, the analogy may not easily accommodate some important parts of positive psychology. For example, trauma, adversity, and mortality all have a place in positive psychology. From the beginning, **resilience** was a core part of justifying and explaining the need for positive psychology. When traumatic events, such as natural disasters, industrial accidents, or assaults, occur we expect that people will suffer enduring and unpleasant consequences. Many do, and they certainly deserve attention. However, other people seem to cope quite well following objectively horrific events. They have relatively little post-traumatic stress, and some people even report psychological benefits (e.g. finding meaning) following trauma (Davis, Wohl, & Verberg, 2007). Positive psychology is definitely about studying these resilient people. Trauma is a key context where our intuition is understandably to focus on the injured, but where learning from the resilient, or 'what goes right', can provide valuable insights (Meredith et al., 2011).

Even if we are most concerned with the troubled, a positive perspective is useful. By analogy, if we wanted to repair a broken machine, having access to a well-functioning example would be very helpful; if we were building a safer automobile, we would examine models that survived crashes, not just those that were crushed. Thus, positive psychology is about more than mere cheerfulness, and calls to more fully examine the 'dark side' of positive psychology have grown as the area develops (e.g. Sheldon, Kashdan, & Steger, 2011; Wong, 2011). This can include unpleasant things that might produce value, for example persistence through adversity, difficulty that builds character, or a sense of mortality that deepens spirituality. It can also mean taking a full look at seemingly pleasant experiences and characteristics, for example the potential disadvantages of extremely high happiness (Oishi, Diener, & Lucas, 2007).

To sum up, in addition to the perspective we take, positive psychology can be described by its topics. These include things that are clearly 'north of neutral' (recall our metaphorical number line), and it also includes 'doing alright under the circumstances' (in contexts that are clearly difficult or unpleasant). In addition, it is important to keep in mind that seemingly or primarily positive experiences, personal characteristics, or circumstances are often more complex than they appear at first glance. Most things in life involve trade-offs; even a clearly preferable option is rarely best in every way and all circumstances. It is important for positive psychology to take a complete view of these 'positive' topics.

By this point, you should have a better sense of positive psychology. Although there is no one single defining rule, considering things like perspective and subject matter helps describe the family resemblance that bonds positive psychology's various parts. To this point I have focused on *where* to put the positive (i.e. intentions, ideology, appreciation, or topics). However, I have neglected one key issue: How do we decide *what* is positive?

ASSESSING POSITIVITY

Defining positivity seems easy, yet a bit of reflection also reveals that people sometimes disagree about what is positive or good. Individuals' judgements of what is desirable may change over time, perhaps even many times during a day. For example, things that were pleasurable when very hungry suddenly shift after a large meal. How, then, can we decide what is positive or good in psychology? First, it is worth noting that much of psychology is neutral (Gable & Haidt, 2005) – topics need not be 'negative' to fall outside positive psychology. Some knowledge about human nature will be useful to positive psychology without being positive psychology per se (e.g. how people think, generally). That said, when we do seek to know whether or not something is positive, we can consider three things: choices, values, and subjective experiences (Diener & Suh, 1997; Gable & Haidt, 2005; Linley, Joseph, Harrington, & Wood, 2006).

Choice

The things that people consistently choose can be viewed as positive, an assumption common in economics. We can infer positivity or desirability from the choice. For example, because Peter decides to ride his bike to school most days (rather than drive a car, take a bus, or walk), we can infer that biking is optimal, at least for Peter in his current circumstances. If there were a better alternative, Peter would choose it instead. His choice reveals his preference, or what is positive for Peter. In a classic demonstration of infants' need (preference) for touch and physical comfort, Harlow (1958) gave baby monkeys raised in the laboratory two choices of surrogate mothers. One 'mother' was constructed from cloth and foam and warmed by a light bulb – soft and warm – but it did not offer any food. The other 'mother' gave food, but was made of wire mesh and was not physically comforting. The infants' choice was very clear: young monkeys spent the vast majority of their time clinging to the soft surrogate mother. Their choice strongly suggests that the cuddly feeling was more positive than food, except during the brief periods of hunger that drove the young monkeys to the wire mother for food. (The result might seem obvious now, but at the time prominent behaviourists argued that the rewards of food explained the bond between mothers and infants.) Developmental psychologists apply similar logic when studying human infants. They make the inference, supported by research, that infants choose to look at things they prefer more (e.g. Quinn, Kelly, Lee, Pascalis, & Slater, 2008). The choice tells us what is positive.

Values

We can also determine what is positive by considering personal or social values. To continue our previous example, perhaps Peter values environmental sustainability and health, and he decides to bike in order to fit his behaviour to these values by getting exercise and producing little pollution. In this case, the values tell us what is good, referring to larger systems such as laws, religious teachings, cultural norms, rational thought, and so on. There are many sources of values, and individuals and cultures look to different authorities and come to different conclusions about which things to prioritize. Psychological science has sometimes been hesitant to study values. In positive psychology, however, avoiding values is difficult. When we seek to understand 'the good life' we must try to understand what people value, what makes life good. This does not mean that the science of positive psychology determines what is good in an objective way, but it must grapple with the issue of what is good.

An early task of positive psychology's founders was to develop a list of values and their associated 'character strengths' (Peterson & Seligman, 2004). They looked to philosophy, religion, literature, children's books, and so on, and across different cultures, trying to identify common themes of universally valued characteristics. The list of strengths – things most people value – can be seen as an early map for the contours of positive psychology. Chapter 4 provides the full list, but examples include curiosity, kindness, fairness, spirituality, and bravery. When we identify what is valued, it helps define those things as positive, and suggests that the processes promoting them are part of positive psychology.

Subjective Experiences

The third way of determining positivity rests on subjective experience. Consider Peter's bike riding again. Perhaps he rides his bike simply because it feels good to do so; the perception of speed and moderate physical exertion give him pleasure. Here we decide that bike riding is positive because the experience is pleasant. Very simply, if it feels good, it is positive (within this criterion). Thinking about subjective experience suggests happiness is central to positive psychology. Of course, happiness does not exhaust the scope of positive psychology (e.g. see previous paragraph), but it is a very important part. Moreover, although some sources of happiness seem completely hedonistic, pleasure often follows from more meaningful endeavours. For example, in one study, researchers tracked people's moods over the course of a few days. Some of the research participants were asked to eat ice cream on two of those days, a second group was asked to write about things for which they were grateful, and a third group was asked to write about the weather. Results showed that eating ice cream and reflecting on gratitude similarly boosted positive moods on those days, compared to writing about the weather (Linley, Dovey, de Bruin, Transler, Wilkinson, Maltby, & Hurling, 2013). Beyond the short-term changes in mood that ice cream or gratitude might facilitate, happiness over the long term also seems to have important consequences. Chapter 3 considers this in more detail, but research suggests that happiness can promote occupational success and even longer life (Diener & Chan, 2011; Lyubomirsky, King, & Diener, 2005).

Our three criteria for knowing what is positive – choice, values, and subjective experience – often agree about what is positive. In the example of Peter's biking, the ways of determining what is good align with one another; choice, values, and experience are congruent. However, this is not always the case. Different ways of determining what is positive can sometimes lead to different conclusions. For example, people often choose things frequently and regularly that are relatively neutral with respect to values or pleasure (e.g. always beginning with the right foot when putting on socks). Sometimes the different approaches lead to opposite conclusions. For example, having sex is typically pleasurable, even when it would be considered negative according to values (e.g. if one is monogamously committed to another person, unmarried, or in a public place). Not everything that feels good 'is' good when we consider values. As is apparent in this last example, people can also disagree about what is good. This is perhaps most obvious when we can identify contradictions in values (e.g. whether it is good or bad or neutral to have sex outside of marriage), but it can also occur in experience (e.g. some people enjoy eating raw fish and others do not). In sum, determining what is good or positive is complex and worthy of discussion in and of itself. Choices, values, and experience can all provide guides, but none provide a definitive answer. Can you think of some examples where they align or conflict?

In Focus

Research-Based Approaches to Describing Positive Psychology

Defining positive psychology is complicated, and some psychologists have tried to address the issue in the way they answer other questions about psychology: with research. That is, they have taken an empirical approach to figuring out what positive psychology is. One effort gathered, coded, and counted the ways in which publications,

(Continued)

researchers, and university courses have considered positive psychology (Hart & Sasso, 2011). With only minor variation across sources (e.g. course outlines vs journal articles), the most frequent topics were happiness and positive features of personality. Slightly less frequently mentioned, but still prominent, were positive interpersonal relationships, sense of meaning, personality growth, and resilience in the face of challenges. As an example, see Table 1.1 for the themes derived from 53 published definitions of positive psychology.

Table 1.1 Positive psychology (PP) themes derived from 53 published definitions

Themes[a]	Frequency[b]	Consensus (%)[c]
Theme 1 views the core of PP as the study of virtues, character strengths, positive personality traits and related attributes and abilities, and talents.	21	39.6
Theme 2 views the core of PP as the study of phenomena indicative of happiness, positive emotional well-being, subjective sense of fulfillment, and satisfaction with the quality of life.	18	34.0
Theme 3 views the core of PP as the study of the developmental process of becoming, growth, fulfillment of capacities, actualization of potential, and development of the highest/authentic self.	11	20.8
Theme 4 views the core of PP as involving the "good life" or "life worth living."	9	17.0
Theme 5 views the core of PP as involving thriving and flourishing.	7	13.2
Theme 6 views the core of PP as involving optimal or adaptive functioning/behaviour, otherwise known as resilience (positive coping under conditions of stress/hardship).	6	11.3

Notes: [a] We adopted a liberal approach to forming the themes. Concepts that were judged to reflect similar underlying content were grouped together. [b] We examined a total of 53 published definitions of positive psychology. The frequency statistic reflects the number of published definitions that included content pertinent to each theme. [c] Given that some of the 53 published definitions that we examined were multi-factorial in nature, the cumulative percent exceeds 100.

Source: Adapted from Hart and Sasso (2011)

Others took a bibliographic, 'big data' approach to find clusters of research topics across 1.7 million published articles (Rusk & Waters, 2013). That is, they identified some core terms that seemed obvious, such as positive psychology, flourishing, gratitude, optimism, virtue, resilience, and so on. To expand the list, they searched published articles to identify other terms that commonly appeared together with the core positive psychology words, and then they added them to the list; for example, altruism, self-efficacy and love. The 233 topics identified in this way are displayed in Figure1.1 as a Wordle.

Figure 1.1   Wordle of positive psychology terms

Note: A Wordle® (www.wordle.net) showing the 233 key PP terms used to identify PP-related documents. The font size of each term is proportional to the square root of the number of times it occurred within the PP-related documents identified. The location of each term has no significance.

Source: Rusk and Waters (2013)

This picture gives a sense of which topics are written about, and how much, in positive psychology. Still, it is good to interpret the details with caution. The procedures relied on computers to do the searching and categorizing (to deal with the 1.7 million potential matches), and the computer algorithm made errors that a human judge would not make. Also, the number of articles is only one indicator of impact or importance. Size is not the only thing that matters. Despite these limitations, the bibliographic analysis

(Continued)

was very clear about another thing: the number of articles published on positive psychology topics has been increasing rapidly over the last 15 years, both in absolute number and as a proportion of all published psychology articles (see also Donaldson, Dollwet, & Rao, 2015). There is no shortage of interesting findings to fill this book, even as there is still much more to study.

POSITIVE PSYCHOLOGY IN CONTEXT

Founders of the positive psychology movement emphasized its differences from traditional psychology (Seligman & Csikszentmihalyi, 2000). This was useful in defining and growing their movement (Yen, 2010), but was also met with some ambivalence, irritation, and critique (Held, 2005; Taylor, 2001). Some felt unfairly excluded, and others pointed to a much longer history of positive topics in psychology. It is clear that positive psychology overlaps considerably with other areas, and many who contribute to it are ambivalent about identifying (exclusively) as positive psychologists. For example, a few years into the movement even its proponents Gable and Haidt (2005) expressed the sentiment, "We do not think of ourselves as rebels, and many of us rarely if ever refer to ourselves as 'positive psychologists.' We merely find that the positive psychology movement helps us study our topics more effectively" (p. 107). Many who contribute to positive psychology see themselves as belonging more to other areas, while having an interest in studying the good life.

Nearly every sub-discipline in psychology rubs up against positive psychology. For example, personality psychology studies the characteristics that differentiate very happy from less happy people. Like positive psychology, health psychology is concerned with human wellness. Both areas share the core notion that health is more than absence of illness, and both have an interest in how prevention can keep people well (e.g. offering support before something goes wrong). Social psychologists have long studied cooperative and prosocial (e.g. helping) behaviour. Cognitive psychology, with its work on creativity, intelligence, and optimal learning strategies, has learned much about clearly positive, valued topics. Developmental psychologists are interested in how all these things unfold over the lifespan. Organizational psychologists and educational psychologists study and apply positive topics in their institutional contexts. Indeed, positive psychology seems to draw from and interact with all areas.

Distinguishing Positive Psychology from Humanistic Psychology

The comparison with humanistic psychology, as a similar movement and sub-discipline, deserves special mention. You may have heard of Maslow's (1943) hierarchy of needs, typically depicted in a pyramid-shaped diagram and topped by the uniquely human need to self-actualize. Carl Rogers (2007) similarly emphasized people's individual uniqueness and the importance of unconditional acceptance from others ('positive regard') in fostering healthy development of the true self. Maslow and Rogers are well-known leaders in humanism, an approach to psychology that shares much with positive psychology. That is, both are prone to an optimistic perspective on human nature. Both focus on helping people thrive, going beyond merely alleviating suffering. Thus, some have argued that positive psychology merely re-branded a long tradition that includes humanistic psychology (Taylor, 2001). Similarly, existential psychology, with a focus on how people find meaning in their lives, is an important predecessor to central topics in positive psychology.

Despite these similarities, distinctions between positive psychology and humanistic or existential psychology are also apparent (see Waterman, 2013). Without a single criterion that defines positive psychology, it is hard to make rigid distinctions from other areas. Nonetheless, the 'family resemblances' of positive psychology and humanistic psychology are a bit different. For example, even when approaching the same topics, the philosophical background, typical methods of gathering information, and the particular research questions tend to differ. Humanistic psychologists are very concerned with the uniqueness of each individual's mental experience (known as phenomenology). For this reason, a person's experience is approached individually; it is seen as very difficult to directly compare it to another person's experience. Research often uses **qualitative methods** (less about numbers) and conclusions are circumscribed, rather than aimed at testing or establishing general truths about humans. In contrast, positive psychologists draw more from **quantitative research** and seek to establish more generalizable truths. These studies frequently compare large groups of people on dimensions that have been defined by the researchers (e.g. scores on a questionnaire) and draw conclusions from statistical tests. Said another way, rather than asking a people where they find meaning in life (and expecting long answers), people might be asked to rate how meaningful life is on a one-to-ten scale, and these scores will be compared to other characteristics, such as religious participation or age. This quantitative approach does not fully capture the richness of individuals, but it does allow positive psychologists to apply the scientific method in ways that are potentially more repeatable and widely applicable.

Much of the distinction between positive and humanistic psychology seems to come down to how much they focus on individual uniqueness versus more general trends. That said, in *applications* of positive psychology (e.g. coaching, counselling), practitioners are often dealing with individual people. I do not mean to suggest that positive psychology practitioners ignore the uniqueness of their clients; instead, they draw insights from the quantitative research of experimental psychology. Much of the positive psychology covered in this book describes what we have learned from this research. However, an important part of positive psychology is what practitioners do with this knowledge (see Chapter 9, which focuses on applications). For example, research shows that positive exercises, such as expressing gratitude, can cause boosts in happiness (Bolier, Haverman, Westerhof, Riper, Smit, & Bohlmeijer, 2013). Practitioners can take these exercises, adjust details to individual needs and contexts, and have relative confidence in the effectiveness of their advice. Ideally, research forms the base of their approach, and some skilful 'art' is employed in its application.

Distinguishing the Science of Positive Psychology from Pop-Culture Advice

Empirical research is a key feature of positive psychology applications, along with the general approach of focusing on strengths rather than weaknesses. This empirical core helps distinguish positive psychology from some other approaches to self-help and advice. Much of 'popular psychology' includes ideas and advice that bear little resemblance to professional or academic psychology. (To make matters even more confusing, popular approaches sometimes co-opt the label 'positive psychology'!) The psychology and self-help sections in bookstores typically contain much that falls outside mainstream psychology as a science and a professional practice. It is certainly possible that some of these gurus offer useful advice, but it is also likely that some others offer useless – or potentially even harmful – advice too (Bergsma, 2008a). A defining feature of (positive) psychology is that it relies on science to arbitrate these things.

Much self-help and popular psychology is not tested or supported in this way. Psychology is a science, and positive psychology very explicitly so (Seligman & Csikszentmihalyi, 2000). Said another way, positive psychology is about collecting data that provides evidence for or against ideas about human flourishing. This is important because other sources, such as common sense, religion, and gurus' intuitions, often offer conflicting advice (Bergsma, 2008b). Research can help determine which (or when) bits of common sense or tradition are correct.

Of course, positive psychologists do not agree about everything either. As in any science, there are sometimes ferocious debates about particular approaches or findings (e.g. see Brown, MacDonald, Samanta, Friedman, & Coyne, 2014; Cole & Fredrickson, 2014). There is also a tension between the desire to rapidly share what psychology is learning about the good life and a slower approach that waits for scientific consensus. These debates are not just at the fringes of positive psychology either. For example, Kashdan and Steger (2011) found it curious that positive psychology founder Martin Seligman published the popular book *Authentic Happiness* only two years after calling for a more positive psychology. Had we learned enough in two years to publicize these 'answers'? Despite these internal debates, virtually all agree that there are many questions that still need to be addressed by research. The key thing, however, is that we agree to sort out unanswered questions and disagreements by gathering research findings. This core value distinguishes positive psychology from other approaches to well-being.

The science of positive psychology is making progress. There are areas where enough evidence has accumulated to make some popular claims untenable. For example, we know that people are not 'blank slates' when it comes to their well-being; dispositions and inheritance matter greatly, though change is still possible (Diener, 2000). Similarly, although not without nuance to explore further, we know that social relationships are essential to human well-being (Peterson, 2006). Meditating atop a mountain in complete isolation may have some benefit, but it will not bring happiness. In addition, we now know that unbridled efforts to increase self-esteem (e.g. by praising even poor performance) are unlikely to produce optimal outcomes (Baumeister, Campbell, Krueger, & Vohs, 2003). Finally, it is very clear that optimal learning occurs when studying is distributed over time, and that testing often promotes retention (Dunlosky, Rawson, Marsh, Nathan, & Willingham, 2013). In other words, quizzes help you learn, and it is better to study regularly and repeatedly (even if briefly), rather than cramming just before evaluations.

Finally, it is useful to distinguish the empirical approach of positive psychology from claims that have only the facade of science. For example, we should be very sceptical about accepting claims that crystals will promote happiness (i.e. beyond their aesthetic charms). Crystal therapy cannot be considered part of positive psychology because it has too many features of pseudoscience (see Lilienfeld, 2005). The 'evidence' around crystal therapy lacks peer-reviewed scientific evidence, correction over time, and connection to other established scientific findings, and has a tendency to rely on anecdote and meaningless jargon. Positive psychology distinguishes itself from some other theories, treatments, and advice concerned with wellness (like crystal therapy or grandma's advice) because it is a science. This does not make it immune from disagreements and errors, but these are corrected and resolved with time and more research.

You may be thinking that my emphasis on the scientific nature of positive psychology sounds defensive. You might also feel uneasy about ascribing the same 'science-ness' to psychology as to the 'hard sciences' like chemistry, biology, or physics. Given the complexity of human behaviour and our relatively limited knowledge (so far!), this intuition is common and understandable. However, science refers not to the amount of accumulated knowledge, but rather to the process of acquiring and evaluating that knowledge. In this way, psychology uses the scientific method in ways that are very similar to chemistry. There are some aspects of psychology that are difficult to measure (e.g. consciousness) or where we have not agreed on what constitutes an accurate, or accurate enough, measure. This is not completely unique to psychology; for example, consider the huge expense and effort that goes into trying to measure a Higgs boson. Developing accurate and reliable measurement tools is an essential part of most sciences, and there is certainly room for improvement in psychology. However, there are many things that we can measure with reasonable precision. Psychology methods often lack the patina of science found in chemistry and physics (e.g. lab coats and fancy equipment, though magnetic resonance imaging (MRI) research takes a step in this direction), but the process remains essentially the same. These observations lead Srivastava (2009) to a pun, calling psychology (and his great blog about it) *The Hardest Science*. Positive psychologists certainly face challenges in generating knowledge, but the difficult process is scientific; it follows the scientific method.

Many of the things we will discuss fall somewhere short of having definitive answers. Positive psychology has learned much about human well-being, but there is still much active debate and enquiry, and many relevant topics that have not received serious attention. For this reason, you are invited to engage in the material with a critical stance. You may have questions or concerns about the support for some ideas, and that can be a healthy reaction. However, it is also important to be open minded when encountering new ideas in a class, and to be aware of personal beliefs and biases. Said another way, you do not need to accept the conclusions of every study we discuss. However, contrary intuitions do not constitute strong arguments on their own. Every study has flaws, yet we are more likely to notice them when we disagree with the results. Often flaws in individual studies are convincingly addressed by other studies. It is good to be sceptical of claims – ask questions! Yet complete cynicism is problematic; be careful not to dismiss things out of hand. Sometimes progress in (positive psychological) science is slower than we would like, but our knowledge does accumulate.

METHODOLOGICAL APPROACHES

The scientific approach defines positive psychology, but there are infinite ways it can be applied. The rest of this book will provide many examples, but in this first chapter we consider some general approaches and the logic behind their knowledge claims. At the most abstract level, science is about making systematic observations about the world. As we learn more about phenomena, we refine our measurements and record keeping, and develop clever new ways to make observations. We also develop knowledge, and this knowledge allows us to make and test more specific predictions about future observations, or *hypotheses*. Much research in psychology takes one of two broad approaches: correlational or experimental. Interpreting results correctly requires that we distinguish between them. We will explore these approaches with an example about money and happiness, and introduce some of the jargon psychological scientists use to talk about research methods.

Parents, teachers, and leaders often encourage generosity. The biblical aphorism "It is better to give than to receive" is heard far beyond religious buildings. Outside those buildings, though, a jocular voice may respond "Better for whom?" The not so subtle suggestion is that generosity may not be as advantageous for the giver as our institutional leaders want us to believe. Are there benefits to giving? This question begins the scientific process. The first task is to narrow down what might be tallied up as we consider 'better'. There are many possibilities. For example, our jocular critic might be thinking only of the concrete money, goods, or favours that are exchanged. (In this case, the recipient is clearly better off.) A minister might measure the transaction in terms of progress towards eternal bliss. (Exactly how many good deeds are needed for heaven's cover charge these days?) As positive psychologists, we might look to a different currency: happiness. Indeed, this is what Elizabeth Dunn and colleagues have done in a series of studies on happiness and prosocial spending, or spending money on others (Dunn, Aknin, & Norton, 2014). By focusing on happiness, we have narrowed the question somewhat, something essential to conducting a study. Indeed, most questions require many individual studies before an answer becomes clear. As we will see, even looking at 'better' in narrower terms of *happiness* requires a variety of approaches.

The Correlational Approach

The **correlational approach** focuses on determining whether, and how strongly, two things are linked. To examine the link between prosocial spending and happiness, one study compared the overall amounts that people spent on others with the spenders' levels of happiness. More specifically, a nationally representative group of over 600 Americans rated their annual income, general happiness, and how much they spent monthly on bills, gifts for self, gifts for others, and charities (Dunn, Aknin, & Norton, 2008a). Results revealed an association, or correlation, between spending on others (gifts and charities) and ratings of happiness. On average, the more people spent on others, the more happiness they reported. This kind of association is typically represented as a **correlation coefficient**, communicated with the statistical shorthand 'r'. In this case $r = .11$ (Dunn, Aknin, & Norton, 2008b). You may be thinking that that the correlation between prosocial spending and happiness would only apply in wealthy countries like the USA, but another large study found the correlation in most of the 120 countries studied (Aknin et al., 2013). The US results also held after statistically controlling for annual income; richer people reported more happiness and more spending, but this did not explain the link between prosocial spending and happiness because they also spent more on themselves. Thus, the correlation appears to be robust across different levels of wealth.

These findings are intriguing, but what can we conclude? Might giving money to others benefit the self (with happiness), as the saying suggests? Results are consistent with the idea that spending on others could cause happiness, but they are not strong evidence. This is because the results are equally consistent with another possibility: that happiness causes generosity.

Correlations do not imply causality – this is a key limitation of correlations. Perhaps those already quite satisfied with their lives find it easier to give resources to others. The direction of causation could go either way. In this example, it seems quite plausible that the prosocial spending *or* happiness could cause the other. This situation is not unique. Many associations in psychology could result from causes in either direction (or even both, varying across circumstances). For example, you can probably come up with a way that each item in these pairs might plausibly cause the other: shyness and social exclusion, ability and motivation, self-esteem and success. This ambiguity is known as the directionality problem, and it is common in correlational studies.

In Focus

Interpreting Correlation Coefficients

This book will not focus on statistics, but the correlation coefficient is worth knowing a bit more about because this single number neatly summarizes a few useful things. The **correlation coefficient**, or *r*, describes the strength and direction of association between two things (e.g. prosocial spending and happiness). The values of *r* can range from −1.0 to +1.0, and 0 is a very important place in this range. When $r = 0$, it tells us that there is no association between two things, that they are completely independent. Values that are above 0 (e.g. $r = .11$, as in the prosocial spending study) tell us that the association is positive. This means that as one thing increases (prosocial spending) the other thing also increases (happiness). Values below 0 convey a negative association; as one thing increases (e.g. the number of friends a person has) the other thing decreases (the number of evenings spent home alone). Can you think of two other things that probably have a negative correlation?

Another key feature of the correlation coefficient is how it conveys information about the strength of the association, known as 'effect size'. As values get further from 0, the association is stronger, the effect size larger. Thus, a correlation of $r = .57$ is stronger (larger) than the correlation of $r = .28$. A correlation of $r = −.83$ is stronger than both. Do not be fooled by the negative sign; it tells us about the direction of the association (positive or negative), but distance from zero (or absolute value) tells us about the strength (see Figure 1.2).

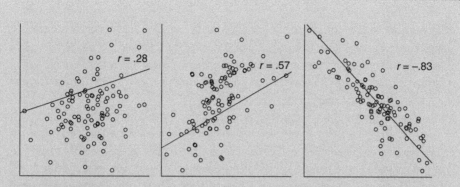

Figure 1.2 Correlation examples

Stronger correlations tell us that two things are more closely related. With stronger correlations, knowing the score on one variable tells you more about the score on the other variable, compared to weaker correlations. (For an interactive visualization of correlation size, see http://rpsychologist.com/d3/correlation/.) As you see more correlations, you will develop a sense of how various associations compare to one another. Returning to our example about prosocial spending and happiness, the correlation of $r = .11$ is considered small in size. As a very rough guide, consider that the *average* effect size in social psychology studies is approximately $r = .21$ (Richard, Bond, & Stokes-Zoota, 2003).

A small correlation does not mean that a finding is unimportant. For example, the correlation between some medications and reduced mortality risk (e.g. aspirin and heart attack) is less than $r = .05$ (Meyer et al., 2001), yet this is enough to save many lives. Rather, a correlation's size tells us how *closely* two things are linked. When reading about the prosocial spending study, you may have thought about someone you know who gives nothing to charity, yet is very happy. There are also examples of miserable people who still give generously. These people go against the average trend, but because the correlation is small, it is not too hard to find them. If the correlation were larger, for example like the $r = .60$ between optimism and happiness, there would be fewer of these exceptions – but some would still exist unless $r = 1$ or -1.

Knowing how strongly two things are correlated, beyond just the direction, is useful. Imagine that you were looking to promote one of your employees to a managerial position. You also know from previous research that success in this position is correlated $r = .14$ with the personality trait of extraversion and $r = .36$ with the personality trait of agreeableness. Assuming you had access to employee's extraversion and agreeableness

(Continued)

scores, which would you prioritize in making your decision? In this hypothetical example, the correct answer seems to be trait agreeableness. The correlation of $r = .36$ tell us that agreeableness is a stronger predictor of job performance than extraversion at $r = .14$. Of course we do not know that extraversion or agreeableness *cause* performance from the correlation, but it does give us something to go on.

Correlations can help us predict things, even if they are ambiguous about causality. They describe regularities in the world, and thus, regardless of the deeper causes, we can exploit those regularities to improve predictions. One more example: if I asked you to predict someone's shoe size, would you rather know her height or her self-esteem level? Height is more strongly correlated with shoe size than self-esteem, so height seems the better choice.

The directionality problem is a common reason why correlations might be ambiguous about causal direction, but it is not the only one. In fact, the directionality problem can be solved in some cases. Typically, this is accomplished by introducing time to a study. If we measure changes over time, we can often rule out one causal direction in that study. Things that occur first cannot be caused by things that happen later – bizarre suggestions from quantum physics aside. Studies conducted across different points in time are called **longitudinal studies**. Research on prosocial spending and happiness has exploited this technique. Dunn et al. (2008a) tracked employees over time. Happiness was measured one month before employees received a large bonus (almost US$5000, on average). Then, six to eight weeks after receiving the bonus, employees again rated their happiness, along with how they had spent the bonus money. Similar to the study described earlier, spending on others was associated (positively correlated) with happiness reported at the end of the study. Because this study could look at changes in happiness over time, it can speak more clearly to the causal direction. The second happiness report happened after the bonuses were spent, so it seems impossible that later happiness could cause the prosocial spending; prior happiness could be statistically controlled. (This particular study was very small, however, so it is still wise to interpret its results cautiously.) In an even clearer demonstration of time ruling out ambiguity about causal direction, Harker & Keltner (2001) correlated positive emotion expressions in college yearbook photos with life outcomes. As one example, women who expressed more positive emotions in their photos were more likely to be married by age 27 ($r = .19$). It is clearly impossible for marriage to influence a photo taken six years earlier!

On the other hand, it also seems impossible for a single smile captured in a photograph to directly cause marriage. Perhaps the emotions expressed in those photos indicated something else about the women? Fortunately, we have some additional information about the women's other characteristics because they also filled out personality questionnaires. It turns out that the more positive photos belonged to women who also scored high on the traits of affiliation and competence, and low on trait negative emotionality (Harker & Keltner, 2001). It seems possible that any one of these traits – or other, unmeasured things – could influence likelihood and age of marriage. This is an example of the **third variable problem**. We cannot conclude a causal link between two things that are correlated, because a 'third variable' may account for correlation – that third variable may cause both parts of the correlation. For example, women high in trait affiliation (the tendency to seek out close bonds with others) might be more prone to making big smiles at the photographer, as well as prioritizing marriage. In this example, trait affiliation causes smiling photos and early marriage; smiley photos do not cause marriage. Even when we do not know what the potential third variables are, we know it is possible that they exist, and so we must avoid narrow causal interpretations of correlations.

To summarize, the correlational approach tells us whether there is an association between two things and, if so, what kind (high scores grouping together or apart, i.e. positive or negative). Many correlations are still ambiguous about why two things are linked. When two things are correlated, the causal direction could go in either direction (the directionality problem). We can sometimes rule out one direction by looking at correlations over time, but we still cannot infer a direct causal relationship between the two things that are correlated because another thing may cause both (the third variable problem). The experimental approach, considered next, typically allows stronger conclusions about causal relationships.

The Experimental Approach

Returning to the prosocial spending example, we have seen that spending on others is correlated with happiness. We have some indication that the correlation is not entirely due to happiness causing prosocial spending, because the longitudinal study (over time) suggests that the prosocial spending can come first, before the happiness increase. However, we still cannot conclude that prosocial spending causes happiness increases because of the third variable problem. Perhaps the especially nice employees responded to their bonuses with a stronger sense of appreciation that increased happiness, and they were also more likely to spend money on others. In other words, trait kindness might be the third variable that explains increased happiness and prosocial spending; we cannot conclude the spending caused the happiness directly. To solve this problem, the researchers turned to the experimental method.

In other words, the researchers contrived a situation where they could ensure that prosocial spenders and selfish spenders did not differ from one another. This did not involve 'personality transplants', but rather a key advantage of the experimental approach: random assignment. In their experimental study, Dunn et al. (2008a) gave research participants $20 in the morning. They randomly split participants into two groups. Half were instructed to spend the $20 on themselves before the end of the day; the other half were instructed to spend the $20 on other people by the end of the day. Splitting participants into groups that will be treated differently is key to the experimental approach. The **experimental approach** differs from the correlational approach because it manipulates something, rather than merely observing it. In contrast to the correlational studies we have seen so far, which compared people who naturally did or who did not engage in much prosocial spending, this experimental study instructed some people to engage in prosocial spending, and others not to. This is the **experimental manipulation**. A key part of this process is that participants are **randomly assigned** to spend on either self or others. This ensures that the two groups are equal in terms of the participants' average backgrounds, personalities, and so on. This might sound strange at first – of course the people in the two groups are different; they are different people. This is true, but each person has an equal chance of being placed in either group (e.g. it might be decided with a coin flip). This means that differences across people will average out, especially as the study size increases. (This is one reason why having larger studies almost always leads to clearer results.) For example, the first particularly nice person might be randomly placed in the 'spending on others' group, but the next nice person has an equal chance of being placed in the 'spending on self' group. As we assign dozens of people, the average personalities between the two groups become quite similar. Even better, when we use random assignment to decide groups, we do not need to measure personality characteristics to infer this. As long as we include enough participants in the study, we can assume that the groups are similar. (Determining exactly how many participants constitutes 'enough' can get complicated and depends on the particular study, so we will leave that aside for now.) Finally, it is essential that the experimenters use a truly random approach to putting participants into groups. Imagine what would happen if they allowed participants to choose which group to be in – it might be hard to fill the 'spending on others' group, and it probably would not include many selfish people.

So what were the results of the prosocial spending experiment? Did the participants who spent money on themselves end the day happier than the participants who had to spend the money on others? Surprisingly, the participants instructed to spend $20 on others reported more happiness at the end of the day (Dunn et al., 2008a). (I say 'surprisingly' because another group of students were asked to predict how happy they would be if spending on either self or others, and they anticipated the opposite.) Because this study used the experimental approach, we have more confidence in concluding that spending money on others caused the increase in happiness. Again, random assignment to groups is what rules out many differences between the other- and the self-spenders. The average personality and background in the two experimental groups should be equal. Also, with the experimental method we do not need to worry about the directionality problem because the outcome – happiness in this study – comes after the experimental manipulation.

As noted previously, some correlational studies use time to avoid the directionality problem, but all experimental studies do this simply by measuring the consequence of a manipulation (which always comes first). This is another reason why experiments can make stronger conclusions about causality. If you are keeping track of the jargon, here are a couple more terms commonly used with the experimental approach: the thing that is being manipulated (self vs other spending in our example) is called the **independent variable**; the outcome or thing that is effected by the manipulation is called the **dependent variable** (end-of-day happiness in our example).

Despite the important strengths of the experimental method, it still has some limitations. (With virtually any single study, there are reasons to be cautious about results.) One limitation of experimental studies stems directly from their central feature and strength: the experimental manipulation. In the spending study, this is easy to see: how many times has someone given you $20 out of the blue, and how often do you let strangers tell you how to spend your money? I feel safe in assuming your answer to both is 'not very often'. Experimental studies are often artificial. They create contrived situations so that the key features can be controlled and manipulated. This allows for more powerful conclusions about causality, but potentially at the cost of studying less naturalistic behaviours, thoughts, and feelings. Perhaps spending $20 on someone else would be less enjoyable if you did not just receive that money from a psychologist. Experimental studies differ in how much they emphasize realism or control, but there is usually a trade-off between the two.

Experimental studies are also not completely immune from the third variable problem we discussed with the correlational approach. Experiments do a good job of ruling out some third variables, particularly those that participants would 'bring to the study' (like personality, gender, and life histories), because random assignment makes experimental groups equivalent in these ways (things average out). However, in psychology, it is very difficult to directly manipulate many of the things we are interested in studying. Thoughts and feelings are internal, so we usually take an indirect route (e.g. showing a happy or sad video to manipulate mood). Also, when we manipulate one thing, we may unintentionally manipulate other things – those other things are like our dreaded third variables in the correlational approach. Imagine you are a participant in the 'spend on others' group of Dunn et al.'s (2008a) spending experiment. You decide to take a friend out for lunch – your treat – and you have a wonderful time. It is easy to see how this might increase your happiness on that day, but is the increased happiness due to the prosocial spending per se, or to the wonderful lunch and time spent together? Said another way, if you arranged to meet your friend for lunch and she paid for her own meal, might it still be wonderful and increase your happiness? Was the prosocial spending really the essential (causal) part of the experience? Perhaps, but similar to correlational results, we must be concerned about what gets manipulated beyond the focal variable in experimental studies. In experimental studies, these potential third variables are called **confounds**. The third variable is 'confounded' with what the experimenter intended to manipulate. Experimenters try to find manipulations that eliminate these confounds, but consumers of research findings must also be vigilant in considering possible confounds.

To summarize, the experimental approach tests whether something we have manipulated (the independent variable) causes differences in something that we have measured (the dependent variable). When enough research participants are randomly assigned to experimental groups, we can rule out many potential 'third variables' (like personality differences), increasing our confidence that the manipulation caused any differences we observe between experimental groups. The strength of this approach – the manipulation – can also be a weakness because it often creates a novel and unnatural situation (especially if in the psychology laboratory!). Also, it is difficult to manipulate most psychological phenomena directly, so we must remain concerned about confounds – things unintentionally manipulated along with our focal variable.

The main distinction between the correlational approach and the experimental approach is that one merely observes the association between things (correlational), whereas the other manipulates something and compares groups that have been treated differently (experimental). We will see many variations and combinations of these general approaches; knowing their general strengths and limitations is helpful in interpreting the findings of individual studies.

SUMMING UP

Historically, the positive psychology movement was valuable in rebalancing psychology's preoccupation with dysfunction. Some have opined or predicted that positive psychology would 'be done' once balance was restored to psychology (e.g. Diener, 2003). It is hard to say whether or not complete balance has been achieved, yet it is clear that significant change has already occurred. Nonetheless, positive psychology as an area does not seem to be fading even as the movement's primary message has been heard (King, 2011; Linley et al., 2006). Scholarship on the core topics in positive psychology continues to grow (Donaldson et al., 2015). Instead of demise, positive psychology is maturing and becoming more balanced itself, for example with recent efforts to integrate nuance and the potential dark sides of seemingly positive phenomena. Accordingly, this text does not simply evangelize the founders' original message or constrain itself to describing their lines of research. It will, at times, take a critical look at core ideas. This approach makes it particularly difficult to clearly define the boundaries of positive psychology. Even without resolution on this point, an undergraduate course or textbook that assembles content around the theme of positive psychology makes for an engaging and potentially life-enhancing approach to learning more about psychology.

TEST YOURSELF

1. What are three criteria that we can use to assess something as 'positive'?

2. What are four ways we can apply the label 'positive' in positive psychology?

3. How is positive psychology similar to and different from other sub-disciplines in psychology (e.g. humanistic, personality, cognitive) and from other forms of self-help advice?

4. Why is it that correlations do not imply causation?

5. What is the key difference between correlational studies and experimental studies?

WEB LINKS

Watch Martin Seligman introduce the positive psychology movement: www.ted.com/talks/martin_seligman_on_the_state_of_psychology

The Positive Psychology Center at the University of Pennsylvania: www.positivepsychology.org

The International Positive Psychology Association: www.ippanetwork.org

The European Network for Positive Psychology: www.enpp.eu

The Canadian Positive Psychology Association: www.positivepsychologycanada.com

FURTHER READING

Read the founders' original description of positive psychology for yourself:

Seligman, M. E. P., & Csikszentmihalyi, M. (2000). Positive psychology: An introduction. *American Psychologist, 55*(1), 5–14.

Examine the history of positive psychology from a more critical perspective:

Yen, J. (2010). Authorizing happiness: Rhetorical demarcation of science and society in historical narratives of positive psychology. *Journal of Theoretical and Philosophical Psychology, 30*(2), 67–78.

Learn how psychologists reflect on positive psychology ten years in (especially Chapters 2, 28, & 30):

Sheldon, K. M., Kashdan, T. B., & Steger, M. F. (eds) (2011). *Designing Positive Psychology: Taking Stock and Moving Forward.* New York: Oxford University Press.

See how positive psychology is described by scholars outside the USA:

Linley, A. P., Joseph, S., Harrington, S., & Wood, A. M. (2006). Positive psychology: Past, present, and (possible) future. *The Journal of Positive Psychology, 1*(1), 3–16.

For an alternative approach to defining positivity, see:

Pawelski, J. O. (2016). Defining the "positive" in positive psychology: Part I. A descriptive analysis. *The Journal of Positive Psychology, 11*, 339–356.

REFERENCES

Aknin, L. B., Barrington-Leigh, C. P., Dunn, E. W., Helliwell, J. F., Burns, J., Biswas-Diener, R., ... Norton, M. I. (2013). Prosocial spending and well-being: Cross-cultural evidence for a psychological universal. *Journal of Personality and Social Psychology, 104*(4), 635–652. http://doi.org/10.1037/a0031578

Batson, C. D. (2014). *The Altruism Question: Toward a Social-psychological Answer.* New York: Psychology Press.

Baumeister, R. F., Campbell, J. D., Krueger, J. I., & Vohs, K. D. (2003). Does high self-esteem cause better performance, interpersonal success, happiness, or healthier life-styles? *Psychological Science in the Public Interest, 4*(1), 1–44. http://doi.org/10.1111/1529-1006.01431

BBC News. (2013). *Happiness index shows "small improvement"* in 2013, ONS says. Retrieved 5 September 2014, from www.bbc.com/news/uk-23501423

Bergsma, A. (2008a). Do self-help books help? *Journal of Happiness Studies, 9*(3), 341–360. http://doi.org/10.1007/s10902-006-9041-2

Bergsma, A. (2008b). The advice of the wise: Afterthoughts about reality checking. *Journal of Happiness Studies, 9*(3), 445–448. http://doi.org/10.1007/s10902-006-9035-0

Bolier, L., Haverman, M., Westerhof, G. J., Riper, H., Smit, F., & Bohlmeijer, E. T. (2013). Positive psychology interventions: A meta-analysis of randomized controlled studies. *BMC Public Health, 13*(1), 119. http://doi.org/10.1186/1471-2458-13-119

Breuer, J., & Freud, S. (1957). *Studies on Hysteria.* New York: Basic Books.

Brown, N. J. L., MacDonald, D. A., Samanta, M. P., Friedman, H. L., & Coyne, J. C. (2014). A critical reanalysis of the relationship between genomics and well-being. *Proceedings of the National Academy of Sciences, 111*(35), 12705–12709. http://doi.org/10.1073/pnas.1407057111

Cole, S., & Fredrickson, B. L. (2014). Errors in the Brown et al. critical reanalysis. *Proceedings of the National Academy of Sciences, 111*(35), E3581.

Csikszentmihalyi, M., & Nakamura, J. (2011). Positive psychology: Where did it come from, where is it going? In K. M. Sheldon, T. B. Kashdan, & M. F. Steger (eds), *Designing Positive Psychology* (pp. 3–8). New York: Oxford University Press.

Davis, C. G., Wohl, M. J. A., & Verberg, N. (2007). Profiles of posttraumatic growth following an unjust loss. *Death Studies, 31*(8), 693–712. http://doi.org/10.1080/07481180701490578

Diener, E. (2000). Subjective well-being: The science of happiness and a proposal for a national index. *American Psychologist, 55*(1), 34–43. http://doi.org/10.1037//0003-066X.55.1.34

Diener, E. (2003). What is positive about positive psychology: The curmudgeon and Pollyanna. *Psychological Inquiry, 14*(2), 115–117.

Diener, E., & Chan, M. Y. (2011). Happy people live longer: Subjective well-being contributes to health and longevity. *Applied Psychology: Health and Well-Being, 3*(1), 1–43. http://doi.org/10.1111/j.1758-0854.2010.01045.x

Diener, E., & Diener, C. (1996). Most people are happy. *Psychological Science, 7*(3), 181–185. http://doi.org/10.1111/j.1467-9280.1996.tb00354.x

Diener, E., & Suh, E. (1997). Measuring quality of life: Economic, social, and subjective indicators. *Social Indicators Research, 40*(1–2), 189–216. http://doi.org/10.1023/A:1006859511756

Donaldson, S. I., Dollwet, M., & Rao, M. A. (2015). Happiness, excellence, and optimal human functioning revisited: Examining the peer-reviewed literature linked to positive psychology. *The Journal of Positive Psychology, 10*, 185–195. http://doi.org/10.1080/17439760.2014.943801

Dunlosky, J., Rawson, K. A., Marsh, E. J., Nathan, M. J., & Willingham, D. T. (2013). Improving students' learning with effective learning techniques: Promising directions from cognitive and educational psychology. *Psychological Science in the Public Interest, 14*(1), 4–58. http://doi.org/10.1177/1529100612453266

Dunn, E. W., Aknin, L. B., & Norton, M. I. (2008a). Spending money on others promotes happiness. *Science, 5870*, 21–23.

Dunn, E. W., Aknin, L. B., & Norton, M. I. (2008b). Supporting material: Spending money on others promotes happiness. *Science (New York, N.Y.), 319*(5870), 1687–1688. http://doi.org/10.1126/science.1150952

Dunn, E. W., Aknin, L. B., & Norton, M. I. (2014). Prosocial spending and happiness: Using money to benefit others pays off. *Current Directions in Psychological Science, 23*(1), 41–47. http://doi.org/10.1177/0963721413512503

Gable, S. L., & Haidt, J. (2005). What (and why) is positive psychology? *Review of General Psychology, 9*(2), 103–110. http://doi.org/10.1037/1089-2680.9.2.103

Harker, L., & Keltner, D. (2001). Expressions of positive emotion in women's college yearbook pictures and their relationship to personality and life outcomes across adulthood. *Journal of Personality and Social Psychology, 80*(1), 112–124. http://doi.org/10.1037//0022-3514.80.1.112

Harlow, H. F. (1958). The nature of love. *American Psychologist, 13*(12), 673–685. http://doi.org/10.1037/h0047884

Hart, K. E., & Sasso, T. (2011). Mapping the contours of contemporary positive psychology. *Canadian Psychology, 52*(2), 82–92.

Held, B. S. (2004). The negative side of positive psychology. *Journal of Humanistic Psychology, 44*(1), 9–46. http://doi.org/10.1177/0022167803259645

Held, B. S. (2005). The "virtues" of positive psychology. *Journal of Theoretical and Philosophical Psychology, 25*(1), 1–34. http://doi.org/10.1037/h0091249

Kashdan, T. B., & Steger, M. F. (2011). Challenges, pitfalls, and aspirations for positive psychology. In K. M. Sheldon, T. B. Kashdan, & M. F. Steger (eds), *Designing Positive Psychology* (pp. 9–24). Oxford University Press.

Kennedy, R. F. (1968). Robert F. Kennedy speeches: Remarks at the University of Kansas, 18 March 1968. Retrieved 8 February 2015, from www.jfklibrary.org/Research/Research-Aids/Ready-Reference/RFK-Speeches/Remarks-of-Robert-F-Kennedy-at-the-University-of-Kansas-March-18-1968.aspx

King, L. (2011). Are we there yet? What happened on the way to the demise of positive psychology. In K. M. Sheldon, T. B. Kashdan, & M. F. Steger (eds), *Designing Positive Psychology* (pp. 439–446). New York: Oxford University Press.

Lilienfeld, S. O. (2005). The 10 commandments of helping students distinguish science from pseudoscience in psychology. *APS Observer, 18*(9), 39–40.

Linley, A. P., Dovey, H., de Bruin, E., Transler, C., Wilkinson, J., Maltby, J., & Hurling, R. (2013). Two simple, brief, naturalistic activities and their impact on positive affect: Feeling grateful and eating ice cream. *Psychology of Well-Being: Theory, Research and Practice, 3*(1), 6. http://doi.org/10.1186/2211-1522-3-6

Linley, A. P., Joseph, S., Harrington, S., & Wood, A. M. (2006). Positive psychology: Past, present, and (possible) future. *The Journal of Positive Psychology, 1*(1), 3–16. http://doi. org/10.1080/17439760500372796

Lyubomirsky, S., King, L., & Diener, E. (2005). The benefits of frequent positive affect: Does happiness lead to success? *Psychological Bulletin, 131*, 803–855.

Maslow, A. H. (1943). A theory of human motivation. *Psychological Review, 50*, 370–396.

Meredith, L. S., Sherbourne, C. D., Gaillot, S. J., Hansell, L., Ritschard, H. V., Parker, A. M., & Wrenn, G. (2011). *Promoting Psychological Resilience in the U.S. Military*. Santa Monica, CA: Rand Corporation.

Mervis, C., & Rosch, E. (1981). Categorization of natural objects. *Annual Review of Psychology, 32*, 89–115.

Meyer, G. J., Finn, S. E., Eyde, L. D., Kay, G. G., Moreland, K. L., Eisman, E. J., … Richey, N. P. (2001). Psychological testing and psychological assessment: A review of evidence and issues. *American Psychologist, 56*(2), 128–165. http://doi.org/10.1037//OOO3-O66X.56.2.128

Musikanski, L. (2014). Happiness and public policy. *Journal of Social Change, 6*(1), 55–85. http://doi.org/10.5590/JOSC.2014.06.1.06

Nelson, L. D. (2014). You know what's on our shopping list. Retrieved 22 May 2014, from http://datacolada.org/2014/05/22/22-you-know-whats-on-our-shopping-list/

Oishi, S., Diener, E., & Lucas, R. E. (2007). The optimum level of well-being: Can people be too happy? *Perspectives on Psychological Science, 2*(4), 346–360. http://doi.org/10.1111/j.1745-6916.2007.00048.x

Pawelski, J. O. (2016). Defining the "positive" in positive psychology: Part I. A descriptive analysis. *The Journal of Positive Psychology, 11*, 339–356. http://doi.org/10.1080/17439760 .2015.1137627

Peterson, C. (2006). *A Primer in Positive Psychology*. New York: Oxford University Press.

Peterson, C., & Seligman, M. E. P. (2004). *Character Strengths and Virtues: A Handbook and Classification*. New York: Oxford University Press and Washington, DC: American Psychological Association.

Quinn, P. C., Kelly, D. J., Lee, K., Pascalis, O., & Slater, A. M. (2008). Preference for attractive faces in human infants extends beyond conspecifics. *Developmental Science, 11*(1), 76–83. http://doi.org/10.1111/j.1467-7687.2007.00647.x.Preference

Richard, F. D., Bond, C. F., & Stokes-Zoota, J. J. (2003). One hundred years of social psychology quantitatively described. *Review of General Psychology, 7*(4), 331–363. http://doi. org/10.1037/1089-2680.7.4.331

Rogers, C. R. (2007). The necessary and sufficient conditions of therapeutic personality change. *Psychotherapy: Theory, Research, Practice, Training, 44*(3), 240–248. http://doi.org/10.1037/0033-3204.44.3.240

Ross, L., Greene, D., & House, P. (1977). The "false consensus effect": An egocentric bias in social perception and attribution processes. *Journal of Experimental Social Psychology, 13*(3), 279–301. http://doi.org/10.1016/0022-1031(77)90049-X

Rusk, R. D., & Waters, L. E. (2013). Tracing the size, reach, impact, and breadth of positive psychology. *The Journal of Positive Psychology, 8*(3), 207–221. http://doi.org/10.1080/1743 9760.2013.777766

Seligman, M. E. P., & Csikszentmihalyi, M. (2000). Positive psychology: An introduction. *American Psychologist, 55*(1), 5–14. http://doi.org/10.1037//0003-066X.55.1.5

Sheldon, K. M. (2011). What's positive about positive psychology? Reducing value-bias and enhancing integration within the field. In K. M. Sheldon, T. B. Kashdan, & M. F. Steger (eds), *Designing Positive Psychology* (pp. 421–429). New York: Oxford University Press.

Sheldon, K. M., Kashdan, T. B., & Steger, M. F. (2011). *Designing Positive Psychology: Taking Stock and Moving Forward*. New York: Oxford University Press.

Sheldon, K. M., & King, L. (2001). Why positive psychology is necessary. *American Psychologist, 56*, 216–217.

Srivastava, S. (2009). Making progress in the hardest science. Retrieved 5 September 2014, from http://hardsci.wordpress.com/2009/03/14/making-progress-in-the-hardest-science/

Stratton, A. (2010). Happiness index to gauge Britain's national mood. Retrieved 10 July 2014, from www.theguardian.com/lifeandstyle/2010/nov/14/happiness-index-britain-national-mood

Taylor, E. (2001). Positive psychology and humanistic psychology: A reply to Seligman. *Journal of Humanistic Psychology, 41*(1), 13–29. http://doi.org/10.1177/0022167801411003

Waterman, A. S. (2013). The humanistic psychology–positive psychology divide: Contrasts in philosophical foundations. *American Psychologist, 68*(3), 124–133. http://doi.org/10.1037/a0032168

Wong, P. (2011). Positive psychology 2.0: Towards a balanced interactive model of the good life. *Canadian Psychology, 52*, 69–81.

Yen, J. (2010). Authorizing happiness: Rhetorical demarcation of science and society in historical narratives of positive psychology. *Journal of Theoretical and Philosophical Psychology, 30*(2), 67–78. http://doi.org/10.1037/a0019103

Zelenski, J. M., & Larsen, R. J. (2000). The distribution of basic emotions in everyday life: A state and trait perspective from experience sampling data. *Journal of Research in Personality, 34*(2), 178–197. http://doi.org/10.1006/jrpe.1999.2275

Part II

Happiness and Positive States

2

Positive Emotions

INTRODUCTION

One day, Matt Frerking, a neuroscientist in his mid-thirties, was taking a shower when he was suddenly overcome by feelings of heaviness in his muscles. His body flopped down and he was unable to stand up or even lift his head. A few minutes later, things returned to normal. Similar episodes started happening more and more. Even as a neuroscientist, Matt did not understand why this was happening. It took years to identify his condition: narcolepsy with cataplexy. Narcolepsy involves involuntary sleep, and cataplexy is a subtype where attacks leave people conscious while unable to control their muscles.

What does this unfortunate condition have to do with positive psychology? As Matt had more attacks, he began to realize what triggered them: positive emotions. Cute puppies, children playing, movie trailers – these were all enough to have Matt drooping over. There are important events in Matt's life that he knows will create unavoidable attacks, such as family weddings or his own anniversary. Matt's family adjusts to accommodate his condition, though his wife will tell you she misses some cuddling. In his day-to-day life, Matt must actively work to keep his positive emotions under control. He speaks slowly to avoid getting excited; he avoids photos that remind him of happy times; he trains himself to remain detached. Occasionally he just gives in and spends time with his wife on the couch – it matters less if his muscles fade out for a while there. More often, Matt is in the unusual position of trying to avoid positive emotions. Even with this goal, and with obvious negative consequences of feeling good, he still cannot avoid happiness. (For a moving and more complete telling of Matt's story, see podcast thisamericanlife.org, episode #409.)

Matt Frerking's experience is suggestive. Imagine trying to get through your day without experiencing pleasant emotions. To have a chance of success with this bizarre goal, you would have to drastically change your activities, avoiding common 'triggers' like pets, friends, music, photos, kind emails, and maybe even insurance advertisements. This is because pleasant emotions are very common in human experience.

People Are Happy Most of the Time

The pervasiveness of pleasant emotions struck me in the first study I helped conduct as a new graduate student. We asked research participants to complete a short questionnaire three times a day over a four-week period (Zelenski & Larsen, 2000). It had questions about current activities and emotions. The many repetitions tracked the ebb and flow of experiences in people's daily lives – a technique known as the **experience sampling method** (Scollon, Kim-Prieto, & Diener, 2003). Across the month, participants reported pleasant emotions like happiness, relaxation, excitement, and interest much more than unpleasant emotions like sadness, guilt, anger, and fear. In one comparison, we identified time periods where one emotion was rated higher than all others, reports with a dominant emotion. Happiness was by far the most common dominant emotion in about 15 per cent of the instances, compared to 1.2 per cent for sadness or 0.2 per cent for fear.

The tendency for people to report pleasant states most of the time is common. In another recent example, MacKerron and Mourato (2013) used smartphones and an app called *Mappiness* to record over one million mood reports from people in the UK. Participants were randomly signalled and asked to rate their momentary happiness on a scale that ranged from 0 to 100. The average rating was well above neutral (50) at 66.4, and the single most common rating was 100 (see Figure 2.1). People were happy most of the time.

People have a **positivity offset**. We do not wander around in a neutral state, waiting for circumstances to move us. Rather, we confront neutrality and ambiguity with a slight sense of optimism and positive evaluation (Cacioppo & Bernston, 1994). We feel good even without pleasant events. These good feelings promote exploration, creativity, sociability, and so on – things that promote healthy functioning (Diener, Kanazawa, Suh, & Oishi, 2014). Our positive bias is the norm – until we get hints that things are not OK. People are also very sensitive to signs of threat. Threats quickly grab our attention – bad is stronger than good in this way – and unpleasant feelings motivate change (Baumeister, Bratslavsky, Finkenauer, & Vohs, 2001).

Indeed, 'negative' emotions are essential to healthy functioning. Although they feel unpleasant, fear, sadness, and disgust get and keep people out of trouble. Immediate demands give negative emotions a privileged place in our consciousness. In this way, negative emotions are more potent, yet positive emotions are more pervasive. Both serve important purposes. (Both can also become unbalanced in maladaptive ways, but that is not our focus in positive psychology.)

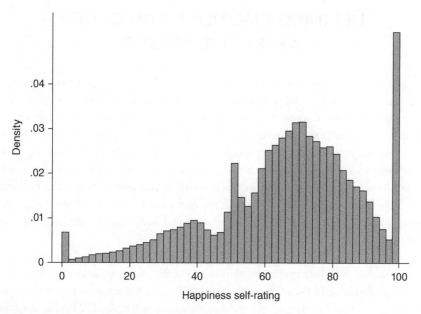

Figure 2.1 Frequency of happiness ratings

Source: Adapted from MacKerron and Mourato (2013)

The abundance of positive emotions in daily life has not been mirrored – until recently – in psychological theory and research. Emotion research may be one of the best examples of how mainstream psychology had become unbalanced by focusing on unpleasant aspects of human experience. Psychology mostly studied unpleasant emotions while neglecting more typical pleasant emotions. You may be familiar with the pioneering research by Ekman and Friesen (1971) on cultural universals in facial expressions. These researchers travelled to remote places to test the notion that all humans – even in isolated hunter-gatherer societies – expressed and understood a few basic emotions in the same way. Try typing 'Ekman faces' into your search engine to retrieve an image with six faces. There, you will find only one positive expression – joy – surrounded by sadness, anger, surprise, fear, and disgust.

In fairness to these important early researchers, many pleasant emotions are not displayed clearly in still photos of faces. For example, emotions like gratitude, amusement, and pride seem to be revealed more in touches, vocalizations, and postures, respectively (Sauter, 2010). Nonetheless, the early focus on facial expressions probably contributed to a lingering neglect of pleasant emotions. Most lists of basic emotions included only one or two pleasant states, and theories provided only vague explanations for positive emotions (Fredrickson, 1998; Ortony & Turner, 1990). Fortunately, balance is returning. Pleasant emotions have been central in the positive psychology movement, and the source of exciting new research questions. See the In Focus box below for a modern list of positive emotions.

DEFINING EMOTIONS AND OTHER AFFECTIVE STATES

Emotions are easily recognized, but hard to define. They emerge when aspects 'come together' in distinct feeling states. **Emotions** involve our physiology, thoughts, subjective feelings, motivation, expressions, and behaviour. During an emotion, these facets of bodily and mental activity suddenly seem to operate in concert. For example, when our hearts beat faster, we feel warmth, our minds go blank except for a deep desire to connect, we lean in close, and we pucker our lips – this is when we recognize a moment of love. Yet just before that emotion episode, hearts were already beating (to circulate blood), the target of affection was already in view, and thoughts filled with the conversation at hand. Something – perhaps a knowing glance or some especially kind words – shifted, and in a moment, an emotion emerged.

Emotions are fleeting. They can occur over just a few seconds, and tend to dissipate or resolve in minutes. We distinguish emotions from other states, such as moods, in this way. Emotions are shorter, and usually more concretely about a particular thing, whereas **moods** are less intense, slower to change, and ambiguously caused (Frijda, 1993). The distinction is loose, however. In research contexts, measurement and manipulation of 'emotions' often seems more like moods. In Chapters 3 and 4, we discuss more long-term differences in feelings. These **emotion traits** describe relatively stable individual differences in average emotional experiences (e.g. some people tend to be happier than others). Finally, **affect** (as a noun) also describes emotion-like phenomena. The term is generic, referring to feelings that differ in pleasantness, but without implying all aspects of an emotion. In this chapter, we consider relatively short-term affective experiences – emotion, mood, and affect – often without sharp distinctions among them.

Fundamental questions about what, exactly, emotions are, or how they come about, are some of the oldest in psychology. In 1884 William James wrote the article "What is an emotion?" and much disagreement remains today (Izard, 2010). Some even question whether 'emotion' is a useful scientific term given the confusion about its meaning (Dixon, 2012). Much of the disagreement centres on the idea of 'basic emotions'. Some view emotions as fixed physiological and behavioural responses produced by distinct brain circuits. The **basic emotion** view identifies a list of discrete, basic emotions that should meet specific criteria, such as having distinct physiology, expressions, experience, and so on (Ekman & Cordaro, 2011). The classic basic emotion list includes sadness, fear, disgust, anger, surprise, and joy. Other lists exist (Ortony & Turner, 1990), and the number of basic emotions has grown over time (Ekman & Cordaro, 2011). Basic emotions are defined narrowly. They have specific causes, are brief, and have automatic consequences. Imagine an instance of intense fear: someone with a knife demands your wallet. This situation evokes a strong, prototypical basic emotion. Other affective experiences, like ambivalence, sympathy, or mild moods, are essentially defined out of 'emotion'. That is, some affective states that do not meet the strict criteria are set aside to have a clear definition of emotion.

The basic emotion approach is intuitive (we all have a sense of sadness, anger, joy, etc.), and it has guided much research on emotions. However, it is not the only approach. In contrast to seeing feelings in distinct categories, an alternative **dimensional perspective** sees more subtle variations and fuzzy boundaries. It arranges emotional experiences in a conceptual space based on their similarities and differences (see Figure 2.2). The arrangement does not have clear categorical boundaries among the many different ways people can experience emotion. For example, distress, anxiety, irritation, and angst have similarities and differences; is one more basic?

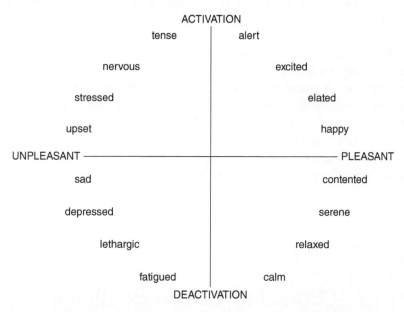

Figure 2.2 The affect circumplex defined by pleasantness and activation dimensions

Source: Adapted from Barrett and Russell (1999)

Some question the very existence of basic emotions. In this view, each 'basic' emotion does not have a distinct brain circuit or fixed expression, but rather is psychologically or socially constructed based on folk ideas about emotions (Gross & Barrett, 2011). Using the terminology of philosophy, basic emotions are not 'natural kinds'; the idea of 'emotions' has meaning only in the way people understand them, not in biology (Barrett, 2006). Others take a variety of more moderate views: "It's been said that there are as many theories of emotions as there are emotion theorists" (LeDoux, quoted in Beck, 2015).

In sum, definitions of emotion vary from fundamental biology to not even existing beyond our ideas of them. Despite contradictory views about the essence of what emotions 'are', psychologists mostly agree that they involve the intersection of a few components, typically:

1. **appraisals**: mental assessments of circumstances, interpreting things;

2. **physiological changes**: in the body (e.g. sweaty palms and racing hearts) and brain;

3. **expressions**: in the face (e.g. a smile), as well as in posture, tone of voice, and touch;

4. **subjective experience**: our personal, first-person, phenomenological feeling;

5. **action tendencies**: motivation to do some things rather than others (e.g. flee or explore).

Much of this chapter is structured around what we have learned about each of these components, with particular emphasis on positive emotions. You will see topics where the basic emotions perspective receives more and less support. Debate continues; evidence is inconclusive.

Fortunately, these theoretical debates do not prevent us from learning other important things about emotions. For example, whether or not the experience of awe depends more on a particular brain circuit or on a shared cultural understanding, we can still study when it is likely to occur and how it might contribute to a fulfilling life. Beyond the basic issues explored here, emotions return in each chapter.

In Focus

Specific Positive Emotions

Early lists of emotions included only one that felt pleasant: happiness, or joy. Things have changed with the positive psychology movement. Here we briefly explore eight different positive emotions. The selection is distilled from commonalities in other recent lists (Campos & Keltner, 2014; Ekman & Cordaro, 2011; Fredrickson, 2013; Shiota, Neufeld, Danvers, Osborne, Sng, & Yee, 2014); it would be possible to add more. For each of these emotions, there is preliminary evidence that they can be distinguished in terms of appraisals, expressions, physiology, or action tendencies, though they also share some common themes.

Joy (happiness) is the pleasant feeling we get when good things happen to us, particularly when they are unexpected or exceed expectations. Joy is invigorating, increasing arousal and activity broadly. (This activity can, in turn, promote learning and skills.)

Love is about social connection and sharing, and typically involves some vulnerability, commitment, and sense of self-expansion (i.e. taking on aspects of another). Love can be further sub-divided based on the target or type of relationship, for example as sexual desire, nurturing (compassion), or attachment to a caregiver (Shiota et al., 2014). We consider love more fully in Chapter 8.

Pride is a confidence that comes from accomplishing socially valued goals. It builds status, and can lead to consumption (taking a reward) or approaching new challenges and taking new risks. Authentic pride can be distinguished from 'hubristic pride', which is not based on actual accomplishment.

Contentment (serenity, relaxation) is a low arousal, pleasant emotion that signals comfort, safety, and ease. It can facilitate reflection on what led to such good circumstances, a sense of appreciation, or savouring of the moment.

Interest (curiosity, enthusiasm) is experienced when people encounter novel situations or information that seems manageable. It promotes exploration, and can help people seize new opportunities. Interest and enthusiasm can narrow attention on a particular object or goal (cf. the broaden and build model). Prolonged absorption with interest is like the state of 'flow', which occurs when the challenges of a situation are matched to a person's skill (Nakamura & Csikszentmihalyi, 2002).

Amusement (humour) occurs in response to the unexpected – mild incongruities that are not threatening. Amusement is associated with playfulness – mentally, physically, and socially – and promotes flexibility, social bonding, and mild risk taking.

Awe (wonder) also stems from novelty, but where the gap between expectations and new information is vast. For example, new scientific discoveries or impressive natural phenomena (e.g. amazing sunsets) promote awe. Awe makes people pause and reconsider assumptions; it can create new ideas about our place in the world and in relation to others.

Gratitude occurs when people receive good fortune and they attribute the cause to another person. The sense of appreciation is often expressed as a desire to 'pay it forward' with prosocial acts. A similar, potentially distinct, emotion – inspiration (elevation) – involves witnessing moral goodness in another person, and instigates morally good or prosocial behaviour in oneself (Algoe & Haidt, 2009).

Appraisals

Appraisals are the cognitive part of emotions. They are individuals' evaluations of immediate circumstances; they assess events' relevance to our well-being and concerns (Moors, Ellsworth, Scherer, & Frijda, 2013). Typically, these evaluations are automatic – rapid and unconscious – or the judgement that spurs an emotion. Appraisals can also be more deliberate, consciously considered assessments, such as when a series of thoughts leads you to a feeling. The mind continuously monitors the environment (including the internal, bodily environment), appraising changes. In appraisal theories, these judgements are the catalyst for emotions. Appraisals are the essential features that determine when and which emotion occurs (Arnold, 1960; Scherer, 2005; Smith & Ellsworth, 1985; Smith & Lazarus, 1993). Other components of emotions (e.g. physiological change, expressions) follow from the appraisal, and as the emotion unfolds, these elements may, in turn, alter ongoing appraisals (Scherer, 2009). For example, imagine you are walking in a forest and you hear rustling in the brush a few meters away. An initial appraisal judges this situation as relevant to your well-being: the noise could be a threat (e.g. a bear) or an opportunity (e.g. a cute bunny) – relevant either way. Other appraisals assess your ability to cope (if a bear), or the certainty you have that it sounded smaller (like a bunny). If you are uncertain or not sure how to deal with a bear, you experience fear. If you are confident that the noise came from something smaller, you experience interest and approach quietly, hoping to catch a glimpse of the little critter.

Some of the most common appraisal dimensions assess the following (Moors et al., 2013):

Is the event relevant to my goals or concerns?

Is the event consistent or inconsistent with my goals or concerns?

How certain am I?

Is the event caused by myself, someone else, or something else?

Can I cope with or control the event?

Other appraisal dimensions include judgements about novelty, fairness, intentionality, urgency, and so on. Positive emotions occur when events are appraised as relevant and consistent with goals. The other appraisal dimensions can further refine positive feelings into more specific emotional experiences (Ellsworth & Smith, 1988). For example, pride involves a sense of personal control and responsibility, whereas awe is associated with a diminished sense of self and external causes (Shiota, Keltner, & Mossman, 2007). Each emotion has a recipe with a unique blend of different appraisals as ingredients.

Appraisals are also personal, or idiosyncratic to individuals. They depend on one's cognitive representations of the world, and thus can explain how two people respond to the same situation with different emotions. Most people who have close encounters with bears in the forest experience fear. However, a naturalist who is searching for bears finds the encounter consistent with her goals and has the resources (skills and experience) to cope. The event is then positive for her. At a safe distance, more of us would enjoy seeing a bear because we would appraise the risk as low. From an appraisal perspective, the particular emotion depends on these appraisals. Appraisals are not just about objective circumstances; they are interpretations that depend on the idiosyncratic goals, skills, and knowledge of the individual making the appraisal.

Measuring and Studying Appraisals

It is difficult to assess appraisals as they are thought to operate in daily life: as ongoing, automatic, unconscious, assessments. However, researchers can still link appraisal patterns with specific emotions. For example, research participants might be asked to recall a past emotional experience, and then to make ratings on appraisal dimensions (e.g. were you responsible, or was the event expected?). Researchers might instead ask for detailed descriptions of past emotion experiences, and have coders, who do not know which emotion was elicited, make the appraisal ratings based on those descriptions. Ratings of appraisals can then be matched to hypotheses about the relevant appraisal dimensions (e.g. amusement is about playfulness with others).

Another technique is to experimentally manipulate relevant features of the situation to see whether this changes self-reported appraisals and emotional experience. As an example, the emotion of interest should, theoretically, involve an appraisal that the event is understandable. In one study, research participants were asked to read an abstract poem, "The Whitest Parts of the Body", from the book *The Life of Haifisch*. Only half of the participants were told that *haifisch* was the German word for shark, and those participants found the abstract poem more interesting – presumably because they appraised it as more understandable due to the extra information (Silvia, 2005). Results were consistent with theory.

None of these research techniques definitively prove that people are continuously and automatically making appraisals in daily life, or that such appraisals cause emotions (cf. Zajonc, 1980). On the other hand, it is hard to imagine a rich emotional experience that is not preceded by some basic cognitive processing that makes sense of perceptions and sensations – something like appraisals. Theory and research on appraisals have articulated the conditions and judgements that people associate with different emotional experiences. This has been particularly useful in recent efforts to expand the list of positive emotions and the distinctions among them.

Physiology

Physiological responses – and internal perceptions of them – are essential to emotions. With emotions, the physiological changes clearly extend beyond the brain to things like heart rate, breathing, muscle tension, moist hands, blushing, and so on – our peripheral physiology. Emotions typically produce increases in arousal, yet some emotions are associated with decreased arousal (e.g. contentment).

As with other components of emotions, the physiological changes are thought to be useful. They prepare the body to meet the needs of the situation. Emotions can be seen as rapid, adaptive responses that helped our ancestors survive (Panksepp, 2011). Indeed, Darwin (1872), and many psychologists since, saw emotions in non-human animals, emphasizing their adaptive value across species. In the prototypical example, seeing a bear in the woods immediately generates fear, which, in part, prepares our bodies for physical challenge (e.g. running away). This would be useful to people and rabbits alike. This bodily preparation appears in our peripheral physiology. We notice it when we experience emotions, and emotion researchers can measure it.

In early theories, bodily changes were viewed as the source of emotions. Working separately in the late 1800s, William James and Carl Lange both proposed that emotions are perceptions of bodily change. In the bear example, our bodies become aroused before we experience fear. The mental state of fear begins with a perception of bodily arousal. Extreme forms of this view seem implausible today, and it was criticized from the beginning (Dixon, 2012). How does the body know to become aroused if no processing occurs in the brain first? Still, the idea that our experiences, choices, and behaviours are shaped by perceptions of our bodily states is still alive and well (Damasio, 1996). Our knowledge and interpretations of situations are essential to emotions, but it seems we also monitor our peripheral physiology to provide some of that information.

Studying Bodily Change

In **psychophysiology**, we measure bodily functions like heart rate, electrodermal activity, finger temperature, and so on, to infer psychological processes (J. T. Larsen, Bernston, Poehlmann, Ito, & Cacioppo, 2008). These measures use a polygraph, the same machines used in lie detection, to simultaneously assess various aspects of physiology. As one example, electrodermal activity (EDA, also known as skin conductance) is measured by placing two electrodes on two different fingers. One of those electrodes produces a small electric current. The second electrode measures that electric current. Because sweat conducts electricity better than dry skin, the second electrode indexes how moist (sweaty) a person's hand is by the amount of electricity it receives. When the electricity received by the second electrode increases, it means there is more sweat. The psychophysiologist can then infer activation of the sympathetic nervous system because it controls sweat glands in the hand (Dawson, Schell, & Filion, 2000).

The bodily nature of emotions combines well with psychophysiological measurement. Researchers have searched for unique profiles of autonomic activity for each basic emotion (cf. James–Lange theory). For example, an early encouraging study found that fear was associated with increased heart rate and decreased finger skin temperature, whereas anger produced both increased heart rate and increased skin temperature (Ekman, Levenson, & Friesen, 1983). Decades of subsequent research have observed some regularities in auto-nomic responses for particular emotions (Cacioppo, Bernston, Klein, & Poehlmann, 1997; Kreibig, 2010). However, these patterns are complex and not robust or distinct enough to strongly suggest clear physiological signatures for all emotions. Peripheral physiological change remains a useful indicator of emotion, but it does not identify particular emotions well on its own (at least not yet). No one could look at a polygraph reading and know it was attached to a person experiencing anger, joy, or any other specific emotion. This is especially true for positive emotions. Few studies have even tried to differentiate among them with physiological measures, so future distinctions remain possible (Shiota & Danvers, 2014).

Rather than having distinct physiological signatures, positive emotions may influence physiology by relieving the arousal of negative emotions. For example, a lab study induced anxiety in participants by telling them they would have 60 seconds to prepare a speech that would be video recorded and evaluated by peers. This produced the predictable anxiety and physiological arousal. In a second phase, some of the research participants were randomly assigned to watch a positive film clip, whereas others viewed neutral or sad film clips. Those who saw the positive clips recovered, physiologically, more quickly than the other groups – even more quickly than those who saw the neutral clip (Fredrickson, Mancuso, Branigan, & Tugade, 2000). Thus, the positive emotions seemed to help 'undo' the physiological effects of anxiety. Findings like this are intriguing, but many other combinations of negative and positive emotions have yet to be tested.

Studying Emotions in the Brain

The embodied nature of emotions has led psychologists to study peripheral physiology. Yet emotions are also psychological states, and this suggests correlations with activity in the brain. One way to assess this is via the electricity generated by the brain itself using electro-encephalography (EEG). The electricity is recorded by a series of electrodes placed on the scalp all around the head. The skull is a barrier that does not conduct electricity well. Thus, EEG recordings are not well suited to localizing specific brain regions, especially those deep in the brain where much emotion processing occurs. Nonetheless, broader patterns of activity – such as the relative activation of right versus left hemispheres – have been suggestive.

In EEG recordings, greater left-side activation correlates with approach motivation and the accompanying emotional experience (Coan & Allen, 2004). For example, putting sugar on newborn infants' tongues increases left (vs right) activation (Fox & Davidson, 1986). In adults, both posed and voluntary (Duchenne) smiles are associated with greater left than right activation (Ekman & Davidson, 1993). Despite these examples, we should not conclude that left hemispheric activation is linked to positive experience per se. Instead, a more nuanced view is required: left activation is associated with approach emotions. Not all pleasant emotions involve approach motivation (e.g. contentment does not). Moreover, some unpleasant emotions do involve approach motivation (e.g. anger), and these emotions are also associated with greater left-hemisphere activation. The clearest evidence for this interpretation comes from studies of anger (Harmon-Jones, 2003), induced, for example, with insulting feedback (Harmon-Jones & Sigelman, 2001). Anger produces greater left-hemispheric activation, similar to more pleasant approach states. Thus, left activation seems to accompany some pleasant states, but indicates approach motivation more than pleasantness itself (Coan & Allen, 2004).

Other brain-imaging techniques allow psychologists to observe changes in more localized parts of the deep brain. These techniques often track changes in blood flow to different regions (Raichle, 1998). For example, with positron emission tomography (PET) radioactive isotopes are injected to the bloodstream and tracked as they flow to different parts of the brain. Functional magnetic resonance imaging (fMRI) uses powerful magnets and pulses of radio waves to measure blood flow based on how much oxygen is in the blood at different locations in the brain. The underlying assumption is that parts of the brain that are more active require more blood to provide oxygen and energy to the neurons. As with studies of peripheral physiology, few brain-imaging studies have yet to differentiate among positive emotions. Still, happiness is often included as a comparison with unpleasant emotions, and this has provided hints about which parts of the brain are more active in pleasant states.

Imaging studies have provided some support for the idea that left-hemisphere activation is associated with approach states, similar to the EEG studies (Murphy, Nimmo-Smith, & Lawrence, 2003). However, they also suggest that the left–right differences become more complex when examining specific areas of the brain (Wager, Phan, Liberzon, & Taylor, 2003). When determining which parts of the brain are especially active during happy states, it is worth considering the question: compared to what? Some areas, such as the medial prefrontal cortex, appear important to many emotions – including happiness – but do not seem to be distinctly associated with happiness (Lindquist, Satpute, Wager, Weber, & Barrett, 2015; Lindquist, Wager, Kober, Bliss-Moreau, & Barrett, 2012). One large analysis found that activation in the rostral anterior cingulate cortex and the right superior temporal gyrus differentiate happiness from other emotions (Vytal & Hamann, 2010). Yet other large analyses, using slightly different techniques, have not observed specific regions that are distinctly associated with happiness – or many other emotions (Lindquist et al., 2012; Murphy et al., 2003; Phan, Wager, Taylor, & Liberzon, 2002).

The key word here is 'distinctly'. Happiness certainly involves some activity in the brain – we knew that even before imaging techniques were invented – yet the activity for happiness is in regions that are also used for other emotions and mental processes (e.g. evaluation in general). For now it seems no single region is dedicated to happiness exclusively. Similar to peripheral physiology, no one could look at a brain scan and know with confidence that a person was experiencing a particular emotion (at least not yet). Still, we are rapidly learning more about the brain correlates of different emotion states under different conditions, making imaging an increasingly powerful technique. Stay tuned for more examples.

Expressions

Emotional expressions are the behavioural component of emotions. For example, smiling faces or arms raised in victory are easily recognized expressions. The term 'expression' implies that they reveal something about internal states. In this way, expressions help communicate those states to other people. Emotions can be expressed in vocalizations (sounds) by varying pitch and tone – and even without speech, such as with sighs, giggles, and grunts (Juslin & Laukka, 2003; Sauter, Eisner, Ekman, & Scott, 2010). Gestures and changes in posture can also signal emotions (Tracy & Robins, 2004), yet most research has focused on the face. Meticulous study has revealed how various combinations of facial muscle movements can express specific emotions. For example, typical expressions of anger involve contracting the brow, and tightening muscles around the eyes and mouth. Detailed facial analyses now allow researchers to objectively code emotion expressions, for example from video recordings. A widely used example is the Facial Action Coding System (FACS; see Ekman, 1982). These nuanced descriptions of facial emotion expressions have also been useful to computer animators.

Some facial expressions can be measured mechanically. Similarly to how a polygraph assesses things like sweaty palms and heart rate, electrodes can be used to measure facial muscle activity (electromyography or EMG). These electrodes are attached to specific places on the face, and they record the electricity generated by muscles just under the skin. Recording muscle activity does a good job of distinguishing pleasant from unpleasant feelings, but typically not more specific emotion expressions. To illustrate, draw an imaginary line between the corner of your mouth and your ear hole. About halfway between, electrodes could measure the activity of your zygomaticus major muscle – one of the main muscles used to produce a smile, and where activity indicates pleasant feelings. (Of course the context is important; activity could also indicate gum chewing!) Just above your eyebrow is another important muscle – the corrugator supercilli – which furrows the brow in expressing unpleasant emotions (Dimberg, 1990; J. T. Larsen, Norris, & Cacioppo, 2003). These EMG recordings can detect very subtle changes in facial muscles – even expressions so small that they are not visible to observers. For example, when shown photos of angry and happy facial expressions, research participants had small contractions in their own corrugator and zygomatic muscles, respectively (Dimberg, Thunberg, & Grunedal, 2002). This subtle mimicry remained even when participants were explicitly instructed to not move their faces. (See a facial EMG study here: www.youtube.com/watch?v=KsTMVzHWSb8.)

Much research on expressions has sought to determine how culturally specific or universal they are. In other words, how well can people from different cultures recognize the emotion expressions of one another? The answer to this question has important implications for central debates about what emotions are (distinct and fixed vs variable and constructed). Much research supports the idea that that people from diverse cultures can recognize facial expressions and vocalizations displayed by people from other cultures (Elfenbein & Ambady, 2002). This appears true for a handful of (mostly unpleasant) specific emotions: anger, disgust, fear, happiness, sadness, and surprise. Correct identifications across cultures are clearly better than chance, but they are also far from perfect. Even people in the same culture can misinterpret emotional expressions, but the results of many studies suggest that people within the same culture recognize one another's expressions better than the expressions of people from other cultures. Thus, there seems to be some culture-specific aspects to understanding expressions too (Elfenbein & Ambady, 2002). Strong claims of either complete universality or social construction appear incorrect.

Nuances of Positive Expressions

As with other components of emotion, distinctions among different positive emotions have not been studied much until recently. Most positive emotions seem to share smiles as part of the expression, but smiles are less common with interest and awe expressions (Campos, Shiota, Keltner, Gonzaga, & Goetz, 2013). Among positive expressions that share the smile, researchers have found hints of other facial movements that could distinguish among states (Mortillaro, Mehu, & Scherer, 2011). Alternatively, positive emotion expressions may be more differentiated in posture or vocalizations (Sauter, 2010). Pride typically involves a small smile with lips together, but also the head tilted back and an expansive posture with hands raised or on the hips (Tracy & Robins, 2004). Studies in the UK, Sweden, and Namibia suggest that people can identify distinct vocal expressions of triumph, amusement, and sexual pleasure; however, understanding these positive vocalizations was more culturally specific, even compared to negative emotions (Sauter & Scott, 2007; Sauter et al., 2011). People in the UK and Namibia did not reliably identify the other culture's positive sounds.

Emotion expressions reveal something about people's internal states, but they are not a direct read-out (Reisenzein, Studtmann, & Horstmann, 2013). Imagine that a respected professor is scolding you about a late assignment, when he suddenly trips over his own feet. Internally this is might seem hilarious, but you will probably put considerable effort into inhibiting an outward expression of amusement. In contrast to inhibition, we also sometimes express emotions that we are not actually feeling. For example, even when you are feeling down, you probably smile when an acquaintance shares good news, or if you are posing for a photograph. People clearly regulate their expressions, and 'unfelt' smiles are particularly common because they signal friendliness.

There are tricks to figuring out when a smile is genuine, however. Smiles involve contracting the zygomaticus muscle in the cheek to pull the sides of the mouth up and back (the one measured with EMG). This is common to all smiles. By using the Facial Action Coding System's detailed analysis, researchers discovered that genuine smiles involve additional facial changes. Specifically, genuine smiles also involve contraction of a muscle around the eye (orbicularis oculi). The visible result is wrinkles, or 'crow's feet', at the outside edge of the eyes (Ekman, 1992; Ekman, Davidson, & Friesen, 1990). The cheek muscles are easy to voluntarily contract, but the eye muscles are more difficult without actual pleasant feelings (Gosselin, Perron, & Beaupré, 2010). These genuine smiles (i.e. with the eye wrinkles) are termed **Duchenne smiles** after the French anatomist who first articulated the distinction in 1862 (but whose work was long overlooked by social scientists).

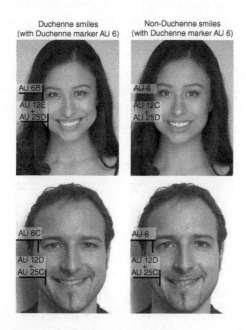

Figure 2.3 Duchenne and non-Duchenne smiles

Photos on the left display Duchenne smiles, whereas photos on the right are non-Duchenne smiles. The key difference is in the muscles at the side of the eyes, coded as action unit six (AU 6) in the FACS approach.

Source: Bogodistov and Dost (2017)

Distinguishing Duchenne smiles has been useful to researchers, especially when they cannot ask people how they feel. For example, in Chapter 1 I wrote about a finding where more intense smiles in yearbook photos predicted positive outcomes many years later (Harker & Keltner, 2001). Let me dissect that result a bit further: all but three of 114 women smiled in their photographs, yet only 50 displayed Duchenne smiles. Including the eye wrinkles was key to differentiating the most intense smiles – it was those 50 women who were more likely to get married. A similar study went back to photos of American baseball players published in 1952. Results seemed to indicate that players who displayed Duchenne smiles lived longer than those who displayed mouth-only smiles (Abel & Kruger, 2010). However, a larger, well-conducted follow-up study found no link between smiles and mortality among baseball players (Dufner, Brümmer, Chung, Drewke, Blaison, & Schmukle, 2018). Sometimes impressive findings – such as predicting death from a single photo – turn out to be flukes. Further studies may shift our understanding again, but the baseball-player phenomenon now seems unlikely. Despite this particular revision, distinguishing Duchenne smiles remains a useful tool.

In Duchenne smile studies, researchers carefully coded facial expressions; yet we all make assessments about the genuineness of others' expressions on some level. Decoding these clues is far from perfect (Krumhuber & Manstead, 2009; Reed, Zeglen, & Schmidt, 2012), but people respond differently to Duchenne smiles, even if they cannot articulate why. For example, Duchenne smiles are rated as more authentic and credible than non-Duchenne smiles (Mehu, Mortillaro, Bänziger, & Scherer, 2012). In another study, photos of actors displaying Duchenne smiles were assessed more positively (e.g. generous and extraverted) compared to non-Duchenne smiles (Mehu, Little, & Dunbar, 2007).

In Focus

Happy Rats?

Emotion research typically takes an evolutionary perspective. Humans' large prefrontal cortex and cognitive capacity make us unique, yet we share much with other species. Studying these similarities – in rats – has produced some surprising insights about pleasure.

One drawback of studying emotion-like processes in animals is that we cannot ask them how they feel (and expect to get a good answer). Yet, as pet owners know, non-human animals seem to express states that seem much like our own emotions. Imagine a dog's excitement as you grab the leash for a walk, or the cat's panic as the vacuum emerges from the closet. Studying human infants presents a similar problem. Yet we can make inferences about their experience and expressions of pleasure by observing which things produce particular expressions.

Applying these methods, psychologists have learned that rats enjoy playing, much like humans do. They even produce distinctive ultrasonic laughs at 50 kHz when they do it. This fun interpretation of rat chirps grew out of a collection of findings. For example, we infer that the 50 kHz trill vocalizations represent pleasure because rats also make them when they are rewarded with electric brain stimulation, drugs like cocaine, and during mating (Burgdorf et al., 2008; Knutson, Burgdorf, & Panksepp, 2002). 'Laughter' seemed appropriate because researchers also prompted 50 kHz trills when they tickled rats. (Yes, the researchers actually tickled the rats, very similarly to how you would tickle a human with rhythmic finger rubs.) The tickling and laughs appear pleasurable for the rats because tickled rats later approached the experimenter more quickly, compared to other rats who were randomly assigned to mere gentle petting (Burgdorf & Panksepp, 2001). To be clear, rat 'laughter' is not equivalent to human laughter (e.g. political satire will not elicit it). Nonetheless, rats seem to have a vocal expression for this pleasant, social, approach state – something that we can recognize as familiar.

Rat expressions have also been used to probe the neuroscience of pleasure (Berridge & Kringelbach, 2011). Fascinatingly, this research suggests that we can want things that we do not actually like. In addition, dopamine may not be the 'pleasure chemical' so often portrayed in popular media. The research actually began by trying to prove the link between dopamine and pleasure, but a unique way of measuring pleasure opened the door to new insights.

Psychologists assume that when rats are willing to work for something (e.g. by pressing a lever), they enjoy the reward that follows (e.g. food, electric brain stimulation, certain drugs, access to sex). But what if we tried to assess pleasure more directly? The researchers found that they could reliably code expressions of pleasure in rats. Similar to human infants and many other mammals, rats produce rhythmic licking movements with their tongues when they taste sweet things; in contrast, they open their mouths wide and shake their heads when they taste bitter things (Berridge, 2007). These expressions vary in frequency and intensity, so researchers can tell when tastes are liked more or less (cf. FACS used for human expressions).

The fascinating findings began when brain manipulations were combined with observations of rats' liking expressions. For example, stimulating or blocking dopamine in the brain (via drugs, surgery, or electrical stimulation) did not seem to change how much rats expressed liking for sweet tastes. If dopamine is responsible for pleasure, it should produce more expressions of liking. This did not occur. In addition, rats clearly expressed pleasure even when dopamine was removed from their brains. Subsequent

(Continued)

research blocked or facilitated other chemicals and found that pleasure was more associated with opioids (similar to morphine) and cannabinoids (similar to marijuana).

Although it may not cause pleasure, dopamine is still important to rewards and their pursuit. Rats who receive amphetamine (which stimulates dopamine) want sweet food rewards more – they work harder for it. Conversely, when dopamine is removed, rats show no interest in pursuing food rewards, and would even starve to death unless fed. However, when these dopamine-depleted rats have food placed in their mouths, they still produce the little licks of enjoyment. Without dopamine, the motivation to seek reward is diminished, but the pleasure of consumption remains. This is a key insight: in the brain, *wanting* things is distinct from *liking* them. Different chemical pathways produce liking versus wanting. (See Kringelbach & Berridge, 2012 for an accessible presentation of the neuroscience.)

When a neuroscientist is not around to alter brain chemistry, wanting and liking typically go together. This explains why dopamine has seemed like a pleasure chemical in so much other research. Yet knowing that wanting and liking can be dissociated in the brain helps us understand psychological phenomena. For example, with drug addiction, wanting drugs of abuse remains very strong, even when the pleasure of their consumption has faded (T. E. Robinson & Berridge, 2003). Addiction seems to change the brain in ways that further dissociate wanting and liking in experience. From a more positive perspective, neuroscientists are now testing the links between the neural structures responsible for sensory pleasure in rats and more sophisticated human pleasures (Berridge & Kringelbach, 2011). There are clear differences between human and rat brains, but also striking similarities. How much might those evolutionarily ancient pleasure circuits underlie venerated human pleasures like the pride of artistic accomplishment? Perhaps you have had the experience of intensely wanting something, but then not enjoying it much once you got it?

Subjective Experience

We all know what emotions feel like, and this internal, first-person experience (or phenomenology) is an important component of emotion. Unconscious emotions may also exist (Winkielman & Berridge, 2004), but most of the time we are aware of our feelings. Subjective experience is measured with self-reports. Essentially, we ask people how they are feeling. The relative ease of this method, compared to physiological assessments or detailed facial analysis, explains some of its popularity. However, equally important is the fact that subjective experience is often the component psychologists are most interested in knowing about.

For example, imagine your friend has an expressionless face, yet tells you he is feeling very sad. Such dissociations between experience and expressions of emotion are not uncommon (Mauss & Robinson, 2009), yet it does not mean we dismiss our friend's feelings. For many, subjective experience alone is enough to identify an emotion.

Assessing subjective experience with self-reports of emotions seems straightforward, yet subtle differences – in when and how things are asked – are crucially important. Additionally, for self-reports to be valid, the reporter must be willing and able to provide accurate information. Some contexts (e.g. highly evaluative ones like job interviews or criminal proceedings) or personal characteristics (e.g. emotional intelligence or verbal ability) can interfere with willingness, ability, or both. Subjective experience is personal; we depend on people's cooperation to assess it.

To obtain self-reports of emotion, one could use a simple open-ended question; for example, "How do you feel?". However, the responses to such a broad question would present problems for a researcher with a large study (Scherer, 2005). First, from angry to zesty, there are hundreds of English words that describe feeling states, so the number of different responses could be overwhelming. Second, if a research participant responded "happy" or "anxious", we would still not know how intensely, and researchers are typically interested in quantitative comparisons across people or circumstances. In order to solve these problems, self-report emotion measures usually present a list of adjectives to be rated on a scale of intensity (see the Try It examples).

Rating scales quantify the intensity of subjective experience, but you may still be wondering how emotion terms are chosen from the hundreds of possibilities. Sometimes the selection is made using a theory. For example, researchers who take the perspective that discrete, basic emotions exist would focus on assessing them. The many other emotion adjectives are then viewed as redundant synonyms, blends of more basic emotions, or other kinds of feelings that do not meet the criteria for a true emotion.

TRY IT

The PANAS Questionnaire

Here are the instructions and some example items from the Positive and Negative Affect Schedule-Expanded Form (PANAS-X; Watson & Clark, 1999).

Instructions: This scale consists of a number of words and phrases that describe different feelings and emotions. Read each item and then mark the appropriate answer in the space next to that word. Indicate to what extent you are feeling this way *right now*, at this moment. Use the following scale to record your answers:

(Continued)

1	2	3	4	5
Very slightly or not at all	A little	Moderately	Quite a bit	Extremely

_____cheerful _____sad _____proud _____enthusiastic

_____surprised _____alert _____jittery _____bold

_____happy _____afraid _____irritable _____interested

Note that the full questionnaire includes 60 individual adjectives; groups of items are averaged to form 13 scales (e.g. general positive affect or more specific states like joviality or fear). Sometimes the instructions are altered to assess more trait level affect, by asking people to report on how they feel in general or on average.

The Dimensional Approach to Affect

Statistical approaches provide another way to reduce the number of emotion words to a manageable number. The process begins by assembling large lists of emotion adjectives, asking people in various circumstances to rate how much they are feeling them, and then using statistical techniques to sort which feelings tend to co-occur (R. J. Larsen & Diener, 1992; Russell, 1980; Watson & Tellegen, 1985). For example, people typically rate 'irritable' and 'angry' highly at the same time, while simultaneously rating 'relaxed' low. Patterns of co-occurrence tell us which emotion terms are more or less similar to each other. These similarities and differences then define a conceptual space where emotion terms are arranged (see Figure 2.2). Much of the similarity and difference among feelings can be represented in a two-dimensional conceptual space (Barrett & Russell, 1998). In this space, feelings that are similar and co-occur appear near one another. Dissimilar feelings that rarely co-occur are at opposite sides of the space. Feelings at 45-degree angles do not correlate with one another; they can co-occur, but not especially often.

In Figure 2.2, we see a dimension from left to right that distinguishes unpleasant (sad) from pleasant (happy) feelings. From bottom to top, activation or arousal increases. Feelings come in all combinations of pleasantness and arousal. Therefore, we see terms scattered all around the two-dimensional space. This pattern is called a circumplex.

With a circular pattern, the defining dimensions are ambiguous. Any two independent dimensions (i.e. at 90 degrees) can define the space. The pleasant–unpleasant and arousal dimensions are an intuitive way to do it. However, a popular alternative is to focus on dimensions rotated 45 degrees in the circle. The widely used Positive and Negative Affect Schedule

(PANAS) questionnaire measures aroused pleasant (e.g. excited) and aroused unpleasant (e.g. nervous) affects (Watson, Clark, & Tellegen, 1988).

Thinking of positive affect and negative affect as two independent dimensions (rather than opposites) implies that positivity and negativity have distinct causes and consequences (Cacioppo & Bernston, 1994). Said another way, what makes people joyful is not simply the absence of what makes them distressed. Looking at the circumplex, we see the opposite of distress is relaxation, not joy. The main idea is that we can be activated in pleasant or unpleasant ways. These two forms of activation are independent of one another. They may reflect our subjective experience of approach or avoidance motivation systems, respectively (Carver, Sutton, & Scheier, 2000; Watson, Wiese, Vaidya, & Tellegen, 1999; Zelenski & Larsen, 1999). In sum, despite ongoing debate about which two dimensions are 'fundamental', the two-dimensional model clearly tells us how various feelings relate to one another. This, in turn, allows for better choices when creating a questionnaire measure.

Memory and Reports of Experience

Time is another important consideration when measuring subjective experience with self-reports. Experience is fleeting. This leads to problems when we try to recall emotions from our past, or when we mentally average feelings over periods of time. For example, if I asked you to indicate how you were feeling at exactly 10:30 on 29 May 2017, could you provide an accurate answer? Not likely. Over time our memories fade. You may even refuse to answer because the question is unfairly hard. However, if I asked you to rate your average moods during May 2017, I suspect you would be more willing to provide an answer. This is odd. Why does it seem more reasonable to report a mental average of moments that we cannot recall individually? Clearly, our mental 'average' is not an actual calculation across many moments, but rather something that is constructed from the information we do have available. Our **experiencing self** – the one who feels things in the moment – is not the same as our **remembering self** – the one who completes self-reports of past experiences (Kahneman & Riis, 2005; M. D. Robinson & Clore, 2002a).

After a week or two it is difficult to actually recall our momentary emotions, and so we rely on other forms of knowledge (M. D. Robinson & Clore, 2002a). Thus, when answering questions about moods from a few weeks ago, people go through a mental process something like "Hmmm, I usually experience moderately pleasant moods, and I think I was on holiday part of that time, so I guess 8 out of 10 on 'joyful'". Rather than a concrete, episodic memory of their past moods, people use beliefs about their dispositions and major life circumstances at the time. As time since the actual experience increases, our reports of emotions include more information about general beliefs (i.e. semantic knowledge) and less about the actual specific, momentary experience (M. D. Robinson & Clore, 2002b). For example, studies have found that when rating current feelings, gender and cultural differences are small or non-existent. However, when recalling those moments later, memories start to conform to stereotypes. That is, in retrospective ratings (only), women are more emotional than men (Barrett, Robin, Pietromonaco, & Eyssell, 1998), and European Americans are happier than Asians (Oishi, 2002). Gender and cultural differences seemed to 'grow' over time in ways that are consistent with the beliefs that people have. This suggests a bias in retrospective ratings of emotional experience.

Biases in distant memories are not especially surprising. Yet even very recent memories are susceptible to distortions. This is because the remembering self pays little attention to time, a phenomenon known as **duration neglect** (Fredrickson & Kahneman, 1993). When remembering experiences, moments are not created equally. Our memories depend particularly on the peak intensity and on how episodes ended (Kahneman, Fredrickson, Schreiber, & Redelmeier, 1993). In a classic study (that stretches the boundaries of positive psychology), patients continuously rated their pain as they underwent a colonoscopy (Redelmeier & Kahneman, 1996). (Colonoscopy was a painful medical procedure where a small camera is inserted into the rectum and moved through the large intestine. Fortunately, modern techniques have eliminated the pain.) An hour after the procedure, patients rated the "total amount of pain experienced". Objectively, patients who experienced longer procedures experienced more pain, because it lasted longer (see Figure 2.4). However, the study found that actual time was unrelated to patients' ratings of 'total

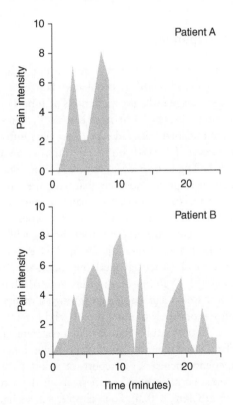

Figure 2.4 Pain ratings over time from Redelmeier and Kahneman (1996)

Real-time recordings from two patients. Each graph displays the intensity of pain recorded each minute by a patient undergoing colonoscopy. The experiences of two individuals are shown (Patient A and Patient B). The x-axis represents time in minutes from the start of the procedure. The y-axis represents the intensity of pain recorded in real-time on a visual analogue scale with ends denoted as 'no pain' and 'extreme pain'. The procedure lasted 8 minutes for Patient A and 24 minutes for Patient B.

pain'. Total pain ratings depended more on how the procedures ended (high or low pain) and how bad the very worst (peak) moment was. A follow-up study asked doctors to try making some colonoscopies last longer – creating objectively more pain – by keeping the camera relatively still in the rectum, and thus creating a mild ending to the procedure. Compared to participants who had regular, shorter, and objectively less painful procedures, the experimental group with mild endings reported substantially less pain (Redelmeier, Katz, & Kahneman, 2003).

Findings like these are not limited to pain (Diener, Wirtz, & Oishi, 2001). In an example more relevant to positive psychology students, Wirtz, Kruger, Scollon, and Diener (2003) studied university students' emotion experiences – and emotion recollections – of spring break trips. During holidays, emotions were rated several times daily (another example of the experience sampling method). Then four days, and then four weeks, after students returned from holidays, they made retrospective ratings of their average emotions during the spring break. Students reported more positive emotions and negative emotions in the retrospective ratings, compared to actual numerical averages of the ratings made during the spring break. Said another way, students' recalled emotions were significantly more intense than their actual experiences. People seem to forget the mundane periods; not all moments are created equally for the remembering self. (People often overestimate the length and intensity of their future emotional reactions too, something discussed in Chapter 6.)

Distinguishing between the experiencing self and the remembering self has a few important implications. First, emotion researchers interested in capturing objective experience need to assess it in the moment (vs with retrospective ratings). Retrospective reports and mental averages over time tell us about remembered experience, which differs somewhat from what actually happened in the moment. Second, we can ask whether it is better to benefit the experiencing self or the remembering self. Should we choose experiences that produce objectively more pleasure (i.e. longer ones), or experiences that we will remember more fondly (i.e. shorter, more intense ones with better endings)? How long does a beach holiday really need to be? In thinking through these questions, it is worth noting that our remembering self is the one that makes decisions about future plans. When it came to colonoscopies and spring break trips, remembered emotions predicted whether or not people would repeat the experience better than momentary (actual) experienced (Redelmeier et al., 2003; Wirtz et al., 2003). Actual experiences are, of course, important to our memories of them. However, when compared, memories have the more lasting impact. Experience is fleeting.

TRY IT

Savouring Positive Experience

This chapter has discussed positive emotions and pleasant states. This exercise asks you to put aside some time to do something pleasurable, and to try to augment that

(Continued)

experience by savouring it. Savouring is a way to manage positive experiences in ways that can enhance them (Bryant, Chadwick, & Kluwe, 2011).

You might plan a little adventure for yourself, a special date with a friend or romantic partner, a phone call to an old friend, a nice meal, etc.

You could also use an unplanned and unexpected positive event (e.g. a compliment, a generous favour, a great song) and try to boost the experience by savouring it.

You are welcome to generate your own ways of fully engaging with your positive experience, and some techniques will work better than others depending on the context. Here are a few ideas (see also http://greatergood.berkeley.edu/article/item/10_steps_to_savoring_the_good_things_in_life):

Try to sharpen your perception by focusing on the relevant details or sensations.

Take a (mental) photograph or a souvenir and return to it later, trying to recall or re-experience the event.

Plan the event for the future, and take some time(s) beforehand to anticipate how nice it will be.

Immerse yourself as much as possible in the event; avoid distractions.

Share this pleasant event with others (do it with them or tell them about it later).

You might also consider how your savouring efforts can effect both your experiencing self (e.g. emphasizing pleasure in the moment and absorbing yourself in it) and your remembering self (e.g. ensuring a good ending, keeping a memento).

Please note that we sometimes try things that don't work out as well as we hope. Some attempts at savouring could backfire, for example by worrying about enjoying something or 'over-thinking' it. That's OK. You can always try savouring again with some adjustments.

Action Tendencies

Action tendencies are the motivational part of emotions (Frijda, Kuipers, & ter Schure, 1989). From an evolutionary perspective, emotions exist because they help organisms respond quickly and adaptively to important circumstances (Tooby & Cosmides, 1990). This response includes a readiness for certain behaviours. For example, because our ancestors responded to snakes with fear and withdrawal, they avoided poisonous bites. Others, who did not share this tendency, were less likely to live long enough to become anyone's ancestors. The physiological changes that accompany emotions are often linked to action tendencies: "Autonomic arousal can be considered the logistic support of certain variants of action readiness" (Frijda et al., 1989, p. 231). Physiological arousal makes the body ready for action. Action tendencies describe that motivation more broadly, and also include cognitive changes and behaviours.

BROADEN AND BUILD MODEL OF POSITIVE EMOTIONS

As we have seen with other components of emotion, the theories fit negative emotions better than positive emotions. Specific behaviour responses seem intuitive for fear (fleeing), anger (fighting), disgust (spitting), and so on. However, as Barbara Fredrickson (1998) noted, the action tendencies for pleasant emotions are less clear. In a seminal article titled "What good are positive emotions?," she proposed a new approach, one that suggested positive emotions function differently, particularly when it comes to their action tendencies and adaptive value. This broaden and build model of positive emotions was a big idea in the emerging positive psychology movement.

According to the **broaden and build model**, positive emotions widen the scope of thoughts and behaviours. This contrasts with the idea of specific action tendencies for negative emotions; they narrow the scope of responses (e.g. flee, fight, or spit). Rather than producing specific responses, positive emotions foster more variety in thoughts and behaviours, such as play, exploration, and social bonding. Over time, these activities are thought to build more lasting skills and resources. This is their adaptive value, or why positive emotions helped our ancestors survive and reproduce. For example, the active play spurred by positive emotions might improve physical fitness and athletic skill. The desire for social connection might foster a friendship that leads to support in the future.

With positive emotions, the 'action tendency' is the immediate broadening of thoughts and behaviours; the adaptive benefit is realized further in the future, compared to negative emotions. Over time, a person who experiences more positive, broadened states will have more opportunities to develop enduring skills and resources – the building part takes time. Fredrickson (2013) describes the broaden and build process as an 'upward spiral': positive emotions promote novel thoughts and activities, which in turn build physical, intellectual, and social skills, which promote healthy functioning and fulfilment, which promote more positive emotions, and on and on.

Experimental studies test the immediate broadening effects of positive emotions. Surprise gifts of candy, pleasant video clips, and mental imagery can effectively produce positive states in the lab. These are compared to neutral control groups or unpleasant emotion inductions. Note that the neutral comparisons are more informative because they tell us about positive emotions per se. When compared only to negative emotions, we do not know whether it is the positive or negative emotion that most accounts for differences. Collectively, these studies suggest that positive emotions broaden our cognition. That is, with positive emotions attention wanders, we consider more creative solutions, and we see the big picture rather than details (Fredrickson, 2013).

RESEARCH CASE

TESTING THE BROADEN AND BUILD MODEL

Early tests of the broaden and build model used laboratory emotion inductions and tested their influence on cognitive processes, such as the breadth of attention. More specifically, the global–local task indicates how much people focus on the big picture (global features) versus smaller details (local features; Kimchi & Palmer, 1982). In this attention task, participants must decide which of two figures is most similar to a target figure, across many examples (see Figure 2.5). Some sets have clear answers, but others are more ambiguous. The ambiguous sets are revealing: the figures can be matched on the smaller, 'local' shapes (individual triangles or squares) or on the overall, 'global' pattern (as arranged in a larger square or triangle). Thus, participants' choices indicate whether they are thinking about the shapes at a narrow or a broad level, individuals or wholes.

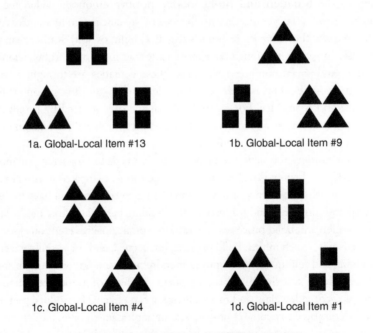

1a. Global-Local Item #13   1b. Global-Local Item #9

1c. Global-Local Item #4   1d. Global-Local Item #1

Example global-local items used in Experiment 1.

Figure 2.5   Global–local task from Fredrickson & Branigan (2005)

In one key study, Fredrickson and Branigan (2005) recruited about 100 student participants and randomly assigned them to watch a video that induced one of the following: amusement (penguins playing), contentment (serene nature scenes), anger (taunting a visible minority), fear (a mountain-climbing accident), or a neutral state (abstract coloured sticks piling up). After the video, participants completed a global–local attention task. There were eight key sets of shapes; the number of 'global' choices were tallied to index broad attentional focus. The results supported the broaden and build model. That is, people who viewed the positive videos (amusement and contentment) made more global choices, compared to people who viewed any of the negative or neutral videos. This study provided early support for the notion that positive emotions broaden attention. Said another way, positive emotions let us see the forest, whereas negative emotions cause us to focus on the trees. Other studies have found similar results with global–local tasks (Gasper & Clore, 2002; Rowe, Hirsh, & Anderson, 2007). Positive emotions seem to broaden attention.

According to the broaden and build model, changes in basic cognitive processes like attention facilitate other kinds of momentary broadening (Fredrickson, 2001). For example, creativity can be defined as making novel connections or finding unusual ways to solve problems (see Chapter 6). Positive emotions improve performance on these kinds of creativity measures (Baas, De Dreu, & Nijstad, 2008; Isen, Daubman, & Nowicki, 1987; Rowe et al., 2007). Beyond creativity, when asked to "Make a list of things you would like to do right now", research participants listed more things if they had just watched a positive film clip, compared to neutral or negative clips (Fredrickson & Branigan, 2005).

Positive emotions seem particularly good at promoting social bonds. Participants induced to feel positive (vs neutral or negative) emotions report wanting to engage in more social activities – even mundane social activities that are no more pleasant than solitary activities (e.g. class group work vs being alone at the beach; Whelan & Zelenski, 2012). Beyond the impulse to socialize, positive emotions seem to facilitate social bonds. For example, induced happiness and gratitude increase feelings of trust (Dunn & Schweitzer, 2005). New university students who reported experiencing more positive emotions also reported feeling more connected to their roommates in the first weeks of living together (Waugh & Fredrickson, 2006). Studies like this bring us from the broadening to the building part of the model. With deeper social bonds comes future support, an enduring 'built' resource.

Because the building happens over longer periods of time, experimental studies (with induced positive emotions) cannot easily assess this part of the model. Much of the research on building has thus relied on correlational techniques. When the correlations are assessed longitudinally (over time) with positive emotions occurring first, it strengthens the interpretation that positive emotions cause the beneficial outcomes (see Chapter 1). Studies measure things like positive coping skills, strong relationships, resilience, work performance, and physical health. They generally find that these resources are more abundant among people who have been experiencing more positive emotions (Cohn, Fredrickson, Brown, Mikels, & Conway, 2009; Fredrickson & Joiner, 2002; Lyubomirsky, King, & Diener, 2005).

In a rare experimental study of resource building, some participants were randomly assigned to practise loving kindness meditation for seven weeks (Fredrickson, Cohn, Coffey, Pek, & Finkel, 2008). Meditation produced an increase in daily positive emotions over time, compared to a control group. Eighteen different resources were also measured before and after the weeks of meditation. Results indicated that positive emotions (produced by meditation) increased scores on nine of the resource measures (e.g. mindfulness, self-acceptance, social support) over time. In addition, the increased resource scores statistically accounted for increases in life satisfaction and decreases in depression symptoms over the study period. Said another way, meditation appeared to begin an upward spiral, producing positive emotions, then resources, and then healthy and happy functioning.

In sum, research generally supports the notion that positive emotions broaden thoughts and behaviours in the moment. It is harder to test how resources are built over time, but correlations are usually consistent with the idea. Despite many supportive findings, the phrase 'broaden and build' is, itself, a broad slogan that glosses over some nuance. As research on positive emotions grows, we are discovering exceptions to this general trend.

Limitations of the Broaden and Build Model

First, the principles of broaden and build probably play out differently for different kinds of positive emotions (Shiota et al., 2014). Joy might facilitate play and physical learning, whereas awe might facilitate thinking about things in a new way. Interest seems to promote exploration and learning, whereas gratitude drives social bonds and prosocial behaviour (Campos et al., 2013; Fredrickson, 2013). With more research attention on positive emotions, distinctions among them have grown. These distinctions suggest some limits to the broadening; each positive emotion promotes openness to only some categories of thoughts and actions. For example, Whelan and Zelenski (2012) found that positive emotions (amusement and inspiration) increased the desire to socialize; yet they simultaneously decreased desire for many solitary activities. (Positive emotions could have increased desire for both kinds.) Thus, although positive emotions do not seem to produce highly specific action tendencies, they may still channel people towards – and away from – some kinds of thoughts and behaviours. Specific positive emotions do not make people simultaneously more open to everything.

Going further, some positive states seem to directly contradict the general trend of broadening. Instead, they narrow attention and behaviour. More specifically, the pleasant feelings that accompany approach motivation narrow attention by causing us to focus on a specific reward (Harmon-Jones, Price, & Gable, 2012). Imagine a neighbour calls to say that he is just about to serve a delicious birthday cake, and offers you a slice if you could please just pick up some candles on your way over. If you are someone who loves cake, this call makes you experience positive emotions. It also gives you a laser-like focus on getting candles to the cake ASAP. In other words, states of desire, excitement, or interest can narrow – rather than broaden – our focus. In one demonstration, research participants were randomly assigned to view a positive film clip: either tempting desserts or funny cat videos (Gable & Harmon-Jones, 2008). They then completed a global–local task (see Figure 2.5 and Research Case box). Participants who viewed the funny cats had a more global focus, consistent with the broadening hypothesis. In contrast, participants who saw the desserts – and reported more desire – had a narrower focus; they noticed the individual shapes more. Conceptually similar results were found in a study that measured attention either just before, or just after, a monetary reward was given. Anticipation seemed to narrow attention, whereas the pleasure after the reward seemed to broaden attention (Gable & Harmon-Jones, 2011). This may be another example of how wanting is different from liking (see In Focus box above): the feelings differ and the focus of attention differs. Some personality characteristics and situational contexts can also reverse positive affect's broadening influence on attention (Gasper, 2004; Huntsinger, Isbell, & Clore, 2014). Thus, 'broaden and build' is useful as a rule of thumb for positive emotions, but it is a rule with exceptions.

SUMMING UP

Positive emotions are common in our experience, and – with the positive psychology movement – have become increasingly common in psychological research. We are learning that positive emotions operate a bit differently than negative emotions do. For example, they seem less differentiated in facial expressions; smiling is common to most. Whereas negative emotions have more specific action tendencies, positive emotions often broaden the scope of thoughts and behaviours. We also see similarities between positive and negative emotions. Appraisal patterns (across dimensions) help distinguish among pleasant feelings as they do among unpleasant feelings. Physiological changes accompany positive emotions, yet as with negative emotions, more work is needed to identify clear and robust patterns that distinguish among them.

Emotions emerge when various bodily and psychological systems come together. These are articulated in the five components of emotions: appraisals, physiological change, expressions, subjective experience, and action tendencies. Although the prototypical emotion includes patterned changes in each component, we have seen that the pattern of change is not always as clear as theory suggests. For example, we can experience an emotion while suppressing its expression; specific physiological signatures for individual emotions are elusive. Each component of emotion seems important, but their coherence is loose. In this way emotions are like a fruit salad. A strawberry, blueberry, banana, kiwi, or grape is not a fruit salad on its own. Yet the combination of any three of these fruits could reasonably be considered a fruit salad. No one component is absolutely necessary. So it is with emotions. The prototypical emotion includes all components, but many of our affective episodes probably include fewer. This state of affairs frustrates clear descriptions and definitions, but seems to be where the research stands at this point. Now that we have explored this complexity, we will be prepared for some emotion shorthand in future chapters.

TEST YOURSELF

1. Briefly describe the five components of emotions.

2. How is the basic emotion approach different from the dimensional approach?

3. What is a Duchenne smile?

4. What is the difference between wanting and liking? Which is more pleasurable?

5. How is the 'experiencing self' different from the 'remembering self'?

6. In the broaden and build model, what is broadened and what is built?

WEB LINKS

Experts in emotion video series with June Gruber: www.youtube.com/playlist?list=PLh9mg-di4rNew731mjlZn43G_Y5otqKzJA

Daniel Kahneman's TED talk on emotional experience, memory, and happiness: www.ted.com/talks/daniel_kahneman_the_riddle_of_experience_vs_memory

FURTHER READING

To learn more about emotion measurements, see:

Mauss, I. B., & Robinson, M. D. (2009). Measures of emotion: A review. *Cognition & Emotion, 23*(2), 209–237.

To read more about using evolutionary theory to differentiate positive emotions, see:

Shiota, M. N., Neufeld, S. L., Danvers, A. F., Osborne, E. A., Sng, O., & Yee, C. I. (2014). Positive emotion differentiation: A functional approach. *Social and Personality Psychology Compass, 8*(3), 104–117.

This brief and accessible article reports the details of the spring break study:

Wirtz, D., Kruger, J., Scollon, C. N., & Diener, E. (2003). What to do on spring break? The role of predicted, on-line, and remembered experience in future choice. *Psychological Science, 14*(5), 520–524.

For a specific example of cross-cultural study of positive emotions (in vocal expressions), see:

Sauter, D. A., Eisner, F., Ekman, P., & Scott, S. K. (2010). Cross-cultural recognition of basic emotions through nonverbal emotional vocalizations. *Proceedings of the National Academy of Sciences of the United States of America, 107*(6), 2408–2412.

Read about the origins of the broaden and build model here:

Fredrickson, B. L. (2001). The role of positive emotions in positive psychology. *American Psychologist, 56*(3), 218–226.

REFERENCES

Abel, E. L., & Kruger, M. L. (2010). Smile intensity in photographs predicts longevity. *Psychological Science, 21*(4), 542–544. http://doi.org/10.1177/0956797610363775

Algoe, S. B., & Haidt, J. (2009). Witnessing excellence in action: The "other-praising" emotions of elevation, gratitude, and admiration. *The Journal of Positive Psychology, 4*(2), 105–127. http://doi.org/10.1080/17439760802650519

Arnold, M. (1960). *Emotion and Personality.* New York: Columbia University Press.

Baas, M., De Dreu, C. K. W., & Nijstad, B. A. (2008). A meta-analysis of 25 years of mood-creativity research: Hedonic tone, activation, or regulatory focus? *Psychological Bulletin*, *134*(6), 779–806. http://doi.org/10.1037/a0012815

Barrett, L. F. (2006). Are emotions natural kinds? *Perspectives on Psychological Science*, *1*(1), 28–58. http://doi.org/10.1111/j.1745-6916.2006.00003.x

Barrett, L. F., Robin, L., Pietromonaco, P. R., & Eyssell, K. M. (1998). Are women the "more emotional" sex? Evidence from emotional experiences in social context. *Cognition & Emotion*, *12*(4), 555–578. http://doi.org/10.1080/026999398379565

Barrett, L. F., & Russell, J. A. (1998). Independence and bipolarity in the structure of current affect. *Journal of Personality and Social Psychology*, *74*(4), 967–984. http://doi.org/10.1037/0022-3514.74.4.967

Barrett, L. F., & Russell, J. A. (1999). The structure of current affect: Controversies and emerging consensus. *Current Directions in Psychological Science*, *8*(1), 10–14. https://doi.org/10.1111/1467-8721.00003

Baumeister, R. F., Bratslavsky, E., Finkenauer, C., & Vohs, K. D. (2001). Bad is stronger than good. *Review of General Psychology*, *5*(4), 323–370. http://doi.org/10.1037/1089-2680.5.4.323

Beck, J. (2015). Hard feelings: Science's struggle to define emotions. Retrieved 22 April 2015 from https://www.theatlantic.com/health/archive/2015/02/hard-feelings-sciences-struggle-to-define-emotions/385711/

Berridge, K. C. (2007). The debate over dopamine's role in reward: The case for incentive salience. *Psychopharmacology*, *191*(3), 391–431. http://doi.org/10.1007/s00213-006-0578-x

Berridge, K. C., & Kringelbach, M. L. (2011). Building a neuroscience of pleasure and well-being. *Psychology of Well-Being*, *1*(1), 1–3. http://doi.org/10.1186/2211-1522-1-3

Bogodistov, Y., & Dost, F. (2017). Proximity begins with a smile, but which one? Associating non-duchenne smiles with higher psychological distance. *Frontiers in Psychology, 8*, 1374.

Bryant, F. B., Chadwick, E. D., & Kluwe, K. (2011). Understanding the processes that regulate positive emotional experience: Unsolved problems and future directions for theory and research on savoring. *International Journal of Wellbeing*, *1*(1), 107–126. http://doi.org/10.5502/ijw.v1i1.18

Burgdorf, J., Kroes, R. A., Moskal, J. R., Pfaus, J. G., Brudzynski, S. M., & Panksepp, J. (2008). Ultrasonic vocalizations of rats (Rattus norvegicus) during mating, play, and aggression: Behavioral concomitants, relationship to reward, and self-administration of playback. *Journal of Comparative Psychology*, *122*(4), 357–367. http://doi.org/10.1037/a0012889

Burgdorf, J., & Panksepp, J. (2001). Tickling induces reward in adolescent rats. *Physiology and Behavior*, *72*(1–2), 167–173. http://doi.org/10.1016/S0031-9384(00)00411-X

Cacioppo, J. T., & Bernston, G. G. (1994). Relationship between attitudes and evaluative space: A critical review, with emphasis on the separability of positive and negative substrates. *Psychological Bulletin*, *115*(3), 401–423. http://doi.org/10.1037/0033-2909.115.3.401

Cacioppo, J. T., Bernston, G. G., Klein, D. J., & Poehlmann, K. M. (1997). Psychophysiology of emotion across the life span. *Annual Review of Gerontology and Geriatrics, 17*, 27–74.

Campos, B., & Keltner, D. (2014). Shared and differentiating features of the positive emotion domain. In J. Gruber & J. T. Moskowitz (eds), *Positive Emotion: Integrating the Light and Dark Sides* (pp. 52–71). New York: Oxford University Press.

Campos, B., Shiota, M. N., Keltner, D., Gonzaga, G. C., & Goetz, J. L. (2013). What is shared, what is different? Core relational themes and expressive displays of eight positive emotions. *Cognition & Emotion, 27*(1), 37–52. http://doi.org/10.1080/02699931.2012.683852

Carver, C. S., Sutton, S. K., & Scheier, M. F. (2000). Action, emotion, and personality: Emerging conceptual integration. *Personality and Social Psychology Bulletin, 26*(6), 741–751. http://doi.org/10.1177/0146167200268008

Coan, J. A., & Allen, J. J. B. (2004). Frontal EEG asymmetry as a moderator and mediator of emotion. *Biological Psychology, 67*(1–2), 7–49. http://doi.org/10.1016/j.biopsycho.2004.03.002

Cohn, M. A., Fredrickson, B. L., Brown, S. L., Mikels, J. A., & Conway, A. M. (2009). Happiness unpacked: Positive emotions increase life satisfaction by building resilience. *Emotion, 9*(3), 361–368. http://doi.org/10.1037/a0015952

Damasio, A. R. (1996). The somatic marker hypothesis and the possible functions of the prefrontal cortex. *Philosophical Transactions of the Royal Society of London. Series B, Biological Sciences, 351*(1346), 1413–1420. http://doi.org/10.1098/rstb.1996.0125

Darwin, C. (1872). *The Expression of the Emotions in Man and Animals*. Oxford: Oxford University Press.

Dawson, M., Schell, A., & Filion, D. (2000). The electrodermal system. In J. T. Cacioppo, L. G. Tassinary, & G. G. Berntson (eds), *Handbook of Psychophysiology* (2nd edn, pp. 200–223). New York: Cambridge University Press.

Diener, E., Kanazawa, S., Suh, E. M., & Oishi, S. (2014). Why people are in a generally good mood. *Personality and Social Psychology Review*, 1–22. http://doi.org/10.1177/1088868314544467

Diener, E., Wirtz, D., & Oishi, S. (2001). End effects of rated life quality: The James Dean Effect. *Psychological Science, 12*(2), 124–128. http://doi.org/10.1111/1467-9280.00321

Dimberg, U. (1990). For distinguished early career contribution to psychophysiology: Award address, 1988. *Psychophysiology, 27*(5), 481–494. http://doi.org/10.1111/j.1469-8986.1990.tb01962.x

Dimberg, U., Thunberg, M., & Grunedal, S. (2002). Facial reactions to emotional stimuli: Automatically controlled emotional responses. *Cognition & Emotion, 16*(4), 449–471. http://doi.org/10.1080/02699930143000356

Dixon, T. (2012). "Emotion": The history of a keyword in crisis. *Emotion Review, 4*(4), 338–344. http://doi.org/10.1177/1754073912445814

Dufner, M., Brümmer, M., Chung, J. M., Drewke, P. M., Blaison, C., & Schmukle, S. C. (2018). Does smile intensity in photographs really predict longevity? A replication and extension of Abel and Kruger (2010). *Psychological Science, 29*(1), 147–153. 95679761773431. http://doi.org/10.1177/0956797617734315

Dunn, J. R., & Schweitzer, M. E. (2005). Feeling and believing: The influence of emotion on trust. *Journal of Personality and Social Psychology*, *88*(5), 736–748. http://doi.org/10.1037/0022-3514.88.5.736

Ekman, P. (1982). Methods for measuring facial action. In K. R. Scherer & P. Ekman (eds), *Handbook of Methods in Nonverbal Behavior Research* (pp. 45–135). New York: Cambridge University Press.

Ekman, P. (1992). Facial expressions of emotion: New findings, new questions. *Psychological Science*, *3*(1), 34–38. http://doi.org/10.1111/j.1467-9280.1992.tb00253.x

Ekman, P., & Cordaro, D. (2011). What is meant by calling emotions basic. *Emotion Review*, *3*(4), 364–370. http://doi.org/10.1177/1754073911410740

Ekman, P., & Davidson, R. (1993). Voluntary smiling changes regional brain activity. *Psychological Science*, *4*(5), 342–345. http://doi.org/10.1111/j.1467-9280.1993.tb00576.x

Ekman, P., Davidson, R. J., & Friesen, W. V. (1990). The Duchenne smile: Emotional expression and brain physiology. *Journal of Personality and Social Psychology*, *58*(2), 342–353. http://doi.org/10.1037/0022-3514.58.2.342

Ekman, P., & Friesen, W. V. (1971). Constants across cultures in the face and emotion. *Journal of Personality and Social Psychology*, *17*(2), 124–129. http://doi.org/10.1037/h0030377

Ekman, P., Levenson, R., & Friesen, W. (1983). Autonomic nervous system activity distinguishes among emotions. *Science*, *221*(4616), 1208–1210. http://doi.org/10.1126/science.6612338

Elfenbein, H. A., & Ambady, N. (2002). On the universality and cultural specificity of emotion recognition: A meta-analysis. *Psychological Bulletin*, *128*(2), 203–235. http://doi.org/10.1037/0033-2909.128.2.203

Ellsworth, P. C., & Smith, C. A. (1988). Shades of joy: Patterns of appraisal differentiating pleasant emotions. *Cognition & Emotion*, *2*(4), 301–331. http://doi.org/10.1080/02699938808412702

Fox, N. A., & Davidson, R. J. (1986). Asymmetry of brain electrical activity in human newborns. *Neuropsychologia*, *24*(3), 417–422.

Fredrickson, B. L. (1998). What good are positive emotions? *Review of General Psychology*, *2*(3), 300–319. http://doi.org/10.1037/1089-2680.2.3.300.What

Fredrickson, B. L. (2001). The role of positive emotions in positive psychology. *American Psychologist*, *56*(3), 218–226. http://doi.org/10.1037/0003-066X.56.3.218

Fredrickson, B. L. (2013). Positive emotions broaden and build. *Advances in Experimental Social Psychology*, *47*, 1–53.

Fredrickson, B. L., & Branigan, C. (2005). Positive emotions broaden the scope of attention and thought-action repertoires. *Cognition & Emotion*, *19*(3), 313–332. http://doi.org/10.1080/02699930441000238

Fredrickson, B. L., Cohn, M. A., Coffey, K., Pek, J., & Finkel, S. M. (2008). Open hearts build lives: Positive emotions, induced through loving-kindness meditation, build consequential personal resources. *Journal of Personality and Social Psychology*, *95*(5), 1045–1062. http://doi.org/10.1037/a0013262

Fredrickson, B. L., & Joiner, T. (2002). Positive emotions trigger upward spirals toward emotional well-being. *Psychological Science, 13*(2), 172–175. http://doi.org/10.1111/1467-9280.00431

Fredrickson, B. L., & Kahneman, D. (1993). Duration neglect in retrospective evaluations of affective episodes. *Journal of Personality and Social Psychology, 65*(1), 45–55. http://doi.org/10.1037/0022-3514.65.1.45

Fredrickson, B. L., Mancuso, R. A., Branigan, C., & Tugade, M. M. (2000). The undoing effect of positive emotions. *Motivation and Emotion, 24*(4), 237–258.

Frijda, N. H. (1993). Moods, emotion episodes, and emotions. In M. L. J. M. Haviland (ed.), *Handbook of Emotions* (pp. 381–403). New York: Guilford Press.

Frijda, N. H., Kuipers, P., & ter Schure, E. (1989). Relations among emotion, appraisal, and emotional action readiness. *Journal of Personality and Social Psychology, 57*(2), 212–228. http://doi.org/10.1037/0022-3514.57.2.212

Gable, P. A., & Harmon-Jones, E. (2008). Approach-motivated positive affect reduces breadth of attention. *Psychological Science, 19*(5), 476–82. http://doi.org/10.1111/j.1467-9280.2008.02112.x

Gable, P. A., & Harmon-Jones, E. (2011). Attentional consequences of pregoal and postgoal positive affects. *Emotion, 11*(6), 1358–1367. http://doi.org/10.1037/a0025611

Gasper, K. (2004). Do you see what I see? Affect and visual information processing. *Cognition & Emotion, 18*(3), 405–421. http://doi.org/10.1080/02699930341000068

Gasper, K., & Clore, G. L. (2002). Attending to the big picture: Mood and global versus local processing of visual information. *Psychological Science, 13*(1), 34–40. http://doi.org/10.1111/1467-9280.00406

Gosselin, P., Perron, M., & Beaupré, M. (2010). The voluntary control of facial action units in adults. *Emotion, 10*(2), 266–271. http://doi.org/10.1037/a0017748

Gross, J. J., & Barrett, L. F. (2011). Emotion generation and emotion regulation: One or two depends on your point of view. *Emotion Review, 3*(1), 8–16. http://doi.org/10.1177/1754073910380974

Harker, L., & Keltner, D. (2001). Expressions of positive emotion in women's college yearbook pictures and their relationship to personality and life outcomes across adulthood. *Journal of Personality and Social Psychology, 80*(1), 112–124. http://doi.org/10.1037//0022-3514.80.1.112

Harmon-Jones, E. (2003). Clarifying the emotive functions of asymmetrical frontal cortical activity. *Psychophysiology, 40*(6), 838–848. http://doi.org/10.1111/1469-8986.00121

Harmon-Jones, E., Price, T. F., & Gable, P. A. (2012). The influence of affective states on cognitive broadening/narrowing: Considering the importance of motivational intensity. *Social and Personality Psychology Compass, 6*(4), 314–327. http://doi.org/10.1111/j.1751-9004.2012.00432.x

Harmon-Jones, E., & Sigelman, J. (2001). State anger and prefrontal brain activity: Evidence that insult-related relative left-prefrontal activation is associated with experienced anger and aggression. *Journal of Personality and Social Psychology, 80*(5), 797–803. http://doi.org/10.1037/0022-3514.80.5.797

Huntsinger, J. R., Isbell, L. M., & Clore, G. L. (2014). The affective control of thought: Malleable, not fixed. *Psychological Review*, *121*(4), 600–618. http://doi.org/10.1037/a0037669

Isen, A. M., Daubman, K. A., & Nowicki, G. P. (1987). Positive affect facilitates creative problem solving. *Journal of Personality and Social Psychology*, *52*(6), 1122–1131. http://doi.org/0.1037/0022-3514.52.6.1122

Izard, C. E. (2010). The many meanings/aspects of emotion: Definitions, functions, activation, and regulation. *Emotion Review*, *2*(4), 363–370. http://doi.org/10.1177/1754073910374661

Juslin, P. N., & Laukka, P. (2003). Communication of emotions in vocal expression and music performance: Different channels, same code? *Psychological Bulletin*, *129*(5), 770–814. http://doi.org/10.1037/0033-2909.129.5.770

Kahneman, D., Fredrickson, B. L., Schreiber, C. A., & Redelmeier, D. A. (1993). When more pain is preferred to less: Adding a better end. *Psychological Science*, *4*(6), 401–405. http://doi.org/10.1111/j.1467-9280.1993.tb00589.x

Kahneman, D., & Riis, J. (2005). Living, and thinking about it: Two perspectives on life. In F. A. Huppert, N. Baylis, & B. Keverne (eds), *The Science of Well-Being* (pp. 285–304). New York: Oxford University Press. http://doi.org/10.1126/science.1103572

Kimchi, R., & Palmer, S. E. (1982). Form and texture in hierarchically constructed patterns. *Journal of Experimental Psychology. Human Perception and Performance*, *8*(4), 521–535. http://doi.org/10.1037/0096-1523.8.4.521

Knutson, B., Burgdorf, J., & Panksepp, J. (2002). Ultrasonic vocalizations as indices of affective states in rats. *Psychological Bulletin*, *128*(6), 961–977. http://doi.org/10.1037/0033-2909.128.6.961

Kreibig, S. D. (2010). Autonomic nervous system activity in emotion: A review. *Biological Psychology*, *84*(3), 394–421. http://doi.org/10.1016/j.biopsycho.2010.03.010

Kringelbach, M. L., & Berridge, K. C. (2012). The joyful mind. *Scientific American*, *307*(2), 40–45. http://doi.org/10.1038/scientificamerican0812-40

Krumhuber, E. G., & Manstead, A. S. R. (2009). Can Duchenne smiles be feigned? New evidence on felt and false smiles. *Emotion*, *9*(6), 807–820. http://doi.org/10.1037/a0017844

Larsen, J. T., Bernston, G. G., Poehlmann, K. M., Ito, T., & Cacioppo, J. T. (2008). The psychophysiology of emotion. In M. Lewis, J. M. Haviland-Jones, & L. Feldman Barrett (eds), *Handbook of Emotions* (3rd edn, pp. 180–195). New York: Guilford Press.

Larsen, J. T., Norris, C. J., & Cacioppo, J. T. (2003). Effects of positive and negative affect on electromyographic activity over zygomaticus major and corrugator supercilii. *Psychophysiology*, *40*(5), 776–785.

Larsen, R. J., & Diener, E. (1992). Promises and problems with the circumplex model of emotion. *Review of Personality and Social Psychology*, *13*, 25–59.

Lindquist, K. A., Satpute, A. B., Wager, T. D., Weber, J., & Barrett, L. F. (2015). The brain basis of positive and negative affect: Evidence from a meta-analysis of the human neuroimaging literature. *Cerebral Cortex*, 1–13. http://doi.org/10.1093/cercor/bhv001

Lindquist, K. A., Wager, T. D., Kober, H., Bliss-Moreau, E., & Barrett, L. F. (2012). The brain basis of emotion: A meta-analytic review. *Behavioral and Brain Sciences*, *35*(3), 121–202. http://doi.org/10.1017/S0140525X11000446

Lyubomirsky, S., King, L., & Diener, E. (2005). The benefits of frequent positive affect: Does happiness lead to success? *Psychological Bulletin*, *131*, 803–855.

MacKerron, G., & Mourato, S. (2013). Happiness is greater in natural environments. *Global Environmental Change*, *23*(5), 992–1000. http://doi.org/10.1016/j.gloenvcha.2013.03.010

Mauss, I. B., & Robinson, M. D. (2009). Measures of emotion: A review. *Cognition & Emotion*, *23*(2), 209–237. http://doi.org/10.1080/02699930802204677

Mehu, M., Little, A. C., & Dunbar, R. I. M. (2007). Duchenne smiles and the perception of generosity and sociability in faces. *Journal of Evolutionary Psychology*, *5*(1), 183–196. http://doi.org/10.1556/JEP.2007.1011

Mehu, M., Mortillaro, M., Bänziger, T., & Scherer, K. R. (2012). Reliable facial muscle activation enhances recognizability and credibility of emotional expression. *Emotion*, *12*(4), 701–715. http://doi.org/10.1037/a0026717

Moors, A., Ellsworth, P. C., Scherer, K. R., & Frijda, N. H. (2013). Appraisal theories of emotion: State of the art and future development. *Emotion Review*, *5*(2), 119–124. http://doi.org/10.1177/1754073912468165

Mortillaro, M., Mehu, M., & Scherer, K. R. (2011). Subtly different positive emotions can be distinguished by their facial expressions. *Social Psychological and Personality Science*, *2*(3), 262–271. http://doi.org/10.1177/1948550610389080

Murphy, F. C., Nimmo-Smith, I., & Lawrence, A. D. (2003). Functional neuroanatomy of emotions: A meta-analysis. *Cognitive, Affective, & Behavioral Neuroscience*, *3*(3), 207–233. http://doi.org/10.3758/CABN.3.3.207

Nakamura, J., & Csikszentmihalyi, M. (2002). The concept of flow. In C. R. Snyder & S. J. Lopez (eds), *The Handbook of Positive Psychology* (pp. 89–105). New York: Oxford University Press. http://doi.org/10.1007/978-94-017-9088-8_16

Oishi, S. (2002). The experiencing and remembering of well-being: A cross-cultural analysis. *Personality and Social Psychology Bulletin*, *28*(10), 1398–1406. http://doi.org/10.1177/014616702236871

Ortony, A., & Turner, T. J. (1990). What's basic about basic emotions? *Psychological Review*, *97*(3), 315–331. http://doi.org/10.1037/0033-295X.97.3.315

Panksepp, J. (2011). The primary process affects in human development, happiness, and thriving. In K. M. Sheldon, T. B. Kashdan, & M. F. Steger (eds), *Designing Positive Psychology* (pp. 51–88). New York: Oxford University Press.

Phan, K. L., Wager, T., Taylor, S. F., & Liberzon, I. (2002). Functional neuroanatomy of emotion: A meta-analysis of emotion activation studies in PET and fMRI. *NeuroImage*, *16*(2), 331–348. http://doi.org/10.1006/nimg.2002.1087

Raichle, M. E. (1998). Behind the scenes of functional brain imaging: A historical and physiological perspective. *Proceedings of the National Academy of Sciences of the United States of America, 95*(3), 765–772. http://doi.org/10.1073/pnas.95.3.765

Redelmeier, D. A., & Kahneman, D. (1996). Patients' memories of painful medical treatments: Real-time and retrospective evaluations of two minimally invasive procedures. *Pain, 66*(1), 3–8. http://doi.org/10.1016/0304-3959(96)02994-6

Redelmeier, D. A., Katz, J., & Kahneman, D. (2003). Memories of colonoscopy: A randomized trial. *Pain, 104*(1–2), 187–194. http://doi.org/10.1016/S0304-3959(03)00003-4

Reed, L. I., Zeglen, K. N., & Schmidt, K. L. (2012). Facial expressions as honest signals of cooperative intent in a one-shot anonymous Prisoner's Dilemma game. *Evolution and Human Behavior, 33*(3), 200–209. http://doi.org/10.1016/j.evolhumbehav.2011.09.003

Reisenzein, R., Studtmann, M., & Horstmann, G. (2013). Coherence between emotion and facial expression: Evidence from laboratory experiments. *Emotion Review, 5*(1), 16–23. http://doi.org/10.1177/1754073912457228

Robinson, M. D., & Clore, G. L. (2002a). Belief and feeling: Evidence for an accessibility model of emotional self-report. *Psychological Bulletin, 128*(6), 934–960. http://doi.org/10.1037/0033-2909.128.6.934

Robinson, M. D., & Clore, G. L. (2002b). Episodic and semantic knowledge in emotional self-report: Evidence for two judgment processes. *Journal of Personality and Social Psychology, 83*(1), 198–215. http://doi.org/10.1037/0022-3514.83.1.198

Robinson, T. E., & Berridge, K. C. (2003). Addiction. *Annual Review of Psychology, 54*, 25–53. http://doi.org/10.1146/annurev.psych.54.101601.145237

Rowe, G., Hirsh, J. B., & Anderson, A. K. (2007). Positive affect increases the breadth of attentional selection. *Proceedings of the National Academy of Sciences of the United States of America, 104*(1), 383–388. http://doi.org/10.1073/pnas.0605198104

Russell, J. A. (1980). A circumplex model of affect. *Journal of Personality and Social Psychology, 39*(6), 1161–1178. http://doi.org/10.1037/h0077714

Sauter, D. A. (2010). More than happy: The need for disentangling positive emotions. *Current Directions in Psychological Science, 19*(1), 36–40. http://doi.org/10.1177/0963721409359290

Sauter, D. A., Eisner, F., Ekman, P., & Scott, S. K. (2010). Cross-cultural recognition of basic emotions through nonverbal emotional vocalizations. *Proceedings of the National Academy of Sciences of the United States of America, 107*(6), 2408–2412. http://doi.org/10.1073/pnas.0908239106

Sauter, D. A., & Scott, S. K. (2007). More than one kind of happiness: Can we recognize vocal expressions of different positive states? *Motivation and Emotion, 31*(3), 192–199. http://doi.org/10.1007/s11031-007-9065-x

Scherer, K. R. (2005). What are emotions? And how can they be measured? *Social Science Information, 44*(4), 695–729. http://doi.org/10.1177/0539018405058216

Scherer, K. R. (2009). The dynamic architecture of emotion: Evidence for the component process model. *Cognition & Emotion, 23*(7), 1307–1351. http://doi.org/10.1080/02699930 902928969

Scollon, C. N., Kim-Prieto, C., & Diener, E. (2003). Experience sampling: Promises and pitfalls, strengths and weaknesses. *Journal of Happiness Studies, 4,* 5–34. http://doi.org/10.1007/978-90-481-2354-4

Shiota, M. N., & Danvers, A. F. (2014). Another little piece of my heart: Positive emotions and the autonomic nervous system. In J. Gruber & J. T. Moskowitz (eds), *Positive Emotion: Integrating the Light and Dark Sides* (pp. 78–94). New York: Oxford University Press.

Shiota, M. N., Keltner, D., & Mossman, A. (2007). The nature of awe: Elicitors, appraisals, and effects on self-concept. *Cognition & Emotion, 21*(5), 944–963. http://doi.org/10.1080/02699930600923668

Shiota, M. N., Neufeld, S. L., Danvers, A. F., Osborne, E. A., Sng, O., & Yee, C. I. (2014). Positive emotion differentiation: A functional approach. *Social and Personality Psychology Compass, 8*(3), 104–117. http://doi.org/10.1111/spc3.12092

Silvia, P. J. (2005). What is interesting? Exploring the appraisal structure of interest. *Emotion, 5*(1), 89–102. http://doi.org/10.1037/1528-3542.5.1.89

Smith, C. A., & Ellsworth, P. C. (1985). Patterns of cognitive appraisal in emotion. *Journal of Personality and Social Psychology, 48*(4), 813–838. http://doi.org/10.1037/0022-3514.48.4.813

Smith, C. A., & Lazarus, R. S. (1993). Appraisal components, core relational themes, and the emotions. *Cognition & Emotion, 7,* 112–269. http://doi.org/10.1080/02699 939308409189

Tooby, J., & Cosmides, L. (1990). The past explains the present emotional adaptations and the structure of ancestral environments. *Ethology and Sociobiology, 11,* 375–424. http://doi.org/10.1016/0162-3095(90)90017-Z

Tracy, J. L., & Robins, R. W. (2004). Show your pride: Evidence for a discrete emotion expression. *Psychological Science, 15*(3), 194–197. http://doi.org/10.1111/j.0956-7976.2004.01503008.x

Vytal, K., & Hamann, S. (2010). Neuroimaging support for discrete neural correlates of basic emotions: A voxel-based meta-analysis. *Journal of Cognitive Neuroscience, 22*(12), 2864–2885. http://doi.org/10.1162/jocn.2009.21366

Wager, T. D., Phan, K. L., Liberzon, I., & Taylor, S. F. (2003). Valence, gender, and lateralization of functional brain anatomy in emotion: A meta-analysis of findings from neuroimaging. *NeuroImage, 19*(3), 513–531. http://doi.org/10.1016/S1053-8119(03)00078-8

Watson, D., & Clark, L. (1999). The PANAS-X Manual for the Positive and Negative Affect Schedule-Expanded Form. *Iowa Research Online,* 1–27. http://doi.org/10.1111/j.1742-4658.2010.07754.x

Watson, D., Clark, L. A., & Tellegen, A. (1988). Development and validation of brief measures of positive and negative affect: The PANAS scales. *Journal of Personality and Social Psychology, 54*(6), 1063–1070.

Watson, D., & Tellegen, A. (1985). Toward a consensual structure of mood. *Psychological Bulletin, 98*(2), 219–235. http://doi.org/10.1037/0033-2909.98.2.219

Watson, D., Wiese, D., Vaidya, J., & Tellegen, A. (1999). The two general activation systems of affect: Structural findings, evolutionary considerations, and psychobiological evidence. *Journal of Personality and Social Psychology, 76*(5), 820–838. http://doi.org/10.1037/0022-3514.76.5.820

Waugh, C. E., & Fredrickson, B. L. (2006). Nice to know you: Positive emotions, self–other overlap, and complex understanding in the formation of a new relationship. *The Journal of Positive Psychology, 1*(2), 93–106. http://doi.org/10.1080/17439760500510569

Whelan, D. C., & Zelenski, J. M. (2012). Experimental evidence that positive moods cause sociability. *Social Psychological and Personality Science, 3*(4), 430–437. http://doi.org/10.1177/1948550611425194

Winkielman, P., & Berridge, K. C. (2004). Unconscious emotion. *Current Directions in Psychological Science, 13*(3), 120–123. http://doi.org/10.1111/j.0963-7214.2004.00288.x

Wirtz, D., Kruger, J., Scollon, C. N., & Diener, E. (2003). What to do on spring break? The role of predicted, on-line, and remembered experience in future choice. *Psychological Science, 14*(5), 520–524. http://doi.org/10.1111/1467-9280.03455

Zajonc, R. B. (1980). Feeling and thinking: Preferences need no inferences. *American Psychologist, 35*(2), 151–175. http://doi.org/10.1037/0003-066X.35.2.151

Zelenski, J. M., & Larsen, R. J. (1999). Susceptibility to affect: A comparison of three personality taxonomies. *Journal of Personality, 67*(5), 761–791. http://doi.org/10.1111/1467-6494.00072

Zelenski, J. M., & Larsen, R. J. (2000). The distribution of basic emotions in everyday life: A state and trait perspective from experience sampling data. *Journal of Research in Personality, 34*(2), 178–197. http://doi.org/10.1006/jrpe.1999.2275

3

Happiness

INTRODUCTION

It was Luke Pittard's lucky day; he had just won $1.3 million in the national lottery. He soon bought a house, spent big on a beautiful wedding, and took a nice holiday with his wife. Then, just two years after his big win, Luke went to work at McDonald's – the fast-food restaurant. This was not because Luke had squandered his windfall. He did it to be happy. Luke had worked at McDonald's before he won the lottery. It is where he met his wife, and he missed his other work friends after quitting. According to Luke, "there is only so much relaxing you can do" (BBC, 2008).

Someone should tell that to Matthieu Richard, a man whose impressive ability to meditate earned him the moniker 'happiest person in the world'. Matthieu's intriguing biography begins in France, where he earned a PhD in biology. Not long after, he made a big change, becoming a Buddhist monk in Nepal, and has spent decades practising meditation. The popular press dubbed him the 'happiest person' after a collaboration with neuroscientists. By practising loving kindness meditation, Matthieu produced the largest left-hemisphere activation the lab had ever seen (this activation is associated with positive and approach emotions; see Chapter 2). He earned the title based on brain waves, but has continued to work with scientists and has written popular books on happiness.

Taking a very different approach, the *New York Times* labelled Alvin Wong the happiest man in America (Rampell, 2011). When he earned the designation in 2011, Alvin was 69 years old, tall, Jewish, Chinese-American, living in Hawaii, owned a small business, and made more than $120,000 a year. This unlikely collection of characteristics was all it took to win the happiness title. The *Times* used polling data to assemble a list of the demographics most associated with happiness. They had not talked to Alvin beforehand, but he confirmed that he was indeed quite happy when they phoned to check. He has since read a lot about happiness and began doing public speaking on the topic.

My hope is that this book helps you learn about happiness, and thus facilitates your well-being. Yet Matthieu and Alvin's experiences suggest that knowing you are happy might also facilitate learning more about it! Perhaps you want to skip ahead to the Try It box to assess your own happiness now?

Luke, Matthieu, and Alvin have intriguing stories that all sound plausible. Yet they also imply quite different things about the causes of happiness, and even what it means to be happy. This chapter describes how psychological scientists have tackled questions about happiness and what they have learned.

WHAT IS HAPPINESS?

Whereas Chapter 2 considered happiness as a brief emotional state, Chapter 3 treats happiness as a more long-term characteristic of people. This is not to say that happiness never changes, but we do want to distinguish a general sense of happiness from more transitory emotions and moods. Very happy people have bad days, and miserable people have pleasant moments. One way to think of this more long-term happiness is as a mental running average of momentary feelings over one's life. Yet, as discussed in Chapter 2, subjective ratings of averaged moments differ somewhat from mathematical averages. Judgements of past emotions are influenced by memory biases.

In addition, the notion that long-term happiness is the accumulation of emotions over time is only part of the story. Philosophers, theologians, and many others have debated happiness for thousands of years. What does it mean to be truly happy? For some, happiness is mainly about feeling good; for others, it is more about living a morally good life; Charles Schultz wrote a book titled *Happiness Is a Sad Song*; the Beatles sang that "Happiness is a warm gun". Because the term happiness can be viewed in different ways, psychologists often replace happiness with the jargon term 'subjective well-being', which is defined more precisely. Subjective well-being is first subjective. It is how individuals view their own well-being, not how a philosopher, psychologist, or other expert would evaluate it. It is personal and in the mind of its subject.

Defining well-being might raise the same thorny issues involved in defining happiness, but with the term subjective well-being, psychologists decided on a specific meaning when they coined it. **Subjective well-being** includes high life satisfaction, experiencing many pleasant emotions, and experiencing few unpleasant emotions (Diener, Suh, Lucas, & Smith, 1999). We discussed pleasant and unpleasant emotions in Chapter 2. Recall that they can be relatively independent – prompted by different things – and thus it is useful to consider both independently. **Life satisfaction** is an individual's judgement that things have gone well and that conditions are good. It can be sub-divided into various domains, such as work satisfaction, relationship satisfaction, leisure-time satisfaction, body satisfaction, and so on. That said, overall life satisfaction judgements are often preferable (Diener, Emmons, Larsen, & Griffin, 1985). When researchers are interested in a particular domain, such as work satisfaction, they will want to assess it separately. On the other hand, when we are interested in someone's overall happiness, it is hard to know which domains will be important to different individuals. One person might value family relationships above all else; for another, wealth is at the top of the priority list. Is there one thing that is essential to your happiness? Do you know people who have a different essential ingredient?

Asking about overall life satisfaction allows people to arrive at a judgement using their own criteria. A proud father might rate his life satisfaction high due to his healthy and loving family; the fact that his family is poor may not matter much for him. A successful athlete might rate her life satisfaction high because she is accomplishing all her professional goals. The subjective nature of subjective well-being suggests that we listen to how people determine their own satisfaction, rather than researchers assuming which domains are most important for them. For example, the Cantril measure of life satisfaction asks people to imagine a ten-step ladder. At the top is the best possible life for you. At the bottom is the worst possible life for you. On which rung would you say you personally feel you stand? Another popular measure of life satisfaction appears in the Try It box.

Collectively, high life satisfaction, many positive emotions, and few negative emotions comprise the construct of subjective well-being. We can think of 'happiness' in the same way. Although the term happiness is often used to describe a pleasant emotional state, happiness can also be understood broadly, something that includes various narrower components (like emotions and satisfaction). These different components generally go together in people – they are correlated (Busseri, 2014). On average, people who experience few unpleasant emotions also tend to be satisfied with their lives. However, the components can also diverge. Imagine a person who spends all his time partying and enjoying the pleasures of life, but feels dissatisfied because he has not accomplished much. Another person might experience the joy of family and the satisfaction of a successful career, yet also be prone to intense anxiety.

These divergences have two important implications. First, the very happiest people have all three components; if we focus on only one indicator, we may be missing part of the complete picture. Second, it can be useful to study the components of subjective well-being as separate entities. They can change differently over time, and events or circumstances can influence one more than others (Diener, Lucas, & Scollon, 2006). For example, wealth is more strongly associated with life satisfaction than it is with positive emotions (Diener, Ng, Harter, & Arora, 2010; Kahneman & Deaton, 2010).

TRY IT

Assessing Happiness

For both questionnaires, rate each statement on a scale where:

7 = Strongly agree

6 = Agree

5 = Slightly agree

4 = Neither agree nor disagree

3 = Slightly disagree

2 = Disagree

1 = Strongly disagree

The Satisfaction with Life Scale (Diener et al., 1985)

_____ In most ways my life is close to my ideal.

_____ The conditions of my life are excellent.

_____ I am satisfied with my life.

_____ So far I have gotten the important things I want in life.

_____ If I could live my life over, I would change almost nothing.

To score, add all your responses together. Scores can range from 5 (least satisfied) to 35 (highest satisfaction possible), with the score 20 as a neutral midpoint. Higher scores indicate more life satisfaction.

The Flourishing Scale (Diener et al., 2009)

_____ I lead a purposeful and meaningful life.

_____ My social relationships are supportive and rewarding.

_____ I am engaged and interested in my daily activities.

_____ I actively contribute to the happiness and well-being of others.

_____ I am competent and capable in the activities that are important to me.

_____ I am a good person and live a good life.

_____ I am optimistic about my future.

_____ People respect me.

To score, add all your responses together. Scores can range from 8 (lowest possible) to 56 (highest possible) with 28 as a neutral midpoint. A high score represents a person with many psychological resources and strengths, consistent with contemporary views of eudaimonia.

Eudaimonia and Broader Views of Well-Being

Subjective well-being, with its facets of emotions and satisfaction, is a useful way to think about and measure happiness. The approach is widely used by researchers, and we have learned much about subjective well-being. However, another popular sentiment among positive psychologists is that subjective well-being is not enough to fully describe the good life. We should also consider things like people's sense of purpose, meaning, authenticity, growth, and so on. These additional features of well-being are often described by positive psychologists with the term **eudaimonia**, though this term means different things to different people.

The ancient Greek philosopher Aristotle first described eudaimonia in his great work *The Nicomachean Ethics*. Eudaimonia is often translated as 'happiness', but Aristotle was describing something a bit different from subjective well-being. Increasingly, eudaimonia is instead translated as 'flourishing'. The term flourishing emphasizes living well; happiness seems more about feeling good. Aristotle explicitly contrasted eudaimonia with feeling good, or hedonia. He viewed simple pleasures as base, far from the pinnacle of eudaimonic well-being. The good life, or eudaimonia, was about living a virtuous life. People who behave in morally valued ways and who fulfil their highest potentials live eudaimonic lives. According to Aristotle, there was nothing subjective about eudaimonia. Virtue and accomplishment should be objectively apparent, for example easily seen by other people, or even as an assessment made at the end of a person's life (Kashdan, Biswas-Diener, & King, 2008). Modern psychologists, however, think of and measure eudaimonia more subjectively, typically using self-report questionnaires. They assume that virtuous living will produce subjective feelings that people can self-report (Huta & Waterman, 2014). The goal of eudaimonia is still virtuous behaviour, but its consequences are assessed as psychological experience.

In psychology, eudaimonia can mean many different things; it lacks the consensus we see with the components of subjective well-being (Huta & Waterman, 2014). A common theme is that indicators of eudaimonia go beyond hedonia, or merely feeling good; they identify other characteristics and experiences of positive mental health and flourishing (e.g. authenticity, meaning). The connection to Aristotle is sometimes loose, but a clear theme is that well-being is distinct from simple pleasure. Said another way, many approaches see Aristotle's notion of eudaimonia as influential, but are not fixed on assessing his eudaimonia precisely. For example, Ryff's (1989) early and popular approach to **psychological well-being** includes six things:

1. Self-acceptance: a positive view of the past and present self that acknowledges good and bad aspects.

2. Positive relations with other people: trusting, intimate, caring relationships with others.

3. Autonomy: independence, authenticity, use of personal standards to guide behaviour, and resistance of social pressures.

4. Environmental mastery: competence, seizing opportunities, finding contexts conducive to needs and values.

5. Purpose in life: clear goals, sense of meaning, important projects, sense that things are worthwhile.

6. Personal growth: openness and sense of continuing development, positive changes over one's lifetime.

More recently, positive psychology founder Seligman (2012) proposed five key aspects of well-being – positive emotion (feeling good), engagement (flow, being absorbed), relationships (strong, healthy ones), meaning (a sense of larger purpose, important reasons for actions), and accomplishment (achieving valued goals) – summarized by the acronym **PERMA**. Positive emotions are hedonic and a component of subjective well-being. The other four aspects stem from Seligman's view that pleasantness is not sufficient; flourishing lives have additional features. As one more example, you can take the Flourishing Scale (Diener et al., 2009) in the Try It box, which asks about meaning, relationships, and mastery.

Psychologists use the idea of eudaimonia to contrast broad ideas of well-being with **hedonia**. The hedonist pursues pleasure above all else – you might be thinking of the prototypical 'sex, drugs, and rock & roll' ethos. However, hedonia is really the goal of maximizing pleasure, rather than the particular means one uses (Huta & Ryan, 2010). If you believe that petting kittens all day will maximize your pleasure, petting kittens is then hedonistic for you. If other people pet kittens because they believe it is kind and virtuous, it is more eudaimonic – even if they get some pleasure from their kindness too.

Favouring eudaimonia over hedonia is a moral judgement that some things are more important than pleasure. This can be taken to a puritanical extreme that explicitly devalues pleasure, but positive psychologists do not go this far. Even if eating chocolate is the greatest pleasure, it may be better – perhaps more fulfilling – to write a poem. To paraphrase the philosopher John Stuart Mill: it is better to be a dissatisfied human than a satisfied pig, or a dissatisfied Socrates than a satisfied fool. You can agree or disagree with Mill; the point is that he is making the value judgement that knowledge is better than satisfaction.

People clearly value things besides simple pleasures. They even sacrifice pleasure in favour of things like authenticity, achievement, or the welfare of other people. For example, climbing mountains leads to intense cold, pain, and exhaustion – not to mention significant risk of death – things that are in no way pleasurable (see Loewenstein, 1999). Yet people voluntarily climb mountains, even after having experienced terrific hardships doing so. It is difficult to argue that the joy of summiting outweighs the pain of climbing if we only consider pleasure. Said another way, if we asked mountaineers why they do it, would 'fun' be the answer?

As other examples, consider people who take religious vows of poverty or medical professionals who trade the comforts of home to volunteer in disaster areas. It seems unlikely that they are driven by pleasure. Finally, take a moment to conduct philosopher Robert Nozick's (1974) famous thought experiment: the experience machine. Imagine that a new machine has been invented. You can have your brain plugged into the machine, and it will simulate any experience you desire. Those experiences can be completely indistinguishable from reality. If you are thinking of the film *The Matrix*, you are on the right track. Your body would live safely in a tank while the machine creates a simulated reality for your mind. That simulation would be full of desirable experiences. If such a machine existed, would you plug in?

When I ask students this question, a few say 'yes' but many more say 'no'. The implication is that we value other things – like authenticity – over pleasure. We want to earn our good feelings. Even when I emphasize that the simulated pleasure feels just as good as genuine pleasure, it is hard to find takers. Many people say they would prefer genuine experiences, even if they were less pleasant than the machine's.

Nozik's experience machine is not very popular. However, even fewer people choose my recently invented 'authentic pain machine'. It hurts you in 100 per cent genuine ways. Would you like to try it? I admit my new pain machine is only a joke; my point here is that pleasure is obviously something we value too (except, perhaps, for those who are puritans). Authentic pleasure is better than authentic pain, and being a satisfied pig is better than being a dissatisfied pig (Diener, Sapyta, & Suh, 1998). Philosophy has a long tradition of debating the merits and truth of hedonism versus eudaimonia, but do we really need to choose? Why not both? The abstract philosophical debate suggests more incompatibility than we observe in day-to-day life (Kashdan et al., 2008). Most positive psychologists would agree that hedonic and eudaimonic pursuits are both important to the good life.

There are times when eudaimonic pursuits will be at odds with maximizing momentary pleasure, but pleasure often follows with time. Delay of gratification can be useful, but eventually that gratification comes – and often in larger amounts because we waited. How do you feel when you accomplish goals, express your true self, or help friends? I bet you feel good. These things are pleasurable. Even though pleasure is not the goal, eudaimonic pursuits often produce it. Some people have a deep sense of meaning, yet experience only few positive emotions; however, such people are uncommon. Eudaimonic constructs, such as Ryff's six aspects listed above, correlate positively and strongly with subjective well-being (Disabato, Goodman, Kashdan, Short, & Jarden, 2015). There are many more people who experience both meaning and pleasant emotions, or a lack of both, together.

Thinking of 'happiness' as subjective well-being (i.e. a pleasant balance of average emotions and high satisfaction) does not imply that it results from a stereotypical 'hedonistic lifestyle'. Pleasant emotions are an important part of subjective well-being, yet they can result from chocolate sprinkles, pony rides, or giving these things to someone else. The rest of this chapter focuses on happiness research with happiness mainly understood as subjective well-being. In other words, I will typically use 'happiness' to refer to subjective well-being. This does not diminish the importance of eudaimonia or other indicators of flourishing. Indeed, studying eudaimonia has highlighted important aspects of the good life beyond feeling good. As you will see, strong social relationships, a sense of meaning, and so on, are very important to subjective well-being. These things are potentially distinct from – yet contribute to – happiness. Other chapters in this book consider aspects of eudaimonia like virtues, authenticity, and positive relationships in more detail. (You will need to consult other sources to learn about sad songs and warm guns.) We now turn to the substantial body of research on subjective well-being.

TRY IT

Eudaimonic and Hedonic Activities

People can pursue activities for reasons that are eudaimonic, such as to develop a skill, to pursue excellence, or express the best of one's self. Other activities might be pursued for mostly hedonic reasons; that is, to find pleasure, enjoyment, relaxation, or fun (Huta & Ryan, 2010). For this exercise, choose one small activity that seems eudaimonic (mostly about being your best self), and another that seems more hedonic (mostly about pleasure). Do them both.

Afterwards, take some time to reflect on the activities. For example, how did you know that they would be eudaimonic or hedonic? How did each make you feel? What were the consequences of each activity? How did other people respond? Any other observations? There are no right or wrong answers here, but psychologists are interested in learning more about how the experience and consequences of hedonic and eudaimonic activities can be similar or different.

WHO IS HAPPY, AND WHERE DOES HAPPINESS COME FROM?

Would you say that you are generally satisfied with your life? Do you experience more pleasant than unpleasant emotions? Most people in the world answer these questions in the affirmative. As we saw in Chapter 2, people tend to experience more positive than negative emotions. This positive balance is also true of life satisfaction, adding up to a generally positive view of overall subjective well-being. As Diener and Diener (1996) titled their review on the subject, "Most People Are Happy". Even people in difficult circumstances often report being reasonably happy. One study assessed 65 French patients with locked-in syndrome – people with near complete paralysis who communicated via eye blinks. Astonishingly, 72 per cent reported being happy! Also, happiness was higher among the people who were locked-in longer (Bruno et al., 2011).

Despite the general trend towards high happiness, there is also considerable variation. For example, on a 1–7 scale of life satisfaction, a sample of rich Americans averaged 5.8, whereas homeless people in California averaged 2.9 – the same as homeless pavement dwellers in the slums of Calcutta (Diener & Seligman, 2004). Research on subjective well-being tries to explain this variation, ultimately trying to determine what causes happiness.

Features of the Person

After many studies, we now know that the best predictors of happiness are personality traits (Diener et al., 1999). Personality can include many things (see Chapter 4), yet key differences among people are commonly summarized with just five dimensions. These traits are known as the **big five**. 'Big' refers to the breadth of each trait – they include many narrower facets. This is how a mere five dimensions can describe so many of the ways that people differ from one another. (With lots of variation in each trait, the particular combination of trait scores is another way that a few primary sources of difference can produce many different people; as an analogy, just three primary colours can combine in different amounts to produce infinite variations.)

One of the big five traits is introversion–extraversion. This trait is made up of components like activity level, sociability, cheerfulness, assertiveness, and excitement seeking. The other big five traits are: emotional stability (vs 'neuroticism' or proneness to negative emotions), agreeableness (trusting, cooperative, sympathetic), conscientiousness (dutiful, tidy, organized, controlled), and openness (to ideas, feelings, aesthetics, sensations) (Digman, 1990). Given that extraversion and emotional stability explicitly include aspects of positive and negative emotionality, it is easy to see why these traits predict subjective well-being, Indeed, these two traits are among the single best predictors of happiness. Beyond their dispositional cheerfulness, extraverts' habit of socializing also boosts their happiness (Srivastava, Angelo, & Vallereux, 2008). Trait agreeableness and conscientiousness have reliable, yet smaller, positive correlations with subjective well-being; openness is less consistently related, but likely positive too (Steel, Schmidt, & Shultz, 2008).

Other personality characteristics, such as optimism and self-esteem, are also strongly correlated with happiness (Lyubomirsky & Lepper, 1999). That is, from a more cognitive perspective, having a positive outlook, believing that things will turn out well, and evaluating oneself positively seems to boost happiness. Of course, being happy can contribute to positive thoughts, but dispositional tendencies towards positive views also seem to facilitate happiness. For example, optimism predicts well-being many years in the future (Carver, Scheier, & Segerstrom, 2010).

Like personality traits, subjective well-being is fairly stable over time. Still, sometimes change does occur, and personality traits seem to change along with happiness (Boyce, Wood, & Powdthavee, 2013). For example, as people become more extraverted, they report more happiness. Nonetheless, the average amount of change is modest. Imagine a group of people: the happiest, most extraverted, and most emotionally stable people in that group are likely to remain the same over time – even across many years (Lucas, 2007). Our dispositions are important to happiness.

In addition to being relatively stable over time, traits and subjective well-being are also heritable. On average, about 40 per cent to 50 per cent of the variation in a group's happiness can be explained by differences in genes. When focusing on the part of happiness that is stable over many years, genetic variation may explain as much as 80 per cent of the differences among people (Lykken & Tellegen, 1996; Nes, Røysamb, Tambs, Harris, & Reichborn-Kjennerud, 2006).

These estimates come from research that uses the twin study method. Monozygotic (identical) and dizygotic (fraternal) twins are compared on characteristics like happiness and traits. Identical twins share the exact same genes – they are essentially clones – and fraternal twins share only half of their genes, like any other siblings. In this way, the different kinds of twins are like a natural experiment where the degree of genetic similarity differs randomly. Thus, when identical twins are more similar in happiness, compared to fraternal twins, we can infer that genetic similarity accounts for some of the similarity in happiness. This is what studies find. It implies that some lucky people – twins or not – possess genes that are more conducive to happiness than others.

Twin studies tell us that genes – collectively – are important to happiness, but they do not tell us which particular genes are important. Without revealing specific genes, twin studies do not suggest specific (physiological) causes of happiness. However, recent advances in genetic research do allow for some general statements. First, it is likely that the same genes that produce differences in the big five traits also contribute to happiness (Weiss, Bates, & Luciano, 2008). Said another way, the heritable part of happiness comes from our personality dispositions. Second, there are likely hundreds, or even thousands, of individual genes that contribute to complex traits like happiness (Chabris, Lee, Cesarini, Benjamin, & Laibson, 2015).

Some studies have linked individual genes to subjective well-being. For example, a gene variant that acts on the neurotransmitter serotonin was correlated with life satisfaction in one study (De Neve, 2011). However, this finding remains preliminary. Because individual genes have very tiny effects on complex traits, it is difficult to detect them reliably. Moreover, even if we do identify a particular gene reliably, it will explain less than 1 per cent of the variation in happiness. Said another way, we are confident that there is no single happiness gene. It is only collectively that genes have a large influence on happiness.

Twin studies provide numeric estimates of how much variation in a group is due to differences in genes. This estimate is called **heritability**. The remaining, unexplained variation is due to differences in life events, parenting, circumstances, choices, and so on. These non-genetic influences are collectively termed 'the environment'. Twin studies estimate both heritability and environmental influences. Also, it is important to keep in mind that heritability refers only to variation in a group. In an individual person, both genes and a developmental environment are essential, so it is impossible to attribute more causation to one or the other. Just as one hand cannot clap, individuals require both genes and environments.

In a group, we can explain how much of the variation across people might be due to genes or environmental influences. These estimates are about the differences between people; again, heritability is defined as the proportion of observed variability in a group that is due to genetic variability. Substantial heritability means that genes are important to variation in happiness. However, whether it is 30 per cent or 50 per cent will vary across studies. The specific number is not particularly important; we expect it to vary. In other words, genetic effects are not fixed or unchanging, nor are they complete explanations for differences across people.

For example, we expect heritability estimates to vary across different populations. The size of a heritability estimate depends on both genes and environments ('nature' and 'nurture') – this is because they must sum to 100 per cent. When there is much environmental variation (e.g. some people growing up in comfort and others in harsh conditions), these differences in environments will create more of the variation. It follows that there is then less variation for genes to explain; the heritability estimate is lower. When environmental variation is less (i.e. high similarity in developmental conditions), differences in genes explain more of the variations that we observe across people. Thus, heritability estimates can change somewhat, depending on the group under study.

A common misconception is that highly heritable traits cannot be changed. This notion may be leading you to a pessimistic conclusion about happiness, but there is reason for hope. The heritability findings on happiness leave plenty of room for people's efforts to increase subjective well-being (Lyubomirsky, Sheldon, & Schkade, 2005).

First, even highly heritable traits can be changed when the environment changes. The best example of this comes from studies of height, which is about 80 per cent heritable (Johnson, 2010). Over the last 150 years, the average height of adults in developed countries has increased by a few centimetres. This is due to the widely available improvements in health and nutrition over time. Height has remained very heritable – even as people have got taller – because better nutrition has been available to most people. Thus, the differences in height are still mostly due to differences in genes – everyone experiences similar growth. Positive psychology hopes to do something like this with well-being. If we can help provide better 'psychological nutrients', perhaps we can increase the average mental health and happiness of societies.

Second, although the heritability of subjective well-being is substantial, it is far less than 100 per cent. Even if 50 per cent of the variation in happiness is due to genes, it leaves 50 per cent of the variation to be explained by other things. It may be possible to systematically change some of them to boost happiness.

Despite this potential, it has been difficult to identify things that explain large portions of the environmental effect (i.e. the influences beyond genes). For example, the historical framing of 'nature vs nurture' has not been very helpful. From it, we might infer that parenting (nurturing) is the other important piece. However, research finds only small effects for the home environment (i.e. parental values and other things that siblings normally share; Turkheimer, 2000). Interestingly, twin and adoption studies have been essential to parenting research. This is because they can separate the influences of parenting practices from the genes that parents also contribute to their children. When genetic similarity is accounted for, parental practices explain little remaining variation. Parenting is an important and complex task, yet most parents end up doing a reasonably good job. The differences do not have a large average influence on adult happiness.

RESEARCH CASE

FINDING THE VERY HAPPY PEOPLE

Good happiness research pre-dates positive psychology, but with the movement came new ways of doing it. In a classic example, Diener and Seligman (2002) collaborated on a study designed to characterize the happiest people. Seligman's background with clinical psychology probably played a role because they borrowed an approach more common with pathology: to identify extreme cases and to compare them to average people. To begin, they recruited a relatively unremarkable sample of 222 students. More impressive, however, was the extensive battery of happiness assessments used to find the very happiest people in this group. This included the facets of subjective well-being: the satisfaction with life scale and measures of positive and negative emotions. Emotions were assessed in a few ways: as participants' ratings of their average affect across 24 adjectives in the last month – twice, as daily ratings of those same adjectives over 51 days, and the same adjectives were rated by five other people who knew each participant as overall averages for the target. In addition, some less direct assessments were used. First was a memory balance measure where participants were given two minutes to write down as many positive events as they could think of, and a similar count of negative events generated in two minutes was subtracted. A trait self-description task forced participants to choose which in a pair of terms described them better – pairs included things like a happiness adjective and an equally desirable personality characteristic. Finally, a measure of suicidal thoughts indicated low happiness.

All these measures were averaged, and the top 10 per cent happiest people were identified. This 'very happy' group was then compared to the bottom 10 per cent and the middle 27 per cent of the sample on many characteristics (personality, social life, habits, demographics, etc.). Consistent with other research, the traits of extraversion and emotional stability were considerably higher in the very happy group; they also scored lower on some Minnesota Multiphasic Personality Inventory (MMPI) pathology scales (e.g. schizophrenia, family conflict, depression, psychopathic). Although the very happy people experienced more positive emotions in day-to-day life (by definition), they were not immune from unpleasant emotions – they experienced the full range. The most striking differences were found in social behaviour. The very happy people seem to have more and better social relationships when assessed by global self-reports (close friends, family, romantic), with peer ratings, and in daily time use (time alone vs time with close others; see Table 3.1). Other seemingly positive features did not uniquely distinguish the very happy people, such as religiosity, physical attractiveness, exercise, grades, sleep – though other studies have found some links with happiness.

Across the many results, researchers concluded that strong social relationships may be a necessary feature of extreme happiness – all of the very happy people had this. Still, strong social relationships were not a sufficient feature either – many average and even some low happiness participants also had good relationships. Thus, extreme happiness seems to require something more – perhaps luck – as no measured feature was sufficient alone.

(Continued)

Table 3.1 Social relationships of the three groups

Measure (Range)	Very Unhappy	Middle	Very Happy
Self-rating of relationships (1–7)			
Close friends	4.1a	5.2b	6.3c
Strong family relationships	3.7a	5.8b	6.4b
Romantic relationship	2.3a	4.8b	6.0c
Peer rating of target's relationships (1–7)	4.2a	5.3b	6.1c
Daily activities (1–10)			
Mean time spent alone	5.8a	5.0ab	4.4b
Mean time spent with family, friends, and romantic partner	3.6a	4.5b	5.1c

Note: Within each measure, groups with different letters differ significantly from one another ($p < .05$). For daily activities, 1 represented 'no time' and 10 represented '8 hours/day'.

Source: Adapted from Diener and Seligman (2002)

Happiness Beyond Personality and Genes

If it is not parenting, what explains the remaining variation in happiness? It turns out that there is not a single or even a small handful of good answers to this question. Rather, it seems that many things account for differences in happiness. In a way, this is similar to how individual genes explain only a very small part of the overall large genetic effect. For example, Diener et al. (1999) conducted a major review of research on subjective well-being over the previous 30 years. They concluded that people's circumstances – things such as education, employment, marriage, etc. – explain some variation in happiness, but their collective contribution is probably smaller than most people would assume. As a rough estimate, these demographic features, altogether, explained about 10–15 per cent of the variation in most societies. Keep in mind that the research was often conducted within a single society, and focused more on Western, industrialized countries. With this caveat, the general trends are as follows:

Gender is not consistently linked to more or less subjective well-being. Although women report higher levels of negative affect and experience higher rates of depression, they also report higher levels of positive emotions, compared to men. Life satisfaction differences are small or non- existent.

Age is also weakly associated with subjective well-being. Emotional intensity may decrease with age, but this applies to both positive and negative emotions. People may value or expect different things at different ages, but happiness appears fairly stable across the lifespan, even in the face of declining income and health. The old are just as happy as the young. This is particularly true in wealthy, English-speaking countries where middle age is associated with a small, temporary dip in happiness (Steptoe, Deaton, & Stone, 2014).

Health is positively associated with happiness, but the link is much stronger for subjective ratings of health, compared to objective health – for example, as rated by physicians or as presence of diseases. Similar to age, people may adjust their expectations to their physical state. Happiness may also promote good health, rather than simply being a consequence of it (Diener & Chan, 2011). Major disability can also significantly hinder happiness for the few people who experience it.

Education has a small positive association with happiness. This link appears stronger among people who are poorer. Education tends to co-vary with status and income, and this is part of the reason educated people are slightly happier. High levels of education might also raise expectations for success, helping explain why it does not have more impact on average levels of happiness.

Intelligence also seems helpful for achieving status and income, yet it has no consistent link with subjective well-being.

Married people tend to be somewhat happier than those who have never married or who have become divorced. Some of this difference is due to happiness before marriage – happier people are more likely to marry and stay married. When looking at changes over time, marriage is associated with a modest increase in happiness, but one that does not last more than a couple of years, on average. However, there are wide differences in the experience of marriage. Some people respond with a lasting increase in happiness, whereas others have a nearly immediate – and lasting – decrease in happiness (Lucas, Clark, Georgellis, & Diener, 2003). In addition, becoming widowed can lead to lasting decreases in happiness. Thus, although marriage contributes to the happiness of many, it is also not a universal key to well-being. All things considered, lifelong singlehood does not preclude a happy life (DePaulo & Morris, 2005).

Parenting has a mixed relationship with happiness. Having children can produce a sense of purpose and some of the best moments in life. Yet extra stress, financial strain, and sleep disturbance are also borne with kids. On balance, children do not seem to have a major, overall influence on happiness. However, this general conclusion over-shadows considerable complexity and debate. A recent comprehensive review made the – perhaps obvious and timid – conclusion that parents are less happy when things go poorly, and happier when they experience more of the joys of children (Nelson, Kushlev, & Lyubomirsky, 2014). In general, men who are somewhat older and married tend to be happier with children, compared to younger, single mothers. Strong social support is helpful, as is having children free of problems or a difficult temperament.

Religion is linked with subjective well-being, but not in a straightforward way. There are no differences among denominations in predicting happiness. For example, Hindus are no more or less happy than Christians, on average; other happiness comparisons also reveal similarity across religions. People who view religion as an important part of their life or who actively participate in a religious community do report higher lev-els of subjective well-being. This seems especially true in difficult circumstances (e.g. poverty, illness) where religion seems to act as a buffer. Among people who would otherwise be unhappy due to their circumstances, religion seems to help.

Money and its link with happiness have been studied a lot. Psychologists have tended to downplay the importance of money for happiness, while economists have argued for a strong link. We can find evidence for both views, because the link between hap-piness and money can vary depending on how you ask the question. Fortunately, we now have a pretty clear picture of this complexity. First, the link between income and happiness is stronger when we define happiness as life satisfaction; the relationship is weaker if we consider emotional experience. Money does less to foster moments of joy, but can generate a sense of satisfaction. Second, although income has an over-all positive correlation with happiness, it is stronger at lower levels of income. Said another way, increasing income has diminishing returns for happiness (see Figure 3.1). An extra $10,000 might improve the satisfaction of a person with low income, but it will do very little for the happiness of a person with high income. At very high levels of income, it takes large amounts of money to improve satisfaction only slightly. Thus, within most countries, the correlation between income and happiness is rel-atively small. In addition, people who are materialistic (i.e. who value money more than other things) tend to be less happy (Dittmar, Bond, Hurst, & Kasser, 2014). This argues against making money the primary goal in one's life. When we look across countries, we see more substantial differences in average income – and the benefits that can come with it. Growing national wealth can improve the well-being of citizens (Inglehart, Foa, Peterson, & Welzel, 2008).

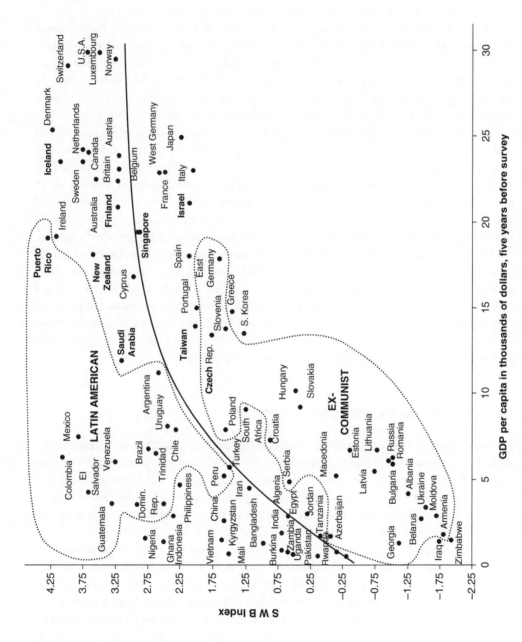

Figure 3.1 Subjective well-being and gross domestic product from Inglehart et al. (2008)

In summary, demographic characteristics like age and gender have weak links with happiness. Also, some of the things that we might assume to be very important – like marriage or income – explain only a small part of happiness. Although these factors' influence is small, at least compared to personality traits, we should not dismiss them altogether.

There are a few reasons to be cautious. First, even when we do not observe an overall difference, a demographic characteristic might combine with other circumstances or traits in important ways. As one example, even though age and gender differences in happiness are tiny overall, young single mothers tend to be significantly less happy than average. In addition, although most people in the USA seem to age happily, older people in Latin America and Eastern Europe do report substantially less happiness (Steptoe et al., 2014).

Second, statistically small effects can sometimes have large practical importance. As an analogy, an increase of a few degrees in the average global temperature would be small compared to the wide variation across climates, yet still catastrophic in its effects. Within countries, the correlation between income and happiness is small; however, when comparing the richest people to the poorest people in a country, the difference in happiness is still noteworthy (a full standard deviation in many countries; Lucas & Schimmack, 2009). Are the rich happier than the poor? Yes – but money is not the most important factor in happiness.

Third, things that are relatively infrequent – such as unemployment – can have a substantial influence on a few individuals' happiness, yet explain only a little of the overall variation in average happiness. The impact on a few individuals is only a small part of the much larger whole; however, it looms very large for those few. Our statistics typically focus on the overall trends, and may gloss over important effects for these smaller sub-groups. In addition, major life events can sometimes produce large changes in happiness, but these changes often fade over time. This idea is captured by the term 'hedonic treadmill'.

Life Events and the Hedonic Treadmill

Because happiness is strongly related to heritable dispositions, and less so to life circumstances, some have claimed that happiness is fixed, that it cannot really be changed. This view goes too far; yet happiness is more stable than many people assume. The relative stability can be for the best. When bad things happen, people typically find a way to cope, and they return to a reasonable level of happiness. People are resilient. However, the flip side of this trend is that good events only boost our happiness temporarily.

People's tendency to return to a 'baseline' level of happiness is known as **adaptation**. With most sensations, we become accustomed to novelty over time. Adaptation is why the first bite of dessert is the sweetest, why we continue to add salt as we make our way through a pile of chips, or why your roommate is shocked at the noise when coming home to the personal dance party that broke out as you turned up the stereo through each new song on your favourite playlist. Said another way, people are sensitive to changes. Once the change has occurred, we adapt to it; it takes more change for us to notice again. It seems people's happiness responds to life events in the same way. We know that our emotions fluctuate with pleasant and unpleasant experiences; these are the kinds of changes we considered in Chapter 2. When it comes to bigger events and longer-term changes in subjective well-being (i.e. beyond daily moods), people also react. Yet people often return to their 'personal normal' after a period of adaptation (Headey & Wearing, 1989; Luhmann, Hofmann, Eid, & Lucas, 2012). This idea has been called the **hedonic treadmill**. Hedonic refers to the pleasantness of experience, and the treadmill implies that we are not really going anywhere.

Tests of the hedonic treadmill view often focus on major life events. In a classic study, people who had won large amounts of money in lotteries were compared to people who were injured in accidents and became paraplegic. A control group of people with similar backgrounds, but no extreme events, was also included (Brickman, Coates, & Janoff-Bulman, 1978). The lottery wins and accidents had occurred between one and 18 months before the data were collected. Participants rated their current happiness, as well as how pleasant they found mundane events like eating breakfast, hearing a joke, or watching TV. Surprisingly, the lottery winners did not report significantly more happiness than the control group. Winners also reported gaining significantly less pleasure from mundane events. These results suggested that winning the lottery did not improve happiness a few months later!

This study is sometimes incorrectly cited with regard to the accident victims – they were not actually equivalent to lottery winners. The victims reported significantly less happiness than both the controls and winners. On the other hand, victims' happiness was still above the midpoint of the happiness scale – this group was not miserable (cf. the locked-in patients described earlier). Moreover, accident victims reported levels of pleasure from mundane events that were similar to the control group and lottery winners. This study had a large impact because it conflicted with people's intuitions. It suggested that major events had only a modest influence on people's happiness.

Since this early and influential study, psychologists have collected much better data. More recent research has clarified the hints of remarkable adaptation – and the limits of adaptation – observed in the classic study. Large studies that track people over many years can tell us about people's happiness both before and after major life events (e.g. see Diener et al., 2006; Headey & Wearing, 1989). They can also tell us about the extent of stability and change in happiness that people typically experience over time. It turns out that people's life satisfaction and average levels of emotion are quite stable over time. In other words, there are moderate to large correlations between individuals' happiness ratings at different points in time, even when ratings are separated by years (Lucas & Donnellan, 2012). However, it is also easy to overstate the degree of stability – the correlations are far from perfect. There are still some fluctuations to explain.

When looking at major life events, such as marriage, serious illness, unemployment, and so on, we see clear influences on happiness. Unsurprisingly, positive events increase happiness, and negative events decrease happiness. Over time, however, we also see evidence of adaptation. The impact of events tends to dissipate. People recover from the sharp decrease in happiness that accompanies things like unemployment and widow-hood. Yet even with this clear recovery, the power of adaptation can also be overstated. Often people's recovery takes years; they remain less happy for a long time after major negative life events. Figure 3.2 summarizes findings from a large German survey that tracked people over many years (Diener et al., 2006). We can see people's yearly life satisfaction ratings from five years before to five years after widowhood, divorce, unem-ployment, and marriage. Findings like these suggest that the hedonic treadmill does not always keep pace with life. Thus, events and circumstances do have some bearing on our happiness, even as adaptation tends to mellow these effects with time (Luhmann et al., 2012). In sum, people's happiness levels are not fixed, but they do seem to resist easy or permanent change.

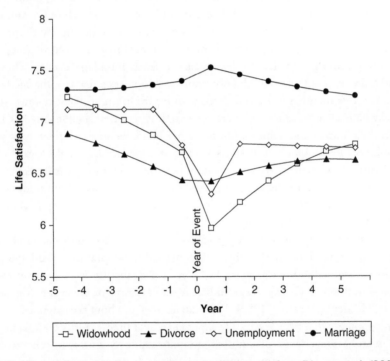

Figure 3.2   Life satisfaction before and after major life events from Diener et al. (2006)

HAPPINESS AROUND THE WORLD

Another persuasive argument against a strong hedonic treadmill comes from international comparisons of happiness. If we compare the average happiness in countries like Denmark,

Australia, and the UK (quite high) to that in countries like Togo, Haiti, and Iraq (quite low) the differences are vast. For example, average life satisfaction, rated on a 10-point scale, is 7.4 in the happiest 10 countries, compared to only 3.4 in the bottom 10 countries (Helliwell, Layard, & Sachs, 2016). Genetic differences do not account for the wide variation across nations. Instead, we see that living conditions, social cohesion, wealth, political stability, liberty, and so on matter a lot when we take a global perspective on subjective well-being. People's happiness does not adapt to everything.

This highlights a key benefit of studying happiness across nations: circumstances differ much more dramatically across nations than within the individual countries where most early research was conducted. For example, in a Swedish sample, much of the variation in happiness will be due to personality and genetic differences. Living conditions are quite good in Sweden, and even the least fortunate citizens are generally able to meet basic needs. As a contrast, imagine looking at a sample that includes half Swedes and half Tanzanians. The living conditions in Tanzania are much more difficult. Because the circumstances of these two countries vary dramatically, those circumstances account for a lot of the variation in happiness when we include both in a comparison. People are, on average, much happier in Sweden than in Tanzania, and these differences are largely due to circumstances. Genetic and personality differences are still present, but now explain less of the variation in happiness, compared to when we considered a group of Swedes only. With wider variation in circumstances, their role in happiness becomes more pronounced. International comparisons show us that the country people live in can contribute to, or detract from, their subjective well-being.

In recent years, our understanding of international differences in subjective well-being has improved dramatically. One important reason for this is the **Gallup World Poll** (GWP). In 2005, the Gallup organization began an annual survey that sought to sample the entire world, and to do so each year for the next 100 years. The scope and scale of this survey were unprecedented. Fortunately, positive psychologists helped design the poll to assess subjective well-being along with other important psychological characteristics and environmental circumstances. The GWP surveys people in 160 nations – it represents views from about 98 per cent of the world's population (see Diener & Tay, 2015). The key questions have been painstakingly translated into many languages and asked the same way in each country. In nations where many people do not have phones, interviewers walk from home to home to survey carefully selected people, revisiting if necessary. That is, about 1000 people are chosen so that they accurately represent the diversity of the population (e.g. on gender, age, geography) in each nation. These survey data are also combined with country-level statistics like gross domestic product (GDP, or wealth), inequality indexes, and so on.

A key advantage of the GWP is the wide range of people it surveys. In addition, it includes questions about each component of subjective well-being. People report their life satisfaction using the ladder measure described earlier; they also indicate whether they experience much enjoyment and laughter (positive emotion), as well as anger, sadness, or stress (negative emotions). Table 3.2 shows some examples of how the components of sub-jective well-being are correlated with people's circumstances (Diener & Tay, 2015). These correlations are based on national averages from the 2005–2013 polls – they include over 1.2 million surveys!

Table 3.2 Nation-level correlations between subjective well-being and societal conditions (2005–2013)

	Life Satisfaction	Enjoyment	Stress
Economic & material needs			
Annual income	.75	.35	.24
Have electricity	.62	.29	.22
Hungry	−.58	−.22	.11
Health			
Life expectancy	.71	.28	.36
Environment quality			
Preservation	.26	.37	.08
Good water	.66	.53	.11
Social quality			
Count on others	.68	.46	.09
Freedom	.53	.53	.07
Honest elections	.39	.27	.10
Equality			
Income inequality	−.44	−.07	−.11

Source: Adapted from Diener and Tay (2015)

Chapter 1 described how we interpret correlation coefficients. To recap, correlations can range from −1 to 1. The sign tells us whether the two things increase together (positive), or whether one increases as the other decreases (negative). Values near 0 suggest that two things are not associated, or that there is no direct link between them. Values closer to −1 or 1 suggest very strong associations. Even correlations of around (−).5 are considered fairly strong, representing a clear, if imperfect, link.

In Table 3.2 – where nations around the world are compared – we see a strong link between annual income and life satisfaction (.75), and a smaller correlation with enjoyment (.35). People report more happiness in richer countries. Interestingly, the correlation between income and stress is also positive (.24). In countries with high income, stress also tends to be higher. Other negative emotions not included in Table 3.2 (e.g. sadness, anger) tend to be lower in places where quality of life is good and income is high. Thus, it seems there is something different about stress; societies that are generally functioning well economically may not reduce stress as efficiently as they provide other psychological benefits.

The correlations in Table 3.2 are consistent with a few ideas already mentioned in this chapter. First, wealth is more strongly associated with life satisfaction than with emotions (.75 is larger than .35 and .24). Second, it is useful to consider different components of subjective well-being because they sometimes suggest different things. Both satisfaction and stress are higher with more income – a mixed bag for overall well-being. As another example, positive emotions – unlike life satisfaction – are more strongly associated with good social relationships and environmental quality, compared to meeting material needs. Third, the link between income and satisfaction is quite strong when we look at national averages. This contrasts with the relatively small correlations between wealth and subjective well-being found when we look at individuals within a single country.

Other aspects of the GWP data extend this idea. Living in a wealthy country seems to contribute to subjective well-being over and above one's individual income (Diener et al., 2010). Wealthier countries tend to have better infrastructure, environmental quality, and less corruption – things that contribute to the well-being of everyone regardless of personal income. Said another way, it is less important to be richer than your neighbours, when it comes to subjective well-being, and more important to live in a place with a generally high quality of life. Again, the conditions in which we live matter for subjective well-being.

Returning to Table 3.2, we see that good circumstances, beyond income, are generally positively correlated with subjective well-being. For example, good environmental quality, being able to count on others, having a sense of personal freedom, and equality are positively correlated with satisfaction and enjoyment. All of these things tend to be higher in wealthier countries; yet statistically controlling for wealth does not eliminate the links. Good social bonds, environments, health, and so on matter beyond their association with money. Countries differ in how they spend their wealth and how they structure their societies. More nuanced statistical analyses show that cultural differences are important to the subjective well-being of nations. When we look at individual countries, we can see these differences. Wealth alone does not ensure the highest quality of life or subjective well-being.

Comparing Individual Countries

A selection of individual nations' well-being is provided in Table 3.3. Each nation has a score, adjusted to a 100-point scale, for subjective well-being, economic and material well-being, health, environmental quality, social quality, and equality. These scores include the example items in Table 3.2, along with others in each category. The subjective well-being column (SWB) combines satisfaction and emotion questions into one score, and the nations are sorted by that score.

Table 3.3 Well-being scores for selected nations

Nation	SWB	Economic/ Material	Health	Environment	Social	Equality
Denmark	**84.0**	**92.9**	84.5	**84.2**	91.3	**77.0**
Netherlands	**82.6**	**90.9**	86.5	81.1	**89.7**	78.0
UK	**78.0**	87.8	88.8	82.9	85.5	70.4
Costa Rica	**77.7**	61.2	86.8	79.8	81.7	70.4
Canada	**77.3**	**90.5**	88.8	76.6	**91.5**	74.2
Germany	76.9	86.6	85.8	**83.2**	79.7	73.5
Mexico	76.7	56.7	85.9	65.6	69.1	70.0
Russia	75.7	62.6	*74.4*	*39.4*	*61.2*	71.3
Brazil	75.7	62.9	83.2	65.7	*32.5*	68.3
China	75.3	63.2	86.2	75.7	86.3	*61.8*
Japan	75.2	85.5	**91.1**	67.8	79.3	**74.3**
Bhutan	74.7	*54.2*	83.5	**89.3**	89.3	75.4
USA	74.3	**89.8**	86.3	76.0	83.5	72.5
South Africa	73.7	*47.6*	*70.3*	65.1	75.8	*58.8*
Singapore	73.4	**89.9**	**93.9**	**90.6**	88.9	74.2
Kenya	73.2	*31.4*	75.5	62.4	70.4	62.3
South Korea	72.5	84.4	87.4	64	66.7	71.1
Qatar	69.4	81.9	**91.3**	88.6	**92.2**	67.7
Israel	*69.3*	80.4	88.9	*56.7*	75.4	**79.9**
India	*68.0*	*47.2*	77.2	69.3	67.1	*67.1*
Greece	*64.5*	69.3	**89.1**	*54.5*	61.6	72.1
Sierra Leone	*56.5*	*22.7*	*61.3*	*48.9*	*59.9*	*59.3*
Iraq	*50.0*	55.7	77.5	*35.3*	*49.7*	72.8

Notes: All values transformed to a 0–100 scale. The top five of selected nations (in this group) on each index are in bold; the bottom five are in italics.

Source: Adapted from Diener and Tay (2015)

The profiles of individual countries are instructive. On average, indicators of quality tend to go together; they are positively correlated. Yet there are also intriguing divergences among the different areas. Positive psychologists argue that these differences make it important to consider subjective well-being itself when making policy decisions. Using only economic indexes, or an index of any one domain alone, would neglect other important aspects of the good life. For example, the USA is the wealthiest nation in the world (though not the best in meeting material needs broadly), yet people there report lower subjective well-being than in many other nations – particularly as it is calculated in Table 3.3. Similarly, Singapore and Japan score very high on meeting economic needs, health, and equality. However, they are not particularly happy, scoring considerably lower on subjective well-being. In contrast, Costa Rica is not a wealthy country, yet ranks among the happiest nations of the world and provides good quality of life in most areas (beyond what we might expect given its modest wealth). This comparison fits with larger trends in cross-cultural studies.

People in Latin America often report more happiness then we would expect, based on their circumstances, whereas people in wealthy East Asian nations often report less. The GWP data are limited in explaining why we see these trends. Given the GWP's wide reach, it is not practical to ask some of the more nuanced questions that would help capture unique features of individual cultures or regions. Indeed, GWP questions are designed to be understood in the same way by everyone. The survey must also be kept brief, thus omitting other potentially interesting questions. Separate studies can help fill this gap. For example, one study suggested that people in Mexico value and express energetic positive emotions more, whereas people in China and Japan value emotional restraint as a route to harmonious social relationships (Ruby, Falk, Heine, Villa, & Silberstein, 2012). Perhaps these cultural ideals help explain some national differences in subjective well-being. More studies are needed to fully understand such cultural differences, and they will need to go deeper than the GWP is able to do.

Changes over Time

The GWP has now been conducted yearly for long enough to look at how things have changed over time. In Table 3.3, Greece stands out as a European country with lower subjective well-being than many nations on the continent. The scores in Table 3.3 are averages across 2005 to 2013; when we look at individual years, we see considerable change over time (Diener & Tay, 2015). Greek society fell into turmoil over a debt crisis during this period, to the point where its membership of the European Union came into doubt. Economic indicators in Greece were not good during this time. Yet even more dramatic changes were seen in people's sense of freedom, satisfaction, sadness, and stress. Other countries that experienced instability, such as Egypt and Syria, also reported sharp declines in well-being during this period. Thus, we see that changes in people's well-being mirror changes in national circumstances. Patterns like this remind us that some of the things that contribute to our happiness, like a stable and free society, can go unnoticed – until they go away.

Even without such extreme circumstances, the ebb and flow of nations' fortunes seem to impact people's happiness. Often, this change is positive. In the GWP, as well as other large international studies that go back 30 years, we see that people's life satisfaction tends to increase as nations become wealthier over time (Diener, Tay, & Oishi, 2013; Inglehart et al., 2008; Oishi & Kesebir, 2015). With economic development, we often see increases in democracy, social tolerance, sense of freedom, optimism, and financial satisfaction too. These changes are important to realizing the happiness benefits of increased wealth. Said another way, national wealth does not translate directly into citizens' happiness. Growing economic prosperity improves satisfaction when it is distributed more equally and strengthens societies. When increases in wealth go to only a small portion of the population (usually the very rich), the national well-being gains do not materialize. High levels of income inequality are associated with lower well-being. Wealth that increases inequality is less helpful to national happiness.

Beyond Satisfaction: Meaning and Religion

We see a recurring theme when comparing nations: wealth is associated with high subjective well-being. However, if we take a broader view of happiness, we see some exceptions to this trend. Stress is one example; it is often high in places that are otherwise doing well. Even more dramatic, however, is the more eudaimonic indicator of meaning in life. In the GWP, poorer countries report having more meaning in life than rich countries (Oishi & Diener, 2014). Said another way, the correlation between life satisfaction and meaning is negative when we look at national averages around the world. The rich countries tend to be more satisfied; the poor countries tend to experience more meaning. (This contrasts with a strong positive correlation between satisfaction and meaning when we look at people within a single country.) It seems there are major differences between societies when it comes to finding meaning.

There are a few possible explanations. For example, poor countries that report high meaning also have higher fertility rates and less education. It may be that having children contributes to meaning, while higher education prompts more questions than answers about the meaning of life. Another major difference across societies is religiosity. In many countries, such as Bangladesh, Malawi, Thailand, and Saudi Arabia, over 95 per cent of people report that religion is an important part of their daily life. In contrast, many developed countries, particularly in Northern Europe, have rates around 30 per cent, and as low as 16 per cent in Sweden (Diener, Tay, & Myers, 2011).

Religious countries report more meaning in life, and poorer countries are more likely to be religious. Statistically, nations' religiosity seems to account for much of the higher meaning. To illustrate, both Haiti and Yemen are similarly poor countries. However, Yemen is more religious than Haiti, and meaning in life is higher in Yemen than Haiti (Oishi & Diener, 2014). We see this trend repeated across nations. Wealthy countries with higher religiosity (like the USA) also report more meaning than wealthy countries with less religiosity (like France). Religion is more closely tied to meaning than wealth is. It appears that poor countries report more meaning in life largely because they are more religious (though education, fertility, etc. probably play some role too).

People in poor, religious societies report a lot of meaning, but still less subjective well-being than people in wealthy countries. What does this imply about the link between religion and happiness? To answer this question, we need to consider people's circumstances. Religiosity is associated with higher subjective well-being at the individual level, especially in very religious societies. There is not one faith that is more conducive to happiness than the others, but religious people tend to be happier than non-religious people when all else is equal. Yet across the world, the more religious countries tend to be less economically prosperous, on average. We have seen that poorer countries tend to be less happy than wealthier countries. Thus, many religious people live in harsh conditions, and they tend to report low satisfaction (along with high meaning). Still, religion – and the sense of meaning it gives – seems to provide some benefit to subjective well-being. This is especially true in places with the most difficult circumstances. We can tease apart the influence of religion and wealth by comparing countries.

Among the poorest and least educated nations, the more religious nations report higher satisfaction than the less religious nations (cf. Yemen vs Haiti). Religion and meaning seem to help with satisfaction. This trend, however, is not as strong in wealthier nations that otherwise have good quality of life (cf. USA vs France). Thus, from the GWP we might conclude that religion facilitates happiness more in difficult circumstances (Diener et al., 2011). Said another way, religion helps buffer against the unhappiness of difficult circumstances. This may also explain why rates of religiosity are declining in many highly developed countries. In these places, it seems people can find high levels of satisfaction in other ways – even if meaning is more elusive.

A FEW LINGERING QUESTIONS

We have discussed definitions of happiness and some of the important predictors of happiness. Psychologists have learned a lot about who reports higher or lower levels of subjective well-being. However, a few frequent – and important – questions about happiness remain. We tackle those questions in this section.

Can We Trust Self-Report Measures of Happiness?

Most happiness research uses self-reports as the primary measurement tool. This raises questions about **validity**: can we trust what people tell us? Similar to self-reports of emotions (considered in Chapter 2), accurate assessment depends on the participants' ability and willingness to report on their happiness. Normally this is not a problem – people easily rate their happiness – but there are sources of bias that can influence answers (see review by Diener, Inglehart, & Tay, 2013). When and how we ask questions about subjective well-being can influence the answers we get.

Subjective well-being is defined as a relatively stable characteristic of people; we explicitly contrast it with the daily fluctuations of moods and emotions. Theoretically then, reports of subjective well-being should not change much from day to day or be influenced by immediate context. Yet some studies suggest that momentary circumstances can influence ratings of overall subjective well-being. When moods, certain life domains, or events are made salient, they can be weighted too strongly in making an overall satisfaction judgement, thus biasing answers. For example, a large telephone survey of Americans asked questions about politics and about well-being. People reported lower well-being if the political questions came just before the well-being questions, compared to other orderings (Deaton, 2011). Presumably, being reminded of the typically dissatisfying domain of politics made people think about it too much when judging their overall well-being. People's ratings of their subjective well-being are not as fixed as theory suggests they should be. The order of questions and context of the assessment can influence answers. Does this mean that measures of subjective well-being are completely invalid? Fortunately, the answer here is a clear "no".

Although questions' order can sometimes make a difference, the influence is usually quite small. Detailed analyses show that subjective well-being scores mostly represent stable judgements (as they should), with momentary conditions accounting for about 10 per cent of the score (Schimmack & Oishi, 2005). In addition, biases can also be corrected or controlled. In the example above, adding a single 'buffer' question after the politics questions removed the effect on well-being ratings. The buffer question simply asked people to consider their personal lives in general, thus allowing other important domains to be considered appropriately.

Although it is not difficult to ask questions about happiness, there are better and worse ways to do it. As a general guideline, better approaches will ask about subjective well-being early in a study and will use procedures that keep testing conditions similar for everyone. Multiple measures and sophisticated statistical techniques can also improve precision (e.g. Kim, Schimmack, & Oishi, 2012).

Our confidence in the validity of happiness questionnaires also comes from decades of corroborating research findings. That is, the measures must be reasonably reliable and valid in order for happiness research to find many of the things already reviewed in this chapter. Happiness scores correlate highly when re-tested across many years, correlate strongly with personality traits, and are moderately heritable (e.g. in twin studies). Differences in societal conditions across nations are associated with substantial differences in subjective well-being, and changes in societal conditions are mirrored by changes in reports of subjective well-being. Self-reports of happiness are also sensitive to major changes in life circumstances (e.g. marriage, divorce, unemployment). In addition, self-reports correlate with a wide range of alternative methods of assessing well-being, such as physiological functioning (Steptoe & Wardle, 2005), family and friends' ratings of happiness (Schneider & Schimmack, 2009), positivity of online posts (Seder & Oishi, 2012), economic indicators of life quality (Oswald & Wu, 2010), and how quickly people recall positive life events (Diener & Seligman, 2002). This large collection of findings strongly supports the notion that self-reports of happiness are generally valid.

Despite the validity of self-report happiness measures, some are still hesitant to trust them. Would it not be better to use an objective measure? Should we yearn for a future with a happiness blood test? Such a tool might be useful, but it will never replace self-reports. Keep in mind that we define well-being as subjective. We care about individuals' judgements. What if the blood test told me you were very happy, yet you told me you were not? Should I trust the blood test more? Unless you are lying, the answer is no; we each know our own subjective well-being best. Philosophers can debate whether or not it is possible to be wrong about your happiness (defined more broadly), but the idea of subjective well-being requires self-reports. There will always be some error when using self-report measures, but this is true of every other measurement in science too. Research in positive psychology strives to further improve our self- report measurement techniques. It also pursues alternative approaches that rely on physiology, internet behaviour, and so on, but these cannot fully replace self-reports.

Is It Good to Be Happy?

Happiness is typically associated with good (valued) things. It is obviously pleasant, and it is something people desire (King & Napa, 1998). Happiness is also correlated with health and success across a variety of domains. Happier people tend to act more prosocially and are more productive. In this way, happiness may even be seen as morally good. The correlates of high happiness include cardiovascular, immune, and endocrine health, as well as better health behaviours, longevity, productivity at work, creativity, cooperation, higher income, delay of gratification, number and quality of social relationships, volunteering and donating, and many others (De Neve, Diener, Tay, & Xuereb, 2013; Lyubomirsky, King, & Diener, 2005).

The many positive associations with happiness are clear; the bigger question is whether happiness is merely a consequence of these desirable things, or if it might also be a cause of them. Major reviews of the scientific literature suggest that happiness is both a cause and a consequence (De Neve et al., 2013; Diener & Chan, 2011). For example, it is easy to imagine that getting married might make a person happier. On the other hand, people who are already happy are more likely to get and stay married (Luhmann, Lucas, Eid, & Diener, 2013); it seems that happiness increases the chances of good marriages. When happiness comes – or is measured – well beforehand, it suggests that happiness can facilitate desirable outcomes. As another example, a large longitudinal study found that positive affect and life satisfaction measured at ages 16, 18, and 22 predicted income at age 29

(De Neve & Oswald, 2012). Happier adolescents became wealthier adults. It is possible that 'third variables' help explain this correlation. For example, the traits of extraversion, optimism, and low neuroticism accounted for some of the link between happiness and later income. Happier young people were also more likely to earn a university degree, become employed, and get promoted. Findings like these help us understand why happiness could be helpful to future success.

Causal links among happiness, health, and success are also inferred from experiments where happiness is manipulated. Typically, such studies manipulate positive emotions in the short term, as opposed to the long-term happiness of subjective well-being. Nonetheless, it seems positive emotion states facilitate many desirable things. As we saw in Chapter 2, positive emotions often broaden thought–action repertoires that help build resources (Fredrickson, 2013). For example, they can promote social bonding, approach goals, creativity, and generosity. Experimental manipulations provide stronger evidence of causality, compared to correlational studies, but there is a gap with long-term subjective well-being. That gap is narrowed by the fact that people with high subjective well-being experience positive emotion states frequently. Happy people have more happy moments – where we have confidence about the causal direction. Thus, it seems that happiness not only feels good, it is often good for you and for those around you.

Is It Possible to Be Too Happy?

Knowing that I am a happiness researcher, people sometimes send me an advertisement for a new drug; it reads, "Are you annoyingly happy? Despondex could be right for you". Designed to treat people who are "insufferably cheery", this pill is not the latest offering from Pfizer, but rather created by the *The Onion*, a satirical paper. At times happiness can seem uncool or be annoying to jealous frenemies, but is there more substance to the idea that too much happiness is a bad thing? It is easy to think that if happiness is good, more happiness is better. Yet this is an assumption that should be tested.

Overall, the research is convincing: happiness is associated – and very likely can help cause – success and health. This conclusion works well when stated as a general rule, but must not be taken to mean that happiness is a panacea or some magic characteristic that is always good for everything. Happiness will not make you taller, grow or remove hair, nor give you better breath. Broad reviews suggest that happiness is useful more often than not, but this does not mean happiness is the most important factor; it is rarely the single best predictor. Counter-examples – where happy people do more poorly – exist too (see Gruber, Mauss, & Tamir, 2011). This is particularly true when we examine positive states. Some high-intensity positive emotions may tax, rather than mend, physiological systems. Happy moments can make people careless and more prone to stereotyping – positive moods are associated with taking mental shortcuts.

When competing or negotiating, unpleasant emotions can facilitate success. Genuine threats should rarely be met with passive smiles. Keep in mind that emotions – pleasant and unpleasant – are functional; they push us towards adaptive responses. The very happiest people still experience unpleasant emotions in their daily life, just a bit less frequently than unhappy people (Diener & Seligman, 2002). Long-term well-being and success are not the result of constant, inflexible, or delusional positive affect. In sum, there are clearly moments when happiness is not the best way to feel.

It is more difficult to find examples where high subjective well-being – as a long-term characteristic of people – hinders health or success. This does not mean that we should dismiss the idea entirely; it is hard to imagine that anything – even happiness – can be a universal and unmitigated good. It seems plausible that high happiness could hinder some artistic or critical endeavours, or produce unwarranted optimism or complacency. There are some empirical hints that more happiness is not always better. Such findings seem to depend on whether we consider achievement or good relationships. Across a collection of large data sets, Oishi, Diener, and Lucas (2007) found that very high happiness was associated with close relationships and volunteering without limit – the happiest people had the richest social and most prosocial lives. The trend was different for measures of achievement, however. Subjective well-being was positively associated with income and achievement in school, yet with an exception for the very highest levels of happiness. Over time, the happiest people tended to earn less money than the moderately happy people (but both earned more than unhappy people). Said another way, when it comes to achievement, the optimal level of happiness might be more like 8.5 – rather than 10 – on a 10-point scale. For good relationships, 10 may well be best.

SUMMING UP

Happiness can mean many things, so psychologists coined the term subjective well-being to describe the combination of positive life evaluations and a pleasant average emotional balance. Eudaimonia and flourishing refer to additional aspects of the good life, such as having a sense of meaning, authenticity, positive relationships, personal growth, autonomy, and so on. It can be useful to distinguish among these various facets of well-being, though they often correlate positively. Research suggests that we can measure happiness with reasonable accuracy. In addition, studies suggest that happiness not only feels good, it likely contributes positively to personal and societal health.

Both internal and external factors influence happiness. Genes, personality, and outlook are among the best predictors of happiness. Still, they leave plenty of room for people's circumstances to play an important role. Basic demographic features (e.g. gender, age, education), parenting practices, and life events have a surprisingly small impact on long-term happiness, on average. Nonetheless, international comparisons show us that societal circumstances – such as meeting basic material needs, strong social connections, and personal liberty – play a major role in humanity's well-being.

Taken together, you might wonder whether there is much individuals can do to increase their happiness. After all, it is impossible to change your genes (though their expression can be altered), and unusual to drastically change personality or outlook. You probably already live in a nation where things are pretty good, and if not, emigrating is extreme and likely difficult. Gaining education, a spouse, or money might improve happiness a little, but the hedonic treadmill can take those gains back. There is no single, simple method that will transform everyone's happiness.

Still, there are very good reasons to be optimistic about the potential for improvement. For example, this chapter has not said much about potentially important factors in happiness: people's efforts and choices (Lyubomirsky, Sheldon, & Schkade, 2005). The way people spend leisure time, enjoy or suffer through their job, and pursue personal goals are not automatic consequences of genes or circumstances. As Brian Little (2014) noted, people's well-being often depends on 'well-doing'. How we pursue life's projects – large and small – are important to happiness. Our personal goals and our pursuit of them leave plenty of room for choices and change. They are also idiosyncratic and thus difficult to capture in a broad survey of happiness. Future chapters of this book dive deeper into the psychology of how thoughts, feelings, circumstances, and behaviours come together, often speaking to the potential for increased happiness.

TEST YOURSELF

1. What is subjective well-being? How does it differ from eudaimonia?

2. What does it mean to say that happiness is heritable?

3. How is money associated with subjective well-being?

4. Why does happiness resist easy change?

5. What are some of the desirable outcomes associated with happiness?

WEB LINKS

World Happiness Report (including GWP results): http://worldhappiness.report

Veenhoven's World Database of Happiness: http://worlddatabaseofhappiness.eur.nl

Ed Diener's personal web page: http://internal.psychology.illinois.edu/~ediener/

FURTHER READING

To learn more about measuring happiness, see:

Diener, E., Inglehart, R., & Tay, L. (2013). Theory and validity of life satisfaction scales. *Social Indicators Research, 112*(3), 497–527.

This review of eudaimonia theory and research takes a big step towards integrating the diverse perspectives:

Huta, V., & Waterman, A. S. (2014). Eudaimonia and its distinction from hedonia: Developing a classification and terminology for understanding conceptual and operational definitions. *Journal of Happiness Studies, 15*, 1425–1456.

This article provides a very recent, accessible, and wide-ranging review of happiness research:

Diener, E., Lucas, R. E., & Oishi, S. (2018). Advances and open questions in the science of subjective well-being. *Collabra: Psychology, 4*(1), 15. https://doi.org/10.1525/collabra.115

For an intriguing look at the Gallup World Poll data on religion and happiness, see:

Diener, E., Tay, L., & Myers, D. G. (2011). The religion paradox: If religion makes people happy, why are so many dropping out? *Journal of Personality and Social Psychology, 101*(6), 1278–1290.

This is a seminal review on the links between happiness and positive outcomes:

Lyubomirsky, S., King, L., & Diener, E. (2005). The benefits of frequent positive affect: Does happiness lead to success? *Psychological Bulletin, 131*, 803–855.

REFERENCES

BBC. (2008). Lotto winner's burger bar return. Retrieved 16 October 2014, from http://news.bbc.co.uk/2/hi/uk_news/wales/south_east/7311542.stm

Boyce, C. J., Wood, A. M., & Powdthavee, N. (2013). Is personality fixed? Personality changes as much as "variable" economic factors and more strongly predicts changes to life satisfaction. *Social Indicators Research, 111*(1), 287–305. http://doi.org/10.1007/s11205-012-0006-z

Brickman, P., Coates, D., & Janoff-Bulman, R. (1978). Lottery winners and accident victims: Is happiness relative? *Journal of Personality and Social Psychology, 36*(8), 917–927.

Bruno, M.-A., Bernheim, J. L., Ledoux, D., Pellas, F., Demertzi, A., & Laureys, S. (2011). A survey on self-assessed well-being in a cohort of chronic locked-in syndrome patients: Happy majority, miserable minority. *BMJ Open, 1.* http://doi.org/10.1136/bmjopen-2010-000039

Busseri, M. A. (2014). Toward a resolution of the tripartite structure of subjective well-being. *Journal of Personality, 83*, 413–428. http://doi.org/10.1111/jopy.12116

Carver, C. S., Scheier, M. F., & Segerstrom, S. C. (2010). Optimism. *Clinical Psychology Review, 30*(7), 879–889. http://doi.org/10.1016/j.cpr.2010.01.006

Chabris, C. F., Lee, J. J., Cesarini, D., Benjamin, D. J., & Laibson, D. I. (2015). The fourth law of behavior genetics. *Current Directions in Psychological Science, 24*(4), 304–312. http://doi.org/10.1177/0963721415580430

De Neve, J. (2011). Functional polymorphism (5-HTTLPR) in the serotonin transporter gene is associated with subjective well-being: evidence from a US nationally representative sample. *Journal of Human Genetics, 56*(6), 456–9. http://doi.org/10.1038/jhg.2011.39

De Neve, J., Diener, E., Tay, L., & Xuereb, C. (2013). The objective benefits of subjective well-being. In J. F. Helliwell, R. Layard, & J. Sachs (eds), *World Happiness Report* (pp. 54–79). New York: UN Sustainable Development Solutions Network.

De Neve, J., & Oswald, A. J. (2012). Estimating the influence of life satisfaction and positive affect on later income using sibling fixed effects. *Proceedings of the National Academy of Sciences of the United States of America, 109*(49). http://doi.org/10.1073/pnas.1211437109

Deaton, A. S. (2011). The financial crisis and the well-being of Americans. *National Bureau of Economic Research.* http://doi.org/10.1017/CBO9781107415324.004

DePaulo, B., & Morris, W. (2005). Singles in society and in science. *Psychological Inquiry, 16*(2), 57–83. http://doi.org/10.1207/s15327965pli1602&3_01

Diener, E., & Chan, M. Y. (2011). Happy people live longer: Subjective well-being contributes to health and longevity. *Applied Psychology: Health and Well-Being, 3*(1), 1–43. http://doi.org/10.1111/j.1758-0854.2010.01045.x

Diener, E., & Diener, C. (1996). Most people are happy. *Psychological Science, 7*(3), 181–185. http://doi.org/10.1111/j.1467-9280.1996.tb00354.x

Diener, E., Emmons, R. A., Larsen, R. J., & Griffin, S. (1985). The satisfaction with life scale. *Journal of Personality Assessment, 49*(1), 71–75. http://doi.org/10.1207/s15327752jpa4901_13

Diener, E., Inglehart, R., & Tay, L. (2013). Theory and validity of life satisfaction scales. *Social Indicators Research, 112*(3), 497–527. http://doi.org/10.1007/s11205-012-0076-y

Diener, E., Lucas, R. E., & Oishi, S. (2018). Advances and open questions in the science of subjective well-being. *Collabra: Psychology, 4*(1), 15. https://doi.org/10.1525/collabra.115

Diener, E., Lucas, R. E., & Scollon, C. N. (2006). Beyond the hedonic treadmill: Revising the adaptation theory of well-being. *The American Psychologist, 61*(4), 305–314. http://doi.org/10.1037/0003-066X.61.4.305

Diener, E., Ng, W., Harter, J., & Arora, R. (2010). Wealth and happiness across the world: Material prosperity predicts life evaluation, whereas psychosocial prosperity predicts positive feeling. *Journal of Personality and Social Psychology, 99*(1), 52–61. http://doi.org/10.1037/a0018066

Diener, E., Sapyta, J. J., & Suh, E. (1998). Subjective well-being is essential to well-being. *Psychological Inquiry, 9*(1), 33–37. http://doi.org/10.1207/s15327965pli0901

Diener, E., & Seligman, M. E. P. (2002). Very happy people. *Psychological Science, 13*, 413– 438.

Diener, E., & Seligman, M. E. P. (2004). Beyond money: Toward an economy of well-being. *Psychological Science in the Public Interest, 5*, 1–31. http://doi.org/10.1126/science.1191273

Diener, E., Suh, E., Lucas, R. E., & Smith, H. (1999). Subjective well-being: Three decades of progress. *Psychological Bulletin, 125*(2), 276–302.

Diener, E., & Tay, L. (2015). Subjective well-being and human welfare around the world as reflected in the Gallup World Poll. *International Journal of Psychology, 50*(2), 135–149. http://doi.org/10.1002/ijop.12136

Diener, E., Tay, L., & Myers, D. G. (2011). The religion paradox: If religion makes people happy, why are so many dropping out? *Journal of Personality and Social Psychology, 101*(6), 1278–1290. http://doi.org/10.1037/a0024402

Diener, E., Tay, L., & Oishi, S. (2013). Rising income and the subjective well-being of nations. *Journal of Personality and Social Psychology, 104*(2), 267–276. http://doi.org/10.1037/a0030487

Diener, E., Wirtz, D., Tov, W., Kim-Prieto, C., Choi, D., Oishi, S., & Biswas-Diener, R. (2009). New well-being measures: Short scales to assess flourishing and positive and negative feelings. *Social Indicators Research, 97*(2), 143–156. http://doi.org/10.1007/s11205-009-9493-y

Digman, J. (1990). Personality structure: Emergence of the five-factor model. *Annual Review of Psychology, 41*, 417–440.

Disabato, D. J., Goodman, F. R., Kashdan, T. B., Short, J. L., & Jarden, A. (2015). Different types of well-being? A cross-cultural examination of hedonic and eudaimonic well-being. *Psychological Assessment, 27*(3), 1–12.

Dittmar, H., Bond, R., Hurst, M., & Kasser, T. (2014). The relationship between materialism and personal well-being: A meta-analysis. *Journal of Personality and Social Psychology*, *107*(5), 879–924. http://doi.org/10.1037/a0037409

Fredrickson, B. L. (2013). Positive emotions broaden and build. *Advances in Experimental Social Psychology*, *47*, 1–53.

Gruber, J., Mauss, I. B., & Tamir, M. (2011). A dark side of happiness? How, when, and why happiness is not always good. *Perspectives on Psychological Science*, *6*(3), 222–233. http://doi.org/10.1177/1745691611406927

Headey, B., & Wearing, A. (1989). Personality, life events, and subjective well-being: Toward a dynamic equilibrium model. *Journal of Personality and Social Psychology*, *57*(4), 731–739. http://doi.org/10.1037/0022-3514.57.4.731

Helliwell, J. F., Layard, R., & Sachs, J. (2016). *World Happiness Report* (Vol. I). https://world-happiness.report/ed/2016/

Huta, V., & Ryan, R. M. (2010). Pursuing pleasure or virtue: The differential and overlapping well-being benefits of hedonic and eudaimonic motives. *Journal of Happiness Studies*, *11*(6), 735–762. http://doi.org/10.1007/s10902-009-9171-4

Huta, V., & Waterman, A. S. (2014). Eudaimonia and its distinction from hedonia: Developing a classification and terminology for understanding conceptual and operational definitions. *Journal of Happiness Studies*, *15*, 1425–1456. http://doi.org/10.1007/s10902-013-9485-0

Inglehart, R., Foa, R., Peterson, C., & Welzel, C. (2008). Rising happiness. *Perspectives on Psychological Science*, *3*(4), 264–285. http://doi.org/10.1111/j.1745-6924.2008.00078.x

Johnson, W. (2010). Understanding the genetics of intelligence: Can height help? Can corn oil? *Current Directions in Psychological Science*, *19*(3), 177–182. http://doi.org/10.1177/0963721410370136

Kahneman, D., & Deaton, A. (2010). High income improves evaluation of life but not emotional well-being. *Proceedings of the National Academy of Sciences of the United States of America*, *107*(38), 16489–16493. http://doi.org/10.1073/pnas.1011492107

Kashdan, T. B., Biswas-Diener, R., & King, L. (2008). Reconsidering happiness: The costs of distinguishing between hedonics and eudaimonia. *The Journal of Positive Psychology*, *3*(4), 219–233. http://doi.org/10.1080/17439760802303044

Kim, H., Schimmack, U., & Oishi, S. (2012). Cultural differences in self- and other-evaluations and well-being: A study of European and Asian Canadians. *Journal of Personality and Social Psychology*, *102*(4), 856–873. http://doi.org/10.1037/a0026803

King, L., & Napa, C. K. (1998). What makes a life good? *Journal of Personality and Social Psychology*, *75*(1), 156–165. http://doi.org/10.1037/0022-3514.75.1.156

Little, B. R. (2014). Well-doing: Personal projects and the quality of lives. *Theory and Research in Education*, *12*(3), 329–346. http://doi.org/10.1177/1477878514545847

Loewenstein, G. (1999). Because it is there: The challenge of mountaineering for utility theory. *Kyklos*, *52*, 315–343.

Lucas, R. E. (2007). Personality and the pursuit of happiness. *Social and Personality Psychology Compass, 1*(1), 168–182. http://doi.org/10.1111/j.1751-9004.2007.00009.x

Lucas, R. E., Clark, A. E., Georgellis, Y., & Diener, E. (2003). Reexamining adaptation and the set point model of happiness: Reactions to changes in marital status. *Journal of Personality and Social Psychology, 84*(3), 527–539. http://doi.org/Doi 10.1037/0022-3514.84.3.527

Lucas, R. E., & Donnellan, M. B. (2012). Estimating the reliability of single-item life satisfaction measures: Results from four national panel studies. *Social Indicators Research, 105*(3), 323–331. http://doi.org/10.1007/s11205-011-9783-z

Lucas, R. E., & Schimmack, U. (2009). Income and well-being: How big is the gap between the rich and the poor? *Journal of Research in Personality, 43*(1), 75–78. http://doi.org/10.1016/j.jrp.2008.09.004

Luhmann, M., Hofmann, W., Eid, M., & Lucas, R. E. (2012). Subjective well-being and adaptation to life events: A meta-analysis. *Journal of Personality and Social Psychology, 102*(3), 592–615. http://doi.org/10.1037/a0025948

Luhmann, M., Lucas, R. E., Eid, M., & Diener, E. (2013). The prospective effect of life satisfaction on life events. *Social Psychological and Personality Science, 4*(1), 39–45. http://doi.org/10.1177/1948550612440105

Lykken, D., & Tellegen, A. (1996). Happiness is a stochastic phenomenon, *Psychological Science, 7*(3), 186–189. http://doi.org/10.1111/j.1467-9639.1991.tb00167.x

Lyubomirsky, S., King, L., & Diener, E. (2005). The benefits of frequent positive affect: Does happiness lead to success? *Psychological Bulletin, 131*, 803–855.

Lyubomirsky, S., & Lepper, H. (1999). A measure of subjective happiness: Preliminary reliability and construct validation. *Social Indicators Research, 46*, 137–155.

Lyubomirsky, S., Sheldon, K. M., & Schkade, D. (2005). Pursuing happiness: The architecture of sustainable change. *Review of General Psychology, 9*(2), 111–131. http://doi.org/10.1037/1089-2680.9.2.111

Nelson, S. K., Kushlev, K., & Lyubomirsky, S. (2014). The pains and pleasures of parenting: When, why, and how is parenthood associated with more or less well-being? *Psychological Bulletin, 140*(3), 846–895. http://doi.org/10.1037/a0035444

Nes, R. B., Røysamb, E., Tambs, K., Harris, J. R., & Reichborn-Kjennerud, T. (2006). Subjective well-being: Genetic and environmental contributions to stability and change. *Psychological Medicine, 36*(7), 1033–1042. http://doi.org/10.1017/S0033291706007409

Nozick, R. (1974). *Anarchy, State, and Utopia* . New York: Basic Books.

Oishi, S., & Diener, E. (2014). Residents of poor nations have a greater sense of meaning in life than residents of wealthy nations. *Psychological Science, 25*(2), 422–430. http://doi.org/10.1177/0956797613507286

Oishi, S., Diener, E., & Lucas, R. E. (2007). The optimum level of well-being: Can people be too happy? *Perspectives on Psychological Science, 2*(4), 346–360. http://doi.org/10.1111/j.1745-6916.2007.00048.x

Oishi, S., & Kesebir, S. (2015). Income inequality explains why economic growth does not always translate to an increase in happiness. *Psychological Science, 26*, 1630–1638. http://doi.org/10.1177/0956797615596713

Oswald, A. J., & Wu, S. (2010). Objective confirmation of subjective measures of human well-being: Evidence from the U.S.A. *Science (New York, N.Y.), 327*(5965), 576–579. http://doi.org/10.1126/science.1180606

Rampell, C. (2011). Discovered: The happiest man in America. Retrieved 25 June 2016, from www.nytimes.com/2011/03/06/weekinreview/06happy.html

Ruby, M. B., Falk, C. F., Heine, S. J., Villa, C., & Silberstein, O. (2012). Not all collectivisms are equal: Opposing preferences for ideal affect between East Asians and Mexicans. *Emotion, 12*(6), 1206–1209. http://doi.org/10.1037/a0029118

Ryff, C. D. (1989). Happiness is everything, or is it? Explorations on the meaning of psychological well-being. *Journal of Personality and Social Psychology, 57*(6), 1069–1081.

Schimmack, U., & Oishi, S. (2005). The influence of chronically and temporarily accessible information on life satisfaction judgments. *Journal of Personality and Social Psychology, 89*(3), 395–406. http://doi.org/10.1037/0022-3514.89.3.395

Schneider, L., & Schimmack, U. (2009). Self-informant agreement in well-being ratings: A meta-analysis. *Social Indicators Research, 94*(3), 363–376. http://doi.org/10.1007/s11205-009-9440-y

Seder, J. P., & Oishi, S. (2012). Intensity of smiling in Facebook photos predicts future life satisfaction. *Social Psychological and Personality Science, 3*(4), 407–413. http://doi.org/10.1177/1948550611424968

Seligman, M. E. P. (2012). *Flourish: A Visionary New Understanding of Happiness and Well-Being.* New York: Simon & Schuster.

Seligman, M. E. P., Steen, T. A., Park, N., & Peterson, C. (2005). Positive psychology progress: Empirical validation of interventions. *American Psychologist, 60*(5), 410–421. https://doi.org/10.1037/0003-066X.60.5.410

Srivastava, S., Angelo, K. M., & Vallereux, S. R. (2008). Extraversion and positive affect: A day reconstruction study of person–environment transactions. *Journal of Research in Personality, 42*(6), 1613–1618. http://doi.org/10.1016/j.jrp.2008.05.002

Steel, P., Schmidt, J., & Shultz, J. (2008). Refining the relationship between personality and subjective well-being. *Psychological Bulletin, 134*(1), 138–161. http://doi.org/10.1037/0033-2909.134.1.138

Steptoe, A., Deaton, A., & Stone, A. A. (2014). Subjective wellbeing, health, and ageing. *The Lancet, 385*(9968), 640–8. http://doi.org/10.1016/S0140-6736(13)61489-0

Steptoe, A., & Wardle, J. (2005). Positive affect and biological function in everyday life. *Neurobiology of Aging, 26*, 108–112. http://doi.org/10.1016/j.neurobiolaging.2005.08.016

Turkheimer, E. (2000). Three laws of behavior genetics and what they mean. *Current Directions in Psychological Science, 9*(5), 160–164. http://doi.org/10.1111/1467-8721.00084

Weiss, L. A., Bates, T. C., & Luciano, M. (2008). Happiness is a personal(ity) thing. *Psychological Science, 19*(3), 205. http://doi.org/10.1111/j.1467-9280.2008.02068.x

Part III

Personality Processes

4

Personality

INTRODUCTION

Debbie Baigrie was walking to her car when a voice behind her demanded money. As she turned around a gun went off – she was shot in the face. During the long and painful reconstruction of her jaw, she learned more about the person who shot her. He was Ian Manuel, a 13-year-old boy who already had a long history of illegal activities. Prosecutors argued that Ian was a budding sociopath, and he was sentenced to life in prison for the shooting.

Surprisingly, Debbie spent years trying to free Ian, and supported him at many court appearances before he was finally released after 25 years. What motivates a victim to advocate for her attacker? We often look to people's personalities to explain such unique behaviours. Debbie seems particularly forgiving. She also has a strong sense of fairness, believing that Ian's punishment was excessive, particularly for someone so young.

Ian has some unusual strengths too. Despite his early history of criminality, Ian reached out to Debbie with an apology; he did not see himself as someone who shot other people. Although he endured 25 hard years in prison, much of it in solitary confinement, he emerged as a caring person with a good sense of humour. Debbie and Ian have become friends. Ian's development from troubled youth to thoughtful adult and his resilience through prison are remarkable.

Ian and Debbie came together in unusual circumstances, but it was their unique characteristics that produced such a heart-warming story. There was something inside each of them – their personalities – that fostered a friendship where many others would have lived with enduring resentment. Moreover, those special circumstances seem to have also changed

Debbie and Ian in positive ways. Each now has a rosier view of human potential, a special result for victims of violent crime and harsh imprisonment. (You can listen to a touching joint interview at www.cbc.ca/radio/asithappens, the 21 November 2016 episode.)

In this chapter, we consider personality and positive psychology. **Personality** refers to the individual, internal characteristics that produce regularities in thoughts, feelings, and actions. Debbie and Ian's story is instructive because it highlights how individuals behave in unique ways – there were many alternative paths their stories could have taken. It also shows the importance of experiences in how personality develops over time.

Early positive psychology drew a lot from personality. More than other areas, personality psychology was historically prone to balance because a primary goal was to map and measure all dispositions (Noftle, Schnitker, & Robins, 2011). This included as much positive as anything else. In addition, many personality psychologists devoted careers to understanding valued characteristics such as optimism, self-efficacy, or creativity. For example, the previous chapter on happiness is largely about personality, and describes work that had a strong start long before positive psychology formed as a new sub-discipline.

Personality psychology is central to positive psychology. It is also larger. I had a mentor who described psychology as a sub-discipline of personality, rather than the other way around. Underlying his bold statement was the idea that understanding personality requires contributions from the basic biology of neuroscience and genetics, to the anthropology and sociology of different cultures. Whether or not you agree with my mentor, personality psychology is clearly much bigger than first impressions might suggest – it has more to offer than just trait questionnaires. Personality psychologists also seek to understand whole people – how our different parts develop and come together into personalities (McAdams & Pals, 2006). This lofty goal remains more aspirational than fully realized; yet it is in the thoughts of many working personality psychologists.

We are interested in personality psychology as it relates to positive psychology. This too engages with some pretty broad issues. We can find valued aspects of people at many levels, from genes that nudge us towards joy, to stories of whole lives well lived. We want to know how basic urges come together with high-minded values to produce satisfying experiences. We wonder why some people seem so naturally contented, while others spend their lives struggling to find meaning. These are specific, positive psychology examples of the thorny issues personality psychologists explore.

Accordingly, this chapter takes an approach similar to Chapter 2 on emotions. We will try to understand the area in general, but with special attention to and examples from the positive parts. In Chapter 2 we saw that positive psychology spawned new ideas about emotion, for example the broaden and build model and new basic emotions. In personality, the positive approach has shined a light on a new set of valued characteristics – character strengths – that are considered at the end of this chapter. Personality is broad and returns in every chapter; this chapter focuses on the core issue of understanding personality itself.

PERSONALITY: THE BIG PICTURE

The scope of human personality was well articulated in a mid-century book by an anthropologist and an early personality psychologist, Kluckhohn and Murray (1948). To paraphrase their now classic formulation, "Every person is in certain respects: a) like all other people, b) like some other people, and c) like no other person." This observation has become a touchstone for highlighting the breadth of personality.

At a basic level, all humans share capacities and needs. Shaped by our evolutionary history, these are species-level universals. As an example relevant to positive psychology, **self-determination theory** (Ryan & Deci, 2000) assumes that all humans have three basic needs: for **competence** (to be capable and master new things), for **autonomy** (to pursue individual, intrinsic desires freely), and for **relatedness** (to feel connected, having good interpersonal relationships with close others). The idea is that all people strive to fulfil these psychological needs, and all experience well-being when their efforts or their circumstances meet the needs. Other parts of one's personality might facilitate or hinder pursuit of basic needs. For example, a generous, sociable, and affectionate person might find it easy to connect with others and effortlessly satisfy the need for relatedness. Nonetheless, all people – even prickly loners – will reap psychological benefits when the need for relatedness is met (Sheldon & Schüler, 2011).

Beyond self-determination theory, virtually all people have human capacities – for example language, basic emotions – even if the details of their expression vary from place to place or person to person. These are part of human personality. In sum, this first level of personality focuses on commonalities across all people; yet, differences may arise in how universal capacities develop or how people meet universal needs.

Those differences bring us to the second level, where we can see dimensions of difference that apply across many people. This middle level is probably what first comes to mind when you think of personality. It is about differences between people, and where we find a natural unit of personality: traits. For example, when we say that Anne is extraverted, we mean that she is different from some other people – those who are more introverted – and similar to others – those who share her tendencies towards talkativeness and exuberance. This middle level is crowded. Beyond traits, it includes the psychology around basic demographic differences (gender, ethnicity), as well as most other individual differences, such as in values, attitudes, attachment styles, and interests. Despite personality psychology's vast breadth, much of it focuses on this middle level of individual differences, as does this chapter.

The middle level allows for much variety across people, yet still neglects individual uniqueness, which fits on a third level. Every person has some characteristics that are completely idiosyncratic. We can understand some of this as the particular combination of an individual's middle-level units (traits, attitudes, etc. – recall the analogy of how vast variety comes from combinations of only three primary colours). Yet there are also individual characteristics – quirks – that are simply unique. For example, there may be something special in the way any particular individual, let's call him Maurice, pronounces the word 'scallops', hits the notes when singing popular songs, or imagines what Buddha looked like sitting under the bodhi tree.

Occasionally, personality psychologists will make in-depth case studies of individuals to understand their idiosyncrasies, and how the various parts of personality come together in a whole person (e.g. Nasby & Read, 1997). More often, psychologists combine qualitative methods (that solicit open-ended stories or descriptions) with quantitative methods (that ask subjects or experts to rate those responses on numeric scales). This allows for statistical comparisons, and creates a bridge from idiosyncratic characteristics to themes that are common across people (though at the cost of losing some individual uniqueness). For example, people have their own **life stories**, that is, the collection of experiences that define them (McAdams & Guo, 2015).

Take a moment to think about your life as a novel or film; try to recall a key scene that represented a turning point; think about the important people or characters in your story, and how you have interacted with them. As you articulate these things, you are revealing your own life story. The way people see and tell their individual life stories can influence how they create the next chapter. For example, one study focused on people who told life stories emphasizing personal redemption; that is, using personal good fortune to successfully address the suffering of another person. People with personal redemption narratives were especially motivated to make things better for the next generation; they also reported higher psychological well-being (McAdams & Guo, 2015).

As another example of individual uniqueness, consider the particular collection of tasks each person is currently working on; these are known as **personal projects**. For example, Sarah may be trying to bench press 160 pounds, sabotage her sister's rocky marriage, and get a passing grade in art history. The particular set of personal projects is unique to each person. However, the way people experience progress towards their personal goals predicts scores on common well-being questionnaires (McGregor & Little, 1998).

Although less research focuses on the individual uniqueness level (vs traits at the middle level), these personal details seem essential to really understanding a person. There is a tension between quantitative approaches that reveal general trends and the personal foibles we notice in those we know well or appreciate in a good biography. Individual characteristics are also very important to counsellors and coaches who are concerned with helping specific individuals, not just the 'average person' or even the 'average extravert'.

Where Do Personalities Come From?

In trying to understand the whole and parts of personality, it is useful to consider how personality develops. Although there are many views on this issue, there is still relative consensus on the basic ideas among contemporary researchers (e.g. see Caspi, Roberts, & Shiner, 2005 for a classic developmental review, and for broad models, see Little, 2015; McAdams & Pals, 2006; McCrae & Costa, 1999; Mischel & Shoda, 1995; Roberts, 2009).

All people begin with their genes, and these genes have evolved over millions of years. It follows that some understanding of human nature can be gleaned by considering human evolution. It is also useful to keep in mind that evolution occurred in environments that differed from modern times, for example with lower population density and less technology. Evolutionary processes can produce commonalities among people (e.g. human abilities like spoken language), as well as differences (e.g. due to consistent costs and benefits of risky vs conservative strategies). In fact, we can see the three levels of personality in genes. All humans share many genes (some of which are also shared with non-human animals) – these are universal. There are also gene variants that we share with some people, but not others. For example, about 57 per cent of people have a gene variant that makes serotonin functioning more efficient, whereas 43 per cent have a version that is slightly less efficient (De Neve, 2011). Collectively, many small genetic differences like this contribute to more substantial and observable individual differences, such as the trait of emotional stability. People are also completely unique in their particular combinations of gene variants – one's individual genome. The one exception is identical (monozygotic) twins, who share all genes. Still, genes are but the first step. Moments after conception, the pre-natal environment begins to shape development, and that environment can differ even for identical twins in the same womb (e.g. in terms of nutrition or exact location).

When babies are born, they have temperamental features that developed via genes interacting with the pre-natal environment. (New findings in epigenetics suggest the intriguing possibility that parents' pre-conception experiences, such as extreme stress, could be encoded in egg or sperm cells; this, in turn, could influence which genes are expressed in their offspring's early development. We do not have any clear examples with human personality yet, however.) Temperamental differences are apparent right away. For example, some newborns are fussy, and others are quieter. These very early temperamental features have links to adult personality; yet there is still much development and growth that will occur, and thus adult characteristics are not pre-determined at this early stage. Influences include the efforts of parents and how they respond to the child's temperament, the random events that occur in everyone's life, and the cultural regularities that each person encounters. As people have and seek out experiences, some characteristics are reinforced and others are changed. The norm is for continuity in personality from childhood to adulthood, but this does not preclude dramatic changes at times.

Maturation also occurs. As children grow, new parts of personality develop. For example, newborns have no sense of self, and young children know only the basics about themselves (e.g. age, gender). The self-concept becomes more complex as children become adolescents. Youth develop new interests, notions of how they differ from other people, and evaluations of those differences (e.g. self-esteem). Self-concepts continue to change throughout adulthood. This is but one example of how many things, such as concerns, habits, goals, and abilities, differ across the life course, both in ways that are common across people and unique to individuals. Personality development and change are most apparent before adulthood, yet continue throughout the lifespan. People find themselves in new situations, facing new challenges, meeting new people, learning new things, and so on. Some of these reinforce personal characteristics and others foster change.

In sum, personalities include basic temperamental influences, as well as the results of early and ongoing experiences. This includes emotional tendencies, beliefs, learned habits, and other factors that guide behaviour. All of these are encoded in physiology at some level. Our personalities are inside us; they are what we bring with us (bodily) from situation to situation. However, this also implies that our physiology is prone to change as we have additional experiences. Our genes themselves do not change; yet they may be expressed or blocked differentially over the life course and in response to experiences.

Most people have a sense – and research supports this notion – that we are in many ways the person we were in the past, and yet that we have also changed. The paradox is not unique to personality. Consider Theseus's ship as described by the ancient Greek writer Plutarch. Over the years, this wooden ship needs to have individual boards replaced as they wear out. After many years, and many, many repairs, every original board has been replaced with a new one. Is it still the same ship? If not, when did it become a different ship? The same issue applies to people. At a literal level, the molecules that make up the cells in our bodies are replaced with new ones, coming mostly from the food we eat. Depending in part on how much we eat, the general shape of our bodies may also change. Even with this change, we remain recognizable. Personality is similar; there is both continuity and change. We are who we have become.

PERSONALITY AT THE MIDDLE LEVEL: DESCRIBING THE DIFFERENCES

Despite the vastness of personality across levels, and the complexity of its development over time, we often want personality psychology to deliver a simple answer to the question: what is this person like? Answers typically put us at the middle level of personality; that is, how a person is like some people and unlike others. There are a few good directions we could take at this level, but the most intuitive path is to begin by listing traits.

Traits and the Big Five Model

Traits are descriptive labels that refer to regularities in thoughts, behaviours, and feelings, and that differentiate among people. For example, if you describe a person as reliable, curious, and shy, you are talking about traits. Furthermore, when we describe someone as reliable, we mean that she shares this characteristic with some other people, who are different in this way from other, less dependable people.

A list of all possible traits would be overwhelming. Early on, personality psychologists Allport and Odbert (1936) went through the entire English dictionary and found thousands of trait terms, which they then listed alphabetically – from 'abandoned' to 'zetetic'. Over the years, this immense list was edited and condensed to create a more manageable set (Goldberg, 1993). Statistical analyses grouped trait terms based on how they correlated with one another. These correlations tell us how traits go together in groups of people, on average. For example, are people described as friendly also likely to be described as assertive or not? The goal was to come up with a map of 'personality space', or to identify the key dimensions of human difference.

Other approaches looked beyond the trait adjectives per se to find key personality differences. They drew on theories and data about physiological differences, the characteristics that differentiated mental health from mental illness, or how people behaved in various psychological tests (e.g. Eysenck & Eysenck, 1985). Over time, the different approaches came to similar conclusions about how the vast scope of trait differences could be summarized by a handful of dimensions. The result was (relative) consensus on a model of personality traits: the five-factor model of traits, also known as the big five (for a broad review, see John, Naumann, & Soto, 2008).

The **big five** traits are commonly labelled: **extraversion**, **neuroticism** (or emotional stability), **agreeableness**, **conscientiousness**, and **openness**. Remembering the list is easy: take the first letter of each trait to spell OCEAN (or CANOE, as we prefer in Canada). The main idea of this model is that these five, broad traits describe much of the variation in human personality. They get at some of the key things that people notice or want to know about others.

With the big five, it is good to keep a particular meaning of 'big' in mind – it refers to the breadth of each trait. In a way, each dimension must summarize around a fifth of all trait differences. They are not specific characteristics; the labels refer to collections of many narrow traits. As a comparison, knowing that a person lives in France gives you some idea about the location, but not nearly as much as knowing that she lives in Bordeaux. Table 4.1 lists the big five traits, along with their **facets**, or narrower parts, of each (see Johnson, 2014). These facets define the broader traits more concretely; a close look at Table 4.1 will help you understand the contents and meaning of the big five traits. The trait facets tend to correlate positively with one another – which is why they are collected in the larger trait – but the correlations are not perfect. For example, someone might score moderately on agreeableness because she is very trusting but not particularly sympathetic. If we only talk about agreeableness, it is a bit like saying someone is from France, as opposed to Bordeaux (like trusting) more specifically.

Table 4.1 The big five traits, facets, and example questionnaire items

Traits and Facets	Example Item
Extraversion	
Friendliness	Make friends easily
Gregariousness	Love large parties
Assertiveness	Wait for others to lead the way (reverse scored)
Activity level	Am always on the go
Excitement seeking	Act wild and crazy
Cheerfulness	Radiate joy
Neuroticism	
Anxiety	Get stressed out easily
Anger	Lose my temper
Depression	Feel comfortable with myself (reverse scored)
Self-consciousness	Am afraid to draw attention to myself
Immoderation	Go on binges
Vulnerability	Become overwhelmed by events
Openness to experience	
Imagination	Love to daydream
Artistic interest	See beauty in the things that others might not notice
Emotionality	Rarely notice my emotional reactions (reverse scored)
Adventurousness	Prefer variety to routine
Intellect	Am not interested in theoretical discussions (reverse scored)
Liberalism	Believe that there is no right or wrong
Agreeableness	
Trust	Trust what people say
Morality	Cheat to get ahead (reverse scored)
Altruism	Am concerned about others
Cooperation	Get back at others (reverse scored)
Modesty	Boast about my virtues (reverse scored)
Sympathy	Sympathize with the homeless

Traits and Facets	Example Item
Conscientiousness	
Self-efficacy	Know how to get things done
Orderliness	Like to tidy up
Dutifulness	Break my promises (reverse scored)
Achievement striving	Work hard
Self-discipline	Carry out my plans
Cautiousness	Act without thinking (reverse scored)

Note: 'Reverse scored' means that people who are high on the trait/facet disagree with that item.

Sources: Adapted from Johnson (2014) and the International Personality Item Pool (ipip.ori.org)

Even when researchers are interested in narrower traits, it is useful to link them with the broader big five model. The common language of the big five promotes communication. For example, one psychologist's studies on persistence can be linked to another researcher's studies on stick-to-it-iveness more easily with the big five model. Both can be clear that they are studying a narrower trait in the broad domain of conscientiousness. A popular characteristic in positive psychology – grit – could be added to that grouping; it too shares much similarity with conscientiousness (Duckworth & Quinn, 2009; Rimfeld, Kovas, Dale, & Plomin, 2016).

The big five provide a set of dimensions where we can locate most other traits. This is similar to how latitude and longitude on a map define a space where specific places can be located. In this way, some traits fall in between the big five dimensions; they are combinations of different big five traits. For example, trait emotional intensity could be understood as a mix of three big five traits (or their facets): extraversion's positive emotions, neuroticism's negative emotions, and openness's awareness of emotions.

Locating traits in 'big five space' allows us to draw on what others have learned. For example, someone interested in grit might infer that people who score high are also be likely to live longer. This is because conscientiousness is associated with longevity (Kern & Friedman, 2008). Of course, it is also good to confirm these inferences with direct tests. Perhaps the longevity association is due to parts of conscientiousness that grit does not share, or perhaps grit also includes some elements of other traits that work against longevity.

Although narrower traits offer more nuance, there is also value in taking a broad approach to personality traits. Assessing the big five at a global level provides a manageable set of key differences which, in turn, can be linked with other things such as occupational achievement or well-being. Given pragmatic limitations – you can only measure so much – the big five allows us to consider many parts of personality at once, rather than focusing on only a few specific characteristics. Indeed, much research assesses the broad big five dimensions without the nuance of facets.

In Focus

Why Does It Feel Like I Am Both? Part 1: Traits as Continuous and Normally Distributed

People love to take personality tests, from the 'Which Disney princess are you?' quiz, to the Myers–Briggs Type Indicator (MBTI). Even when we suspect a lack of scientific rigour, a sense that these tests can provide some sort of insight often remains. This is curious given that the quiz scores are based on things we know about ourselves and that we provide as straightforward answers. Is there really much mystery as to what "I prefer to skip loud parties to stay at home with a good book" is getting at? Unpacking our attraction to these tests teaches two important lessons about personality traits: the dimensional nature of traits (part 1) and the state–trait distinction (part 2).

One reason personality quizzes are so appealing is that we often experience uncertainty when presented with typologies. Are you a thinker or a doer? More of an Ariel or an Aurora? An introvert or an extravert? Even though we have considerable self-knowledge, it can be difficult to pigeonhole our personalities in one of two options. Often we think we are a bit of both. That intuition has merit.

When researchers use personality questionnaires, they typically derive a numerical score. Typically, this score is a simple average of ratings, or a sum of 'yes' responses. Such numbers contain more information, compared to the categorical types that often come from internet quizzes – or the MBTI, which shares this flaw. For example, if a test merely classifies people as 'introvert' or 'extravert', there are only two possible outcomes. With a numeric score, we can see more nuance. Imagine a 'yes/no' extraversion questionnaire with 20 items; it is given to five people and their scores are 2, 7, 9, 12, and 19. If I classify the <10s as introverts and the >10s as extraverts, I lose a lot of information about the other differences. I also make a pretty arbitrary distinction in the middle of the scale. For example, the person who scores 9 ('introvert') is in a different category than the person who scores 12 ('extravert'); yet those two people are more similar (only three points apart) than the people who scored 9 and 2 (seven points apart) who were both put in the introvert category. Putting people into categories obscures the numerical differences, and can lead to some wacky conclusions about who are more similar and different.

And it gets worse! Across most personality questionnaires, the numeric scores of a group of people tend to be normally distributed. That is, the distribution looks much more like the left panel (normal curve), and not like the right panel in Figure 4.1. Many people score near the middle of the scale. If you think of the individual questionnaire items that generate these scores, there is a mix of 'yes' and 'no' responses. Most people report having some characteristics of both introversion and extraversion; the extreme profiles are rare. Thus, drawing an arbitrary line in the middle of this cluster is likely to misclassify some people. Every measure has a bit of error; if being off by a point or two means a whole new category, it magnifies that error.

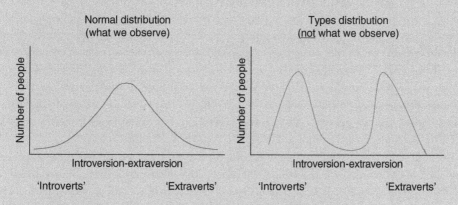

Figure 4.1 Distinguishing between normal distributions and 'types'

The main message here is that it is best to think of personality traits as dimensions of difference, rather than types or black-and-white categories. Moreover, most people tend to be moderate on most traits. Extreme scores are less frequent. You might actually be 'a bit of both' because you score near the middle of a trait dimension. (Despite this, psychologists often use terms that sound categorical, for example 'extraverts'. Among researchers – and in this book – such labels are a linguistic shorthand for 'people who score relatively high on an extraversion scale, as compared to those who score low'. With phrasing like that you can see the attraction of the imperfect shorthand terms!)

Research on the Big Five Traits

As the consensus model of personality traits, there are thousands of studies using the big five. This section briefly touches on the basics of their scope and usefulness. In essence, it describes some key reasons why the big five model is accepted as a good map of personality; these include wide applicability, heritability, stability over time without rigidity, and predictive power.

At a broad level, the big five traits are found in most languages. People in diverse cultures understand the traits, and the correlations among questionnaire items are similar to those found in English (McCrae & Costa, 1997). That said, a model adding a sixth broad trait – about honesty and humility – also works well across diverse languages (Ashton et al., 2004; Saucier, 2009). The big five are even found in non-human animal species, with traits coded by human observers or caretakers (Gosling, 2008). However, only genetically close species, such as chimpanzees, seem to have all five traits. In sum, the big five traits are widely applicable.

The big five traits, like many personality characteristics, are moderately heritable (Bouchard & Loehlin, 2001). Genetic variation explains a substantial part of observed variation in traits; yet this does not argue against the notion that development and experience are also important (see Chapter 3 for more on interpreting heritability). On average, trait scores are remarkably stable over time, with sizable correlations between measurements taken decades apart (Roberts & DelVecchio, 2000). Nonetheless, we can also observe individual change (i.e. when a person's trait score increases or decreases over time) and normative changes (i.e. patterns of average or typical change with age). The normative trait changes can be viewed as maturation, and are observed throughout adulthood. For example, neuroticism tends to decrease over time in early adulthood (Roberts, Walton, & Viechtbauer, 2006).

Because traits are generally stable over long periods of time, we can use them to predict important life outcomes (Ozer & Benet-Martínez, 2006; Roberts, Kuncel, Shiner, Caspi, & Goldberg, 2007; Soto, 2019). Even when assessed years before, traits scores can indicate who is more likely to get and keep a good job, be happy, remain married, or live a long and healthy life. For example, the traits of low conscientiousness, emotional stability, and agreeableness predict divorce far better than low socioeconomic status; also, the big five traits (collectively) predict occupational status almost as well as general intelligence (Roberts et al., 2007). Especially relevant to positive psychology, extraversion and emotional stability are the best predictors of subjective well-being within a nation, even over long periods of time (Diener, Suh, Lucas, & Smith, 1999).

Traits as Personality Processes: What Makes Someone Extraverted?

Researchers have linked big five traits with differences in the size or activity of brain structures (DeYoung, Hirsh, Shane, Papademetris, Rajeevan, & Gray, 2010). This work is still far from having complete biological explanations of traits. Nonetheless, research at the intersection of psychologically defined traits and neuroscience has generated promising theories about cores of extraversion and neuroticism – the two traits most strongly associated with subjective well-being.

Briefly, extraversion may result from stronger sensitivity to potential rewards in the environment (Gray, 1987). That is, extraverts' friendliness, excitement seeking, activity level, and so on stem from their tendency to notice and pursue positive stimuli, and they experience larger mood boosts when they do. In contrast, introverts are less likely to see the appeal of skydiving, chatting up a stranger, or taking charge, and may even experience less pleasure when doing so. These tendencies (i.e. extraversion) have been linked to neurotransmitters and brain structures that deal with rewards (Depue & Collins, 1999). This, in turn, suggests a particular reason for extraverts' characteristic behaviours, and thus can help hone predictions. Extraverts are more prone to socializing, but perhaps this is limited to circumstances that are likely to be rewarding (Lucas & Diener, 2001). For example, if dinner with the in-laws is typically unpleasant, the fact that it is social does not make it attractive to extraverts. Extraverts' sensitivity to rewards seems to play out in their thoughts too; they tend to interpret ambiguous information in positive ways, judge hypothetical events more positively, and rate positive things as more likely to occur in the future (Zelenski, 2007) – extraverts are more optimistic.

RESEARCH CASE

TRAITS AND COGNITIVE BIASES

As psychologists began to see extraversion and neuroticism as related to reward and punishment systems, it suggested new hypotheses. For example, these systems might also exert influence over cognitive processes, biasing people high in extraversion towards positive information, and people high in neuroticism towards negative information. Rusting (1999) tested this idea in some clever ways.

In one study, she recruited about 150 students and measured their traits with standard questionnaires. Those people were then invited to the lab a couple weeks later, seemingly for an unrelated study, where they performed various cognitive tasks. In one task, participants listened to a recording where 90 individual words were spoken, one every three seconds. The participants were asked to write down those words

(Continued)

as part of a 'spelling test'. The spelling was important, but not in the way participants probably assumed. A subset of 16 critical words were homophones – words that sound the same, but have different spellings and meanings. These special homophones had either a positive or negative version, or a more neutral version. For example, key homophones included: rose–rows, won–one, peace–piece, mourning–morning, bored–board, fined–find. At the end of the spelling task, participants were also asked to write definitions of each word to ensure the positive, negative, or neutral interpretations were intended, rather than actual spelling errors. The positive and negative interpretations were then added up, and these scores were correlated with trait extraversion and neuroticism.

A couple of other cognitive tasks were included in the study too (in various randomized orders): a memory task that included positive, negative, and neutral words, and a story-completion task where participants wrote from ambiguous prompts, such as "John is resting his head on his hands". These tasks were also scored for their positive and negative content (i.e. words recalled, or story themes scored by two judges). Table 4.2 shows the correlations between extraversion and neuroticism and the cognitive tasks. We see that these traits predicted (correlated with) how people performed on positive versus negative content in the task. Extraversion was associated with more positive, and neuroticism with more negative interpretations and recall. It seems these traits are associated with some biases in thinking, beyond motivation and emotional experience per se.

Table 4.2   Correlations between traits and cognitive task performance

	Extraversion	Neuroticism
Positive homophones	.20*	−.25*
Negative homophones	.01	.26*
Positive word recall	.27*	−.19*
Negative word recall	−.15	.26*
Positive story score	.24*	−.18*
Negative story score	−.17*	.22*

Note: Statistically significant correlations ($p < .05$) indicted with *.

Source: Adapted from Rusting (1999)

Extraverts seem more attuned to pleasure seeking. This makes them happier on average; yet it can also get them into trouble at times (e.g. more accidents, drug abuse). In contrast, trait neuroticism reflects a sensitivity to threats and potential punishments. This can help keep people high in neuroticism safe, but with the costs of frequent anxiety and some missed opportunities (Nettle, 2006). Neuroscience suggests that rewards and punishments are processed separately; the brain systems are largely independent (Corr, 2004). Similarly, trait extraversion and neuroticism do not correlate with one another. Some people are high on both, low on both, or high on one in roughly equal proportions.

In any given situation, the reward and punishment systems are both evaluating things. For example, imagine a stranger gives you a delicious-looking cupcake. The reward-sensitive tendency is to eat it – yum! The punishment-sensitive tendency is to wonder whether it has been poisoned – hmm? The balance of these tendencies produces a decision about whether to eat or to toss the treat. Across many situations and decisions, the strength of reward and punishment sensitivity is revealed as trait extraversion and neuroticism, respectively. From this perspective, traits not only describe regularities in behaviour, they also represent specific causal processes.

In Focus

Why Does It Feel Like I Am Both? Part 2: States, Traits, and Within-Person Variability

Pigeonholing our personalities into rigid types is difficult when we consider individual moments. Occasionally, even the most outrageous extravert will sit quietly, and timid introverts will sometimes stand up and be heard. In this way too, 'both' is a valid intuition when you consider which kind of person you are.

This brings us to the state–trait distinction. **Traits** refer to average tendencies over time. They are inside people; that is, they are the long-term inclinations that people carry with them to each situation. Yet in each moment we have thoughts, feelings, and behaviours that can vary quite a bit; these are states. **States** are temporary and sensitive to the immediate context; they are short-term units. For example, watching a funny video might put you in a happy state, but we can distinguish this state from your

(Continued)

characteristic happiness (like a trait), which is considerably more difficult and slower to change.

The distinction is important; yet states and traits are still linked. For example, different people respond to the same situation in different ways. This is due, at least in part, to their traits. In this way, we can use states to learn more about traits. That is, we often infer people's traits based on a collection of moments. It is important to have a large collection; for example, one aggressive action alone does not make a person a jerk. Yet over longer periods of time, traits are revealed in the average of many states.

Psychologists have used the experience sampling method to clarify the links between states and traits. This approach asks people to rate their behaviour many times per day over the course of a couple weeks. These are ratings of states; for example, 'How [active, talkative, assertive, etc.] are you right now?' When these state ratings are averaged over time, people show clear differences. Those average differences are remarkably consistent over time – as we expect with traits. A person's average of extraverted behaviours in one week typically correlates >.9 with the average of extraverted behaviours in the next week (Fleeson, 2004). The weekly averages also correlate strongly with conventional trait questionnaires (Fleeson & Gallagher, 2009). Thus, it seems traits do a good job of describing average behaviours in day-to-day life.

Despite the remarkable consistency of trait averages, those averages obscure an equally remarkable pattern of variability in momentary behaviours. In experience sampling studies, most people use the full range of ratings. For example, even people who are, on average, very introverted sometimes report behaving in very extraverted ways, and vice versa. If we look at the full distribution of momentary behaviours, we see lots of variety – even in one person. For example, Figure 4.2 plots the distribution of momentary ratings separately for trait introverts and extraverts (defined here as having average scores one standard deviation above or below the mean – this is arbitrary, but makes for a clear figure). There is a clear average difference (i.e. the trait part), but also considerable overlap in the day-to-day behaviours these people report. Both report a wide range of introverted–extraverted momentary behaviours. Similar patterns are found even when objective observers make the ratings – in one study, across 20 hours of in-lab activities (Fleeson & Law, 2015). The same patterns of consistency and variability apply to all big five traits and their relevant behaviours.

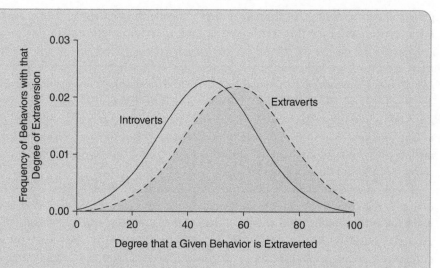

Figure 4.2 Density distributions of extraverted behaviour from Fleeson and Gallagher (2009)

Clearly, people do not always behave in accordance with their dispositions. Rather, dispositions reveal themselves only in long-term averages across situations. In any given moment, there are many things that can influence behaviour; traits are only one small part. This also helps explain why we rely on questionnaires to resolve uncertainty about our personalities. We can all recall times when we behaved like a raving extravert or a quiescent introvert – probably within the last couple days. In this way, we truly are 'both' in day-to-day life. Nonetheless, we can also look to average tendencies – as good personality questionnaires do – to reveal some important ways in which we differ from others over the long term.

Individual Differences beyond Traits

Knowing where people stand on the big five traits tells us quite a bit about their personalities; yet it does not seem comprehensive. We have already touched on human universals and individuals' idiosyncrasies as additional levels of personality. Still it seems there are many parts to people, even within the middle level of individual differences. There are conscious parts and unconscious parts; there are emotional parts and logical parts; there are parts that seem constant and parts that seem ever changing. Can traits capture all this diversity?

Beyond the narrower facets they subsume, there is another way in which the big five traits are broad: we infer traits by drawing on a wide variety of psychological phenomena (Zillig, Hemenover, & Dienstbier, 2002). For example, the questionnaire items in Table 4.1 extend across thoughts ('believe there is no right or wrong'), feelings ('radiate joy'), behaviours ('go on binges'), and desires ('like to tidy up'). Yet traits are often seen as but one kind of individual difference variable. Other units of individual difference include goals, attitudes, motives, self-evaluations, values, abilities, strengths, interests, and so on (see the In Focus box below).

These other units seem distinct from traits, even if the boundaries are a bit fuzzy. For example, many studies have been conducted on the need for achievement. People with high **need for achievement** are driven by a deep desire to obtain excellence, and they tend to do well in business (McClelland, 1965). Need for achievement is also seen as an individual difference – some people have more of it than others. (This is in contrast to the idea of a universal need for competence in self-determination theory.) Although we can distinguish between needs and traits, the need for achievement sounds very similar to the achievement striving facet of trait conscientiousness. That facet is measured with questionnaire items like 'works hard' or 'does more than what's expected'.

To see the distinction between need and trait, consider that people might regularly work hard for various reasons, such as to impress parents, a strong sense of duty, or because they are gifted with super-focused attention. The need for achievement describes something more specific; it is not indicated by the mere presence of hard work, but only when that work is motivated by the particular need. In contrast, big five traits like conscientiousness are usually viewed as primarily descriptive, part of a broad map of individual differences. The trait model is mostly agnostic about deeper causes – at least for now. That said, research is suggesting deeper causes, such as the notion that extraversion is caused by reward sensitivity.

Other kinds of units are usually more specific in their definitions and claims; for example, when a pattern of hard work results from the specific need for achievement. As another example, people's self-esteem is inherently subjective. That is, the **self-concept** is more about perceptions of reality than about objective reality per se (Markus & Wurf, 1987). For example, individuals' beliefs about competence and worth define self-esteem. Beliefs and reality are usually similar, but important differences can emerge too. In contrast to the subjective self, we view traits as something people have; traits do not depend on subjective interpretations. (This view is in conflict with the widespread use of self-report trait questionnaires, and a reason why observer reports are often used to assess traits too.) In our example, a high-achieving person might have high trait conscientiousness (at least as rated by others) even while having low self-esteem. The subjective evaluation of self-esteem differs from the typical behaviours of high trait conscientiousness.

Having different kinds of units (e.g. traits, needs, self) helps us understand apparent contradictions and conflicts in personality, such as the high achiever with low self-esteem.

Ultimately, it is difficult to know exactly why thoughts, feelings, or behaviours occur, especially when we are interested in the personality variables that describe regularities across many situations. For this reason, it is also difficult to draw clear lines between different kinds of individual difference units (e.g. traits vs needs). Sometimes it seems we have more units than are necessary. For example, people's subjective views of themselves usually align well with their traits; people who see themselves as talkative usually *are* pretty talkative. Often, we are content to simply measure big five traits, and not assess self-concepts about those characteristics separately. Other times, distinctions among units are important, such as when there is a contradiction or a domain where people are prone to defensiveness (Vazire & Carlson, 2010). In addition, traits are not always the most useful thing to know about someone. Imagine you are buying a gift for a person who you do not know well. Would you rather know that the person is high in agreeableness and openness, or that he loves to go fishing and collects lures? Here, interests (around fishing) seem more relevant than traits. The most useful personality unit is often determined by the context or our particular research question.

Said another way, personality psychologists have a valuable consensus on the big five model of traits; that is, an overarching map for the domains of extraversion, neuroticism, agreeableness, openness, and conscientiousness. However, there is less consensus on a model for personality units beyond traits. Most agree that traits are insufficient on their own, but it is hard to know exactly where traits begin and end in terms of thoughts, feelings, beliefs, desires, and so on. Traits seem to overlap other units' territories.

In addition, the task of making clear rules about the distinctions between different kinds of units is often complicated by the results of research. For example, traits had been historically defined as highly heritable and stable through adulthood; traits were something that people had, an unchanging core of personality. A major problem with this view is that traits can and do change somewhat in adulthood (even with much stability too; Roberts et al., 2006). In addition, virtually all the other individual difference units turn out to be moderately heritable, just like traits (Polderman, Benyamin, de Leeuw, Sullivan, van Bochoven, Visscher, & Posthuma, 2015; Turkheimer, 2000). This applies to things that we intuitively think should have more to do with nurturing, education, and experiences, such as life satisfaction, values, attachment styles, and religiosity (e.g. Donnellan, Burt, Levendosky, & Klump, 2008; Koenig, McGue, Krueger, & Bouchard, 2005). Such findings challenged initial ideas about how traits might differ from other units (i.e. in heritability). However, this is not to say that we cannot make conceptual distinctions across different units – the following In Focus box provides some useful descriptions in that regard. Additional research will help us understand the true distinctions, but accurately carving nature at its joints is hard!

In Focus

Personality Units at the Middle Level

This box lists and briefly describes some of the common personality units. There are many examples within these categories; for example, need for achievement is one of many potential needs.

Traits describe regularities in thoughts, feelings, and behaviours (McCrae & Costa, 1999). They may be broad (e.g. big five extraversion) or narrower (e.g. talkative). Specific causes of these regularities are typically not assumed, but may be proposed or studied.

Needs (or Motives) produce motivation and behaviour towards their satisfaction (Sheldon & Schüler, 2011). For example, the need for affiliation prompts social relationships – analogous to food, hunger, and eating. Gratifying behaviours are variable and depend on situational triggers, momentary satiation of the need, and general strength of the need.

Goals are the things people want to accomplish (McGregor & Little, 1998; Roberts & Robins, 2000). They can range from idiosyncratic personal projects (e.g. work up the courage to ask Gretchen for a date) to broad life aspirations (e.g. get married and raise a family).

Interests are the activities or domains that attract us (e.g. sports, art, books, gardening). Interests are often assessed as broad vocational domains (e.g. working more with people vs things; Prediger, 1982).

Values are concepts seen as universally important, positive, and useful, yet prone to individual (and cultural) differences in their relative ranking. For example, values include fairness, benevolence, power, hedonism, loyalty, etc. (Graham et al., 2011; S. H. Schwartz & Bardi, 2001).

Character strengths describe positive, valued characteristics (Peterson & Seligman, 2004). They are trait-like in being relatively stable and including regularities in thoughts, feelings, behaviours, and desires. This distinguishes strengths from values, which, although all positive, are described more narrowly as the ideals people prioritize.

Attitudes are the relatively consistent evaluations of things, ideas, people, etc. (Howe & Krosnick, 2017). For example, you may have a positive or negative view of Liberal Party members, Italian food, or bell-bottom trousers. Some attitudes are strong and personally important, such as about the environment for an activist.

Attachment styles are mental models about interpersonal relationships which influence behaviours in relationships and beyond (Mikulincer & Shaver, 2007). For example, people with a secure attachment believe close others would support them, and feel comfortable pursuing novel activities.

Self-concept is the subjective understanding or beliefs about one's own characteristics, which may differ somewhat from objective reality (Markus & Wurf, 1987). Some aspects of the self-concept are measured as individual differences, such as self-esteem, self-compassion, or self-efficacy.

Abilities are the skills people have, such as intelligence, the components of verbal, spatial and quantitative ability, or of other 'multiple intelligences' such as in music or athletics (Gardner & Hatch, 1989).

To navigate the uncertain territory of near infinite personality constructs, it is wise to keep two ideas in mind: the jingle fallacy and the jangle fallacy. The **jangle fallacy** is thinking that two nearly identical things are different because they have different names. For example, some have argued that conscientiousness and grit are so similar that having two separate names is more confusing than helpful (Credé, Tynan, & Harms, 2016). In this view, the distinction between conscientiousness and grit is an instance of the jangle fallacy. In contrast, the **jingle fallacy** is thinking that two actually different things are the same because they share a name. For example, optimism has been measured in two different ways: 1) with questionnaires about general future expectations (e.g. 'in uncertain times, I usually expect the best'; Scheier, Carver, & Bridges, 1994), or 2) by coding the way people explain the reasons for good and bad events (e.g. as being due to internal vs external or controllable vs uncontrollable reasons; Peterson, 1991). In the second approach, the idea is that people who see good events as controllable and caused by the self are more optimistic than people who see good things as due to luck and forces beyond their control. Although both measurements can reasonably be called optimism, they are not highly correlated with one another, and they sometimes predict different things (Reilley, Geers, Lindsay, Deronde, & Dember, 2005). They are not both the same optimism; the shared name is a jingle fallacy.

Keep the jingle and jangle fallacies in mind when you encounter a new personality construct. Knowing about the fallacies will not tell you where, exactly, to draw distinctions, but it will prompt useful questions. Ultimately, we rely on research to guide decisions about what is too similar or sufficiently distinct. However, there is still much research to be done, and the answer sometimes depends on the task at hand. The big five provide an overarching map of personality differences. Yet we often want to be more specific, either with a narrower trait/facet, or to specify a particular kind of personality unit, such as a need, an interest, or – the focus of our next section – a character strength.

POSITIVE PSYCHOLOGY'S PERSONALITY UNIT: CHARACTER STRENGTHS

Developing the Strengths Model

Early in the positive psychology movement, the founders sought to map the domain of positive individual differences (Peterson & Seligman, 2004). They had observed that psychology put great effort into describing, defining, and categorizing hundreds of mental disorders, such as major depression, hypoactive sexual desire disorder, and even nicotine dependence (i.e. smoking). These were articulated in places like the widely used *Diagnostic and Statistical Manual of Mental Disorders*. As an antidote to this pessimistic and narrow focus, the positive psychology founders wanted to craft a new 'manual of the sanities', a list of the ways people thrive and excel, the things that are good about human nature – **strengths**.

The list was guided by Aristotle's notion of eudaimonia (see Chapter 3). Rather than focusing on merely pleasant things, it targeted morally valued characteristics. Researchers have tended to avoid moral pronouncements – for good reason – yet the founders believed it was still possible to find a set of virtues that everyone could agree were beneficial; the goal was more to describe, rather than prescribe, them. They looked far and wide in crafting this list, across many cultures to great thinkers in literature, philosophy, and religion; they also considered more prosaic sources like Boy Scout and Girl Guide texts, greeting cards, bumper stickers, and other pop culture. Of course, they surveyed social science theory and research, including psychology.

Many positive characteristics were filtered through a set of criteria and were only retained if most criteria were met. For example, the criteria stated that strengths should contribute to fulfilment, be valued themselves (vs just their consequences), not diminish other people, be trait-like, be distinct from other strengths, be encouraged by social institutions, and so on. In the end, 24 strengths were included, organized according to six broader **virtues**. (This is similar to the idea of narrower facets making up the broader big five traits.) The virtues and strengths are listed in Table 4.3 with brief descriptions. They are known as the **VIA classification of character strengths**. (VIA stands for values in action, but is rarely articulated anymore.)

Table 4.3 The VIA virtues and character strengths

Virtue and strength	Definition
1 **Wisdom and knowledge**	Cognitive strengths that entail the acquisition and use of knowledge
Creativity	Thinking of novel and productive ways to do things
Curiosity	Taking an interest in all of ongoing experience
Open-mindedness	Thinking things through and examining them from all sides
Love of learning	Mastering new skills, topics, and bodies of knowledge
Perspective	Being able to provide wise counsel to others
2 **Courage**	Emotional strengths that involve the exercise of will to accomplish goals in the face of opposition, external or internal
Authenticity	Speaking the truth and presenting oneself in a genuine way
Bravery	*Not* shrinking from threat, challenge, difficulty, or pain
Persistence	Finishing what one starts
Zest	Approaching life with excitement and energy
3 **Humanity**	Interpersonal strengths that involve "tending and befriending" others
Kindness	Doing favors and good deeds for others
Love	Valuing close relations with others
Social intelligence	Being aware of the motives and feelings of self and others
4 **Justice**	Civic strengths that underlie healthy community life
Fairness	Treating all people the same according to notions of fairness and justice
Leadership	Organizing group activities and seeing that they happen
Teamwork	Working well as member of a group or team
5 **Temperance**	Strengths that protect against excess
Forgiveness	Forgiving those who have done wrong
Modesty	Letting one's accomplishments speak for themselves
Prudence	Being careful about one's choices; *not* saying or doing things that might later be regretted
Self-regulation	Regulating what one feels and does

(Continued)

Table 4.3 (Continued)

6	Transcendence	Strengths that forge connections to the larger universe and provide meaning
	Appreciation of beauty and excellence	Noticing and appreciating beauty, excellence, and/or skilled performance in all domains of life
	Gratitude	Being aware of and thankful for the good things that happen
	Hope	Expecting the best and working to achieve it
	Humor	Liking to laugh and tease; bringing smiles to other people
	Religiousness	Having coherent beliefs about the higher purpose and meaning of life

Source: Seligman et al. (2005), or see: www.viacharacter.org

The six guiding virtues are **wisdom, courage, humanity, justice, temperance,** and **transcendence**. Each virtue includes a few strengths that are more specific instances of, or potential paths to, that virtue. For example, the virtue of wisdom includes the strengths of creativity, curiosity, open-mindedness, love of learning, and perspective. One might enact the virtue of wisdom in any of these ways. For example, perspective could involve giving good advice; curiosity helps propel one towards the knowledge that might make giving good advice possible. With 24 different strengths and the many ways each can be expressed, the VIA classification outlines a broad territory. In this chapter, we focus on the VIA system as a whole; other chapters explore individual strengths in more detail (e.g. authenticity in Chapter 5, or creativity in Chapter 6).

As planned, a 'manual of the sanities' was published; it articulated the development and measurement of the strengths model, along with an entire chapter devoted to what was known about each strength (Peterson & Seligman, 2004). This set of characteristics became the foundation for much discussion in positive psychology, especially in its applications (e.g. coaching, counselling, in business, training). The VIA classification lists the important individual differences in positive psychology. Measures of all 24 strengths are collected in a single questionnaire. You can take the questionnaire measure here: www.viacharacter.org. (Rank-order scores are free; paid reports are also available, but no need to pay for those.) There is a similar questionnaire for young people available there too.

Testing the Strengths Model: Similarity and Difference with the Big Five

The virtues and strengths model has much in common with the big five, and has borrowed many findings and good ideas from personality psychology. For example, I have already noted the hierarchical idea that narrower strengths can be organized as parts of broader virtues (like facets and traits), and that one criterion for strengths is that they are trait-like and dimensional (vs diagnostic categories). Research has supported the notion that strength scores are relatively stable – like traits – at least over the course of months; long-term studies have not been conducted yet (Peterson & Seligman, 2004). Stability in average scores over time does not mean rigidity, however. It seems that individuals' momentary expressions of strengths also vary widely in day-to-day behaviour, similar to the big five domains (Bleidorn & Denissen, 2015). There are some roles and situations that facilitate expression of particular strengths, and most people express even their least characteristic strengths at times.

Also like the big five traits, strengths are intended as a broad map of (positive) individual differences. The standard questionnaire measure of strengths assesses all 24 at once, giving a complete profile. The standard list of strengths can also facilitate communication among researchers and practitioners because it provides a common language, like the big five.

As intended, the strengths seem widely relevant across cultures. One large online study found very similar rank ordering of scores across 54 nations, suggesting more similarity than cultural difference (Park, Peterson, & Seligman, 2006). The most commonly endorsed strengths tended to be kindness, fairness, gratitude, honesty, and judgement, whereas self-regulation, humility, and prudence were less commonly claimed. In another intriguing study, three very diverse sets of people were compared: isolated Inughuit people in Greenland, traditional Maasai in Kenya, and University of Illinois undergraduates in the USA (Biswas-Diener, 2006). Although some differences emerged in the strengths' relative importance across these groups, there was still substantial agreement that the strengths existed, and that they were desirable aspects of character. Even people in difficult circumstances, such as the homeless, can identify their personal strengths, and they correspond well with the founders' list (Tweed, Biswas-Diener, & Lehman, 2012). In sum, the strengths seem to have wide applicability, again like the big five.

With many similarities between strengths and the big five traits, some question whether there are too many similarities (Noftle et al., 2011). The idea behind strengths was to correct the imbalance in clinical psychology, but the project ended up covering much of the same territory mapped by the big five traits. If we compare Table 4.1 with Table 4.3, some similarity is evident. For example, self-discipline sounds a lot like self-regulation, modesty like humility, and kindness like altruism. In many cases, differing labels for strengths and big five facets may represent more jangle fallacy than substantive difference. This interpretation is supported by studies that have given both trait and strengths questionnaires to the same people. Although not completely redundant, the correlations between traits and strengths are substantial; moreover, traits and strengths largely overlap in predicting various forms of well-being (Noftle et al., 2011; Steger, Hicks, Kashdan, Krueger, & Bouchard, 2007). Nonetheless, there are some aspects of strengths that seem neglected by the big five, for example around spirituality.

Indeed, there is little to distinguish strengths from traits as a different kind of personality unit. We covered how needs and the self-concept are defined more specifically than traits in the same domain (i.e. about particular motive or subjective view, respectively). In contrast, strengths are explicitly defined as trait-like, potentially including thoughts, feelings, and actions. Nonetheless, we can find a couple differences. For example, unlike traits, strengths are all valued aspects of personality. Trait models are broader, mapping both desirable and undesirable characteristics – even to the point where the big five are used to differentiate among personality disorders (Widiger, 2005). As another example, a low score on neuroticism does not connote a strength per se, but rather a mere absence of unpleasant emotions.

In addition, strengths were initially described as more prone to development via education, effort, or nurturing, compared to traits. It is not clear that research will support this intuition, however. As one example, strengths – like most individual differences – are heritable to a similar degree as traits, and evidence of shared environment influences (e.g. parenting) is elusive (Steger et al., 2007; Tucker-Drob, Briley, Engelhardt, Mann, & Harden, 2016).

Still, there are some hints in research that strengths can change or be trained. For example, in the months following the 11 September 2001 attacks, Americans reported more hope, kindness, spirituality, and teamwork than in the previous months (Peterson & Seligman, 2003). Although different people completed the questionnaire before and after the attacks (a limitation of this study), similar differences were not seen among non-American respondents who visited the questionnaire website during the same period. This suggests that proximity to the event may help explain the change in scores. In addition, a large UK study found that most strengths had small positive correlations with age, suggesting that they may reflect positive development and maturity (Linley et al., 2007). There are also a few studies that suggest individual strengths like self-regulation or gratitude can be increased with experimental interventions (Friese, Frankenbach, Job, & Loschelder, 2017; Lambert, Clark, Durtschi, Fincham, & Graham, 2010). However, these approaches are preliminary and require verification with stronger methods before we can conclude that they are successful training techniques.

Although big five traits tend to be stable over time, there are also examples where intentional change or psychological interventions have produced modest changes in trait scores over relatively short periods of time (Hudson & Fraley, 2016; Roberts, Luo, Briley, Chow, Su, & Hill, 2017). Thus, it seems possible to nudge both traits and strengths up or down, but dramatic changes are still rare. Strengths appear similar to traits in the ease and typical amount of change, but we still have very little good data on changing strengths – conclusions are tentative. On the other hand, strengths need not be easily trained to be useful. Positive psychologists often want to simply identify people's strengths and encourage their use.

In Focus

Signature Strengths

A key criterion used to select strengths was that they should contribute to fulfilment. In other words, strengths should go beyond helping people cope with difficulty or to feel good; strengths should enhance well-being broadly by facilitating a virtuous life, similar to the notion of eudaimonia. Along with this comes the idea that some strengths are a deep and intrinsic part of people; these are known as **signature strengths**. That is, people have a handful of strengths that feel strongest and most authentic; those strengths' expression is natural, energizing, and even yearned for. Accordingly, good things happen when engaging these signature strengths, including a boost in subjective well-being (Peterson & Seligman, 2004).

The idea of signature strengths applies to the normal, day-to-day lives of flourishing people. In addition, it was developed into a cornerstone positive psychology exercise. For example, it was among the most promising idea introduced in a classic article on new positive psychology interventions (Seligman et al., 2005). People who completed the strengths exercise reported more happiness and fewer depression symptoms weeks and even months after doing it – especially if they continued using strengths beyond the exercise week. Subsequent experiments have found similar increases in happiness (e.g. Gander, Proyer, Ruch, & Wyss, 2012).

Despite these encouraging results, some questions about the exercise remain (Quinlan, Swain, & Vella-Brodrick, 2012). For example, studies with stronger control groups – those that also include positive expectations and self-relevant activities – often see similar changes in both the strengths and the control groups (Mongrain & Anselmo-Matthews, 2012; Proyer, Gander, Wellenzohn, & Ruch, 2015). Results have also been less consistent for depression symptoms, compared to happiness ratings. Researchers are still trying to determine what the essential ingredients of exercises like this are. It may be that working on signature strengths per se is not the reason the exercise seems to work. For example, one study randomly assigned some people to use their lesser strengths (i.e. the strengths where they scored lowest) in new ways. The lesser strengths group showed improvements in happiness similar to people who used their signature strengths (Proyer et al., 2015). Yet both strengths groups reported more happiness than a control group that wrote about childhood memories. In sum, the signature strengths exercise seems like a positive experience for many people; yet we will need more research to understand exactly why and how much.

Another distinction between traits and strengths is found in the methods used to develop the overall models. Unfortunately, this distinction reveals a potential weakness of the strengths model, specifically the way strengths relate to their virtues. Whereas trait models like the big five relied heavily on statistical techniques to refine lists and develop questionnaires, the approach to strengths was more conceptual. Said another way, rather than looking at correlations to decide which strengths to group together in virtues, the founders used their judgement (based on wide reading and discussions). Since the original strengths questionnaire was developed, millions of people have completed it. With this mountain of data, researchers have been able to examine how individual questionnaire items, strengths, and virtues go together. Without getting into the statistical details, it is fair to say that the questionnaire data do not map onto the VIA classification system well. For example, different analyses – examining over a million people's scores – have suggested that three, four, or five (rather than six) broad virtues fit the data better (McGrath, 2014, 2015; McGrath & Walker, 2016).

In essence, whereas the five-factor model of traits is now fairly robust, the organization of strengths and virtues is still in the early stages of refinement. The standard strengths questionnaires, or the strengths' organization – or both – will likely change in the future. Nonetheless, there is still value in knowing the current organization. It represents the founders' vision and substantial conceptual work. A new consensus will require more than statistical critique and will take considerable effort and time.

Some personality psychologists look at this collection of findings and wonder whether a new set of trait-like strengths is really needed. Is there more jangle fallacy than usefulness in strengths? Despite substantial overlap, I have devoted a section of this chapter to strengths because they do seem to be serving an important purpose. Strengths quickly became central to the practice of positive psychology; the language of the 24 strengths is already widespread in the field. There are valid criticisms that applications and use of the strengths questionnaires have outpaced empirical support – nearly five million people have taken the strengths questionnaire; nonetheless, the 24 strengths articulate individual differences that are widely valued and important to positive psychology.

There is a clear benefit in linking these strengths more directly to the big five – much has already been learned about those traits. Still, some strengths, like spirituality, probably fall outside or awkwardly between big five traits and facets. Naming key characteristics in a list draws attention to strengths that might otherwise remain neglected. Also, the strengths are framed as positive, valued characteristics. This recommends qualities for development and intervention, in contrast to the big five where value judgements are avoided. That said, there are still good questions about whether more of a strength is always better, as opposed to the notion of a more moderate 'golden mean' (Niemiec, 2013; B. Schwartz & Sharpe, 2006). In sum, it seems wise for positive psychologists to be fluent in the languages of both traits and strengths. Both models would benefit from clear translations between them.

TRY IT

Using Your Signature Strengths in New Ways

Encouraging people to build on their strengths is a hallmark of positive psychology practice. This exercise is one example of that. Begin by identifying one of your signature strengths. One way to do this is to take the questionnaire at www.viacharacter.org (again, no need to pay). Signature strengths are the ones people score highest on when they complete the questionnaire. If you prefer to skip the questionnaire, that is fine too. Simply examine the list in Table 4.3 and pick out one that describes you well, and that feels like it is an important part of you. Indeed, when people are asked to simply pick their top strengths from a list, they tend to correspond to the questionnaire scores (Peterson & Seligman, 2004). Even without taking the questionnaire, the VIA webpage might still be helpful in considering your candidate signature strengths; each is described in a bit more detail there.

Once you have identified a signature strength that you would like to work with, commit to using that strength in a new way. For example, you might decide to try something new each day for the next week. It is best to make your own personalized plan – think about your circumstances and how to best deploy your strength. You will be more effective in completing exercises like this if you make some concrete plans about when and how you will do the activities, and how you might overcome inevitable obstacles. For example, if your plan for Tuesday involves taking a walk in a garden to appreciate some beauty, what will you do if it is raining? Is there an alternative activity, or will you just plan to find your umbrella the night before?

SUMMING UP

Personality is very broad, including everything from features of our common humanity (e.g. basic needs and capacities) to the individual quirks that make each person unique. Nonetheless, much of personality psychology focuses on a middle level of difference, or how each individual is like some people and unlike others. Traits are the most common unit at this level, and are typically understood as fitting into a comprehensive, consensus model: the big five. The big five traits are broad in two important ways. First, each includes narrower traits, called facets, such as how openness includes imagination, intellect, artistic interest, and so on. Second, traits include a broad range of relevant psychological phenomena, including thoughts, feelings, behaviours, and desires. This breadth is both a strength and a weakness. The comprehensiveness is useful, but nuance is lost. The big five is like a world map; sometimes we want to zoom in closer.

Other middle-level units, such as needs, values, and attitudes, are defined more specifically. They may overlap (or correlate with) traits in the same domains, yet will have distinct elements. For example, people high in emotional stability tend to have high self-esteem; yet the particular self-view that is self-esteem is much more specific than the generally low levels of negative emotion that define trait emotional stability. We have avoided some deep and tricky questions about such overlap; in this example, is self-esteem part of emotional stability, or better understood as a consequence, or perhaps even partial cause of the trait? Personality psychology still lacks consensus on such issues, but they invite fascinating new research questions.

Positive psychology has created its own model of middle-level units: virtues and character strengths. Strengths are trait-like in being dimensional, relatively stable, and applicable across contexts; however, they are unique in being defined as valued characteristics. Similar individual differences are described by the big five model and the VIA classification of strengths; yet the VIA model uses terminology that is useful to communication and practice in positive psychology. Despite this key advantage, the VIA classification system is quite new (by research standards) with some important aspects still underdeveloped; it is best viewed as a 'work in progress'.

When we focus on personality and individual differences, there is a tendency to see behaviours and longer-term outcomes as the result of individuals' character. Personality is an important piece, to be sure; however, the personality focus can obscure other important contributors. For example, we saw in Chapter 3 how the society in which a person lives (stable and prosperous vs unequal and corrupt) can have a substantial impact on subjective well-being. This is true even while traits like extraversion and emotional stability – and many of the VIA strengths – also strongly predict well-being. Both are important. Personality is powerful, yet so are circumstances.

Moreover, personality is a much better predictor of behaviours when we look over the long term, averaging across many moments. Individual moments are harder to explain. There was a long and acrimonious debate in psychology about whether traits determined behaviours, or whether the momentary context (the situation) was more important (Kenrick & Funder, 1988). Framed as 'either–or', this is a silly question. It clearly takes both. Similar to the way genes need environments in which to develop, personalities need situations for their expression. As examined in the In Focus 'Part 2' box, momentary behaviours are quite variable. For example, even dispositionally agreeable people have moments of rudeness and aggression, and this suggests the importance of situational provocations. Yet it is equally clear that not everyone reacts to the same situation (e.g. the same insult) in the same way – personality is required in order to understand this other kind of variation. Recall the remarkable story of Debbie and Ian that began this chapter.

Personality is the stuff inside us, the traits, goals, and accumulated experience that we bring from situation to situation. It is useful to distinguish personality from situational features, or the stuff outside us. Yet both are essential features in producing behaviour. We unpack more details of situational environments (physical and interpersonal) in future chapters.

TEST YOURSELF

1. Give an example of a personality feature at each level; that is, where everyone is the same, where some people differ, and where everyone differs.

2. Name the big five traits. Can you also list one facet of each trait?

3. What are two reasons why it can be hard to decide whether you are an introvert or an extravert?

4. Describe three kinds of personality units that are not traits.

5. Describe two ways character strengths are like traits, and one way they are different.

6. Name the six virtues, and one related strength for each.

WEB LINKS

The Personality Project (a wealth of information about personality psychology): www. personality-project.org

Take a big five personality inventory (with feedback): www.personal.psu.edu/%7Ej5j/IPIP/

VIA Character Institute (questionnaires and resources on strengths and virtues): www. viacharacter.org

FURTHER READING

To learn more about how contemporary personality theory brings together the many parts, try:

McAdams, D. P., & Pals, J. L. (2006). A new big five: Fundamental principles for an integrative science of personality. *The American Psychologist, 61*(3), 204–217.

This classic review of personality development discusses stability, change, and likely causes:
Caspi, A., Roberts, B. W., & Shiner, R. L. (2005). Personality development: Stability and change. *Annual Review of Psychology, 56*(1), 453–484.

Get a broader perspective on virtues with this guide to them in major religions:

Dahlsgaard, K., Peterson, C., & Seligman, M. E. P. (2005). Shared virtue: The convergence of valued human strengths across culture and history. *Review of General Psychology, 9*(3), 203–213.

To learn more about how character strengths are being used in positive psychology practice, see:

Niemiec, R. M. (2013). VIA character strengths: Research and practice (the first 10 years). In H. H. Knoop & A. Delle Fave (eds), *Well-Being and Cultures: Perspectives from Positive Psychology* (Vol. 3, pp. 11–29). Cham: Springer. http://doi.org/10.1007/978-94-007-4611-4

REFERENCES

Allport, G., & Odbert, H. (1936). Trait-names: A psycho-lexical study. *Psychological Monographs, 47*, 1–171.

Ashton, M. C., Lee, K., Perugini, M., Szarota, P., de Vries, R. E., Di Blas, L., … De Raad, B. (2004). A six-factor structure of personality-descriptive adjectives: Solutions from psycholexical studies in seven languages. *Journal of Personality and Social Psychology, 86*(2), 356–366. http://doi.org/10.1037/0022-3514.86.2.356

Biswas-Diener, R. (2006). From the equator to the North Pole: A study of character strengths. *Journal of Happiness Studies, 7*(3), 293–310. http://doi.org/10.1007/s10902-005-3646-8

Bleidorn, W., & Denissen, J. J. A. (2015). Virtues in action – the new look of character traits. *British Journal of Psychology, 106*(4), 700–723. http://doi.org/10.1111/bjop.12117

Bouchard, T. J., & Loehlin, J. C. (2001). Genes , evolution , and personality. *Behavior Genetics, 31*(3), 243–274. http://doi.org/10.1007/s10519-014-9646-x

Caspi, A., Roberts, B. W., & Shiner, R. L. (2005). Personality development: Stability and change. *Annual Review of Psychology, 56*(1), 453–484. http://doi.org/10.1146/annurev.psych.55.090902.141913

Corr, P. J. (2004). Reinforcement sensitivity theory and personality. *Neuroscience and Biobehavioral Reviews, 28*(3), 317–332. http://doi.org/10.1016/j.neubiorev.2004.01.005

Credé, M., Tynan, M. C., & Harms, P. D. (2016). Much ado about grit: A meta-analytic synthesis of the grit literature. *Journal of Personality and Social Psychology*, 1–20. http://doi.org/10.1037/pspp0000102

De Neve, J. (2011). Functional polymorphism (5-HTTLPR) in the serotonin transporter gene is associated with subjective well-being: Evidence from a US nationally representative sample. *Journal of Human Genetics, 56*(6), 456–459. http://doi.org/10.1038/jhg.2011.39

Depue, R. A., & Collins, P. F. (1999). Neurobiology of the structure of personality: Dopamine, facilitation of incentive motivation, and extraversion. *Behavioral and Brain Sciences, 22*(3), 491–569. http://doi.org/10.1017/S0140525X99002046

DeYoung, C. G., Hirsh, J. B., Shane, M. S., Papademetris, X., Rajeevan, N., & Gray, J. R. (2010). Testing predictions from personality neuroscience: Brain structure and the big five. *Psychologcial Science, 21*(6), 820–828. http://doi.org/10.1177/0956797610370159

Diener, E., Suh, E., Lucas, R. E., & Smith, H. (1999). Subjective well-being: Three decades of progress. *Psychological Bulletin, 125*(2), 276–302.

Donnellan, M. B., Burt, S. A., Levendosky, A. A., & Klump, K. L. (2008). Genes, personality, and attachment in adults: A multivariate behavioral genetic analysis. *Personality & Social Psychology Bulletin, 34*(1), 3–16. http://doi.org/10.1177/0146167207309199

Duckworth, A. L., & Quinn, P. D. (2009). Development and validation of the short grit scale (Grit-S). *Journal of Personality Assessment, 91*(2), 166–174. http://doi.org/10.1080/00223890802634290

Eysenck, H. J., & Eysenck, M. J. (1985). *Personality and Individual Differences: A Natural Science Approach*. Cham: Springer.

Fleeson, W. (2004). Moving personality beyond the person–situation debate. *Current Directions in Psychological Science, 13*, 83–87.

Fleeson, W., & Gallagher, P. (2009). The implications of Big Five standing for the distribution of trait manifestation in behavior: Fifteen experience-sampling studies and a meta-analysis. *Journal of Personality and Social Psychology, 97*(6), 1097–1114. http://doi.org/10.1037/a0016786

Fleeson, W., & Law, M. K. (2015). Trait enactments as density distributions: The role of actors, situations, and observers in explaining stability and variability. *Journal of Personality and Social Psychology, 109*(6), 1090–1104. http://doi.org/10.1037/a0039517

Friese, M., Frankenbach, J., Job, V., & Loschelder, D. D. (2017). Does self-control training improve self-control? A meta-analysis. *Perspectives on Psychological Science, 12*(6), 1077–1099. http://doi.org/10.1177/1745691617697076

Gander, F., Proyer, R. T., Ruch, W., & Wyss, T. (2012). Strength-based positive interventions: Further evidence for their potential in enhancing well-being and alleviating depression. *Journal of Happiness Studies, 14*(4), 1241–1259. http://doi.org/10.1007/s10902-012-9380-0

Gardner, H., & Hatch, T. (1989). Multiple intelligences go to school: Educational implications of the theory of multiple intelligences. *Educational Leadership, 18*(8), 4–10. http://doi.org/10.2307/1176460

Goldberg, L. R. (1993). The structure of phenotypic personality traits. *The American Psychologist, 48*(1), 26–34. http://doi.org/10.1037/0003-066X.48.12.1302

Gosling, S. D. (2008). Personality in non-human animals. *Personality and Social Psychology Compass, 2*, 985–1001. http://doi.org/10.1111/j.1751-9004.2008.00087.x

Graham, J., Nosek, B. A., Haidt, J., Iyer, R., Koleva, S., & Ditto, P. H. (2011). Mapping the moral domain. *Journal of Personality and Social Psychology, 101*(2), 366–385. http://doi.org/10.1037/a0021847

Gray, J. A. (1987). Perspectives on anxiety and impulsivity: A commentary. *Journal of Research in Personality, 21*(4), 493–509. http://doi.org/10.1016/0092-6566(87)90036-5

Howe, L. C., & Krosnick, J. A. (2017). Attitude strength. *Annual Review of Psychology, 68*(1), 327–351. http://doi.org/10.1146/annurev-psych-122414-033600

Hudson, N. W., & Fraley, R. C. (2016). Changing for the better? Longitudinal associations between volitional personality change and psychological well-being. *Personality & Social Psychology Bulletin, 42*(5), 603–615. http://doi.org/10.1177/0146167216637840

John, O. P., Naumann, L. P., & Soto, C. J. (2008). Paradigm shift to the integrative Big Five Trait taxonomy. In O. P. John, R. W. Robins, & L. A. Pervin (eds), *Handbook of Personality: Theory and Research* (pp. 114–158). New York: Guilford Press. http://doi.org/10.1016/S0191-8869(97)81000-8

Johnson, J. A. (2014). Measuring thirty facets of the Five Factor Model with a 120-item public domain inventory: Development of the IPIP-NEO-120. *Journal of Research in Personality, 51*, 78–89. http://doi.org/10.1016/j.jrp.2014.05.003

Kenrick, D. T., & Funder, D. C. (1988). Profiting from controversy: Lessons from the person–situation debate. *American Psychologist, 43*, 23–34.

Kern, M. L., & Friedman, H. S. (2008). Do conscientious individuals live longer? A quantitative review. *Health Psychology, 27*(5), 505–512. http://doi.org/10.1037/0278-6133.27.5.505

Kluckhohn, C., & Murray, H. A. (1948). *Personality in Nature, Society, and Culture*. New York: Knopf.

Koenig, L. B., McGue, M., Krueger, R. F., & Bouchard, T. J. (2005). Genetic and environmental influences on religiousness: Findings for retrospective and current religiousness ratings. *Journal of Personality*, *73*(2), 471–488. http://doi.org/10.1111/j.1467-6494.2005.00316.x

Lambert, N. M., Clark, M. S., Durtschi, J., Fincham, F. D., & Graham, S. M. (2010). Benefits of expressing gratitude: Expressing gratitude to a partner changes one's view of the relationship. *Psychological Science*, *21*(4), 574–80. http://doi.org/10.1177/0956797610364003

Linley, A. P., Maltby, J., Wood, A. M., Joseph, S., Harrington, S., Peterson, C., … Seligman, M. E. P. (2007). Character strengths in the United Kingdom: The VIA Inventory of Strengths. *Personality and Individual Differences*, *43*(2), 341–351. http://doi.org/10.1016/j.paid.2006.12.004

Little, B. R. (2015). The integrative challenge in personality science: Personal projects as units of analysis. *Journal of Research in Personality*, *56*, 93–101. http://doi.org/10.1016/j.jrp.2014.10.008

Lucas, R. E., & Diener, E. (2001). Understanding extraverts' enjoyment of social situations: The importance of pleasantness. *Journal of Personality and Social Psychology*, *81*(2), 343–356. http://doi.org/10.1037/0022-3514.81.2.343

Markus, H. R., & Wurf, E. (1987). The dynamic self-concept: A social psychological perspective. *Annual Review of Psychology*, *38*(1), 299–337. http://doi.org/10.1146/annurev.ps.38.020187.001503

McAdams, D. P., & Guo, J. (2015). Narrating the generative life. *Psychological Science*, *26*(4), 275–483. http://doi.org/10.1177/0956797614568318

McAdams, D. P., & Pals, J. L. (2006). A new big five: Fundamental principles for an integrative science of personality. *The American Psychologist*, *61*(3), 204–217. http://doi.org/10.1037/0003-066X.61.3.204

McClelland, D. (1965). N achievement and entrepreneurship: A longitudinal study. *Journal of Personality and Social Psychology*, *1*, 389–392.

McCrae, R. R., & Costa, P. T. (1997). Personality trait structure as a human universal. *The American Psychologist*, *52*(5), 509–516. http://doi.org/10.1037/0003-066X.52.5.509

McCrae, R. R., & Costa, P. T. (1999). A five-factor theory of personality. In L. A. Pervin & O. P. John (eds), *Handbook of Personality: Theory and Research* (2nd edn.) (pp. 139–153). New York: Guilford Press.

McGrath, R. E. (2014). Scale- and item-level factor analyses of the VIA inventory of strengths. *Assessment*, *21*(1), 4–14. http://doi.org/10.1177/1073191112450612

McGrath, R. E. (2015). Integrating psychological and cultural perspectives on virtue: The hierarchical structure of character strengths. *The Journal of Positive Psychology*, *10*, 407–424. http://doi.org/10.1080/17439760.2014.994222

McGrath, R. E., & Walker, D. I. (2016). Factor structure of character strengths in youth: Consistency across ages and measures. *Journal of Moral Education, 45*, 400–418. http://doi.org/10.1080/03057240.2016.1213709

McGregor, I., & Little, B. R. (1998). Personal projects, happiness, and meaning: On doing well and being yourself. *Journal of Personality and Social Psychology, 74*(2), 494–512. http://doi.org/10.1037/0022-3514.74.2.494

Mikulincer, M., & Shaver, P. R. (2007). Boosting attachment security to promote mental health, prosocial values, and inter-group tolerance. *Psychological Inquiry, 18*(3), 139–156. http://doi.org/10.1080/10478400701512646

Mischel, W., & Shoda, Y. (1995). A cognitive-affective system theory of personality: Reconceptualizing situations, dispositions, dynamics, and invariance in personality structure. *Psychological Review, 102*(2), 246–68. http://doi.org/10.1037/0033-295X.102.2.246

Mongrain, M., & Anselmo-Matthews, T. (2012). Do positive psychology exercises work? A replication of Seligman et al. *Journal of Clinical Psychology, 68*(4), 382–389. http://doi.org/10.1002/jclp.21839

Nasby, W., & Read, N. W. (1997). The life voyage of a solo circumnavigator: Integrating theoretical and methodological perspectives. *Journal of Personality, 65*(4), 787–1068. http://doi.org/10.1111/j.1467-6494.1997.tb00534.x

Nettle, D. (2006). The evolution of personality variation in humans and other animals. *American Psychologist, 61*(6), 622–631. http://doi.org/10.1037/0003-066X.61.6.622

Niemiec, R. M. (2013). VIA character strengths: Research and practice (the first 10 years). In H. H. Knoop & A. Delle Fave (eds), *Well-Being and Cultures: Perspectives from Positive Psychology* (Vol. 3, pp. 11–29). Cham: Springer. http://doi.org/10.1007/978-94-007-4611-4

Noftle, E. E., Schnitker, S. A., & Robins, R. W. (2011). Character and personality: Connections between positive psychology and personality psychology. In K. M. Sheldon, T. B. Kashdan, & M. F. Steger (eds), *Designing Positive Psychology* (pp. 207–227). New York: Oxford University Press.

Ozer, D. J., & Benet-Martínez, V. (2006). Personality and the prediction of consequential outcomes. *Annual Review of Psychology, 57*, 401–421. http://doi.org/10.1146/annurev.psych.57.102904.190127

Park, N., Peterson, C., & Seligman, M. E. P. (2006). Character strengths in fifty-four nations and the fifty US states. *The Journal of Positive Psychology, 1*(3), 118–129. http://doi.org/10.1080/17439760600619567

Peterson, C. (1991). The meaning and measurement of explanatory style. *Psychological Inquiry, 2*, 1–10. http://doi.org/10.1007/s00425-001

Peterson, C., & Seligman, M. E. P. (2003). Character strengths before and after September 11. *Psychological Science, 14*(4), 381–384. http://doi.org/10.1111/1467-9280.24482

Peterson, C., & Seligman, M. E. P. (2004). *Character Strengths and Virtues: A Handbook and Classification.* New York: Oxford University Press and Washington, DC: American Psychological Association.

Polderman, T. J. C., Benyamin, B., de Leeuw, C. A., Sullivan, P. F., van Bochoven, A., Visscher, P. M., & Posthuma, D. (2015). Meta-analysis of the heritability of human traits based on fifty years of twin studies. *Nature Genetics*, *47*(7), 702–709 http://doi.org/10.1038/ng.3285

Prediger, D. J. (1982). Dimensions underlying Holland's hexagon: Missing link between interests and occupations? *Journal of Vocational Behavior*, *21*(3), 259–287. http://doi.org/10.1016/0001-8791(82)90036-7

Proyer, R. T., Gander, F., Wellenzohn, S., & Ruch, W. (2015). Strengths-based positive psychology interventions: A randomized placebo-controlled online trial on long-term effects for a signature strengths- vs. a lesser strengths-intervention. *Frontiers in Psychology*, *6*, 1–14. http://doi.org/10.3389/fpsyg.2015.00456

Quinlan, D., Swain, N., & Vella-Brodrick, D. A. (2012). Character strengths interventions: Building on what we know for improved outcomes. *Journal of Happiness Studies*, *13*(6), 1145–1163. http://doi.org/10.1007/s10902-011-9311-5

Reilley, S. P., Geers, A. L., Lindsay, D. L., Deronde, L., & Dember, W. N. (2005). Convergence and predictive validity in measures of optimism and pessimism: Sequential studies. *Current Psychology*, *24*(1), 43–59. http://doi.org/10.1007/s12144-005-1003-z

Rimfeld, K., Kovas, Y., Dale, P. S., & Plomin, R. (2016). True grit and genetics: Predicting academic achievement from personality. *Journal of Personality and Social Psychology*, *111*(5), 780–789. http://doi.org/10.1037/pspp0000089

Roberts, B. W. (2009). Back to the future: Personality and assessment and personality development. *Journal of Research in Personality*, *43*(2), 137–145. http://doi.org/10.1016/j.jrp.2008.12.015

Roberts, B. W., & DelVecchio, W. F. (2000). The rank-order consistency of personality traits from childhood to old age: A quantitative review of longitudinal studies. *Psychological Bulletin*, *126*(1), 3–25. http://doi.org/10.1037/0033-2909.126.1.3

Roberts, B. W., Kuncel, N. R., Shiner, R., Caspi, A., & Goldberg, L. R. (2007). The power of personality. *Perspectives on Psychological Science*, *2*(4), 313–345. http://doi.org/10.1111/j.1745-6916.2007.00047.x

Roberts, B. W., Luo, J., Briley, D. A., Chow, P. I., Su, R., & Hill, P. L. (2017). A systematic review of personality trait change through intervention. *Psychological Bulletin*, *142*(12), 117–141. http://doi.org/10.1037/bul0000088

Roberts, B. W., & Robins, R. W. (2000). Broad dispositions, broad aspirations: The intersection of personality traits and major life goals. *Personality and Social Psychology Bulletin*, *26*(10), 1284–1296. http://doi.org/10.1177/0146167200262009

Roberts, B. W., Walton, K. E., & Viechtbauer, W. (2006). Patterns of mean-level change in personality traits across the life course: A meta-analysis of longitudinal studies. *Psychological Bulletin*, *132*(1), 1–25. http://doi.org/10.1037/0033-2909.132.1.1

Rusting, C. L. (1999). Interactive effects of personality and mood on emotion-congruent memory and judgment. *Journal of Personality and Social Psychology*, 77(5), 1073–1086. http://doi.org/10.1037/0022-3514.77.5.1073

Ryan, R., & Deci, E. (2000). Self-determination theory and the facilitation of intrinsic motivation. *American Psychologist*, 55(1), 68–78. http://doi.org/10.1037/0003-066X.55.1.68

Saucier, G. (2009). What are the most important dimensions of personality? Evidence from studies of descriptors in diverse languages. *Social and Personality Psychology Compass*, 3(4), 620–637. http://doi.org/10.1111/j.1751-9004.2009.00188.x

Scheier, M. F., Carver, C. S., & Bridges, M. W. (1994). Distinguishing optimism from neuroticism (and trait anxiety, self-mastery, and self-esteem) – a reevaluation of the life orientation test. *Journal of Personality and Social Psychology*, 67(6), 1063–1078.

Schwartz, B., & Sharpe, K. E. (2006). Practical wisdom: Aristotle meets positive psychology. *Journal of Happiness Studies*, 7(3), 377–395. http://doi.org/10.1007/s10902-005-3651-y

Schwartz, S. H., & Bardi, A. (2001). Value hierarchies across cultures: Taking a similarities perspective. *Journal of Cross-Cultural Psychology*, 32(3), 268–290. http://doi.org/10.1177/0022022101032003002

Seligman, M. E. P., Steen, T. A., Park, N., & Peterson, C. (2005). Positive psychology progress: Empirical validation of interventions. *American Psychologist*, 60(5), 410–421. http://doi.org/10.1037/0003-066X.60.5.410

Sheldon, K. M., & Schüler, J. (2011). Wanting, having, and needing: Integrating motive disposition theory and self-determination theory. *Journal of Personality and Social Psychology*, 101(5), 1106–1123. http://doi.org/10.1037/a0024952

Soto, C. J. (2019). How replicable are links between personality traits and consequential life outcomes? The life outcomes of personality replication project. *Psychological Science*, 30(5), 711–727. https://doi.org/10.1177/0956797619831612

Steger, M. F., Hicks, B. M., Kashdan, T. B., Krueger, R. F., & Bouchard, T. J. (2007). Genetic and environmental influences on the positive traits of the values in action classification, and biometric covariance with normal personality. *Journal of Research in Personality*, 41(3), 524–539. http://doi.org/10.1016/j.jrp.2006.06.002

Tucker-Drob, E. M., Briley, D. A., Engelhardt, L. E., Mann, F. D., & Harden, K. P. (2016). Genetically-mediated associations between measures of childhood character and academic achievement. *Journal of Personality and Social Psychology*, 111(5), 790–815. http://doi.org/10.1037/pspp0000098

Turkheimer, E. (2000). Three laws of behavior genetics and what they mean. *Current Directions in Psychological Science*, 9(5), 160–164. http://doi.org/10.1111/1467-8721.00084

Tweed, R. G., Biswas-Diener, R., & Lehman, D. R. (2012). Self-perceived strengths among people who are homeless. *The Journal of Positive Psychology*, 7(6), 481–492. http://doi.org/10.1080/17439760.2012.719923

Vazire, S., & Carlson, E. N. (2010). Self-knowledge of personality: Do people know themselves? *Social and Personality Psychology Compass, 4*(8), 605–620. http://doi.org/10.1111/j.1751-9004.2010.00280.x

Widiger, T. A. (2005). Five factor model of personality disorder: Integrating science and practice. *Journal of Research in Personality, 39*, 67–83. http://doi.org/10.1016/j.jrp.2004.09.010

Zelenski, J. M. (2007). The role of personality in emotion, judgment, and decision making. In K. D. Vohs, R. F. Baumeister, & G. Loewenstein (eds), *Do Emotions Help or Hurt Decision Making? A Hedgefoxian Perspective* (pp. 117–132). New York: Russell Sage Foundation Press.

Zillig, L. M. P., Hemenover, S. H., & Dienstbier, R. A. (2002). What do we assess when we assess a big 5 trait? A content analysis of the affective, behavioral, and cognitive processes represented in big 5 personality inventories. *Personality and Social Psychology Bulletin, 28*(6), 847–858. http://doi.org/10.1177/0146167202289013

5

The Self

INTRODUCTION

Imagine you are in an experiment with some simple tasks: sit quietly and spontaneously move your finger when you feel like it. Also, watch a clock on the wall. After you have moved your finger, report the clock's exact position when you first had the idea to move. This is repeated a few dozen times (Libet, 1985). Although this experiment is pretty boring as a participant, the results have created a lot of excitement. There is one other important detail: during the task, electrodes measure tiny electrical signals in the brain and muscles. These recordings show that brain activity precedes the muscle movement; this is not too surprising. However, a signal in the brain was also observed about a half second before subjects reported being aware of their intention to move their fingers. In other words, the results suggest that a part of our brains – distinct from our conscious selves – decides when to move.

With decades of neuroscience research, it is not controversial to suggest that our thoughts and conscious experience are related to brain functioning. Yet it is still a bit disconcerting to consider that our intentions – our will – follow from the neurons as if our conscious 'choices' are nothing more than reports on what the deep brain has already decided to do (Wegener & Wheatley, 1999). Other psychology findings challenge the notion that we are fully in conscious control of our actions, for example by showing that various subtle, even unconscious, experimental manipulations can alter those choices (e.g. see Krueger & Funder, 2004). Is human experience simply the result of mechanistic inputs and outputs with no room for wilful, conscious intervention?

On the other hand, the fact that people can sometimes be fooled about the causes of their choices does not mean they are complete fools. It is an error to conclude that non-conscious causes in some circumstances mean that there are non-conscious causes in all circumstances. Also, if conscious choice is an illusion, why do people want it so much? As one defender of free will put it:

> It is not as if people would be fine with slavery or prison if only the food were better. Countless people have risked and sacrificed their lives in fighting to achieve and defend freedom, and it is very difficult to find historical instances of uprisings or wars based on a demand for less freedom. (Baumeister, 2008, p. 15)

People do not seem content to let their lives play out, come what may.

The debates around free will and consciousness have kept philosophers in business for centuries; I will not deprive them of their livelihood by resolving things here. These are tricky issues that often hinge on what one means by 'free will' and 'self'. For example, how much of the unconscious self represents who 'you' are? What if it is in conflict with who you think you are? In this chapter, we will mostly sidestep these thorny questions by focusing on one understanding of the self: the self-concept.

DEFINING THE SELF

In grasping the scope of the self, it is useful to make an initial division and clarification in what we mean by 'self', a distinction that goes back to a founding father of psychology, William James (1890). First, the self is a person's consciousness, the self-aware knower, decider, and actor – the 'you' who is directing and aware of thoughts, feelings, and behaviours. James labelled this aspect of self as the 'I'. We have the notion that this self is largely about conscious experience, but may include actions, ideas, or feelings that are not entirely deliberate, such as when you quickly balance yourself after tripping – you still think, 'I did that'. When you turn the page in this book, it is this self, the 'I', an actor who is effecting change in the environment. When you push yourself to continue reading to the end of the section, even though you really need to pee, you are exerting self-control, another thing the self does as an actor. This aspect of self is most wrapped up in issues around free will; it is also very difficult to study. In fact, James merely noted the existence and trickiness of the 'I', and then quickly moved on.

The second way to understand the self takes it as an object to be known; James referred to this as the 'Me'. The term self-concept is used to describe this notion of self (though the shorthand of plain 'self' is also common). The **self-concept** is subjective; it is the mental representations – knowledge, beliefs, evaluations, etc. – about who you are. One assessment tool for the self-concept gives people a sheet of paper with the question "Who are you?" at the top followed by 20 blank lines (Kuhn & McPartland, 1954). In this instance, the 'I' will consider the contents of the 'Me' to answer the question. People write things like "a musical genius", "a giving lover", "too fat", "adventurous", or "an old man". These are all beliefs people have about themselves.

The self-concept includes ideas about many aspects of personality (e.g. traits, motivations, strengths), physical appearance, roles, accomplishments, and so on, but all from a subjective perspective. It is not objective reality per se, but a person's understanding of reality. My self-concept is 'Me'; how I see myself. In this way, we can talk about the 'contents' of the self, or what a person's self-concept includes. Said another way, the self-concept is a theory about the self (Epstein, 1973). For example, self-efficacy – the belief that you can take effective actions – is one feature of the self-concept of particular interest to positive psychology. Similarly, subjective well-being is defined as personal judgements about one's satisfaction and emotional experience; it is subjective and about the self, thus another aspect of the self-concept. A personal sense of meaning and purpose are also parts of the self-concept.

The self-concept includes many things that positive psychology would like to encourage. However, a question remains about whether it is better to focus on changing the self-concept directly, or to change the reality it represents. As we will discuss, this is particularly evident in the ongoing debate around the wisdom of trying to boost self-esteem.

Although we make a distinction between the 'I' and the 'Me', the two aspects of self clearly interact. For example, when people have high self-efficacy for a task (they believe they can do it), they are more likely to actually pursue it and succeed (Bandura, 1977). In this way, the self-concept (e.g. sense of self-efficacy) is important to behaviours and accomplishing goals. As another example, people who see themselves as more closely connected to nature are more likely to engage in environmentally sustainable behaviours (Nisbet, Zelenski, & Murphy, 2009). In both cases, people's views about themselves seem to push the 'I' to act.

The self-concept also guides people's thoughts and shapes the way they process information. In cognitive psychology, the **self-reference effect** is a robust and well-studied phenomenon; it refers to people's ability to remember things better when they are associated with the self-concept (Symons & Johnson, 1997). Interestingly, the information does not even need to be true of the self; simply considering things in relation to the self improves memory. For example, in lab experiments, people are presented with a series of trait adjectives accompanied by the question "Does this word describe you?" and other kinds of questions, such as "Does this word have more than six letters?". In a surprise memory test that follows, the words accompanied by the self-related question are remembered much better than all others. If the terms are actually self-descriptive, memory improves only slightly more – simply asking the question matters more than the answer (Howell & Zelenski, 2017).

Beyond clever lab studies, people's tendency to think more deeply about self-relevant information can be harnessed to improve learning, such as the memory tested on university exams (Dunlosky, Rawson, Marsh, Nathan, & Willingham, 2013). Do you believe it? (See what I did there?) By relating textbook information to experiences you have had, to people you know, or even asking yourself 'Do I agree with that?', the information is retained better. We are all good at thinking about ourselves. When people encounter new information, linking it to the self-concept gives them more opportunity to recall it later. Do you think you should give this technique a try? Are all these questions starting to annoy you? Do you think they will help you remember the self-reference effect?

The self-concept is also important to how people operate in day-to-day life (Markus & Wurf, 1987). Although we have the experience of a unitary self – I am one individual – our self-concepts have different parts. For example, a man might have a somewhat different sense of self as a father, compared to in his work-role as a farmer or as vice-president of the local historical society. Moreover, the immediate context will make some aspects of the self-concept more salient, and thus more likely to guide thoughts and behaviour. For example, seeing a baby might activate notions of a more maternal self. Being in a crowd of very well-dressed people might provoke self-doubts about status and frustrated ambitions. Gazing at a night sky full of stars might provoke thoughts that the self is small in an enormous universe and prompt a quest for deeper meaning. In essence, the self-concept can guide behaviour from the inside out; yet the immediate context also activates different aspects of that internal self-concept. Taking a longer view, day-to-day experiences and feedback can also change the self-concept over time, similar to personality development more generally (Thagard & Wood, 2015).

THE TRUE SELF AND AUTHENTICITY

People do not like hypocrites, and pointing out a rival's inconsistencies is persuasive in arguments. Similarly, we do not like it when other people believe things about us that seem untrue – even when others' views are positive. Underlying this aversion is the notion that each of us has a true self, and that we should behave and speak in ways that express that true self authentically. Nonetheless, we all do things that we would not fully endorse from time to time. When misbehaving, some mental gymnastics often allow us to create psychological distance. For example, you might think that it was not my 'true self' who was laughing at a racist joke, picking my nose, or ignoring those cries for help on a busy street, right? Also, with many possible selves, how do we know which one is 'true'?

The idea that we should get to know and act consistently with our true selves – to be **authentic** – has a long history in Western thought, going back to the Ancient Greeks (Harter, 2002). Before positive psychology, the humanists (e.g. Rogers, Maslow) valued self-actualization, and described how problems can develop when people are pressured into doing things that do not match their self-concepts. The founders of positive psychology represented this idea in the character strength of honesty (also called authenticity or integrity). Authenticity is also a core feature of eudaimonia (i.e. forms of well-being that go beyond merely feeling good) as described and studied by contemporary psychologists (Huta & Waterman, 2014). Research suggests that many forms of well-being (e.g. positive emotions or meaning) are associated with self-concepts and behaviours that are perceived as authentic (Kernis & Goldman, 2006;

Lenton, Slabu, & Sedikides, 2016). Nonetheless, knowing the true self is tricky, and perhaps even impossible from a fully objective perspective.

Most lay people take an **essentialist view** of the true self, the idea that each person contains an immutable essence, a set of necessary defining features, or a singular true self (Schlegel & Hicks, 2011; Strohminger, Knobe, & Newman, 2017). Despite the importance of this essence, it is seen as hidden, something that takes effort to discover and understand (Schlegel, Vess, & Arndt, 2012). The essence is usually seen as unchanging. Even as the self-concept develops, we might understand it as following a pre-determined path towards our true potential. We see the essence as inside us, distinct from and resistant to external influences. It is probably something we are born with. We believe that behaviours can sometimes be inconsistent with the true self, perhaps due to external pressures and compromises. Yet our feelings about those behaviours seem diagnostic of the true self. For example, if we feel bad about doing something, perhaps it was not an expression of our true self. Indeed, the true self is typically seen as moral and good.

It may be impossible to objectively or completely pin down a person's true self. Moreover, essentialist intuitions about the true self are challenged by research and observation. For example, we see contradictions and changes in the self-concept across time; sometimes self-views disagree with what others see; and clever experiments can trick people into believing things about themselves that are demonstrably untrue (Vazire & Carlson, 2010). A true essence may still exist, but knowing it seems prone to error then.

Regardless, psychologists can study people's perceptions of the true self, such as the other characteristics of people who see themselves as authentic, and the conditions that seem to foster feelings of authenticity. As we will see, findings in this area are intriguing and do not always match intuitions. Even if it is hard to know the true self with certainty, should we still try to be true to ourselves?

Where Do We Find Authentic Behaviour?

Self-determination theory provides a bridge from humanistic ideas about healthy self-concepts to contemporary research in positive psychology. They share an assumption that humans are prone to positive growth, unless hampered by poor circumstances. The 'self-determination' refers to people's sense that they are doing things that the self fully endorses – things that are authentic. As noted in Chapter 4, this often involves doing things that meet basic needs for autonomy, competence, and relatedness. The notion of autonomy as a basic need suggests that people thrive when they have a sense of control. Going further, the theory's main focus is on the reasons why people do things (Deci & Ryan, 2000). It contrasts **intrinsic motivation** – where things are done for enjoyment and where the desire is for fully internal reasons – with **extrinsic motivation**, where there is some external pressure. Extrinsic motivation is always less self-determined than intrinsic motivation, but it covers a wide range, from modest to extreme external influences. For example, voluntarily doing something to help a loved one is less extrinsic (i.e. somewhat internalized even if guilt also plays a role), compared to working at a horrible job for the pay cheque (i.e. motivated purely by the external reward of money).

Extrinsic incentives can motivate people, but they do not help with the expression of the true self. As such, they produce motivation only as long as the external incentive is in place. No one continues working at a horrible job if the payment stops. In contrast, intrinsically motivated behaviours do not depend on outcomes. If Bernice intrinsically loves to paint landscapes, she will continue to do it whether or not she can sell her paintings. In addition, external incentives are often more ephemeral than intrinsic motivations. When the external incentives are less salient, their influence fades. Research suggests that when people pursue personal goals (e.g. to cook with fresh vegetables, or learn to play guitar) for more intrinsically motivated reasons, they are also more likely to accomplish those goals (Sheldon, 2014; Sheldon & Elliot, 1999). Moreover, accomplishing intrinsic goals produces more positive emotions and satisfaction, compared to accomplishing extrinsic goals.

According to self-determination theory, and consistent with these findings on goals, intrinsic motivation promotes psychological health (positive experience) and personal growth (including accomplishing those important goals; Deci & Ryan, 2000). The theory also provides one way of understanding which behaviours and goals are expressions of the true self. That is, authentic behaviours are those that people experience as intrinsically motivated, the things that people do for personal enjoyment, rather than because of external pressures. These also tend to be things that meet the three basic needs for autonomy, relatedness, and competence (Ryan & Deci, 2000).

Measuring Authenticity

Similar ideas have been incorporated into questionnaire measures of authenticity that go beyond needs, motivation, and goals. **Dispositional authenticity** questionnaires assess characteristics that reflect or seem conducive to authentic experiences (Kernis & Goldman, 2006; A. M. Wood, Linley, Maltby, Baliousis, & Joseph, 2008). They assess the degree to which people think they generally behave in authentic ways. For example, some items ask about whether people feel like they know their true selves. Others ask about how much they feel influenced by other people, or about how often they put on a 'false face' in social situations (see Try It box).

TRY IT

The Authenticity Scale

Here are the items that make up a dispositional authenticity questionnaire (A. M. Wood et al., 2008). They are mainly provided for you to better understand how dispositional

(Continued)

authenticity is assessed. As a research instrument, there are no clear guidelines on how to interpret individual scores. That said, you can try completing the questionnaire by rating the items on a 1 (does not describe me at all) to 7 (describes me very well) scale. Reverse-scored items mean that people with high authenticity give low ratings to these items (i.e. reverse of the others).

1. I think it is better to be yourself than to be popular.

2. I don't know how I really feel inside (reverse scored).

3. I am strongly influenced by the opinions of others (reverse scored).

4. I usually do what other people tell me to do (reverse scored).

5. I always feel I need to do what others expect me to do (reverse scored).

6. Other people influence me greatly (reverse scored).

7. I feel as if I don't know myself very well (reverse scored).

8. I always stand by what I believe in.

9. I am true to myself in most situations.

10. I feel out of touch with the real me (reverse scored).

11. I live in accordance with my values and beliefs.

12. I feel alienated from myself (reverse scored).

Fully knowing the true self seems like it should include both desirable and undesirable aspects of one's self (assuming the true self is not perfect). Nonetheless, measures of dispositional authenticity mostly correlate with other desirable characteristics, such as self-esteem, purpose in life, positive affect, and life satisfaction (Kernis & Goldman, 2006; A. M. Wood et al., 2008). Of course, there are good theoretical reasons to think that self-awareness and authentic living do actually promote well-being (or conversely, that happy people could perceive their great lives accurately). On the other hand, perhaps people who are prone to overly positive self-views are simply lumping authenticity in with their collection of amazing self-reported qualities. After all, would people with poor self-knowledge actually know that they are biased?

Researchers have turned to momentary experiences – or state authenticity – to help tease apart these possibilities. **State authenticity** is the perception or feeling that one is currently behaving in accordance with the true self; it varies from moment to moment. Experience sampling studies – where people rate things like momentary moods, state authenticity, self-esteem, and satisfaction of needs for competence, autonomy, and relatedness – find positive correlations among these things, similar to disposition-level studies (Heppner , Kernis, Nezlek, Foster, Lakey, & Goldman, 2008; Lenton et al., 2016). That is, people report feeling authentic when they feel good, confident, and when meeting important needs. Moments of inauthenticity seem to co-occur with unpleasant emotions, especially when being judged by others or facing difficult situations (Lenton, Bruder, Slabu, & Sedikides, 2012).

Some differences emerge between state and dispositional authenticity too. In contrast to the dispositional questionnaires that score influence from others as hindering authenticity, authentic moments are positively correlated with accepting influence from others (Lenton et al., 2016). This apparent contradiction might be resolved by understanding the influence as a matter of degree. Taking some helpful advice now and then may facilitate personally important goals, and thus feel authentic. On the other hand, feeling like other people have a strong influence on how you live your life overall may be too much. Even studies of state authenticity find that feeling a lack of control or low in social power is associated with inauthenticity (Heppner et al., 2008; Kraus, Chen, & Keltner, 2011); yet control and power can be distinguished from accepting some (helpful) influence from others.

The experience sampling method has produced other findings that might contrast with your intuitions about feelings of authenticity. Consider Dawn, who is dispositionally quite introverted. Do you think that she feels more authentic when she behaves in more introverted ways, or in more extraverted ways? When students were asked this question, they believed that feelings of state authenticity would be higher when behaving in ways that are consistent with their big five traits (Fleeson & Wilt, 2010); that is, when Dawn is acting more introverted in this example. However, results of experience sampling studies – where trait-relevant behaviours and authenticity were rated together in the moment – showed that people's dispositional traits were not important to state authenticity. Rather, people felt more authentic when they behaved in extraverted, stable, open, agreeable, and conscientious ways, regardless of their dispositions. Said another way, for introverted, disagreeable, etc. people, behaving contrary to their traits seemed to feel more authentic! The results tell us that Dawn the introvert is likely to feel more authentic when she behaves in more extraverted ways. (Recall from Chapter 4 that most people engage in a wide range of momentary behaviours, even while traits describe average tendencies well.) Roni the extravert also feels authentic when behaving in extraverted ways – it seems there is something about extraverted (and open, agreeable, etc.) behaviour that promotes authenticity, regardless of one's trait level (Fleeson & Wilt, 2010).

In another study, the big five traits were compared across different roles (Sheldon, Ryan, Rawsthorne, & Ilardi, 1997). That is, people rated their extraversion, agreeableness, etc. separately for contexts where they were students, employees, family members, and so on. Similar to the experience sampling studies, results indicated that self-reports of authenticity were not associated with having more consistency in trait ratings (i.e. similar trait levels across roles). However, in both studies, reporting more authenticity was associated with positive emotions.

If our big five dispositions are part of the true self, these findings are puzzling. On the other hand, people's traits may be less important to them – not key parts of the self-concept – compared to other self-relevant and valued goals (Little, 2015). When you think about the things that are most important about yourself, are those things your big five traits? If not, perhaps fulfilling other important aspects of the self-concept require some flexibility in trait-related behaviours. For example, a person who is deeply committed to stand-up comedy will probably have more success with an extraverted approach. On average, open, agreeable, conscientious, stable, and extraverted behaviours seem more conducive to accomplishing valued goals (though with some variation, depending on the goal and situation). Moreover, people are more likely to see their ideal selves as having more, rather than less, of these traits (Whelan & Zelenski, 2012). Behaviours that take us closer to a personal ideal, as opposed to reflecting typical habits or dispositions, may better represent the true selves we imagine (Strohminger et al., 2017).

In this light, the state authenticity results make more sense. Authenticity seems to follow from expresssions of personally valued, rather than all, aspects of the self. There may still be value in accurately knowing about undesirable aspects of our selves, but their mere expression is less likely to produce momentary feelings of authenticity.

Going beyond correlational methods, experiments have more convincingly suggested that state authenticity can be caused by behaving in ways that express important values. In one experiment, participants were randomly assigned to argue either for or against the idea that it is good and right to help family and friends – in other words, to express support (or not) for the value of benevolence (Smallenbroek, Zelenski, & Whelan, 2017). Recall from Chapter 4 that values are defined by the fact that virtually all people see them as good, even though people still differ in which values they rank as more important than others. Participants who argued for benevolence felt substantially more state authenticity, compared to those who argued against. Their moods also improved somewhat. Moreover, the difference in state authenticity was even larger for people who prioritized benevolence over other values (such as achievement, power, or security). These results support the notion that behaving in ways that are consistent with one's self- concept can produce authenticity. In this way, values seem to differ from traits when it comes to momentary behaviours and authenticity. Behaving contrary to values reduces authenticity, whereas behaving contrary to traits can sometimes promote authentic feelings.

Across all the studies mentioned so far, state authenticity seems to co-occur with positive emotions. Other studies have even found that experimentally inducing positive moods with non-self-relevant manipulations (e.g. with videos or music) can increase feelings of state authenticity – people seem to infer authenticity when they are feeling good (Lenton, Slabu, Sedikides, & Power, 2013). Yet if authenticity is about representing valued aspects of the true self, it should be possible to feel authentic and unpleasant at the same time. The idea is very similar to the distinction between hedonic definitions of well-being and eudaimonic definitions of well-being more generally; one is about feeling good and the other is about virtuous actions.

Value-congruent behaviour can occur even in unpleasant circumstances. For example, standing up for a core belief even when others disagree, or resisting a potentially pleasant but immoral temptation, are expressions of the true self that occur along with some unpleasantness. People are able to recall such situations, that is, times when they behaved in ways that express values even though the circumstances were unpleasant. Moreover, people report experiencing more state authenticity in these value-consistent moments, compared to when they behaved in ways that contradicted values, even if those circumstances were more pleasant (Smallenbroek et al., 2017). In sum, although state authenticity often co-occurs with pleasant moods, it remains even more tightly linked to behaviour that expresses valued aspects of the true self.

SELF-VIEWS: -EFFICACY, -ESTEEM, AND -COMPASSION

Many aspects of the self-concept are idiosyncratic. We each have a unique set of beliefs about who we are and our abilities, interests, quirks, and so on. This uniqueness is important, but difficult to study, especially with quantitative methods. There are also aspects of the self-concept that are relevant across people, or where individuals can be rank-ordered in terms of differences along a common dimension. The notion of dispositional authenticity is an example of this: we treat it as an individual difference; we compare people with higher and lower scores on this aspect of the self-concept. In this section, we consider three more dimensions of self-views that are important in positive psychology: self-efficacy, self-esteem, and self-compassion. These are all aspects of the 'Me', the self-concept; yet they have important implications for what the 'I' does in day-to-day life.

Self-Efficacy

The notion of self-efficacy was developed as part of a broader social-cognitive approach to psychology in the 1970s (Bandura, 1977, 2011). This approach critiqued behaviourism's focus on immediate rewards and punishments, and its central ideas later became foundational in positive psychology. (Recall the bibliometric word cloud in Chapter 1 where self-efficacy was the largest, or most mentioned, term related to positive psychology.)

In the social-cognitive approach, the 'social' part emphasizes the importance of other people (e.g. the famous 'Bobo doll study' on how people learn by watching others); the 'cognitive' part emphasizes people's thoughts and subjective experience. Self-efficacy is key to understanding well-being because it directs people towards active engagement with meaningful pursuits. **Self-efficacy** is the personal belief that one can successfully enact behaviours that will lead to desirable outcomes. People have many different efficacy beliefs; they are separate for the particular domain or task at hand. For example, you may have high self-efficacy for completing a 10k race, while having low self-efficacy for playing "God Save the Queen" on the trombone. These might also change with new circumstances; for example, if you sprain your ankle or begin music lessons. High self-efficacy connotes a sense of being able to overcome challenges, but beliefs are also updated based on circumstances.

Across many studies, people's engagement and success are substantially higher when they have a sense of self-efficacy (Bandura, 2011). That is, we tend to avoid activities with low self-efficacy, and take up pursuits where self-efficacy is high, where we believe we can enact the important behaviours. This applies throughout day-to-day activities, yet social scientists have been especially interested in areas that contribute to strong societies. For example, workplaces are contexts where motivated engagement with tasks has important pay-offs, and self-efficacy is a good predictor of job performance (Stajkovic & Luthans, 1998). Similarly, academic achievement is strongly predicted by self-efficacy (Schneider & Preckel, 2017). People with low self-efficacy for an activity (e.g. work or school) are unlikely to give as much effort, and are then, predictably, less likely to succeed. In this way, a belief about the self ('I think I can do it') spurs desirable action.

Self-efficacy has also been important to theories of health behaviour and change (Sheeran et al., 2016). People who successfully stop smoking, increase exercise, and remember to apply sunscreen regularly, as examples, have – or have developed – high self-efficacy for these activities. Most research on self-efficacy has been correlational, and the findings are thus ambiguous about causality. Although the theory is clearly about causality (i.e. self-efficacy causes behaviour), this is often difficult to test in the real world because such tests require a manipulation that increases self-efficacy, and then following people over time to observe changes in behaviours. However, in the health domain these difficult criteria have been met. That is, multiple studies with random assignment and control groups suggest that interventions that increase self-efficacy also cause increases in relevant health behaviours (Sheeran et al., 2016).

Given self-efficacy's role in predicting important outcomes, psychologists are keen to understand the sources of self-efficacy (Bandura, 2011; Maddox, 2009). Personal experiences are most important – a history of past successes makes one confident and optimistic about future successes in similar circumstances. That said, successfully coping with some difficulty along the way can foster a more resilient efficacy. Some challenge is helpful, but repeated failures weaken self-efficacy.

Before one has any experience, or where an initial attempt went poorly, there are still ways to gain self-efficacy. The broader social-cognitive perspective suggests that other people can boost or detract from our sense of self-efficacy. Through vicarious experience, we can see someone else succeed, and infer that we would have similar results, especially if that person is similar to us. Verbal persuasion can also have an effect, for example when others tell us they think we can or cannot do things. Persuasion is weaker than direct experience, and also depends on the credibility of the source. Finally, mood and physiological states can have momentary effects on efficacy beliefs. For example, fatigue can reduce efficacy. Pleasant moods often boost self-efficacy; indeed, the social cognitive perspective argues that increased self-efficacy is an important reason why positive emotions often facilitate desirable outcomes (Bandura, 2011).

Identifying the sources of self-efficacy suggests ways that psychologists can design interventions to increase it (Maddox, 2009). For example, the perception of successful personal experience can be enhanced when small, concrete goals are assessed frequently and with clear feedback. The use of 'models' can demonstrate others succeeding, in person or even in videos. Similarly, support groups allow people to share experiences of success in coping or in reaching common goals. A counsellor, employer, or health-care worker might provide a persuasive 'pep talk' along with information about how to succeed. Relaxation techniques can encourage a frame of mind conducive to higher self-efficacy in otherwise difficult circumstances. In sum, a variety of techniques that encourage self-efficacy's sources are now common parts of therapy, coaching, and other behavioural interventions.

RESEARCH CASE

INTERVENING TO PROMOTE HEALTH BEHAVIOUR SELF-EFFICACY

Health psychologists commonly assess self-efficacy when they test health behaviour interventions. Strategies vary widely in how much they focus on self-efficacy per se, but sometimes it is the main target for change. For example, Luszczynska, Tryburcy, & Schwarzer (2007) tested an online intervention to promote healthy eating. They recruited a sample of adults with webpage advertisements. Interested participants filled out an initial questionnaire which included items about self-efficacy for healthy eating (e.g. "How certain are you that you are able to maintain a healthy diet, even if you would have to change habits regarding grocery shopping?"). They were then randomly assigned to a control group, a self-efficacy condition, or a third condition that combined self-efficacy with a planning exercise.

About a month later, the control group participants were emailed some general information about the importance of nutrition, and how support from family or friends can be helpful when failing to meet nutritional goals. The self-efficacy groups received information about the usefulness of high self-efficacy in meeting goals, and some brief exercises designed to improve self-efficacy for healthy eating. For example, they received

(Continued)

personal feedback about their scores (high, low, or about average), along with some appropriate encouragement (e.g. "Even if it may seem a bit low, one can easily strengthen these beliefs in order to reach one's own goals easier and faster…"). Persuasion and reminders of past success were also used; participants were asked to recall and write about some specific instances where they were successful in resisting unhealthy foods and/or choosing healthier options. Participants were then asked to view these examples as indications of past success, and to reflect on how such experiences feel good. Participants in another experimental group received all of this, plus some instructions to make an action plan about when, where, and how they would maintain a healthy lifestyle.

About six months after the intervention, participants were contacted again to report on self-efficacy, plans, and how many fruits and vegetables they had been eating over the last two weeks. As predicted, self-efficacy for healthy eating increased more in the groups that received the intervention. In addition, these participants reported eating more fruits and vegetables over time, compared to the control group (see Figure 5.1). Statistical analyses suggested that the increases in self-efficacy accounted for the increases healthy eating. The eating changes were not enormous (i.e. all groups falling between one and two per day), but keep in mind that the intervention was relatively minimal, all online, and occurred months earlier.

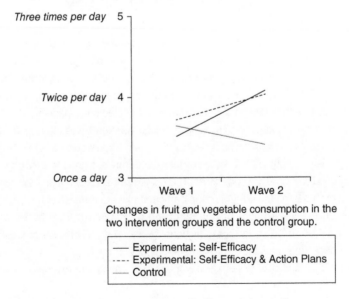

Changes in fruit and vegetable consumption in the two intervention groups and the control group.

—— Experimental: Self-Efficacy
---- Experimental: Self-Efficacy & Action Plans
.... Control

Figure 5.1   Results of the healthy eating self-efficacy intervention

You may also be thinking that the hypothesis of the study was obvious to the participants in the self-efficacy conditions. Perhaps they reported increasing self-efficacy merely because they were told it would be helpful. It is hard to rule out this concern, but other studies with less obvious foci on self-efficacy often find that it still explains positive changes in health behaviours. For example, the 'Body and Soul' intervention was designed to promote healthy eating via African-American churches (Resnicow et al., 2004). The intervention included cookbooks, health fairs, cooking classes, and various forms of encouragement (videos, counsellors, church groups), but none of these had a very direct focus on self-efficacy per se. Nonetheless, these activities seemed to increase self-efficacy, along with healthy eating. With so much going on in the 'Body and Soul' intervention, it is hard to pin down self-efficacy change as the primary factor. Nonetheless, this study nicely complements the more direct, or obvious, self-efficacy interventions. Collectively, there are good reasons to think that healthy eating can be promoted by increasing people's self-efficacy for it.

Self-Esteem

Self-esteem sounds similar to self-efficacy, but it is distinct. **Self-esteem** is a positive evaluation of the self; it is having a sense of worth, competence, and personal satisfaction in valued domains. It is also subjective – about what one believes, rather than objective reality. Normally, we think of self-esteem as an overall, general self-evaluation. This contrasts with self-efficacy which is typically more specific, about a particular goal or set of behaviours. Exceptions to this trend do exist; that is, one can assess general self-efficacy or narrower evaluations of esteem in particular domains. However, this is far less common and less consistent with their theoretical origins.

There are additional ways in which efficacy and esteem differ. Whereas self-esteem is largely a feeling of positivity about the self, self-efficacy is more a cognitive judgement about ability. In addition, self-esteem depends on feeling competent in areas that are personally valued; self-efficacy is simply the judgement that the behaviours can be enacted, regardless of importance. For example, Sean may have high self-efficacy for doing arithmetic, and low self-efficacy for making shots in basketball. These are assessments of what he can do. Sean's general self-esteem will be higher or lower depending on how important success in arithmetic or basketball is to his sense of self. If basketball is unimportant, the low basketball self-efficacy and poor performance are irrelevant to Sean's self-esteem. Of course there are some things that most people do care about, such as having strong interpersonal relationships; these domains are thus commonly important to self-esteem (Leary & Baumeister, 2000).

Self-esteem has been studied extensively in recent decades, and studies find some clear and desirable correlates (Baumeister, Campbell, Krueger, & Vohs, 2003; Swann, Chang-Schneider, & Larsen McClarty, 2007). For example, self-esteem is strongly associated with subjective well-being and lower rates of depression. People with high self-esteem tend to persist more on difficult tasks, especially when there are indications that such persistence is likely to pay off. Although the correlations are considerably smaller, self-esteem also predicts occupational status, income, and health (Orth, Robins, & Widaman, 2012). In adolescence, low self-esteem is associated with aggression problems; it also predicts criminality in adulthood (Donnellan, Trzesniewski, Robins, Moffitt, & Caspi, 2011; Trzesniewski, Donnellan, Moffitt, Robins, Poulton, & Caspi, 2006).

Despite the pattern of desirable correlations, social scientists still debate the wisdom of trying to increase self-esteem directly (Baumeister et al., 2003; Swann et al., 2007). To be clear, almost all agree that it is more desirable for a person to have high, as opposed to low, self-esteem. The argument against pursuing high self-esteem is more about the direction of causation, the methods of trying to increase it, and early overblown claims about the potential benefits. Some history is useful here. In the 1970s and 1980s there was a strong societal and policy push to increase self-esteem, especially for children in the USA. This was supported by social scientists' theoretical – but largely untested – claims about how high self-esteem could increase academic performance and mental health, and reduce delinquency. Programmes were developed to encourage self-esteem, but they yielded little supportive data. This was in part because they were not designed to be strong experimental tests, but also because self-esteem is hard to change. The wide range of hypothesized benefits now seems overly optimistic.

By the 2000s, more data had accumulated and influential reviews began to argue against the prudence of striving for higher self-esteem (Baumeister et al., 2003; Crocker & Park, 2004). They noted that self-esteem was only weakly or inconsistently associated with some important outcomes. For example, the correlations between academic performance and self-esteem are small, and self-esteem does not seem to protect against early experimentation with sex or drugs in adolescence. More importantly, however, the reviews questioned the direction of causation when correlations were found. Rather than self-esteem causing success, it may be that success causes increases in self-esteem. Or that a third variable, such as ability, causes both success and self-esteem.

Similarly, people who are dispositionally happy may include their self-concepts in their lists of things to feel good about, rather than high self-esteem actively causing happiness. Critics also pointed out how self-esteem can be desirable, even while some methods of maintaining or encouraging it are problematic. Hints from laboratory studies suggested that protecting or striving for high self-esteem could make people act defensively. For example, ignoring indications of poor performance can prolong good feelings, but it works against improvement; derogating others can preserve self-esteem with unfair comparisons, but also brings social costs such as bigotry (Crocker & Park, 2004). Moreover, attempts to encourage self-esteem with excessive praise, as opposed to rewarding only real accomplishments, might encourage narcissism, distorted expectations, reduced effort, and poor performance in the future (Baumeister et al., 2003). In sum, after initial enthusiasm for encouraging high self-esteem, many psychologists have become sceptical about the value of such efforts. Pursuing self-esteem may even entail some costs.

The debate is tricky, but not impossible to reconcile. Observational studies 'in the real world' find correlations between high self-esteem and many – but not all – desirable outcomes. There are now strong longitudinal studies showing that desirable and objectively measured outcomes, such as income, health, and low aggression, are preceded in time by high self-esteem (e.g. Donnellan et al., 2011; Orth et al., 2012). This pattern, supported by rigorous statistical analyses, argues for self-esteem as a cause of future benefits. It may be that high self-esteem causes well-being, health, or success under normal conditions, even if past intervention studies have not produced the same desirable outcomes. That is, naturally occurring self-esteem may be helpful, even if past interventions failed to produce it. New studies with experimental methods (manipulations and control groups) would certainly bolster the argument for self-esteem as a cause of desirable outcomes, but the latest and best longitudinal studies remain suggestive about self-esteem's benefits.

Unfortunately, we still do not know how to increase self-esteem reliably. That is, interventions designed to increase self-esteem are typically ineffective, short-lasting, or too complex to isolate the effects of self-esteem. As we learn more, it seems that increasing self-esteem will be difficult. Beyond previous failed interventions, longitudinal studies suggest that self-esteem tends to be quite stable, similar to personality traits (Kuster & Orth, 2013). This does not mean that change is impossible, but perhaps focusing on self-esteem is not the best way to encourage its desirable correlates. For example, if we want to increase well-being or academic performance, it may be easier to teach coping or study skills, rather than taking the seemingly difficult route of trying to first change self-esteem. Moreover, it is possible that some methods of increasing self-esteem will not have the same benefits as naturally occurring high self-esteem. Artificial enhancements do not always work the same way. For example, consider height and basketball performance as an analogy: it is uncontroversial to suggest that being taller promotes success in basketball; yet artificially (or experimentally) boosting height with high-heel shoes would not have the same effect.

In addition, research suggests that some intuitive ideas about boosting self-esteem backfire for people who lack it. For example, one study asked people to repeat positive statements to themselves (e.g. 'I'm a loveable person'); this task made people with high self-esteem feel a little better, but made people with low self-esteem feel worse (J. V. Wood, Perunovic, & Lee, 2009). Similarly, when Dutch children with low self-esteem were asked to make a drawing and then given excessive praise (i.e. "You made an incredibly beautiful drawing!"), it was not helpful. They were subsequently less likely to accept an educational challenge (i.e. to draw additional pictures described as difficult but where much would be learned), compared to after receiving less praise, or to children with high self-esteem (Brummelman, Thomaes, Orobio de Castro, Overbeek, & Bushman, 2014). It seems that people with low self-esteem are uncomfortable with overly positive information that contradicts their self-views. In sum, boosting self-esteem is difficult, and may be especially difficult for the low-self-esteem people who have the most to gain.

Finally, some of the arguments against trying to boost self-esteem stem from concerns that attempts might instead promote narcissism (Baumeister et al., 2003). Narcissism is similar to high self-esteem in that both share positive evaluations of the self. However, narcissism also includes a sense of superiority and entitlement – not only being good, but being better than others and deserving of special treatment. People high in narcissism are overconfident, and they respond to challenges and treats to self-worth with aggression (Bushman et al., 2009). We do not want to promote these characteristics, and some argue that excessive praise will do just that. However, as with self-esteem, research remains unclear on what actually changes narcissism over time.

The definition of self-esteem does not include superiority or entitlement, but people with these qualities – the narcissists – can still score high on measures of self-esteem. For example, the questionnaire item "I feel I have a number of good qualities" gets strong agreement from people with high self-esteem; yet narcissists strongly agree too, perhaps thinking "Not just good, all my qualities are tremendous, and better than all those other losers out there". Thus, healthy high self-esteem and problematic narcissism can produce the same high scores on some questionnaires.

Researchers are now measuring more nuanced self-views separately, differentiating among the various cousins of self-esteem. Narcissism is a noxious example. Our next topic, self-compassion, purports to be a healthier version of positive self-views.

TRY IT

Example Items Used to Measure Self-Esteem and Self-Compassion

Completing the questionnaire involves rating one's level of agreement with the statements.

Self-Esteem (Rosenberg, 1965):

1. On the whole, I am satisfied with myself.

2. I wish I could have more respect for myself (reverse scored).

3. I feel that I have a number of good qualities.

4. I certainly feel useless at times (reverse scored).

Self-Compassion (Neff, 2003):

1. I'm tolerant of my own flaws and inadequacies.

2. When I see aspects of myself that I don't like, I get down on myself (reverse scored).

3. I try to see my failings as part of the human condition.

4. When I fail at something that's important to me I tend to feel alone in my failure (reverse scored).

5. When something painful happens I try to take a balanced view of the situation.

6. When I fail at something important to me I become consumed by feelings of inadequacy (reverse scored).

Note: 'reverse scored' means that people who score high disagree with the item.

Self-Compassion

Like self-esteem, self-compassion is a positive perspective on the self; however, self-compassion entails a different way of understanding the self-concept. **Self-compassion** is a self-view defined by three components: kindness towards the self, an awareness of common humanity, and a mindful approach to negative parts of the self (Neff, 2003, 2011). Whereas self-esteem is an evaluation, self-compassion is a particular way of relating to the self; it is less judgemental and more accepting. By recognizing a common humanity – that all people share many qualities and faults – self-compassionate thinking is less critical: if everyone makes mistakes, it is not so bad when I do too. Similarly, a mindful approach involves taking a step back to see things in a more objective or balanced way. Negative aspects are acknowledged, but they are not taken as grist for endless rumination; they do not require lengthy analysis and further evaluation. (Like mindfulness, the idea of self-compassion borrows from Buddhism.)

Self-compassion is in clear contrast to a critical approach to oneself; instead it extends kindness to the self. In an illustrative exercise, people are asked to write down how they would respond to a good friend who is going through a tough time (Neff, n.d.). Next, they are asked to write down what they think and do when they feel bad about themselves. Often a clear contrast emerges: we are kind with our good friends, but can be quite critical of our own failings. The self-compassionate response is to treat the self as we would treat a good friend – with kindness. As an individual difference, people high in self-compassion are prone to this response, whereas people low in self-compassion are more self-critical.

As you may be gathering, self-compassion is especially relevant in difficult circumstances. People high in self-compassion cope well when they inevitably screw up. For example, one study asked people to vividly imagine hypothetical failure scenarios, such as creating a long, awkward pause during a stage performance by forgetting their lines (Leary, Tate, Adams, Allen, & Hancock, 2007). People high in self-compassion reported fewer unpleasant emotions and self-critical thoughts (e.g. 'I'm such a loser') after imagining these failures. Moreover, individual differences in self-compassion predicted these merciful responses better than self-esteem. To be clear, self-compassion and self-esteem are positively and substantially correlated (about $r = .60$) – people tend to be high or low on both together (Neff & Vonk, 2009). However, when the two are compared, there are hints that the self-compassionate response may be the more useful element in coping with failure, compared to the mere positive evaluations of self-esteem (Leary et al., 2007).

Self-compassion seems to help people feel better in the face of failure, but this raises questions about motivation. Perhaps people need to feel the sting of defeat to work hard in the future; does a self-compassionate response make people complacent or lazy? Although these questions come easily, they confuse compassion with indulgence. Conceptually, people high in self-compassion still want the best for themselves; they just avoid adding critical thoughts to actual failure. At the empirical level, self-compassion is positively correlated with self-esteem (which, in turn, is associated with persistence), trait conscientiousness (which includes achievement striving), academic mastery goals (which connote a motivation to develop skills), and curiosity (Neff, Hsieh, & Dejitterat, 2005; Neff, Rude, & Kirkpatrick, 2007). This collection of desirable correlations argues against the notion that self-compassion merely provides excuses for idleness. Unsurprisingly, self-compassion also correlates with subjective well-being.

The proponents of self-compassion argue that it offers a better goal for intervention, compared to self-esteem (Neff, 2011). That is, the two constructs share many positive associations, but whereas striving for self-esteem can sometimes involve derogating rivals and other defensive behaviours, self-compassion avoids these maladaptive properties. In addition, there are some indications that self-compassion can be increased with workshops or psychotherapy (Gilbert & Procter, 2006; Neff & Germer, 2013). In short, self-compassion appears promising as a positive self-view worth fostering. However, it is also important to keep in mind that the research on self-compassion is still preliminary. Part of the reason why there are questions around promoting self-esteem is because so many studies have explored its costs and benefits. Self-compassion has received a tiny fraction of that research attention. I have focused on the positive potential of self-compassion with supportive examples, but even the basic claims require further testing. Thus, it is best to think of self-compassion as an intriguing idea with potential – not as something that has been clearly demonstrated as more adaptive than self-esteem.

TRY IT

How Would You Treat a Friend?

The main text briefly described an exercise that helps people to think in a more self-compassionate way by considering how they respond to their good friends. For this exercise, slow down and actually go through each step in the process; write down your answers:

1. Think of situations where a good friend feels bad about him or herself. How do you ideally respond? What is your tone?

2. Think of how you typically respond when you feel bad about yourself. What do you do and say? What is the tone?

3. Is there a difference between responses to a good friend and yourself? What factors lead you to treat yourself differently than you would treat a friend?

4. What might change if you treated yourself more like a good friend when you are suffering?

You can find this exercise and others, including guided meditations, at: http://self-compassion.org/category/exercises/

CULTURAL CAUTIONS ABOUT THE SELF-CONCEPT

The distinction between self-esteem – which is mainly about seeing the self positively – and self-compassion – which involves seeing the self as like others and with a balance of good and bad – mirrors broader culture differences in the self-concept. That is, self-esteem seems prototypically American with its abundance of positive attitude. In contrast, the notion of self-compassion draws from Buddhism and includes a subdued sense of personal importance that is more common in Asia. (However, self-criticism is also prominent in some Asian cultures, so we should not infer massive continental differences in self-compassion.) Indeed, cultural psychologists have focused on the self-concept as an important window on cultural differences. Their findings suggest that we use caution in applying the ideas covered in this chapter beyond the North American and Western European nations, where most studies have been conducted. Culture provides a lens through which people interpret the world, including their self-concepts.

It is important to recognize that cultures vary in many ways, and that each culture is distinct. Moreover, even within a single culture, things change over time, and there are wide variations among people's self-concepts – not all Canadians or all Japanese are the same as others in their respective cultures. That said, psychologists have highlighted prominent cultural differences in two self-related processes: independence and interdependence (Markus & Kitayama, 2010). **Independence** is about seeing the self as unique and pursuing personal goals autonomously; North Americans and Western Europeans tend to have more independent self-concepts. In contrast, **interdependence** is about social bonds, fitting into groups and thereby considering others' wishes and social norms before acting. East Asians tend have more interdependent self-concepts. (The terms individualist and collectivist, respectively, are commonly used to describe very similar differences in cultures, rather than selves per se; see Oyserman, Coon, & Kemmelmeier, 2002.)

Cultural differences in the self-concept can reveal themselves on the Twenty Statements Test. In one study, research participants in Japan and the USA were given a piece of paper with the question "Who are you?" at the top followed by 20 lines that began "I am…". When given this broad question, the Euro-Americans were more likely to describe themselves with abstract trait terms (e.g. honest, moody, easy-going), whereas the Japanese were more likely to write about social roles or socially defined statuses (e.g. in the gymnastics club, a college student, a ballerina) (Cousins, 1989). Said another way, Japanese self-concepts were more relational and American self-concepts more individual.

These cultural differences may extend to people's perceptions of the true self and authenticity. An independent self-concept suggests a strong, distinct, and unique self that persists in the face of various situational pressures. An interdependent sense of self places more emphasis on context. For example, it is easier to see an interdependent self as serious at school, silly with friends, sarcastic in debate club, and obedient with family, all without a sense of contradiction. Each of these may be an appropriate response to the social context. Of course cultural differences in the self-concept are a matter of degree – we can all see some consistency and some variation in our behaviours over time – yet people with independent self-concepts may have a more essentialist view of the true self; they may expect that consistent expressions of inner dispositions are more important to authenticity and well-being, compared to people with an interdependent self-concept. People in Western cultures are often surprised by research that suggests that accepting help from others or behaving in counter-dispositional ways can still feel authentic (Fleeson & Wilt, 2010); perhaps this would seem more natural to people with more interdependent senses of self?

In one comparison between Korean and American students, the Koreans saw themselves as more flexible across situations, and this flexibility was mostly unrelated to well-being or positive perceptions from others (Suh, 2002). In contrast, seeing oneself as consistent across situations predicted higher well-being and more positive perceptions from others among the American students. This study did not measure subjective authenticity directly, but it does hint at ways in which the true self might be viewed differently across cultures.

Consistent behavioural expressions seem both more common and more desirable in the individualist culture.

Although cultural differences in authenticity are quite speculative, there has been more research comparing self-esteem across cultures. East Asian samples often score lower on measures of self-esteem than Western samples (Heine & Hamamura, 2007). Other findings suggest that East Asians are less prone to self-enhancement more generally. For example, in the Twenty Statements Test, East Asian students tend to have a lower ratio of positive to negative self-descriptors, compared to American students (Heine & Hamamura, 2007). In another comparison, students from Singapore were less likely to describe themselves as better than average in terms of intelligence, honesty, health, and so on, compared to Israeli students with more independent self-concepts (Kurman, 2003). In addition, Singapore students were less likely to overestimate their academic performance when self-reports were compared to actual evaluations. Turning to well-being, a large study compared students across 31 nations and found that self-esteem was positively correlated with life satisfaction in all of them (Diener & Diener, 1995). However, the correlation was much stronger among individualist, compared to more collectivist, cultures. In other words, self-esteem seems more conducive to happiness in cultures that value independence.

Psychologists have interpreted findings like this in two different ways. One view is that **self-enhancement**, the tendency to see oneself in a positive way, is primarily a Western cultural phenomenon (Heine, Lehman, Markus, & Kitayama, 1999). Others suggest that all people have a motive to self-enhance, but that people do it differently, depending on their cultural norms (Sedikides, Gaertner, & Vevea, 2005). For example, people in more independent cultures may inflate their views of personal abilities, whereas people in more interdependent cultures may enhance beliefs about the quality of their relationships.

In addition, some comparisons may depend more on the specifics of particular cultural comparisons (e.g. USA vs China), rather than the broader dimension of independence–interdependence per se (Oyserman et al., 2002). For example, one large study found substantial variation in the average levels of self-esteem across 53 nations, but these differences correlated only $r = .02$ with an index of individualism (Schmitt & Allik, 2005). It also found that mean levels of self-esteem fell above the midpoint of the scale in most cultures – 'average' self-esteem tended to be a bit better than average. On the one hand, this suggests that most cultures self-enhance; on the other, the variation also suggests that some cultures do it more than others, at least in terms of self-esteem. (Still, the variation was not predicted by individualism in this large study.)

In sum, people's self-concepts are rich in individual and cultural differences. Even if there are some universals (perhaps a need to self-enhance), these almost certainly play out differently based on people's experiences in a particular culture. Self-concepts are the home of core ideas in positive psychology. Much would be gained by extending our knowledge about cultural differences in how people come to understand themselves, for example in terms of authenticity, subjective well-being (Suh, Diener, Oishi, & Triandis, 1998), and a sense of meaning in life (Steger, Kawabata, Shimai, & Otake, 2008).

SUMMING UP

We began with a distinction between two important aspects of the self: the active self that does things ('I'), and our subjective understanding of the self-concept ('Me'). For psychologists, understanding the self-concept is important because it guides the ways people process new information and how they behave. For example, people tend to pursue goals when they believe they can perform the behaviours needed for success – when they have high self-efficacy. The self-concept is multi-faceted, including ideas about who we were in the past, who we might become, and how we evaluate our various characteristics. Different circumstances bring to mind the parts of the self-concept that are most relevant at the time.

Despite this self-complexity, most people still believe they have one 'true self'. It is probably impossible to know or measure the true self in an objective way, but most people value behaviour that is perceived as reflecting their true selves. When people behave authentically – in ways that are subjectively consistent with the true self – they also tend to report well-being and accomplishment. Self-determination theory describes these authentic behaviours as intrinsically motivated and as meeting basic needs for autonomy, relatedness, and competence.

Self-esteem is an evaluative part of the self-concept. Although it is not a panacea, people with high self-esteem tend to be happier, healthier, and more persistent. Despite these desirable correlates, efforts to increase self-esteem have not produced clear benefits. Moreover, some argue that prioritizing self-esteem, or giving undeserved praise to others, could actually promote nasty, defensive behaviours and narcissism. High self-compassion may be a healthier and more prosocial goal as it involves less critical evaluation and a sense of common humanity.

Finally, much research in psychology has focused on Western, educated, industrialized, rich, and democratic societies (summarized with the playful acronym **WEIRD**; Henrich, Heine, & Norenzayan, 2010). This leaves many gaps in our understanding, but cultural psychologists have begun to study differences in self-concepts, such as how much people emphasize independence or interdependence. This, in turn, has potentially important implications for the parts of the self-concept central to positive psychology such as views of the true self, the desirability of self-esteem, and sources of meaning. We should be cautious in extending research findings across different cultures.

TEST YOURSELF

1.   How is the 'I' part of the self different from the 'me' part of the self, and how are they linked?

2. How does self-determination theory describe authentic behaviours?

3. Note one similarity and one difference in the correlates of dispositional authenticity and state authenticity.

4. Give one good reason for, and one good reason against, efforts aimed at increasing self-esteem.

5. Describe the key differences between the independent aspect and the interdependent aspect of the self-concept.

WEB LINKS

Radiolab stories about the neuroscience of self: www.radiolab.org/story/91496-who-am-i/

A wealth of information on self-determination theory: http://selfdeterminationtheory.org

Information, measures, and exercises on self-compassion: http://self-compassion.org

FURTHER READING

To engage with an accessible discussion of free will, consciousness, and extensions to morality, see:

Cave, S. (2016). There's no such thing as free will. *The Atlantic*, www.theatlantic.com/magazine/archive/2016/06/theres-no-such-thing-as-free-will/480750/

Go back to a classic and engaging treatise on the self-concept with:

Epstein, S. (1973). The self-concept revisited or a theory of a theory. *American Psychologist, 28*, 404–416.

Take a deeper look at research on how well, and in what domains, we know ourselves:

Vazire, S., & Carlson, E. N. (2010). Self-knowledge of personality: Do people know themselves? *Social and Personality Psychology Compass, 4*(8), 605–620.

This article provides a nice review of self-efficacy and thoughts on positive psychology from a leader in the social-cognitive movement:

Bandura, A. (2011). A Social Cognitive perspective on Positive Psychology. *International Journal of Social Psychology, 26,* 7–20.

To further explore the link between culture and self-concept, see:

Markus, H. R., & Kitayama, S. (2010). Cultures and selves. *Perspectives on Psychological Science, 5*(4), 420–430.

REFERENCES

Bandura, A. (1977). Toward a unifying theory of behavioral change. *Psychological Review, 84*(2), 191–215. http://doi.org/10.1037/0033-295X.84.2.191

Bandura, A. (2011). A Social Cognitive perspective on Positive Psychology. *International Journal of Social Psychology, 26,* 7–20. http://doi.org/10.1174/021347411794078444

Baumeister, R. F. (2008). Free will in scientific psychology. *Perspectives on Psychological Science, 3*(1), 14–19. http://doi.org/10.1111/j.1745-6916.2008.00057.x

Baumeister, R. F., Campbell, J. D., Krueger, J. I., & Vohs, K. D. (2003). Does high self-esteem cause better performance, interpersonal success, happiness, or healthier lifestyles? *Psychological Science in the Public Interest, 4*(1), 1–44. http://doi.org/10.1111/1529-1006.01431

Brummelman, E., Thomaes, S., Orobio de Castro, B., Overbeek, G., & Bushman, B. J. (2014). "That's not just beautiful—that's incredibly beautiful": The adverse impact of inflated praise on children with low self-esteem. *Psychological Science, 25*(3), 728–735. http://doi.org/10.1177/0956797613514251

Bushman, B. J., Baumeister, R. F., Thomaes, S., Ryu, E., Begeer, S., & West, S. G. (2009). Looking again, and harder, for a link between low self-esteem and aggression. *Journal of Personality, 77*(2), 427–446. http://doi.org/10.1111/j.1467-6494.2008.00553.x

Cousins, S. D. (1989). Culture and self-perception in Japan and the United States. *Journal of Personality and Social Psychology, 56*(1), 124–131. http://doi.org/10.1037/0022-3514.56.1.124

Crocker, J., & Park, L. E. (2004). The costly pursuit of self-esteem. *Psychological Bulletin, 130*(3), 392–414. http://doi.org/10.1037/0033-2909.130.3.392

Deci, E. L., & Ryan, R. M. (2000). The "what" and " why" of goal pursuits: Human needs and the self-determination of behavior. *Psychological Inquiry, 11*(4), 227–268. http://doi.org/10.1207/S15327965PLI1104

Diener, E., & Diener, M. (1995). Personality processes and individual differences: Cross-cultural correlates of life satisfaction and self-esteem. *Journal of Personality and Social Psychology, 68*(4), 653–663.

Donnellan, M. B., Trzesniewski, K. H., Robins, R. W., Moffitt, T. E., & Caspi, A. (2011). self-esteem is related to antisocial behavior, aggression, and delinquency. *Psychological Science, 16*(4), 328–335.

Dunlosky, J., Rawson, K. A., Marsh, E. J., Nathan, M. J., & Willingham, D. T. (2013). Improving students' learning with effective learning techniques: Promising directions from cognitive and educational psychology. *Psychological Science in the Public Interest, 14*(1), 4–58. http://doi.org/10.1177/1529100612453266

Epstein, S. (1973). The self-concept revisited or a theory of a theory. *American Psychologist, 28*, 404–416.

Fleeson, W., & Wilt, J. (2010). The relevance of big five trait content in behavior to subjective authenticity: Do high levels of within-person behavioral variability undermine or enable authenticity achievement? *Journal of Personality, 78*(4), 1353–1382. http://doi.org/10.1111/j.1467-6494.2010.00653.x

Gilbert, P., & Procter, S. (2006). Compassionate mind training for people with high shame and self-criticism: Overview and pilot study of a group therapy approach. *Clinical Psychology and Psychotherapy, 13*(6), 353–379. http://doi.org/10.1002/cpp.507

Harter, S. (2002). Authenticity. In C. R. Snyder & S. J. Lopez (eds), *Handbook of Positive Psychology* (pp. 382–394). New York: Oxford University Press.

Heine, S. J., & Hamamura, T. (2007). In search of East Asian self-enhancement. *Personality and Social Psychology Review, 11*(1), 4–27. http://doi.org/10.1177/1088868306294587

Heine, S. J., Lehman, D. R., Markus, H. R., & Kitayama, S. (1999). Is there a universal need for positive self-regard? *Psychological Review, 106*(4), 766–794. http://doi.org/10.1037/0033-295X.106.4.766

Henrich, J., Heine, S. J., & Norenzayan, A. (2010). The weirdest people in the world? *Behavioral and Brain Sciences, 33*, 61–83. http://doi.org/10.1017/s0140525x0999152x

Heppner, W. L., Kernis, M. H., Nezlek, J. B., Foster, J., Lakey, C. E., & Goldman, B. M. (2008). Within-person relationships among daily self-esteem, need satisfaction, and authenticity. *Psychological Science, 19*(11), 1140–1145.

Howell, G. T., & Zelenski, J. M. (2017). Personality self-concept affects processing of trait adjectives in the self-reference memory paradigm. *Journal of Research in Personality, 66*, 1–13. http://doi.org/10.1016/j.jrp.2016.12.001

Huta, V., & Waterman, A. S. (2014). Eudaimonia and its distinction from hedonia: Developing a classification and terminology for understanding conceptual and operational definitions. *Journal of Happiness Studies, 15*, 1425–1456. http://doi.org/10.1007/s10902-013-9485-0

James, W. (1890). *The Principles of Psychology* (Vols. 1 & 2). New York: Henry Holt & Co. (Vol. 118). http://doi.org/10.1037/10538-000

Kernis, M. H., & Goldman, B. M. (2006). A multicomponent conceptualization of authenticity: Theory and research. *Advances in Experimental Social Psychology, 38*(6), 283–357. http://doi.org/10.1016/S0065-2601(06)38006-9

Kraus, M. W., Chen, S., & Keltner, D. (2011). The power to be me: Power elevates self-concept consistency and authenticity. *Journal of Experimental Social Psychology, 47*(5), 974–980. http://doi.org/10.1016/j.jesp.2011.03.017

Krueger, J. I., & Funder, D. C. (2004). Towards a balanced social psychology: Causes, consequences, and cures for the problem-seeking approach to social behavior and cognition. *Behavioral and Brain Sciences, 27*(3), 313–327. http://doi.org/10.1017/S0140525X04000081

Kuhn, M. H., & McPartland, T. S. (1954). An empirical investigation of self-attitudes. *American Sociological Review, 19*(1), 68. http://doi.org/10.2307/2088175

Kurman, J. (2003). Why is self-enhancement low in certain collectivist cultures? An investigation of two competing explanations. *Journal of Cross-Cultural Psychology, 34*(5), 496–510. http://doi.org/10.1177/0022022103256474

Kuster, F., & Orth, U. (2013). The long-term stability of self-esteem. *Personality and Social Psychology Bulletin, 39*(5), 677–690. http://doi.org/10.1177/0146167213480189

Leary, M. R., & Baumeister, R. F. (2000). The nature and function of self-esteem: Sociometer theory. In M. P. Zanna (ed.), *Advances in Experimental Social Psychology* (pp. 1–62). San Diego, CA: Academic Press. http://doi.org/10.1016/S0065-2601(00)80003-9

Leary, M. R., Tate, E. B., Adams, C. E., Allen, A. B., & Hancock, J. (2007). Self-compassion and reactions to unpleasant self-relevant events: The implications of treating oneself kindly. *Journal of Personality and Social Psychology, 92*(5), 887–904. http://doi.org/10.1037/0022-3514.92.5.887

Lenton, A. P., Bruder, M., Slabu, L., & Sedikides, C. (2012). How does "being real" feel? The experience of state authenticity. *Journal of Personality, 81*(3), 276–289. http://doi.org/10.1111/j.1467-6494.2012.00805.x

Lenton, A. P., Slabu, L., & Sedikides, C. (2016). State authenticity in everyday life. *European Journal of Personality, 30*(1), 64–82. http://doi.org/10.1002/per.2033

Lenton, A. P., Slabu, L., Sedikides, C., & Power, K. (2013). I feel good, therefore I am real: Testing the causal influence of mood on state authenticity. *Cognition & Emotion, 27*(7), 1202–1224. http://doi.org/10.1080/02699931.2013.778818

Libet, B. (1985). Unconscious cerebral initiative and the role of conscious will in voluntary action. *Behavioral and Brain Sciences, 8*(4), 529–539. http://doi.org/10.1017/S0140525X00044903

Little, B. R. (2015). The integrative challenge in personality science: Personal projects as units of analysis. *Journal of Research in Personality, 56*, 93–101. http://doi.org/10.1016/j.jrp.2014.10.008

Luszczynska, A., Tryburcy, M., & Schwarzer, R. (2007). Improving fruit and vegetable consumption: A self-efficacy intervention compared with a combined self-efficacy and planning intervention. *Health Education Research, 22*(5), 630–638. http://doi.org/10.1093/her/cyl133

Maddox, J. E. (2009). Self-efficacy: The power of believing you can. In S. J. Lopez and C. R. Snyder (eds), *The Oxford Handbook of Positive Psychology* (pp. 335–344). New York: Oxford University Press.

Markus, H. R., & Kitayama, S. (2010). Cultures and selves. *Perspectives on Psychological Science*, *5*(4), 420–430. http://doi.org/10.1177/1745691610375557

Markus, H. R., & Wurf, E. (1987). The dynamic self-concept: A social psychological perspective. *Annual Review of Psychology*, *38*(1), 299–337. http://doi.org/10.1146/annurev.ps.38.020187.001503

Neff, K. D. (n.d.). Self-compassion exercise 1: How would you treat a friend? Retrieved 19 August 2017, from http://self-compassion.org/exercise-1-treat-friend/

Neff, K. D. (2003). The development and validation of a scale to measure self-compassion. *Self and Identity*, *2*(3), 223–250. http://doi.org/10.1080/15298860309027

Neff, K. D. (2011). Self-compassion, self-esteem, and well-being. *Social and Personality Psychology Compass*, *5*(1), 1–12. http://doi.org/10.1111/j.1751-9004.2010.00330.x

Neff, K. D., & Germer, C. K. (2013). A pilot study and randomized controlled trial of the mindful self-compassion program. *Journal of Clinical Psychology*, *69*(1), 28–44. http://doi.org/10.1002/jclp.21923

Neff, K. D., Hsieh, Y.-P., & Dejitterat, K. (2005). Self-compassion, achievement goals, and coping with academic failure. *Self and Identity*, *4*(3), 263–287. http://doi.org/10.1080/13576500444000317

Neff, K. D., Rude, S. S., & Kirkpatrick, K. L. (2007). An examination of self-compassion in relation to positive psychological functioning and personality traits. *Journal of Research in Personality*, *41*(4), 908–916. http://doi.org/10.1016/j.jrp.2006.08.002

Neff, K. D., & Vonk, R. (2009). Self-compassion versus global self-esteem: Two different ways of relating to oneself. *Journal of Personality*, *77*(1), 23–50. http://doi.org/10.1111/j.1467-6494.2008.00537.x

Nisbet, E. K., Zelenski, J. M., & Murphy, S. A. (2009). The nature relatedness scale: Linking individuals' connection with nature to environmental concern and behavior. *Environment and Behavior*, *41*(5), 715–740. http://doi.org/10.1177/0013916508318748

Orth, U., Robins, R. W., & Widaman, K. F. (2012). Life-span development of self-esteem and its effects on important life outcomes. *Journal of Personality and Social Psychology*, *102*(6), 1271–1288. http://doi.org/10.1037/a0025558

Oyserman, D., Coon, H. M., & Kemmelmeier, M. (2002). Rethinking individualism and collectivism: Evaluation of theoretical assumptions and meta-analyses. *Psychological Bulletin*, *128*(1), 3–72. http://doi.org/10.1037/0033-2909.128.1.3

Resnicow, K., Kramish Campbell, M., Carr, C., McCarty, F., Wang, T., Periasamy, S., … Stables, G. (2004). Body and soul: A dietary intervention conducted through African-American churches. *American Journal of Preventive Medicine*, *27*(2), 97–105. http://doi.org/10.1016/j.amepre.2004.04.009

Rosenberg, M. (1965). *Society and the Adolescent Self-Image*. Princeton, NJ: Princeton University Press.

Ryan, R., & Deci, E. (2000). Self-determination theory and the facilitation of intrinsic motivation. *American Psychologist, 55*(1), 68–78. http://doi.org/10.1037/0003-066X.55.1.68

Schlegel, R. J., & Hicks, J. A. (2011). The true self and psychological health: Emerging evidence and future directions. *Social and Personality Psychology Compass, 5*(12), 989–1003. http://doi.org/10.1111/j.1751-9004.2011.00401.x

Schlegel, R. J., Vess, M., & Arndt, J. (2012). To discover or to create: Metaphors and the true self. *Journal of Personality, 80*(4), 969–93. http://doi.org/10.1111/j.1467-6494.2011.00753.x

Schmitt, D. P., & Allik, J. (2005). Simultaneous administration of the Rosenberg self-esteem scale in 53 nations: Exploring the universal and culture-specific features of global self-esteem. *Journal of Personality and Social Psychology, 89*(4), 623–642. http://doi.org/10.1037/0022-3514.89.4.623

Schneider, M., & Preckel, F. (2017). Variables associated with achievement in higher education: A systematic review of meta-analyses. *Psychological Bulletin, 143*(6), 565–600. http://doi.org/10.1037/bul0000098

Sedikides, C., Gaertner, L., & Vevea, J. L. (2005). Pancultural self-enhancement reloaded: A meta-analytic reply to Heine (2005). *Journal of Personality and Social Psychology, 89*(4), 539. http://doi.org/10.1037/0022-3514.89.4.539

Sheeran, P., Maki, A., Montanaro, E., Avishai-Yitshak, A., Bryan, A., Klein, W. M. P., … Rothman, A. J. (2016). The impact of changing attitudes, norms, and self-efficacy on health-related intentions and behavior: A meta-analysis. *Health Psychology, 35*(11), 1178–1188. http://doi.org/10.1037/hea0000387

Sheldon, K. M. (2014). Becoming oneself: The central role of self-concordant goal selection. *Personality and Social Psychology Review, 18*(4), 349–365. http://doi.org/10.1177/1088868314538549

Sheldon, K. M., & Elliot, A. J. (1999). Goal striving, need satisfaction, and longitudinal well-being: The self-concordance model. *Journal of Personality and Social Psychology, 76*(3), 482–497. http://doi.org/10.1037/0022-3514.76.3.482

Sheldon, K. M., Ryan, R. M., Rawsthorne, L. J., & Ilardi, B. (1997). Trait self and true self: Cross-role variation in the big-five personality traits and its relations with psychological authenticity and subjective well-being. *Journal of Personality and Social Psychology, 73*(6), 1380–1393. http://doi.org/10.1037//0022-3514.73.6.1380

Smallenbroek, O., Zelenski, J. M., & Whelan, D. C. (2017). Authenticity as a eudaimonic construct: The relationships among authenticity, values, and valence. *Journal of Positive Psychology, 12*, 197–209. http://doi.org/10.1080/17439760.2016.1187198

Stajkovic, A. D., & Luthans, F. (1998). Self-efficacy and work-related performance: A meta-analysis. *Psychological Bulletin, 124*(2), 240–261. http://doi.org/10.1037/0033-2909.124.2.240

Steger, M. F., Kawabata, Y., Shimai, S., & Otake, K. (2008). The meaningful life in Japan and the United States: Levels and correlates of meaning in life. *Journal of Research in Personality, 42*(3), 660–678. http://doi.org/10.1016/j.jrp.2007.09.003

Strohminger, N., Knobe, J., & Newman, G. (2017). The true self: A psychological concept distinct from the self. *Perspectives on Psychological Science, 12*(4), 551–560. http://doi.org/10.1177/1745691616689495

Suh, E. M. (2002). Culture, identity consistency, and subjective well-being. *Journal of Personality and Social Psychology, 83*(6), 1378–1391. http://doi.org/10.1037/0022-3514.83.6.1378

Suh, E. M., Diener, E., Oishi, S., & Triandis, H. C. (1998). The shifting basis of life satisfaction judgments across cultures: Emotions versus norms. *Journal of Personality and Social Psychology, 74*(2), 482–493. http://doi.org/10.1037/0022-3514.74.2.482

Swann, W. B., Chang-Schneider, C., & Larsen McClarty, K. (2007). Do people's self-views matter? Self-concept and self-esteem in everyday life. *American Psychologist, 62*(2), 84–94. http://doi.org/10.1037/0003-066X.62.2.84

Symons, C. S., & Johnson, B. T. (1997). The self-reference effect in memory: A meta-analysis. *Psychological Bulletin, 121*(3), 371–394. http://doi.org/10.1037/0033-2909.121.3.371

Thagard, P., & Wood, J. V. (2015). Eighty phenomena about the self: Representation, evaluation, regulation, and change. *Frontiers in Psychology, 6*, 334. http://doi.org/10.3389/fpsyg.2015.00334

Trzesniewski, K. H., Donnellan, M. B., Moffitt, T. E., Robins, R. W., Poulton, R., & Caspi, A. (2006). Low self-esteem during adolescence predicts poor health, criminal behavior, and limited economic prospects during adulthood. *Developmental Psychology, 42*(2), 381–390. http://doi.org/10.1037/0012-1649.42.2.381

Vazire, S., & Carlson, E. N. (2010). Self-knowledge of personality: Do people know themselves? *Social and Personality Psychology Compass, 4*(8), 605–620. http://doi.org/10.1111/j.1751-9004.2010.00280.x

Wegener, D. M., & Wheatley, T. (1999). Apparent mental causation. *American Psychologist, 54*(7), 480–492.

Whelan, D. C., & Zelenski, J. M. (2012, July). Subjective authenticity and counterdispositional behavior: Exploring the relation between behaving extraverted and feeling authentic, International Network on Personal Meaning conference, Toronto, Canada.

Wood, A. M., Linley, A. P., Maltby, J., Baliousis, M., & Joseph, S. (2008). The authentic personality: A theoretical and empirical conceptualization and the development of the authenticity scale. *Journal of Counseling Psychology, 55*(3), 385–399. http://doi.org/10.1037/0022-0167.55.3.385

Wood, J. V., Perunovic, W. Q. E., & Lee, J. W. (2009). Positive self-statements: Power for some, peril for others. *Psychological Science, 20*(7), 860–866. http://doi.org/10.1111/j.1467-9280.2009.02370.x

6

Thinking

INTRODUCTION

Johannes Kepler was an eminent seventeenth-century astronomer and mathematician whose ground-breaking laws of planetary motion described elliptical orbits. His passion for astronomy began early as a young boy, and this led to him being noted as a prodigy for the character strength 'love of learning' (Peterson & Seligman, 2004). Kepler's high intelligence and scientific creativity make him a good case study to introduce a chapter on cognition and thinking, but the story I want to share reveals more problematic thinking, an episode lacking in wisdom (see Krulwich, 2014).

At the age of 40, Kepler found himself in need of a wife; he was recently widowed and had young children who required care. (In seventeenth-century Germany, a new wife was the clear way to deal with this situation.) His plan was to meet with 11 candidates, keep notes, and then select the best choice from this group. He started meeting the women, but things did not begin well. The first three were not to his liking because of bad breath, other lovers, or expensive tastes. He thought the fourth and fifth women were quite attractive, but his process moved too slowly for them, so they moved on from him. Women six through 11 repeated these patterns; they were either unattractive to Johannes, or they did not want to wait for him to make a decision and rejected him first. After more than two years, he was still without a wife. This seemed especially tragic given that he had met – but lost – three good matches along the way. The man who understood planetary forces so well had more trouble in the sphere of human attractions.

Fortunately, Kepler's story does not end sadly. After his failed search, he redoubled his efforts to woo bachelorette five, and ended up with a long and happy marriage to her.

We still talk about the long road Kepler took to romantic bliss because the story was so delicious to other mathematicians who studied what is known as the 'marriage problem'. This is ultimately a problem about decision making. Kepler was pursuing a strategy of **maximizing**; that is, his goal was to choose the very best wife. Even in his limited universe of 11 potentials, the time and effort needed to determine which one was best undermined his ability to make a choice and realize his goal of getting married. Complete maximizing is often impossible (there are simply too many options), but even in a more limited set, the costs of a full search often outweigh the marginal benefits of selecting the single best option. Instead, it can be better to choose the reasonably good option that presents itself sooner. Choosing a reasonable (if not optimal) option is called **satisficing**; it is something people do often.

Mathematicians have studied the marriage problem, and they have come up with a solution that works well, most of the time. It can be applied to any similar problem with a set number of options. The strategy involves knowing when to stop searching. In essence, you consider the first 36.8 per cent of options, but do not select any. After that first group, you assess more options one by one, and you select the next option that is better than the first group – you stop looking because … maths.

Perhaps we should be wary of mathematicians' advice when choosing romantic partners (see Chapter 8 for more on what psychology has learned); yet the formula would have worked well for Kepler, leading him to choose the fifth woman as soon as he met her. More generally, psychologists agree with the mathematicians about the perils of maximizing, and the drawbacks extend beyond wasted time. When assessed as an individual difference, the tendency to maximize is associated with lower subjective well-being (Oishi, Tsutsui, Eggleston, & Galinha, 2014; Schwartz, Ward, Lyubomirsky, Monterosso, White, & Lehman, 2002). It is not clear that having many choices is problematic on its own – we often want more choices (Simonsohn, Nelson, & Simmons, 2014) – but people who weigh each option in pursuit of perfection are less happy. The alternative is to use satisficing strategies, that is, to choose a 'good enough' option more quickly (even if not taking the formal 36.8 per cent approach).

In this chapter we consider topics that are mostly about thinking. Although it is difficult – and often unwise – to fully dissociate cognition from emotion, a clear link to happiness is not required for something to count as positive psychology. Valued characteristics and exceptional accomplishment can be hedonically neutral and yet still very useful. For example, intelligence lacks a consistent link with happiness, but it is important to many of humanity's greatest accomplishments. We will also consider creativity – which can benefit from positive moods – and wisdom – which may help produce them. Yet we do not value creativity and wisdom primarily for the happiness links, but rather because they provide so much more. Understanding these thought processes enriches our knowledge of the good life. All that said, the final topic of this chapter, affective forecasting, deals with how we think about happiness per se. Affective forecasts are judgements about feelings; they have important consequences for our decisions and how we pursue well-being.

CREATIVITY

What can you do with a brick? Take a moment to come up with as many uses as you can. There are the obvious answers, such as start building a wall. You might also think about using it to hold down some paper in the wind, crack open a nut, as a weapon, as a way to raise funds (where a donor 'buys' it), put it in a toilet tank to conserve water, and so on. This task is one way that psychologists assess the slippery concept of creativity, and it can be repeated over a variety of objects; it is known as the 'alternative uses' task.

Psychologists define **creativity** as the combination of uniqueness and usefulness. Ideas that are novel and unusual are an important start, but they do not count as truly creative if they have no function or work poorly (Simonton, 2009). For example, a sponge raincoat is unique, but not functional. That said, the purpose of artistic work is evaluated differently. In an art exhibition the sponge raincoat may indeed be very creative if it is effective in prompting deep thought or emotions, for example about drought.

Finding an ideal assessment of creativity is less straightforward than describing it in the abstract. The alternative uses task is one approach, but the broader scope of creativity is revealed by four Ps: processes, products, persons, and press (Rhodes, 1961; Runco, 2004). That is, creativity can be considered as the particular kinds of thought processes, the creative works themselves – products (e.g. inventions, songs), the personality characteristics of creative people, and the environmental press; that is, the external forces that facilitate or hinder creativity. The alternative uses task is about generating products (i.e. the list of uses), but apart from research contexts, it is not really the kind of 'product' we would care much about. As such, the alternative uses task is typically used to study the other features of creativity; for example, what personality traits predict coming up with many unusual uses? Or, does sitting near a large box (i.e. 'outside the box') produce more unusual lists? (There was actually a study similar to this – results were supportive, but controversial.) We will look into each of the four Ps a bit more.

Process

When approaching creativity as a process, psychologists are usually seeking cognitive explanations (Simonton, 2009). Creative thinking differs from other approaches to solving problems or accomplishing tasks. **Divergent thinking** is a mental approach that takes many paths to solutions, as opposed to a single logical path to one best solution, and it is a key feature of creativity (Runco & Acar, 2012). For example, the scoring for the alternative uses task rewards divergent thinking with points for generating many different and original answers across various categories of use (Silvia et al., 2008). Divergent thought is helpful for creative solutions, and contrasts with the **convergent thinking** needed to solve problems with straightforward or single best answers. For example, divergent thinking might help an architect consider novel designs for a new bridge. Later these designs might be tested with convergent thinking that applies formulas for calculating how much weight each bridge design can handle before collapsing. Recall that truly creative works must be both novel and useful. Divergent thinking is needed for the novelty, but some 'solutions' will later be dismissed for the bad ideas they are.

Another creativity test – the remote associates test (Bowden & Jung-Beeman, 2003; Mednick, 1962) – highlights an additional cognitive process that underlies creativity: the ability to 'connect the dots', even when they are far apart. In this task people are given three words, and must come up with a single word that can be clearly linked to each. We can contrast this with pure divergent thinking because there is a single correct answer. However, getting to the answer requires one to think in many directions at once, to see connections between otherwise unrelated concepts, to connect the 'remote associates'. For example, what single word links fish, mine, and rush? The answer is 'gold' (goldfish, gold mine, gold rush). The Try It box includes 12 more problems that you can use to quiz your creative thinking.

TRY IT

Remote Associates Problems

Remote associates are often used to assess creative thought. See if you can solve these puzzles by finding one new word that links the three others. That is, the same one word can create a compound word with all three words in the list. (Answers appear at the bottom of the box – no peeking!)

1. cream/skate/water

2. horse/human/drag

3. test/runner/map

4. mill/tooth/dust

5. date/alley/fold

6. mail/board/lung

7. tooth/potato/heart

8. end/line/lock

(Continued)

9. wet/law/business

10. right/cat/carbon

11. tank/hill/secret

12. dive/light/rocket

These items are adapted from Bowden and Jung-Beeman (2003). The article includes many others, and also reports on how many people solved the problems across different time deadlines, giving an indication of average difficulty.

Answers: 1. ice; 2. race; 3. road; 4. saw; 5. blind; 6. black; 7. sweet; 8. dead; 9. suit; 10. copy; 11. top; 12. sky

---

Divergent thinking can also follow from the way attention is deployed (Ansburg & Hill, 2003; Carson, Peterson, & Higgins, 2003). That is, people differ in the extent to which they focus all attention sharply on a task, or devote some attention to peripheral (off-task) information. In research contexts, participants might be asked to memorize a list of words from a sheet of paper while other distracting words are played on a speaker that the participants are told to ignore. The amount of distraction can be assessed in a subsequent test where the previously irrelevant (auditory) words are now the correct answers to anagrams (i.e. scrambled words like MRADSBELC). People who allowed extraneous information into their minds with poorly focused attention on the first task now perform better on the second task – the 'distraction' turned out to be useful after all. Most of the time, when we are not hanging out in sneaky psychologists' labs, distractions are unhelpful. People generally do a pretty good job of automatically blocking out irrelevant information. It happens unconsciously and is called **latent inhibition**. Low latent inhibition can be problematic; for example, it plays a role in some mental disorders. However, creativity may be an exception where reduced latent inhibition is helpful. Allowing a little more random information into the mind seems to help people think in divergent, creative ways. For example, one study found that students with low latent inhibition scored higher on the remote associates task (Ansburg & Hill, 2003). Another study found that low latent inhibition was associated with having more lifetime creative accomplishments in a group of high-achieving students (Carson et al., 2003).

Products

Using lifetime creative accomplishments as an outcome measure introduces the second P: creativity as the products themselves. This approach has some unique benefits, such as being able to study the creativity of people who have been dead for hundreds of years. In one example, the career trajectories of 120 classical music composers were examined by tallying their compositions over time (Simonton, 1991). There are both advantages and disadvantages to counting products (e.g. melodies, scientific papers, patents, paintings). On the one hand, the tallies are very objective and easy to agree on; on the other, tallies may assess productivity more than exceptional creativity per se – the amount versus the quality. For example, Matt Farley has released more than 14,000 songs via online streaming services. They are played enough to generate modest income, but is he a creative genius? It can be tricky to decide which contributions are more creative; yet it is hard to dismiss the notion that there are real differences in degree of creativity, for example between one of Mozart's great works and one of Matt Farley's many songs about poop.

A central issue in defining creative products is deciding who gets to assess whether or how much something is creative. In the study of composers, this was addressed by incorporating an expert's ratings of musical quality; some songs were judged as better than others. One could also count the number of performances, the times streamed online, the likelihood that works appear in university course outlines, and so on. Choosing one best indicator is hard, but collecting a variety of measures provides a reasonable picture of differences in creativity. These indicators can draw on raw counts, subjective impressions, popularity, and influence.

Creative products can also be assessed with self-report questionnaires (Silvia, Wigert, Reiter-Palmon, & Kaufman, 2012). These ask people to indicate whether they have done a variety of creative things, such as invented a game, designed an experiment, made a webpage, or decorated a room (Batey, 2007). Others give additional points for creative accomplishments that are more significant. For example, in the domain of culinary arts, a person would get one point for indicating that they often experiment with recipes, and more points if they have had recipes used in restaurants, won awards, or published them nationally (Carson, Peterson, & Higgins, 2005). Self-report scales have the advantage of covering many different kinds of creativity quickly and easily, and they can assess 'everyday' instances of creativity that lack objective public records (e.g. notebook doodles). Indeed, not all creative products need to be famous; focusing on accomplishment or excellence adds an extra criterion. Self-reports can also allow people to inflate their creative accomplishments (i.e. to lie), but this is probably not a major problem. Most people report relatively modest levels of creative accomplishment. People seem willing to admit, for example, that they have absolutely no expertise or training in things like theatre, architecture, dance, or inventing (Silvia et al., 2012).

Personality

Among the big five personality traits (see Chapter 4), openness is most strongly linked to creativity (Kandler et al., 2016). Open people's tendencies towards unusual experiences, deep thought, aesthetic appreciation, and so on seem to put them in creative mindsets and contexts. In particular, they are prone to some of the cognitive processes that drive creativity, such as divergent thinking and reduced latent inhibition. One study found that tests of divergent thinking correlated with trait openness measured 20 years later, even if openness was rated by spouses or peers (McCrae, 1987). Creative accomplishments across many domains (art, science, film, creative writing, inventions) are also predicted by trait openness (Kaufman et al., 2016). Because these links unfold over long periods of time, they suggest some stability in creativity; it is trait-like, as we would expect for a character strength.

In addition, intelligence is associated with creative accomplishment, especially in the sciences (Simonton, 2012). Psychologists have even debated whether creativity is the same as intelligence, but current consensus is that creativity provides something more – there are highly intelligent people who are not very creative (i.e. good at convergent, but not divergent, thinking). In addition, relevant expertise is needed in most areas. For example, you will not produce an excellent oil painting on your first try, nor will you advance particle physics theory without first learning a lot about physics.

An interesting counterpoint to the need for expertise and intelligence is the exceptional creativity of children. We are not talking about great works of art or scientific accomplishment here; yet spending time with young people quickly reveals their knack for divergent thinking (e.g. coming up with odd and sometimes hilarious ideas). This has even been formalized in tests of problem solving that are geared towards children's strengths. As people age, we learn things about the world. This is normally helpful, but it narrows the possibilities we consider. Adults dismiss improbable answers, and this can interfere with creative problem solving. For example, the 'candle problem' is a classic creativity task where a person must attach a candle to the wall using only a book of matches and a box of tacks. How would you do this? (The solution is to use the box as a support, pinning it to the wall to create a little shelf.) In one study, five-year-old children were faster to solve this problem than six- or seven-year-old children, but only when the tacks were in their box (German & Defeyter, 2000). That is, seeing the box used for another purpose (to hold tacks) seemed to hinder older children's ability to see it in a new way (as a mini-shelf); younger children were less hindered by that constraint. Another study found that adults performed more poorly than four-year-old children when the task involved learning unusual causal relationships – how to make a novel machine work (Gopnik et al., 2017). It seems that adults rely more on prior beliefs, whereas children are more open to unusual evidence that can lead to the (correct) creative solutions.

Press

Press refers to the external influences on a person, and how they are perceived. That is, the objective circumstances can have different effects, depending on how individuals view them. This, in turn, can promote or hinder creativity. For example, work environments that make employees feel short on time, controlled, disrespected, and in competition seem to also reduce creativity (Runco, 2004). In contrast, creative performance is higher when leaders clearly value and reward it (Byron & Khazanchi, 2012).

Positive moods can also facilitate creativity. For example, early studies found that comedy videos and gifts of candy (that presumably boost mood) produced better performance on the candle task and the remote associates task (Isen, Daubman, & Nowicki, 1987). Indeed, findings like this helped inspire the broaden and build theory of positive emotions (Fredrickson, 1998). As you may recall from Chapter 2, this theory states that the purpose of positive emotions is to broaden thought–action repertoires – things that are very conducive to divergent thinking and creativity. Getting more specific, it seems that high arousal positive states – feeling happy, upbeat, and elated – are likely the best for creative thinking, as opposed to low-energy relaxation (or unpleasant) states (Baas, De Dreu, & Nijstad, 2008).

The external environment can also be a source of novel ideas that help spur creativity. For example, there are hints that gaining multicultural experiences (e.g. living abroad, diversity education) can increase creativity (Leung, Maddux, Galinsky, & Chiu, 2008). In addition, laboratory studies suggest that doing one task in an unusual way can produce creativity on subsequent tasks. For example, in one study Dutch participants were asked to assemble a breakfast sandwich of butter and chocolate sprinkles by following a series of instructed steps (Ritter, Damian, Simonton, van Baaren, Strick, Derks, & Dijksterhuis, 2012). Apart from the explicit instruction, this was not unusual – the breakfast is popular in the Netherlands. Some participants made it in the usual way, following a familiar sequence of buttering bread, adding chocolate on top, and so on. Other participants were instructed to follow more unusual steps: put the chocolate on a plate, butter the bread, and then put it butter side down on the plate to gather chocolates, and so on. After this, all participants did the alternative uses task (i.e. what can you do with a brick?). Participants who made breakfast in the unusual way generated more unusual uses for the brick. The implication is that some environments will push people out of their habitual ways of behaving, and this, in turn, will facilitate creativity. This is a technique you could try; perhaps a novel activity could get you out of an inspiration rut?

WISDOM

As noted in Chapter 4, wisdom is one of the six virtues used to organize the 24 character strengths. It is the most cognitive of the virtues, and it encompasses the narrower strengths of curiosity, judgement, creativity, love of learning, and perspective (Peterson & Seligman, 2004). Recall that the virtue labels were meant to collect similar strengths in only a loose way – there is not a strong theory or research to insist that these are the essential features of wisdom when approaching the topic more generally. Of the narrower strengths, perspective and judgement are most prototypical of wisdom. For example, researchers often assess **wisdom** as a tendency towards thinking in ways that include multiple perspectives and that recognize uncertainty. Wisdom is revealed in proverbs, advice, and good choices that are sensitive to individuals' circumstances. Wisdom includes knowledge about the pragmatics of life – how to live a good life – and a motivation to apply this beyond narrow self-interest. One can use intelligence for evil, but wisdom is good by definition.

As such, the term wisdom is a fine choice to collect various strengths into a larger virtue. Strengths like curiosity and creativity can be distinguished from wise reasoning, yet they probably contribute to learning important life lessons and applying them well, part of wisdom's 'extended family'. In this chapter we consider wisdom and creativity at a similar level of analysis. Creativity is not a subset of wisdom as described in this section; this is a narrower wisdom than the VIA virtue label.

The strengths and virtues are presented as all being equally valuable, but some have argued that a form of wisdom – practical wisdom – is most important, a master virtue (Schwartz & Sharpe, 2006). To illustrate, imagine that a good friend asks you "Do I look good in this dress?". You think that she does not. What do you say? You might express your strength of honesty or your strength of kindness, but it would be difficult to do both in this situation. Moreover, the best course of action may depend on the particular circumstances, for example whether another dress is available or whether your friend will benefit more from optimal appearance or a confidence boost in this situation. This is just one example of how individual strengths can conflict with each other. Try to think of times when these pairs might also be at odds: self-regulation and zest, fairness and kindness, humility and leadership. Practical wisdom is about being able to understand and balance the many trade-offs involved when straightforward answers are elusive. Whether or not you agree that practical wisdom is the most important virtue, Schwartz and Sharpe's (2006) dress example shows us that wise people must be nimble in their thinking. Indeed, the notion of balancing among competing ideals, perspectives, interests, and strategies is common to most theories and assessments of wisdom (Baltes & Staudinger, 2000; Grossmann, 2017; Sternberg, 1998).

Measuring Wisdom

Like many interesting psychological phenomena, wisdom is easy to recognize, yet hard to define in a way that can be easily measured. Self-report questionnaires are sometimes used to measure wisdom and its associated traits. The VIA strengths and virtues questionnaire is a staple among positive psychologists, and other standalone wisdom questionnaires exist as well (Staudinger & Glück, 2011). Such questionnaires have the advantage of being easy to administer; yet the domain of wisdom prompts some special concerns about relying on self-judgements. Scholars see true wisdom as including modesty and an awareness of limits to self-knowledge, so the wisest people may not strongly agree with items like "I really understand how life works", or "My decisions are better than other people's". Instead, naïve people with high self-esteem may rate such items higher than the truly wise would. To be fair, many self-report questionnaire items are actually less direct and evaluative, compared to these illustrations. For example, one questionnaire gives points for claiming difficult life experiences and frequent reminiscences – not very evaluative, but which presumably contribute to wisdom (Webster, 2007). Still, wisdom researchers tend to be wary of global self-assessments, and they have created some intriguing alternatives.

In the Berlin wisdom paradigm (Baltes & Staudinger, 2000), people are presented with scenarios and asked to 'think out loud' as they reason through the dilemmas. These responses are recorded and then scored by trained coders who assess wise reasoning. Wisdom is indicated by strong knowledge (both the facts and how to apply them), a sense of relativism (i.e. that values and priorities differ across ages, cultures, etc.), and an appreciation for uncertainty (i.e. limits to knowledge).

For example, one scenario poses the dilemma, "A 15-year-old girl wants to get married right away. What should one/she consider and do?". Here is an answer indicating low wisdom:

A 15-year-old girl wants to get married? No, no way, marrying at age 15 would be utterly wrong. One has to tell the girl that marriage is not possible. [After further probing] It would be irresponsible to support such an idea. No, this is just a crazy idea. (Baltes & Staudinger, 2000, p. 136)

In contrast, a high-wisdom answer is:

Well, on the surface, this seems like an easy problem. On average, marriage for 15-year-old girls is not a good thing. But there are situations where the average case does not fit. Perhaps in this instance, special life circumstances are involved, such that the girl has a terminal illness. Or the girl has just lost her parents. And also, this girl may live in another culture or historical period. Perhaps she was raised with a value system different from ours. In addition, one has to think about adequate ways of talking with the girl and to consider her emotional state. (Baltes & Staudinger, 2000, p. 136)

The differences in uncertainty and relativism are vast in these examples.

A recent approach strikes a middle ground between global self-reports and expert-coded scenarios (Brienza et al., 2017). The approach relies on people's ratings, but these ratings are based on specific events, and they target components of wise reasoning; these include considering a variety of perspectives, uncertainty, and compromise. That is, people are asked to recall recent events from their own lives (e.g. an interpersonal conflict). They then use a 5-point scale to rate how much they did or thought things, in that moment, such as:

1. Put myself in the other person's shoes.

2. Believed the situation could lead to a number of different outcomes.

3. Double-checked whether my opinion on the situation might be incorrect.

4. Tried my best to find a way to accommodate both of us.

5. Tried to see the conflict from the point of view of an uninvolved person.

Higher ratings indicate more wise reasoning on all of these items. Because the ratings apply to a single episode, a more dispositional assessment of wisdom (i.e. as a character strength or virtue) requires soliciting multiple events across different kinds of circumstances. People are often wiser in some contexts than in others; yet the wisest people reason this way consistently (Brienza et al., 2017).

Finding Wisdom

If looking for wisdom, your first instinct is likely to go to an older person. Indeed, many wisdom researchers came to the topic by looking for examples of healthy aging. When asked to nominate wise individuals, lay people typically choose older adults, and wisdom is one of few positive features of elderly stereotypes (Staudinger & Glück, 2011). Although scholars agree that life experience is essential to developing wisdom, the data tell a somewhat more complicated story in linking age and wisdom.

In essence, there are not clear and consistent age differences in wisdom measures across adulthood (Baltes & Staudinger, 2000; Brienza et al., 2017; Grossmann, 2017; Staudinger & Glück, 2011). To be clear, individual studies sometimes find age differences, but they tend to be small, both increasing and decreasing over the lifespan, or vary by topic and culture. On the other hand, if we compare wisdom to other kinds of cognitive processes, older people do seem especially resilient with wisdom. That is, memory and processing speed tend to decline with age; thus, the lack of similar decline in wisdom is telling. Wisdom likely suffers too with serious cognitive decline, and among older people there may be a mix of both the exceptionally wise and others who are losing that capacity. In addition, before making too much of small age effects in wisdom, we should mind the gap between real world wisdom and the artificial tasks used to assess it (Baltes & Staudinger, 2000). Despite these cautions, most agree that wisdom requires more than the mere accumulation of years, and some older adults still lack wisdom.

Beyond age, are there other individual differences more associated with wisdom? Of the big five traits, openness is most consistently correlated with various measures of wisdom (Brienza et al., 2017; Staudinger & Glück, 2011). Narrower personality characteristics such as emotion regulation, social intelligence, mindfulness, perspective taking, and so on also correlate with wisdom, though some of these characteristics begin to overlap with self-report measures of wisdom itself.

General intelligence is also positively correlated with wisdom (Staudinger, Lopez, & Baltes, 1997). Although wisdom is seen as going beyond raw intellect – particularly in terms of practical applications – intelligence is often seen as a pre-condition of wisdom. Yet intelligence and wisdom differ in important ways. For example, unlike intelligence, wisdom is typically associated with psychological well-being. The link goes back to Aristotle, who saw practical wisdom as a master virtue and eudaimonia as about living a virtuous life. Contemporary research supports this notion by linking measures of wisdom and well-being, especially a sense of personal growth (Wink & Staudinger, 2016).

Some contexts and momentary mindsets also seem more conducive to wise reasoning than others. In particular, self-focus or ego-centric perspectives may impair wisdom. Hints of this are found when comparing cultural differences in individualism or power; wise reasoning seems more prevalent when these are lower (Grossmann, 2017). In addition, lab studies suggest that momentary manipulations can have similar effects. In one example, participants were asked to consider a scenario where a romantic partner had sex with the person's close friend (Grossmann & Kross, 2014). Half of the participants were randomly assigned to consider this happening to themselves, whereas the other half imagined this happening to another person. They then rated items indicating wise reasoning (similar to the five example items in the previous section). Wise reasoning was lower when thinking about the self, compared to someone else. Perhaps this is why we often go to others for advice – their thinking may be wiser because they have some distance, asking more questions and considering broader perspectives.

In summing up, let us consider wisdom by borrowing the '4 Ps' framework from creativity research. Measures of wise reasoning get at the process (especially the non-self-report measures that give points for balancing many perspectives). As a strength, wisdom is an aspect of personality, and is associated with trait openness and intelligence (similar to creativity). In terms of press, it seems that contexts and cultures that reduce an ego-centric perspective help promote wise reasoning. Unfortunately, the remaining P – products – is elusive in wisdom research; studying important and impactful instances of real world wisdom presents significant challenges. Perhaps some clever readers will take up this challenge as the next generation of researchers.

INTELLIGENCE

Few topics in psychology generate as much controversy as intelligence. I suspect that much of the strong feeling around intelligence comes from the fact that we value it so highly – even among those who argue against the widespread use of intelligence tests. This high value makes intelligence important to positive psychology. Despite the controversies, it seems clear that some people are cleverer than others, and this describes differences in **intelligence**. Individual differences are at odds with a desire for equality, but this situation is not new to us. We have considered other aspects of positive psychology where people clearly differ and where one end of the spectrum is more desirable. For example, subjective well-being and character strengths are highly valued, and we readily acknowledge pervasive individual differences. What society does about these differences depends on value judgements that go beyond what science can tell us. Intelligence shares other similarities with happiness and virtues (and traits). As we will see, all have a hierarchical structure, strong heritability, and sensitivity to environmental influences.

Who has higher intelligence, Bobbie, a whiz at mathematics, or Chris, whose immense vocabulary includes words like zetetic, obdurate, and enervate? This is a difficult question to answer because maths skills and vocabulary seem quite different from one another. On the other hand, would you be surprised to learn that Chris is also great at solving logical puzzles, and Bobbie is fluent in four languages? Probably not, because people who are clever in one area often do well in others. Two competing notions – distinct abilities versus one broad intelligence – have caused a lot of debate among people who study intelligence. Fortunately, we can avoid the minutia of these arguments by focusing on an overarching consensus: intelligence is best viewed as having a hierarchical structure (Deary, 2012). We can distinguish between different cognitive skills, but they often co-occur in people. Figure 6.1 presents the hierarchical model.

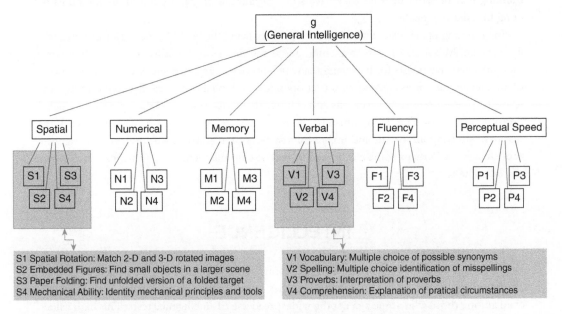

Figure 6.1   A hierarchical model of intelligence. (See main text for further explanation.)

Figure 6.1 displays a hierarchical model of intelligence. Substantial debate remains around the details (i.e. the particular groupings and labels); this model is a hybrid intended to convey the general ideas with relatively accessible labels (see Johnson & Bouchard, 2005). At the bottom level are individual tests (i.e. S1, S2, etc.). Specific test examples and brief descriptions are provided for spatial and verbal abilities. Dozens of specific tests could be included if this was a comprehensive model. Individual tests are grouped at a level just above to represent categories of particular skills (i.e. spatial, numeric, etc.). A difficulty here is that any one test may draw upon multiple skills (e.g. as in a verbal description of a maths problem), so the figure oversimplifies things somewhat. Still, with many tests and sophisticated statistics, researchers make sense of the underlying ability groups. At the top of the hierarchy is 'g', the general factor of intelligence. IQ tests assess a variety of narrower abilities to arrive at this single, broad score.

Researchers find consistent positive correlations across many different tests of ability (e.g. maths, language, logic, spatial, processing speed, memory, knowledge; for example tests and items, see: https://icar-project.com/ICAR_Catalogue.pdf). Thus, it is reasonable to average across these tests and arrive at a single, overall general intelligence score (often referred to as 'g'). General intelligence is at the top of the hierarchy. It is also possible to distinguish among the parts, or separate abilities, a step down in the hierarchy. For example, tests of vocabulary correlate more strongly with reading comprehension than with tests of algebra, which, in turn, correlate more strongly with tests of geometry. That is, we can assess a verbal ability that is separable from numerical ability (even as they share a modest positive correlation). The situation is very similar to how we understand subjective well-being. Life satisfaction is distinct from positive emotions, but on average, the same people tend to experience lots of both – there is a positive correlation, but it is not perfect. The big five traits, made up of their narrower facets, share a conceptually similar hierarchical structure.

As such it is possible and useful to measure the thing at the top of the hierarchy (e.g. general intelligence, happiness, agreeableness), or the more specific components at other times. As an example, overall intelligence does a good job of predicting the magnitude of accomplishments such as earning advanced degrees, patents, job performance, high income, and so on (Kell, Lubinski, & Benbow, 2013; Schmidt & Hunter, 1998). Yet the profile of different abilities predicts which field people pursue. For example, relatively higher verbal ability predicts accomplishment in arts and humanities, whereas higher maths and spatial ability predicts accomplishment in engineering and physical sciences (Wai, Lubinski, & Benbow, 2009).

Controversy also surrounds the notion that intelligence is heritable, but much of the tension can be eased with a clear understanding of heritability. Chapter 3 went into some detail on what heritability means for subjective well-being, and the same ideas apply to intelligence. It is very clear that a substantial part of variation in intelligence is due to variation in genes, but the specific genes are hard to identify and there are likely hundreds involved (Chabris, Lee, Cesarini, Benjamin, & Laibson, 2015; Johnson, 2010). Also, a substantial heritability does not imply that intelligence is fixed or that development and environments are not also essential elements. People are not blank slates, but circumstances are also very important. With intelligence, we have a good idea of what accounts for some of this environmental influence, and it is something that society can control: education. You are, right now, engaging with the single best method for increasing intelligence – congratulations. See the Research Case box to learn more about how researchers demonstrated the importance of education.

In addition, the average intelligence of people has increased substantially over the last 100 years – about 30 IQ (intelligence quotient) points (Pietschnig & Voracek, 2015). This change is surprisingly large. IQ has a mean of 100 and standard deviation of 15. (The mean is still 100 because the scale is periodically adjusted based on current test scores.) Said another way, the average IQ test performance of 100 years ago would border on mental disability today. Although the causes for this increase are still debated, the trend appears across many nations (e.g. Germany, Kenya, Japan, UK, Sweden, Brazil, USA). Very similar to height, we observe strong heritability along with strong mean-level increases over the twentieth century in IQ. Some people have a genetic advantage when it comes to intelligence or height, but this does not negate the importance of education and nutrients.

RESEARCH CASE

DOES EDUCATION INCREASE INTELLIGENCE?

Testing the impact of education on intelligence has required some clever approaches. The link might seem obvious – it is not hard to see the correlation between years of education and intelligence – but we also know that it is folly to infer a causal link from a correlation alone. In this case, it is easy to imagine the opposite direction of causation. That is, clever people may stay in school longer, and even be selected by educators to do so because they are already intelligent. Other 'third variables' could explain the link too; for example, wealth can contribute to tutors, health, and other advantages, along with years of education via postgraduate tuition. Deciding among these various explanations is difficult. Moreover, it is unethical and impractical to conduct a true experiment, for example, by randomly assigning some students to receive less education than others.

Fortunately, researchers have identified some natural experiments that get pretty close to random assignment (Ritchie & Tucker-Drob, 2018). For example, schools typically implement a birthday cut-off for entering school, and as a result children with similar chronological ages will end up with different years of education, relative to their ages. For example, if 31 October is the deadline, young Sally, born 28 October, enters school, while young Samantha, born 2 November, does not. We can then compare scores on intelligence tests to see whether students like Sally score higher than students like Samantha. With large groups and careful comparisons, intelligence differences can be attributed to the extra year of education.

In other cases, societies make more dramatic shifts in policy by changing the years of mandatory education. For example, in the 1960s Norway increased mandatory schooling from seven years to nine years. Also during this period, all draft-eligible men were given standardized intelligence tests at age 19 by the military. This allowed researchers to compare intelligence scores for men in years just before and just after the policy change; the length of schooling was 'manipulated' by government policy – much like the otherwise impossible experiment we would want (Brinch & Galloway, 2012).

Recently, researchers collected all the clever studies like these they could find – these included over 600,000 participants – and combined them using a technique called meta-analysis (Ritchie & Tucker-Drob, 2018). In essence, **meta-analysis** takes a sophisticated average of all the studies conducted on a topic. The idea is that idiosyncrasies (or weaknesses) of individual studies balance out, and we are left with a reasonable estimate of the overall finding. When it comes to education and intelligence, they estimated that each additional year of education adds between one and five points to a person's IQ. A couple of IQ points may sound unimpressive, but it adds up over many years of schooling. The estimated range of IQ points is wide due to some variability across the different kinds of studies (e.g. birthday method vs policy change), and the kind of intelligence test. Interestingly, however, the intelligence gains seemed to apply to both the kinds of things taught explicitly in school (e.g. general knowledge and vocabulary, often called **crystalized intelligence**), as well as more basic or abstract abilities (e.g. processing speed and memory, often called **fluid intelligence**).

In sum, the results of many clever studies suggest that education does indeed have a positive influence on general intelligence. Of course it is also likely that more intelligent people stay in school longer – both of these things can be true and contribute to the correlation. Yet the studies considered in this meta-analysis are unique in more clearly testing the causal role of education.

Despite the consensus that a hierarchical model best describes the domain of intelligence and ability, there is still some debate about the implications for learning, and about how far the boundaries of intelligence should extend. For example, Howard Gardner has been influential among educators in suggesting the idea of 'multiple intelligences', emphasizing the distinctiveness of different abilities, rather than the commonalities (see Gardner & Moran, 2006). Many of the intelligences he proposes seem to easily fit within the hierarchy of general intelligence (e.g. linguistic, spatial, and logical), but others may be more distinct (e.g. musical, or bodily – as indicated by good balance; Visser, Ashton, & Vernon, 2006).

In education, it can be useful to teach concepts in multiple ways so as to engage various abilities and thus produce a deeper understanding. This general truism contrasts slightly with the notion of learning styles, or the idea that different people will always learn best with particular kinds of instruction (e.g. visual learners vs auditory learners – many different styles have been proposed). Although the notion of multiple intelligences implies different modes of learning, even Gardner has been critical of learning styles (Gardner, 2013). Moreover, research has not identified much benefit in teaching to individuals' styles; that is, by matching instruction style to the person (Kozhevnikov, Evans, & Kosslyn, 2014). Instead, having a flexible strategy for teaching and learning seems to work best – different concepts and tasks will require different modes of thinking. For example, some information is best conveyed visually; trying to translate to an audio-only approach is unlikely to help anyone, even if that person has strong musical ability.

The notion of emotional intelligence also stretches the boundaries of intellectual ability. **Emotional intelligence** includes the abilities to perceive, understand, and regulate emotions adaptively (Roberts, MacCann, Matthews, & Zeidner, 2010). For example, you might notice someone smirk during your oral presentation, realize that it is generating feelings of hostility, which you then manage to supress during this important meeting. Each of these steps draws on parts of emotional intelligence. Individual differences in emotional intelligence are less about emotion experience per se, and more about the ability to recognize and use emotions well (which may, in turn, impact future feelings). Emotional intelligence seems to straddle a domain somewhere between cognitive ability and personality traits (e.g. self-control, empathy, emotional stability). Depending on how emotional intelligence is measured, it can overlap with either ability or personality. Yet there seems to be some unique aspects of emotional intelligence that predict job performance in emotionally demanding roles (Joseph & Newman, 2010). Emotional intelligence is also positively associated with well-being more generally, though the correlations are often of modest size (Roberts et al., 2010).

This brings us to our final controversial topic (though there are others not considered here): does intelligence predict important life outcomes, and how does it compare with non-cognitive factors? Although people – especially students – often disparage aptitude and intelligence tests, research clearly shows that they predict a variety of desirable outcomes (Deary, 2012; Hambrick & Chabris, 2014; Kuncel & Hezlett, 2010; Schmidt & Hunter, 1998). For example, they predict higher grades in school, degree completion, creativity, leadership, and job success. There are even indications that intelligence predicts better health over time (Deary, 2012; Wrulich, Brunner, Stadler, Schalke, Keller, & Martin, 2014). Moreover, ability tests predict these important outcomes even after taking socioeconomic status into account – it is clearly not the case that IQ is merely a rough proxy for family advantage; cognitive ability matters. In addition, intelligence still matters at the extreme high end of the scale. Even among just the top 1 per cent of IQ, people with the highest scores (i.e. 99.9 per cent vs 99.1 per cent) are more likely to achieve a PhD, scientific and literary publications, patents, and high income (Lubinski, 2009).

The value of intelligence is sometimes belittled by comparing it to other important predictors of success. For example, the positive psychology canon includes a study that pitted self-discipline against IQ in predicting future grades among about 150 American grade 8 students (Duckworth & Seligman, 2005). The study found that self-discipline was a better predictor than IQ. These results underscore an important point: personality and effort matter greatly to success. However, this study likely overestimates the importance of self-discipline relative to IQ – most other research suggests that both are similarly important. For example, a meta-analysis (summarizing many studies) found that IQ and trait conscientiousness (which includes self-discipline) predict academic success equally well, along with substantial variation in these links depending on age, academic level, and so on (Poropat, 2009). In addition, study habits and skills are also good predictors of academic success (Crede & Kuncel, 2008). Collectively, the research makes it hard to persuasively argue that intelligence, personality, or effort is the single key to success. Rather, all of these are important, and combine to produce accomplishment in school and well beyond (Lubinski, 2004).

In Focus

Optimal Learning Techniques

We think of intelligence as an individual difference, something that can develop over years with education. In education, we focus on learning over shorter timeframes. Cognitive and educational psychologists study various approaches to learning, ultimately generating knowledge about which techniques work better than others. In a major review, ten learning techniques were compared and categorized in terms of their effectiveness and potential for broad application (Dunlosky, Rawson, Marsh, Nathan, & Willingham, 2013). Although their conclusions include substantial nuance, some techniques stood out as more or less useful.

The two best techniques were practice testing and distributed practice. Practice tests are low stakes and informal, including things like student-generated flash cards or attempting textbook-based questions (e.g. see the end of each chapter in this book). Distributed practice refers to repetition spaced out over different study times. Flash cards are again a good example, if they are reviewed repeatedly. Reading content in a book that is repeated in a lecture also counts. Distributed learning is typically contrasted with cramming (e.g. the day before an exam). Research clearly shows

(Continued)

that breaking the same amount of time into separate sessions spread over days and weeks produces superior learning. Thus, both of the strongest techniques emphasize coming back to material multiple times.

The review put three techniques in a 'moderate' category because they seemed promising, but with some limits. That is, these techniques' effectiveness seemed limited to narrower domains, they were more difficult to implement, or there was less research available. First, interleaved practice can be contrasted with blocked studying. Here, different kinds of material are mixed in a study session (interleaved), and this seems to promote learning beyond studying the different topics separately in different sessions. Elaborative interrogation and self-explanation are both techniques that involve generating links to other knowledge. With elaborative interrogation, one comes up with explanations for why a stated fact is true (e.g. why is IQ correlated with income?). In self-explanation, the learner links new information to things s/he already knows (cf. the self-reference effect in Chapter 5). Self-explanation also includes (mentally) describing how a problem can be solved as it is approached (e.g. first I sort by size, then I transform, then … OK, go). Collectively, then, mixing topics and trying to elaborate on concepts while studying appear effective (but perhaps less than practice testing and avoiding last-minute cramming).

Finally, five techniques received low utility ratings. This is not to say that they will never be helpful, but rather that evidence is unavailable or weak, that successful applications are narrow, or that alternative approaches work better in head-to-head comparisons. In particular, highlighting (or underlining) text while reading is a common technique among students, but studies find that it typically fails to improve learning. The other weak techniques are complete re-reading of text, writing summaries of text, using keywords as memory triggers, and generating imagery from text-based materials while reading. If your favourite techniques fall in this category, you could consult the Dunlosky et al. article to read more details about their limitations. You might also consider adjusting your study habits to see whether you can reap the benefits of the other techniques more supported by research.

PREDICTING THE FUTURE: AFFECTIVE FORECASTING

This chapter focuses on cognition. Cognition is often contrasted with emotion; yet finding examples of thinking that are completely devoid of feelings is more difficult than the common contrast suggests. For example, high levels of creativity, wisdom, and emotional intelligence all imply a knack for dealing with emotions. In this section we focus directly on how people think about emotions, or more specifically how people predict their future emotions, especially happiness. These mental assessments of future emotions or happiness are known as **affective forecasts**, and they are important because the forecasts help people make decisions. That is, we often make decisions that we think will maximize our (future) happiness, or plan activities based on how we think we will feel (e.g. avoiding a difficult conversation on a day we expect to be grouchy already).

Many affective forecasting studies suggest that people overestimate how much influence various events will have on future happiness. For example, imagine how happy you will be next week if your favourite football team wins the big weekend game. Despite many people's intuitions of a more lasting effect, a study of World Cup games found that German supporters enjoyed somewhat boosted moods on winning game days, but those boosts did not persist beyond one day (Stieger, Götz, & Gehrig, 2015). As another example, people currently in romantic relationships tend to think that a break-up would cause them to be quite unhappy for months. Yet people who have actually experienced break-ups in recent months have levels of happiness that are very similar to those who are still coupled. In other words, we tend to overestimate how long the sorrow of a break-up will stick with us (Gilbert, Pinel, Wilson, Blumberg, & Wheatley, 1998). Similar overestimates have been found for the results of pregnancy tests, professors' tenure decisions, and students' assignment to preferred residence halls (Wilson & Gilbert, 2005).

People's tendency to overestimate the intensity or duration of how much events will change happiness is known as the **impact bias**. We might think that buying the newest tablet computer will cause a substantial and lasting boost to happiness, but this is probably wishful thinking. To be clear, people are not deluded about what constitutes good and bad events. It feels better to get a new tablet than to have one stolen. However, neither of these events is likely to change our overall happiness as much as we anticipate that it would beforehand. This prediction error is the impact bias.

There are few common reasons for the impact bias. The first one is related to the hedonic treadmill (see Chapter 3). As we have seen, even major life events' influence on happiness fades over time. Simply becoming accustomed to change explains some of the adaptation over time. For example, the lightning speed of our new wireless internet connection is soon taken for granted, and we wonder how we ever lived with the now painfully slow older version. With time, the improvement no longer brings pleasure or appreciation; it is the new normal. People often fail to consider adaptation when predicting their future happiness. In addition, people take active steps to deal with unpleasant events, both consciously and unconsciously, and others often assist too with social support. Soon after you are dumped, your best friend may plan a special day together; you begin to remind yourself of how that ex could be selfish and annoying at times; you notice how nice that attractive acquaintance has been to you lately, and so on. When people consider the impact of a negative event, they often fail to think about all the things they will do to (successfully) cope with it. This tendency has been called **immune neglect**; it is the notion that we underestimate the effectiveness of our 'psychological immune system' to cope with changes and return us to well-being (Gilbert et al., 1998).

Another reason for the impact bias is focalism, or the **focusing illusion**. When people consider how much a future event or set of circumstances will influence their happiness, they tend to weight that particular thing too much. If I ask you to rate your general happiness if you earned perfect course grades this term, grades would be in the front of your mind. You might neglect other important things such as the busy period at your part-time job, the poor health of a favourite uncle, the heavy course load of the next term, and so on. People probably engage in focalism in spontaneous thought too. Features that are most obvious can have undue influence on our predictions of future happiness. For example, a study recruited students at either Midwestern US universities or Southern Californian universities (Schkade & Kahneman, 1998). When these students were asked to rate the happiness of "someone like them" in either the Midwest or California, most thought that the Californians would be happier. There was, in fact, no difference in average happiness across the locations. A series of other questions revealed the focusing illusion. In participants' minds there was an obvious difference between these two locations – California's very pleasant weather – and it had a major influence on forecasts of happiness. However, when probed further (after the happiness ratings), many of the most important things, such as job prospects, social life, personal safety, and so on, did not favour California. Yet these did not seem to come to mind when people predicted the happiness of those in the different locations. Although the weather in California is lovely, weather has little influence on life satisfaction (Lucas & Lawless, 2013); it was weighted too heavily in the affective forecasts.

As we have seen, the causes of happiness are many, and our intuitions about them are not always correct. The focusing illusion can make us pay too much attention to obvious, but relatively unimportant, contributors – like weather – when deciding how to maximize our happiness. As a rule of thumb, any single thing is unlikely to be as important to happiness as it seems while we are thinking about it (and simultaneously failing to consider all the other influences).

Research on affective forecasting suggests that people make errors when predicting their future happiness, and that this leads to some suboptimal decisions (Hsee & Hastie, 2006). With the focus on errors, we might ask whether this line of research really fits in positive psychology. It is about happiness, but it also seems to suggest pervasive human failings in decision making. Chapter 1 revealed the complexity in deciding what is and what is not positive psychology. There are also ways to take a more positive perspective on affective forecasting findings.

First, it is important to recognize exceptions to the impact bias. Some experiences seem to boost people's moods more than we anticipate. These include having conversations with strangers (Epley & Schroeder, 2014), spending money on other people (Dunn, Aknin, & Norton, 2008), and spending time in nearby nature (Nisbet & Zelenski, 2011). Although these are forecasting errors, such findings suggest that doing more of these things might improve happiness. There is a positive prescriptive message if we identify under-appreciated experiences. Similarly, knowing about common errors like the focusing illusion may help people improve decisions and thus happiness. For example, taking time to consider the bigger picture can reduce the biased decisions that would follow from a more narrow focus (Wilson, Wheatley, Meyers, Gilbert, & Axsom, 2000). Again, this is news you can use.

Finally, it is not clear that all forecasting errors are a bad thing. Although adaptation and coping shorten the emotional impact of events, they do not eliminate the initial response (Levine, Lench, Kaplan, & Safer, 2013). Overestimating the impact of positive and negative events can be motivational, and it may ultimately lead to preferable outcomes. For example, believing that you would be miserable following a break-up may cause you to treat your partner better. Surely the road to happiness is not the 'wise' realization that "It will all be OK" or "Nothing will make me happier for very long, so why bother". Some forecasting 'errors' may be useful – healthy little mental fictions that get us to do the right thing.

SUMMING UP

This chapter focuses on the more cognitive parts of positive psychology – domains where thinking is of central importance. In creativity, the cognitive processes include divergent thinking, making remote connections, and reduced latent inhibition. These processes are more common among some people, such as those who score highly on the trait of openness. Circumstances can also promote creative thought by altering moods (positive is helpful) or sparking atypical mindsets (e.g. new cultures or breaking habits). Ultimately, we are interested in the output of creative thought: ideas, solutions, and works of art that are both novel and useful. The four Ps framework outlines the broad scope of creativity, and it can also help frame research on wisdom.

Similar to creativity, wisdom involves particular kinds of momentary thought processes. Wise reasoning includes strong knowledge, along with broad perspective and having a good sense of limits to one's knowledge. Wisdom can be facilitated by strategically pursuing other perspectives, such as considering things for another person, or taking an outsider's perspective on your own dilemmas. Although wisdom is seen as a hallmark of healthy aging, it is found at similar levels across adulthood. Finally, and again like creativity, wisdom is more common among people high openness and intelligence.

As the links with wisdom and creativity suggest, intelligence is a common ingredient of human thriving and accomplishment. People with high IQs produce more creative works, are more educated, perform better in most work roles, and are rewarded with higher incomes. Intelligence is best thought of in a hierarchical way, where various narrower abilities (e.g. spatial, verbal, quantitative, processing speed) correlate positively, and are sensibly combined into an overarching general intelligence (g, or assessed as IQ). Like most individual differences, intelligence is substantially heritable. Still, circumstances and development – and particularly education – are also important to reach (or thwart) the genetic potential. Arguments against the utility of IQ tests are much more common than data that support them. IQ scores do a good job of predicting success in many domains. Still, this does not detract from equally strong data showing important roles for personality, effort, motivation, and specific skills (e.g. study skills in school performance).

Whereas intelligence is the least emotion-related topic we considered, affective forecasts are the most – they are thoughts about emotions. People use anticipated feelings as a way to make decisions and guide behaviour. Interestingly, there are some systematic errors in judgements about future happiness. People tend to overestimate how intense or how long the impact of events will be. This often happens because we focus too narrowly on a particular event or domain, not considering the full breadth of influences on our future happiness. Some overestimates may actually be useful in motivating desirable behaviours. In other domains, however, decisions can be improved by correcting biases (e.g. avoiding the undeserved attraction of nicer climates).

The topic of affective forecasts helps reiterate the intimate connection between cognition and emotion. These topics' separation into different chapters should not imply a robust independence in psychological processes. Chapter 2 described how cognition was essential to emotions. Specifically, the way people (cognitively) interpret their circumstances often determines their emotional responses (e.g. is that rustling in the brush threatening or intriguing?). Conversely, many thought processes depend deeply on emotions. Our feelings influence judgements and cognitive performance. For example, people's reasoning about moral issues (e.g. is it ethical to eat a particular thing?) can hinge on feelings, with rationalization used to support those intuitions (Haidt, 2001). Much of what we learn is driven by the more emotional processes of interest and curiosity. Truly exceptional accomplishment and creative achievements occur when high ability combines with intense emotional drive (and perhaps a bit of luck).

TEST YOURSELF

1. Use a short phrase to describe each of the four Ps in creativity research.

2. Name two individual differences that predict both creativity and wisdom well.

3. Describe at least two features of wise reasoning.

4. What does it mean to say that intellectual ability is hierarchical?

5. Explain why we devote so much energy to education when intelligence is highly heritable.

6. Compare and contrast immune neglect and the focusing illusion.

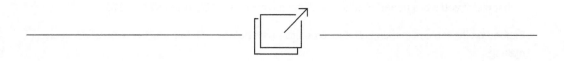

WEB LINKS

A collection of creativity measures curated by Paul Silvia: https://osf.io/4s9p6/

Finding the Next Einstein: a blog on education, intelligence, and accomplishment by Jonathan Wai: www.psychologytoday.com/blog/finding-the-next-einstein

Flynn's entertaining TED talk on increases in intelligence over time: www.youtube.com/watch?v=9vpqilhW9uI

FURTHER READING

This article provides a comprehensive and accessible review of creative genius:

Simonton, D. K. (2012). Creative genius as a personality phenomenon: Definitions, methods, findings, and issues. *Social and Personality Psychology Compass, 6*(9), 691–706.

For a brief review and critical perspective on the malleability of cognitive ability:

Moreau, D., Macnamara, B. N., & Hambrick, D. Z. (2019). Overstating the role of environmental factors in success: A cautionary note. *Current Directions in Psychological Science, 28*(1), 28–33.

This paper reviews a large study that followed very talented people over decades:

Lubinski, D., & Benbow, C. P. (2006). Study of mathematically precocious youth after 35 years. *Perspectives on Psychological Science, 1*(4), 316–345.

This article argues that biases in thinking lead people to overestimate the impact of money on happiness:

Kahneman, D., Krueger, A. B., Schkade, D., Schwarz, N., & Stone, A. A. (2006). Would you be happier if you were richer? A focusing illusion. *Science, 312*(5782), 1908–1910.

Expand on the topic of thinking related to positive psychology with this article on moral decision making:

Conway, P., & Gawronski, B. (2013). Deontological and utilitarian inclinations in moral decision making: A process dissociation approach. *Journal of Personality and Social Psychology, 104*(2), 216–235.

REFERENCES

Ansburg, P. I., & Hill, K. (2003). Creative and analytic thinkers differ in their use of attentional resources. *Personality and Individual Differences, 34*(7), 1141–1152. https://doi.org/10.1016/S0191-8869(02)00104-6

Baas, M., De Dreu, C. K. W., & Nijstad, B. A. (2008). A meta-analysis of 25 years of mood-creativity research: Hedonic tone, activation, or regulatory focus? *Psychological Bulletin, 134*(6), 779–806. https://doi.org/10.1037/a0012815

Baltes, P. B., & Staudinger, U. M. (2000). Wisdom: A metaheuristic (pragmatic) to orchestrate mind and virtue toward excellence. *American Psychologist, 55*(1), 122–136. https://doi.org/10.1037//0003-066X.55.1.122

Batey, M. (2007). *A Psychometric Investigation of Everyday Creativity.* University College, London.

Bowden, E. M., & Jung-Beeman, M. (2003). Normative data for 144 compound remote associate problems. *Behavior Research Methods, Instruments, & Computers, 35*(4), 634–639. https://doi.org/10.3758/BF03195543

Brienza, J. P., Kung, F. Y. H., Santos, H. C., Bobocel, D. R., Grossmann, I., Brienza, J. P., ... Grossmann, I. (2017). Wisdom, bias, and balance: Toward a process-sensitive measurement of wisdom-related cognition. *Journal of Personality and Social Psychology.*

Brinch, C. N., & Galloway, T. A. (2012). Schooling in adolescence raises IQ scores. *Proceedings of the National Academy of Sciences, 109*(2), 425–430. https://doi.org/10.1073/pnas.1106077109

Byron, K., & Khazanchi, S. (2012). Rewards and creative performance: A meta-analytic test of theoretically derived hypotheses. *Psychological Bulletin, 138*(4), 809–830. https://doi.org/10.1037/a0027652

Carson, S. H., Peterson, J. B., & Higgins, D. M. (2003). Decreased latent inhibition is associated with increased creative achievement in high-functioning individuals. *Journal of Personality and Social Psychology, 85*(3), 499–506. https://doi.org/10.1037/0022-3514.85.3.499

Carson, S. H., Peterson, J. B., & Higgins, D. M. (2005). Reliability, validity, and factor structure of the creative achievement questionnaire. *Creativity Research Journal, 17*(1), 79–98. https://doi.org/10.1207/s15326934crj1701

Chabris, C. F., Lee, J. J., Cesarini, D., Benjamin, D. J., & Laibson, D. I. (2015). The fourth law of behavior genetics. *Current Directions in Psychological Science, 24*(4), 304–312. https://doi.org/10.1177/0963721415580430

Crede, M., & Kuncel, N. R. (2008). Study habits, skills, and attitudes. *Perspectives on Psychological Science, 3*(6), 425–454.

Deary, I. J. (2012). Intelligence. *Annual Review of Psychology, 63*, 453–482. https://doi.org/10.1146/annurev-psych-120710-100353

Duckworth, A. L., & Seligman, M. E. P. (2005). Self-discipline outdoes IQ in predicting academic performance of adolescents. *Psychological Science, 16*(12), 939–944. https://doi.org/10.1111/j.1467-9280.2005.01641.x

Dunlosky, J., Rawson, K. A., Marsh, E. J., Nathan, M. J., & Willingham, D. T. (2013). Improving students' learning with effective learning techniques: Promising directions from cognitive and educational psychology. *Psychological Science in the Public Interest, 14*(1) 4–58. https://doi.org/10.1177/1529100612453266

Dunn, E. W., Aknin, L. B., & Norton, M. I. (2008). Spending money on others promotes happiness. *Science, 5870*, 21–23.

Epley, N., & Schroeder, J. (2014). Mistakenly seeking solitude. *Journal of Experimental Psychology: General, 143*, 1980–1999.

Fredrickson, B. L. (1998). What good are positive emotions? *Review of General Psychology, 2*(3), 300–319. https://doi.org/10.1037/1089-2680.2.3.300.

Gardner, H. (2013). "Multiple intelligences" are not "learning styles", *The Washington Post.* Retrieved 9 July 2015, from https://www.washingtonpost.com/news/answer-sheet/wp/2013/10/16/howard-gardner-multiple-intelligences-are-not-learning-styles

Gardner, H., & Moran, S. (2006). The science of multiple intelligences theory: A response to Lynn Waterhouse. *Educational Psychologist, 5*, 227–232. https://doi.org/10.1207/s15326985ep4104

German, T. P., & Defeyter, M. A. (2000). Immunity to functional fixedness in young children. *Psychonomic Bulletin & Review, 7*(4), 707–712. https://doi.org/10.3758/BF03213010

Gilbert, D. T., Pinel, E. C., Wilson, T. D., Blumberg, S. J., & Wheatley, T. P. (1998). Immune neglect: A source of durability bias in affective forecasting. *Journal of Personality and Social Psychology, 75*(3), 617–638. https://doi.org/10.1037/0022-3514.75.3.617

Gopnik, A., O'Grady, S., Lucas, C. G., Griffiths, T. L., Wente, A., Bridgers, S., … Dahl, R. E. (2017). Changes in cognitive flexibility and hypothesis search across human life history from childhood to adolescence to adulthood. *Proceedings of the National Academy of Sciences, 114*(30), 7892–7899. https://doi.org/10.1073/pnas.1700811114

Grossmann, I. (2017). Wisdom in context. *Perspectives on Psychological Science*, *12*(2), 233–257. https://doi.org/10.1177/1745691616672066

Grossmann, I., & Kross, E. (2014). Exploring Solomon's paradox: Self-distancing eliminates the self-other asymmetry in wise reasoning about close relationships in younger and older adults. *Psychological Science*, *25*(8), 1571–1580. https://doi.org/10.1177/0956797614535400

Haidt, J. (2001). The emotional dog and its rational tail: A social intuitionist approach to moral judgment. *Psychological Review*, *108*(4), 814–834.

Hambrick, D. Z., & Chabris, C. (2014). What do SAT and IQ tests measure? General intelligence predicts school and life success. Retrieved 16 April 2014, from www.slate.com/articles/health_and_science/science/2014/04/what_do_sat_and_iq_tests_measure_general_intelligence_predicts_school_and.single.html

Hsee, C. K., & Hastie, R. (2006). Decision and experience: Why don't we choose what makes us happy? *Trends in Cognitive Sciences*, *10*(1), 31–37. https://doi.org/10.1016/j.tics.2005.11.007

Isen, A. M., Daubman, K. A., & Nowicki, G. P. (1987). Positive affect facilitates creative problem solving. *Journal of Personality and Social Psychology*, *52*(6), 1122–1131. https://doi.org/0.1037/0022-3514.52.6.1122

Johnson, W. (2010). Understanding the genetics of intelligence: Can height help? Can corn oil? *Current Directions in Psychological Science*, *19*(3), 177–182. https://doi.org/10.1177/0963721410370136

Johnson, W., & Bouchard, T. J. (2005). The structure of human intelligence: It is verbal, perceptual, and image rotation (VPR), not fluid and crystallized. *Intelligence*, *33*(4), 393–416. http://doi.org/10.1016/j.intell.2004.12.002

Joseph, D. L., & Newman, D. A. (2010). Emotional intelligence: An integrative meta-analysis and cascading model. *Journal of Applied Psychology*, *95*(1), 54–78. https://doi.org/10.1037/a0017286

Kandler, C., Riemann, R., Angleitner, A., Spinath, F. M., Borkenau, P., & Penke, L. (2016). The nature of creativity: The roles of genetic factors, personality traits, cognitive abilities, and environmental sources. *Journal of Personality and Social Psychology*, *111*, 230–249. https://doi.org/10.1037/pspp0000087

Kaufman, S. B., Quilty, L. C., Grazioplene, R. G., Hirsh, J. B., Gray, J. R., Peterson, J. B., & Deyoung, C. G. (2016). Openness to experience and intellect differentially predict creative achievement in the arts and sciences. *Journal of Personality*, *84*(2), 248–258. https://doi.org/10.1111/jopy.12156

Kell, H. J., Lubinski, D., & Benbow, C. P. (2013). Who rises to the top? Early indicators. *Psychological Science*, *24*(5), 648–659. https://doi.org/10.1177/0956797612457784

Kozhevnikov, M., Evans, C., & Kosslyn, S. M. (2014). Cognitive style as environmentally sensitive individual differences in cognition: A modern synthesis and applications in education, business, and management. *Psychological Science in the Public Interest*, *15*(1), 3–33. https://doi.org/10.1177/1529100614525555

Krulwich, R. (2014). How to marry the right girl: A mathematical solution [Krulwich Wonders blog]. Retrieved 15 May 2014, from www.npr.org/blogs/krul wich/2014/05/15/312537965/how-to-marry-the-right-girl-amathematical-Solution

Kuncel, N. R., & Hezlett, S. A. (2010). Fact and fiction in cognitive ability testing for admissions and hiring decisions. *Current Directions in Psychological Science*, *19*(6), 339–345. https://doi.org/10.1177/0963721410389459

Leung, A. K., Maddux, W. W., Galinsky, A. D., & Chiu, C. (2008). Multicultural experience enhances creativity: The when and how. *American Psychologist*, *63*(3), 169–181. https://doi.org/10.1037/0003-066X.63.3.169

Levine, L. J., Lench, H. C., Kaplan, R. L., & Safer, M. A. (2013). Like Schrödinger's cat, the impact bias is both dead and alive: Reply to Wilson and Gilbert (2013). *Journal of Personality and Social Psychology*, *105*(5), 749–756. https://doi.org/10.1037/a0034340

Lubinski, D. (2004). Introduction to the special section on cognitive abilities: 100 years after Spearman's (1904) "'General Intelligence,' Objectively Determined and Measured". *Journal of Personality and Social Psychology*, *86*(1), 96–111. https://doi.org/10.1037/0022-3514.86.1.96

Lubinski, D. (2009). Exceptional cognitive ability: The phenotype. *Behavior Genetics*, *39*(4), 350–358. https://doi.org/10.1007/s10519-009-9273-0

Lucas, R. E., & Lawless, N. M. (2013). Does life seem better on a sunny day? Examining the association between daily weather conditions and life satisfaction judgments. *Journal of Personality and Social Psychology*, *104*(5), 872–884. https://doi.org/10.1037/a0032124

McCrae, R. R. (1987). Creativity, divergent thinking, and openness to experience. *Journal of Personality and Social Psychology*, *52*(6), 1258–1265. https://doi.org/10.1037/00223514.52.6.1258

Mednick, S. (1962). The associative basis of the creative process. *Psychological Review*, *69*(3), 220–232. https://doi.org/10.1037/h0048850

Moreau, D., Macnamara, B. N., & Hambrick, D. Z. (2019). Overstating the role of environmental factors in success: A cautionary note. *Current Directions in Psychological Science*, *28*(1), 28–33.

Nisbet, E. K., & Zelenski, J. M. (2011). Underestimating nearby nature: Affective forecasting errors obscure the happy path to sustainability. *Psychological Science*, *22*(9), 1101–1106. https://doi.org/10.1177/0956797611418527

Oishi, S., Tsutsui, Y., Eggleston, C., & Galinha, I. C. (2014). Are maximizers unhappier than satisficers? A comparison between Japan and the USA. *Journal of Research in Personality*, *49*, 14–20. https://doi.org/10.1016/J.JRP.2013.12.001

Peterson, C., & Seligman, M. E. P. (2004). *Character Strengths and Virtues: A Handbook and Classification.* New York: Oxford University Press and Washington, DC: American Psychological Association.

Pietschnig, J., & Voracek, M. (2015). One century of global IQ gains: A formal meta-analysis of the Flynn effect (1909-2013). *Perspectives on Psychological Science*, *10*(3), 282–306. https://doi.org/10.1177/1745691615577701

Poropat, A. E. (2009). A meta-analysis of the five-factor model of personality and academic performance. *Psychological Bulletin, 135*(2), 322–338. https://doi.org/10.1037/a0014996

Rhodes, M. (1961). An analysis of creativity. *The Phi Delta Kappan, 42*(7), 305–310. https://doi.org/10.2307/20342603

Ritchie, S., & Tucker-Drob, E. (2018). How much does education improve intelligence? A meta-analysis. *Psychological Science, 29*(8), 1358–1369. https://doi.org/10.1177/09567976 18774253

Ritter, S. M., Damian, R. I., Simonton, D. K., van Baaren, R. B., Strick, M., Derks, J., & Dijksterhuis, A. (2012). Diversifying experiences enhance cognitive flexibility. *Journal of Experimental Social Psychology, 48*(4), 961–964. https://doi.org/10.1016/j.jesp.2012.02.009

Roberts, R. D., MacCann, C., Matthews, G., & Zeidner, M. (2010). Emotional intelligence: Toward a consensus of models and measures. *Social and Personality Psychology Compass, 4*(10), 821–840. https://doi.org/10.1111/j.1751-9004.2010.00277.x

Runco, M. A. (2004). Creativity. *Annual Review of Psychology, 55*(1), 657–687. https://doi.org/10.1146/annurev.psych.55.090902.141502

Runco, M. A., & Acar, S. (2012). Divergent thinking as an indicator of creative potential. *Creativity Research Journal, 24*(1), 66–75. https://doi.org/10.1080/10400419.2012.652929

Schkade, D. A., & Kahneman, D. (1998). Does living in California make people happy? A focusing illusion in judgments of life satisfaction. *Psychological Science, 9*(5), 340–346. https://doi.org/10.1111/1467-9280.00066

Schmidt, F. L., & Hunter, J. E. (1998). The validity and utility of selection methods in personnel psychology: Practical and theoretical implications of 85 years of research findings. *Psychological Bulletin, 124*(2), 262–274. https://doi.org/10.1037/0033-2909.124.2.262

Schwartz, B., & Sharpe, K. E. (2006). Practical wisdom: Aristotle meets positive psychology. *Journal of Happiness Studies, 7*(3), 377–395. https://doi.org/10.1007/s10902-005-3651-y

Schwartz, B., Ward, A., Lyubomirsky, S., Monterosso, J., White, K., & Lehman, D. R. (2002). Maximizing versus satisficing: Happiness is a matter of choice. *Journal of Personality and Social Psychology, 83*(5), 1178–1197. https://doi.org/10.1037//0022-3514.83.5.1178

Silvia, P. J., Wigert, B., Reiter-Palmon, R., & Kaufman, J. C. (2012). Assessing creativity with self-report scales: A review and empirical evaluation. *Psychology of Aesthetics, Creativity, and the Arts, 6*(1), 19–34. https://doi.org/10.1037/a0024071

Silvia, P. J., Winterstein, B. P., Willse, J. T., Barona, C. M., Cram, J. T., Hess, K. I., … Richard, C. A. (2008). Assessing creativity with divergent thinking tasks: Exploring the reliability and validity of new subjective scoring methods. *Psychology of Aesthetics, Creativity, and the Arts, 2*(2), 68–85. https://doi.org/10.1037/1931-3896.2.2.68

Simonsohn, U., Nelson, L. D., & Simmons, J. P. (2014). p-Curve and effect size: Correcting for publication bias using only significant results. *Perspectives on Psychological Science, 9*(6), 666–681. https://doi.org/10.1177/1745691614553988

Simonton, D. K. (1991). Emergence and realization of genius: The lives and works of 120 classical composers. *Journal of Personality and Social Psychology, 61*(5), 829–840. https://doi. org/10.1037/0022-3514.61.5.829

Simonton, D. K. (2009). Creativity. In S. J. Lopez & C. R. Snyder (eds), *The Oxford Handbook of Positive Psychology* (2nd edn, pp. 261–270). New York: Oxford University Press.

Simonton, D. K. (2012). Creative genius as a personality phenomenon: Definitions, methods, findings, and issues. *Social and Personality Psychology Compass, 6*(9), 691–706. https://doi. org/10.1111/j.1751-9004.2012.00455.x

Staudinger, U. M., & Glück, J. (2011). Psychological wisdom research: Commonalities and differences in a growing field. *Annual Review of Psychology, 62*(1), 215–241. https://doi. org/10.1146/annurev.psych.121208.131659

Staudinger, U. M., Lopez, D. F., & Baltes, P. B. (1997). The psychometric location of wisdom-related performance: Intelligence, personality, and more? *Personality and Social Psychology Bulletin, 23*, 1200–1214.

Sternberg, R. J. (1998). A balance theory of wisdom. *Review of General Psychology, 2*(4), 347–365. https://doi.org/10.1037/1089-2680.2.4.347

Stieger, S., Götz, F. M., & Gehrig, F. (2015). Soccer results affect subjective well-being, but only briefly: A smartphone study during the 2014 FIFA World Cup. *Frontiers in Psychology, 6*, 497. https://doi.org/10.3389/fpsyg.2015.00497

Visser, B. A., Ashton, M. C., & Vernon, P. A. (2006). Beyond g: Putting multiple intelligences theory to the test. *Intelligence, 34*(5), 487–502. https://doi.org/10.1016/j.intell.2006.02.004

Wai, J., Lubinski, D., & Benbow, C. P. (2009). Spatial ability for STEM domains: Aligning over 50 years of cumulative psychological knowledge solidifies its importance. *Journal of Educational Psychology, 101*(4), 817–835. https://doi.org/10.1037/a0016127

Webster, J. D. (2007). Measuring the character strength of wisdom. *The International Journal of Aging and Human Development, 65*(2), 163–183. https://doi.org/10.2190/AG.65.2.d

Wilson, T. D., & Gilbert, D. T. (2005). Affective forecasting: Knowing what to want. *Current Directions in Psychological Science, 14*(3), 131–134. https://doi.org/10.1111/j.0963-7214.2005.00355.x

Wilson, T. D., Wheatley, T., Meyers, J. M., Gilbert, D. T., & Axsom, D. (2000). Focalism: Source of durability bias in affective forecasting. *Journal of Personality and Social Psychology, 78*(5), 821–836. https://doi.org/10.1037/0022-3514.78.5.821

Wink, P., & Staudinger, U. M. (2016). Wisdom and psychosocial functioning in later life. *Journal of Personality, 84*(3), 306–318. https://doi.org/10.1111/jopy.12160

Wrulich, M., Brunner, M., Stadler, G., Schalke, D., Keller, U., & Martin, R. (2014). Forty years on: Childhood intelligence predicts health in middle adulthood. *Health Psychology, 33*(3), 292–296. https://doi.org/10.1037/a0030727

Part IV

Social, Psychological,
and Physical
Environments

7

Social and Physical Environments

INTRODUCTION

Imagine Leningrad, Soviet Union in 1941. The city is under siege with Nazi soldiers invading from the south and Finnish soldiers blocking the north. The siege will last for more than two years. Food, water, and other essentials of life will become incredibly scarce. Yet in this chaos and mass starvation sits a building full of food that is not eaten. It is a seed bank created by Nikolai Vavilov. Ironically, the purpose of this collection was to prevent hunger. Years earlier Vavilov realized how much human well-being depended on natural forces after witnessing crop failures and mass starvations. He embarked on a project to collect, study, and preserve thousands of crop seeds (rice, beans, wheat, etc.) that could withstand various harsh and unpredictable growing conditions. At the time of the siege, Vavilov was in prison – the reason was little more than having misguided but powerful enemies in Stalin's government – but he had already recruited a team of followers who were caring for the secret seed collection as the Nazi army threatened the city. As the siege went on, those guardians literally began to starve to death. People were found dead still clasping the envelopes of beans and rice that they could have eaten to save their lives. They literally chose personal starvation to ensure that the seed collection – which had so much potential to prevent mass starvations in the future – was preserved. Vavilov also died of starvation in prison. Their heroic sacrifices played out over years, but the seed bank did survive. (For a full version of the story consult the Endless Thread podcast: www.wbur.org/endlessthread/2018/01/26/the-vault)

The Leningrad seed bank story touches on key themes addressed in this chapter. Vavilov was inspired to collect seeds because he recognized the importance of nature in meeting human needs. We will discuss less dramatic and more positive ways that nature, from house-plants to forests, can contribute to well-being. In addition, the guardians of Vavilov's seeds show how people (sometimes) perform dramatic altruistic acts, sacrificing themselves for the greater good. We will consider acts like these, along with the considerably more mundane ways people get along with one another in day-to-day life. Connecting these ideas – nature and prosociality – is the notion that the contexts we find ourselves in – physical and social environments – matter greatly for people's individual and collective well-being. Currently, Vavilov's legacy is evident in a massive international seed vault in Svalbard, Norway. Here, seeds from North Korea sit peacefully right next to seeds from South Korea, Sudan, and so on, preserving genetic biodiversity in a world threatened by changing climate. As one more link, human cooperation is becoming essential to preserving environmental health.

SOCIAL ENVIRONMENTS: HUMAN NATURE AND COOPERATION

Other people create contexts with profound effects on our choices, behaviour, and well-being. For example, when you wake up in the morning, you might keep quiet if someone is sleeping in the next room. As you choose breakfast items, you might consider others' preferences in making choices, or be frustrated that someone else took the last of your favourite. When you decide about your seat on the bus, which side of the path you will walk down, and whether or not you will whistle while you work, it will depend on the people around you. Even when others are not physically present, they exert an influence through social norms, expectations, or imagined future consequences. These social forces are particularly evident in our close relationships, but they come from complete strangers too.

Perhaps you are someone who does not think much about these things (i.e. low in 'social mindfulness'; see Van Doesum, Van Lange, & Van Lange, 2013). Still, other people's choices create and constrain the opportunities you have, be it small things like an open bus seat or more consequential things like an available spot in your preferred university programme. More broadly, the food you eat, clothes you wear, and bed you sleep in all depend on other people linked via complex social systems. The obvious point here is that even the most solitary or self-centred people cannot detach themselves from pervasive social influences. Humans are amazingly interconnected.

As such, every chapter of this book touches on social relationships in some way. Our focus in this chapter is on how people get along with one another, and to examine this issue with our customary focus on the positive. This chapter is less about close relationships (e.g. love and positive relationship dynamics are the focus of Chapter 8), and more about how people cooperate via loose or anonymous ties. We will consider how the context of social problems prompts solutions (or not), noting roles for personality and underlying thought processes along the way.

Evolutionary Perspectives

Humans' extreme interconnectedness is indisputable; yet the form of those connections is described in deeply divergent ways. For example, some see human nature as ultimately selfish and competitive with individuals striving to get ahead of others. Others argue that people are driven by cooperative motives to get along and help others thrive collectively. Take a moment to consider your assumptions here: do you think human nature is generally more competitive or more cooperative?

When thinking about this question, it is easy to find anecdotal examples on both sides: exceptional altruism and devastating cruelty. Characterizing human nature as simply cooperative or competitive makes it difficult to explain both extremes. You might expect a positive psychology textbook to argue forcefully for niceness (cooperation) in human nature – and some of that argument is coming. However, ignoring interpersonal struggle seems unwise too. Recall Chapter 1's warning against making an ideological assumption about human nature. As a scientific enterprise, positive psychology should examine rather than assume. Moreover, the important goal of balancing pre-positive psychology is lost if the darker sides are denied, swinging the pendulum too far in the opposite direction.

So, let us begin with the notion that people have some tendencies towards selfishness, competitiveness, and perhaps even cruelty. Keep in mind that these impulses are not always dark. We value power and victory (e.g. in business, politics, sport) – even when it imparts costs to others, so long as those costs are not too extreme or unfair. However, we also value generosity, compassion, and helping. Recent arguments and research in (positive) psychology suggest that these prosocial impulses may be equally basic to human nature. Clever experiments show that people's impulses are sometimes cooperative; doing the nice thing does not always require overriding a selfish desire. In sum, this section does not quibble with the idea that human nature is selfish (in part), but rather argues that it is also prosocial. In this domain, humans seem to have dual natures.

Despite the potential complexity of dual competitive and cooperative natures, social scientists can account for both with a few relatively simple ideas from evolutionary theory. You may be surprised to see evolution being invoked as a basis for human generosity. Evolution is often characterized in more competitive terms, such as 'survival of the fittest' or about 'selfish genes'. However, the competition among genes need not translate into combat between human beings. Popular imagination (as evidenced by internet image searches) seems to interpret 'survival of the fittest' as predator–prey action sequences and hot human bodies, but there are other strategic routes to survival and flourishing. For example, human children require an exceptional amount of nurturing – that nurturing is an adaptation shaped by evolution.

In his book *Born to be Good*, Dacher Keltner (2009) argues for a positive human nature, and notes that Darwin himself was a softie when it came to highlighting humanity's compassionate tendencies. Both suggest that there are adaptive benefits of feeling sympathy for others, and that humans have exploited this social niche. Taking a step back, natural selection occurs when some genes are passed to future generations more frequently than others. In addition to survival, reproduction is key. More adaptive genes become more common in future generations (better survival and more offspring); less helpful genes decline and perhaps even disappear in future generations. In this way, genes are selfish and competitive. Natural selection works as some genes win out over others. Fitness, however, describes any effective strategy, be it a killer instinct, camouflage, helping, or love.

While we are clarifying terms, it is important to keep in mind that **prosocial behaviour** refers to anything that increases another's well-being, such as helping, sharing, or cooperation. If that behaviour also increases the actor's well-being, it is still counts as prosocial – even if personal gain motivated the prosocial behaviour. For example, giving a gift to someone is a prosocial act whether or not it comes just before asking a big favour. Here, we can make a distinction with **altruism**, where actions benefit someone else, without clear personal benefit, or even at a potential cost to the actor. Given the many potential indirect benefits of prosocial behaviour (e.g. good moods, earned gratitude, reputation) it is difficult to know conclusively that an act is unambiguously altruistic. As such, the definition of altruism is commonly expanded to include prosocial behaviours that are performed without (conscious) regard to potential personal benefits, even if they may eventually accrue. A classic approach in social psychology – the **empathy– altruism model** – articulates this view: people sometimes help without regard to personal costs and benefits, and this happens when they have empathetic concern for a person in need (Batson, Ahmad, & Lishner, 2009). Still, even if not part of the immediate decision making, the long view of evolutionary theory suggests some personal benefits can accrue from such 'altruistic' acts (Curry, Rowland, Van Lissa, Zlotowitz, McAlaney, & Whitehouse, 2018).

An expansive view of prosocial behaviour makes it easier to see how it could evolve from selfish genes. That is, to the extent that personal benefits also accrue from kindness, that kindness can be an adaptation. By giving, I (and my genes) might also succeed. To be more specific, the clearest form of adaptive prosociality is when people help members of their biological family. Parents give much to their children, but those children share many genes with their parents. From an evolutionary point of view, those genes are helping themselves. This logic spreads through the family tree. In fact, studies suggest that people's degree of helpfulness depends on genetic relatedness. We are more apt to help close relatives (who share more genes) than distant relatives (who share fewer genes), all else being equal (Burnstein, Crandall, & Kitayama, 1994). The term **kin altruism** describes prosocial actions directed towards genetic relatives which, in turn, helps propagate shared genes.

Kin altruism follows easily from evolutionary theory with its clear genetic benefits, but much prosocial behaviour is directed towards non-relatives. To explain this prosociality, evolutionary theories invoke two ideas: reciprocal altruism and competitive altruism. (Both of these jargon terms again use 'altruism' loosely, where actors do ultimately gain fitness via their prosociality.)

Reciprocal altruism is the idea that people will help one another, over time (Trivers, 1971). This is an adaptation because people who exchange favours and cooperate will succeed more than those who do not. Imagine our hominid ancestors who shared food, fire, and protection in ways that increased survival for all, compared to the non-cooperators. There are also potential costs or risks in giving to others. It follows that people have evolved some sensitivity to noticing cheaters – those who only take but do not reciprocate – to mitigate these risks. As a result, prosociality will vary across contexts and with the trustworthiness of targets. Reciprocal altruism suggests that we are more likely to engage in prosocial behaviour with people who will be able to reciprocate, such as those who we will see again or are part of our in-group. However, reciprocal altruism has a harder time explaining generous acts towards strangers, such as giving a meal to travellers as they pass through town. Evolutionary theory has a different answer for these forms of prosociality: competitive altruism.

Competitive altruism (or 'costly signalling') describes prosocial acts where the individual benefits are indirect; they accrue via improvements to one's reputation (Gintis, Smith, & Bowles, 2001). For example, if a person throws lavish parties and gifts generously, it signals that the person has many resources – an attractive quality in a mate (friend) or a mate (lover). Just as the peacock's enormous tail is adaptive in signalling health, rather than its raw survival value, generous acts can signal fitness and boost status. If other people see you helping a stranger, you may gain a positive reputation which ultimately translates into your genes being passed on to the next generation (e.g. you become attractive to that cutie next door). The stranger may not reciprocate herself (e.g. she is just passing through town), but the prosocial act boosts status and signals to others that you are a good cooperation partner in the future. Risky and heroic acts of bravery can similarly generate status, signalling that this is a capable, prosocial person to have around.

To be clear, bravery and compassionate help do not imply consciously selfish or sexual motives. The long-term evolutionary benefit is not the same as the momentary (conscious) processes that facilitate it. In the moment, feeling empathy for the person in need prompts a desire to help – a tendency shared by some close non-human evolutionary relatives like chimpanzees (de Waal, 2008). The ultimate evolutionary goal (increasing genes in future generations) is distinct from the immediate experience (feeling empathy and helping). As another example, most sex is pursued for pleasure (momentary) rather than procreation (ultimate evolutionary benefit). Interestingly, research on sex supports the notion that prosocial behaviour is an adaptation. Recent studies found that people who self-reported more prosocial behaviour, or demonstrated it in a lab setting, also reported more lifetime sex, dating partners, offspring, and income (Arnocky, Piché, Albert, Ouellette, & Barclay, 2017; Eriksson, Vartanova, Strimling, & Simpson, 2018). Evolutionary selection allows these characteristics to become part of human nature and may even help explain why we morally value altruism (i.e. it is good for the genes). However, survival and reproduction are often far from the minds of prosocial actors. The genes can be selfish, even while the humans have altruistic intentions. It is also possible for prosocial impulses to be non-adaptive in particular circumstances (e.g. perhaps heroism leading to death); evolution is about long-term averages, not single situations. Finally, to the extent that prosocial behaviour is indeed adaptive, it is likely to feel good (Buss, 2000). Research supports the notion that prosocial behaviours improve moods (Curry et al., 2018).

In sum, nurturing, cooperation, and helping are all compatible with evolution and can be seen as useful human adaptations. (Again, this does not negate the idea that violence too can be an adaptation in other circumstances.) Researchers sometimes draw on evolutionary theory to make more specific predictions about where we will find more and less cooperation (i.e. the circumstances where it was better or worse for genes, on average). Things become complex at they get specific, so we will leave evolution here the broad level, and turn to describing some of the social circumstances that tempt both selfish and prosocial aspects of human natures.

Social Dilemmas

Setting aside the grandiose language around basic human nature, many situations present a choice between selfish and more prosocial actions. For example, if you find a wallet full of cash on the street, do you take the money, return the wallet, or both? Beyond such mini moral dilemmas, the conflict between immediate self-interest and the larger collective good underlies many important social issues, such as traffic, taxation, and trade. In order to live together in thriving societies, people must (sometimes) act in prosocial ways, giving up opportunities to maximize short-term individual gains. **Social dilemmas** are these situations where individuals must choose between maximizing immediate personal benefit or contributing to collective well-being, and where the system breaks down unless enough people cooperate.

The oft-used phrase 'tragedy of the commons' describes a failure of cooperation, such that an important resource is lost (Hardin, 1968). In the classic example, individual farmers share a common pasture with a limited capacity. Every individual farmer faces a temptation to graze more cows, thereby increasing profits. However, if too many cows graze the shared pasture, all the grass dies – the cows and people could follow soon after. When too many people make the selfish choice, tragedy ensues.

Shared pastures are not among our most urgent issues today, but the collective logic has many parallels, for example with climate change (where cows remain an issue due to their 'emissions'). Nations, industries, and individuals must consider driving their productivity with fossil fuels against the environmental and economic damages of climate change. As with the common pasture, avoiding tragedy requires broad cooperation (i.e. limited emissions), and each individual's fate depends on others' behaviour. Global climate change is a grand challenge, but humans have faced similar collective problems throughout history. Fortunately, people often find ways to work collectively and thus sustain common resources (Ostrom, 2009). This observation – at odds with the notion that people behave in narrowly selfish ways unless restrained by a government – won Elinor Ostrom the Nobel Prize in Economics.

Social dilemmas are studied broadly across the social sciences (e.g. by economists, anthropologists, and sociologists) because the logic of dilemmas applies to so many important issues. Positive psychology can contribute too. Solving social dilemmas is ultimately about healthy interpersonal relationships, and human flourishing depends on successful solutions. Also, not all dilemmas are about avoiding tragedy; some describe the cooperation needed to create new benefits.

Social scientists identify two broad categories of social dilemmas: common pool resources and public goods (Van Lange, Joireman, Parks, & Van Dijk, 2013). In **common pool resource dilemmas**, some good already exists and people can draw from that good; they are called 'take some' dilemmas. Most natural resources (e.g. pastures, water, oil, fish) fit this description, as do most environmental issues. For example, creating pollution might be necessary to create a product, but there is a limit to how much pollution the environment can absorb, and everyone suffers from poor environmental conditions. (Here a clean environment is a resource that is 'consumed'.) As long as people take from a common pool at a sustainable rate, there is no problem. However, a dilemma arises when individuals are tempted to take more. If too many over-harvest the resource, it vanishes – we see the tragedy of the commons. These dilemmas are especially difficult at large scales. For example, it is hard to imagine how one individual's choices could have any meaningful impact on global fish stocks; however, if everyone takes this truism to mean that their behaviour does not matter – tragedy.

Problems with common pools develop over time. At the beginning, the resource is abundant, and it is easy to take. It is tempting to take a little extra because the negative consequences are diffuse and shared by all. Moreover, there is uncertainty about how others will behave. Even if you consume at a sustainable rate, others may still over-harvest the resource to the point of depletion. These challenges make sustaining a common resource difficult, but it can be done.

In contrast to resource dilemmas, **public goods dilemmas** are about creating a benefit that does not yet exist; some people contribute resources to create a good that benefits everyone, regardless of individuals' contribution levels. Public goods dilemmas are thus called 'give some' dilemmas. For example, things like libraries, bridges, and charity programmes are public goods. Once created, they are open to all who need them. As another example, democratic government requires voting, time, and resources (via taxes) – it is a public good (most of the time). Yet, as with other public goods, people who dodge the costs (taxes and voting) still benefit from the stable society that government creates.

With public goods dilemmas, there is a delay between contributing and reaping the benefit. In addition, they often include some uncertainty that enough resources will be gathered to actually create the good. This is exacerbated by the 'free rider' problem. For any one individual, it seems irrational to contribute to a public good when it is possible to enjoy the benefits without contributing. Of course, if everyone thinks this way, the good will not exist – hence the dilemma. In contrast to common pool dilemmas, the challenge of public goods is in getting started; yet once started, the good persists easily. As such, public goods dilemmas are sometimes called social fences (the challenge is upfront), whereas common resource dilemmas are called social traps (problems develop with time).

Although real world social dilemmas are abundant, researchers often adapt them to the psychology laboratory for more controlled study. For example, groups of research participants might 'go fishing' in a simulation where they are paid for each fish they harvest, and where the fish are replenished over time depending on how many are left (much like spawning in a real lake). Participants face choices about how many fish to catch, and at what rate, while considering what other fishers might do. Harvesting can be sustainable, but with rapid gathering the fish will go extinct. This is an example of a common resource dilemma, translated to a lab simulation (J. Gifford & Gifford, 2000). Various features can be altered (e.g. number of fishers, allowing communication or not, rate of replenishment) to determine which influence cooperation and sustainable harvesting. (See the Research Case box later for an example of a public goods dilemma.)

In social dilemmas, people are collectively better off with cooperation. Social scientists have learned much about the factors that seem to promote or hinder these prosocial behaviours. Some of the important factors have more to do with the dilemma itself. For example (adapted from review by Parks, Joireman, & Van Lange, 2013):

- Cooperation is higher when the dilemma is framed as an ethical decision, and lower when framed as a business decision.

- Cooperation is lower when there is uncertainty about the size of resources or the rate of replenishment (common resources), or uncertainty about exactly how much is needed to provide a public good.

- Cooperation is higher when resources are seen as owned by a community, rather than as private property.

- Cooperation is higher when people believe they will interact repeatedly (vs a one-time decision). Actual past experience with the dilemma also promotes cooperation.

In addition to the dilemma itself, aspects of the social situation can promote or hinder cooperation. For example (again, see Parks et al., 2013 for details):

- Allowing communication among people promotes cooperation.

- Smaller groups tend to be more cooperative than larger groups.

- Cooperative norms and knowing that similar others cooperate help promote prosocial choices.

- Adding rewards for cooperation or punishments for non-cooperation increases cooperation.

- Respect from leaders and fair treatment within groups promotes cooperation.

- Cooperation increases within a group when competing against another out-group.

Finally, personality plays a role in when and how much people cooperate. People who are higher in trust (a facet of big five agreeableness) tend to cooperate more (Balliet & Van Lange, 2013), as do people prone to thinking more about the future (associated with big five conscientiousness; Kortenkamp & Moore, 2006). More directly related to social dilemmas, the Try It box demonstrates a questionnaire measure of **Social Value Orientation (SVO)**. Individual differences in SVO predict how people respond in other social dilemmas – both lab-based and in real world volunteering, charity, and pro-environmental behaviours (Balliet, Parks, & Joireman, 2009). Three orientations are typically distinguished: prosocial, individualist, and competitive. People with a prosocial orientation tend to be more cooperative in general. Their primary goal is to maximize the collective good, and they prefer equality. People who are more individualist oriented seek to maximize their personal gains, without much regard for others' outcomes. Their choices are sometimes seen as 'rational' because they fit with the simplest economic assumptions about self-interest, or 'homo economicus', at least in the short term. People with a competitive orientation are even less prosocial; they seek to maximize a relative advantage over others, even if it means they give up some personal benefit in absolute terms. For example, competitive people prefer to allocate $50 to self and $10 to another ($40 advantage) than $60 to self and $40 to another (potentially more to self, but only $20 advantage).

As with most things, personality differences can also interact with features of particular situations. For example, prosocials tend to cooperate more when a dilemma is framed as 'give-some' (by giving more), whereas individualists cooperate more with a 'take-some' framing (by taking less; De Dreu & McCusker, 1997). Moreover, social value orientations describe general personality tendencies, but some circumstances will exert stronger influence – even competitively oriented people will sometimes cooperate.

TRY IT

The Social Value Orientation Slider

Here are the instructions and some example items from a questionnaire-based measure of social value orientation (Murphy, Ackermann, & Handgraaf, 2011). For additional information see: http://ryanomurphy.com/styled-2/index.html

(Continued)

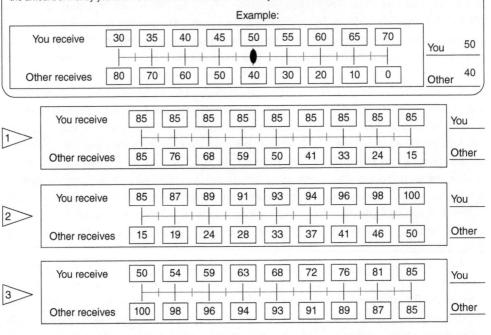

Figure 7.1

Solving Social Dilemmas

Social scientists, policy makers, and most other people try to discover and generate the circumstances that promote cooperation. One obvious way to increase cooperation is to change the incentives of the dilemma. A government might create tax incentives for reducing pollution, thus making it more attractive to industry. A roommate might begin nagging incessantly, making it less pleasant to leave dirty dishes lying around. Beyond changing the actual incentives (i.e. the raw cost–benefit analysis), such actions can also change perceptions of social norms and what others will do. For example, knowing that punishment looms for those who do not cooperate makes it seem more likely that others will comply, even for anonymous others in large groups. This, in turn, makes it easier to cooperate because the collectively successful outcome (i.e. preserving a resource or providing a new public good) seems more likely – others will follow incentives too. In other words, believing that others will cooperate helps remove some individual psychological barriers. Moreover, when cooperation is seen as normative, social pressure works towards a prosocial default. It is uncomfortable to be the lone jerk who fails to cooperate. Without cooperative social norms, pressure can work the other way – no one wants to be a naïve chump either. In sum, adding incentives, sanctions, or enforcement changes both the raw calculation and the social pressures.

Across many studies, rewards and punishments typically work well in nudging people towards more cooperative behaviours (Balliet, Mulder, & Van Lange, 2011). That said, every instance is unique, and incentives can backfire by reducing people's intrinsic motivation for prosocial behaviours (Deci & Ryan, 2000); in other words, the good behaviour becomes contingent on the reward, rather than motivated by a deeper personal desire. Similarly, punishment in the form of fees can change an ethical decision to an economic calculation, which can then make prosocial behaviour less likely. For example, one study found that adding a fee for late day-care pickups seemed to increase their occurrence (Gneezy & Rustichini, 2000) – the interpretation here is that busy parents were willing to pay when a price was set, but had experienced guilt about being late without the fee.

Depending on the particular dilemma, the lists in the previous section might suggest other feasible routes to better cooperation, such as promoting communication, linking people in repeated choices, or providing concrete information or goals. Even with these features, much of the challenge in social dilemmas is the uncertainty about how others will behave. Thus, increasing trust is often key to their solutions.

Trust develops via positive experiences with cooperation, and people are often willing to give cooperation a try. However, negative experiences are particularly powerful. Trust builds slowly via mutual cooperation, compared to how quickly it erodes with cheating. For this reason, relatively infrequent moments of greed – or even miscommunication and accidents – can derail cooperation among people who would actually prefer to do it. One successful way to combat the effects of infrequent cheating is with generosity. That is, even for people who are seeking to maximize personal benefit, generosity is a wise tactic – within limits. Of course it makes sense to stop cooperating with people who never reciprocate; however, both computer simulations and experiments with people suggest that responding to some initial or infrequent cheating with more cooperation often elicits reciprocity (Klapwijk & Van Lange, 2009; Wu & Axelrod, 1995). Ultimately, it is beneficial to cooperate with people who will (usually) reciprocate – this produces better outcomes than going it alone. However, when people are quick to retaliate against bad behaviour, they inhibit potential cooperation in cases where cheating is based on errors or temporary circumstances, rather than unwillingness to cooperate over the long term. In the real world, apologies and forgiveness play an important role in repairing cooperative relationships (R. Fehr, Gelfand, & Nag, 2010), a topic ripe for further exploration by positive psychologists.

Cooperation and trust are also more frequent among people who share a common identity. For example, one experiment asked psychology students to consider a situation where another student would allocate money to them. When they were told the other student was also a psychology major (shared in-group), students believed they would get larger allocations, compared to when they thought the allocator was a nursing or economics major (Foddy, Platow, & Yamagishi, 2009). Such group biases are a double-edged sword. They promote cooperation with in-group members, but hinder cooperation with out-group members. Still, both tendencies can be harnessed towards the greater good.

Inter-group competition might be harnessed towards prosocial ends by making those ends the measure of victory. For example, a campus charity event might award a prize to the student group that raises the most funds. Groups compete, but the charity benefits. Social dilemma researchers suggest that even global issues like climate change might be solved when nations compete against one another for moral high ground or green economic development (Van Lange, Joireman, & Milinski, 2018). National goals might then trickle down to competitions between cities, or even to contests to reduce energy use across different university residence buildings. Even if working towards a common national goal, smaller group identities might provide a basis for helpful competition.

Alternatively, policy makers and persuaders might focus on building towards larger common identities. People can see themselves as part of a family, neighbourhood, city, gender, religion, sports team, and so on, and these different identities are not mutually exclusive. By using larger and more inclusive identities – such as a common humanity – the scope of cooperation can be increased across narrower identities that would otherwise suggest outgroups. Rather than stoking competition, this approach seeks to build trust though unity. Believing that all humans have an interest in reducing climate change may foster trust, making it easier to endure some cost in reducing individual emissions. Taking this idea a step further still, some people include relationships with animals and the natural environment as part of their identity; animals are not cooperation partners here, but this broad, interconnected identity contributes to a sense that the environment deserves protection and fair treatment (Clayton & Opotow, 2003).

In sum, social dilemmas describe many situations where cooperation provides the greatest collective good, but where there is some challenge in balancing individual, short-term benefit against long-term, collective well-being. Features of the dilemma, the broader situation, and personalities all contribute to how things unfold.

Leaders often attempt to promote successful resolution of dilemmas. As one more example, the UK's 'nudge unit' (more formally called the Behavioural Insights Team) has gained attention for using incentives or reframing decisions to promote things like paying taxes, insulating homes, and charity donations. In a nutshell, they use the acronym EAST to advocate interventions that are easy, attractive, social, and timely (see Service et al., 2014). For example, at tax time they sent out nice letters which stated that most people paid their taxes on time. The people who received this letter (which emphasized the social norm of paying) were themselves more likely to pay on time.

Before moving on to the next section, think of a local social dilemma that is not working ideally (e.g. litter, traffic jams on campus, creating a new public good in your community). What are some specific steps that might improve the greater good by solving your social dilemma?

Intuitive Prosociality

Earlier, I asked you to consider your assumptions about human nature. Perhaps it was hard to decide whether people are usually naughty or nice; it seems we have elements of both. Given that people are nice at least some of the time, let us now consider a more detailed question: how do the prosocial behaviours come about? For example, when a person finds a wallet full of cash, is there a strong impulse to take the money? Does it require self-control (i.e. overriding a selfish impulse) to return the wallet with all its contents? In social dilemmas, is the first impulse to free ride? Many assume that people's initial instincts are selfish (think of Freud's id), and that we get to prosocial behaviours by overriding this impulse with reflective self-control – we need to think about resisting urges before we do the nice thing.

Although there are certainly times when self-control helps people behave prosocially (e.g. resisting the last piece of pizza), psychological research suggests that people's first impulses might be prosocial – not selfish – in some circumstances. This notion is termed **intuitive prosociality**; that is, when our initial impulse is to improve another person's well-being (Zaki & Mitchell, 2013).

Heroic deeds provide a particularly dramatic example of intuitive prosociality. Asking heroes (e.g. who pulled strangers from a burning car, saved a person from a bull by attacking it, or faced down a speeding train to help someone who had fallen on the tracks) why they performed their extreme acts elicits a common answer. They say things like "I didn't think about it, I just did it". (For an academic analysis of these heroes see Rand & Epstein, 2014; for a compelling telling of their stories, listen to this Radiolab podcast: www.wnycstudios.org/story/how-be-hero.) It seems these heroes acted prosocially on impulse, not after careful deliberation or by resisting urges to protect their own safety. Perhaps these people are simply special (super heroes?). Their particular experiences are clearly unique; however, some mundane psychology experiments with average people also find prosocial impulses. For example, studies of social dilemmas suggest that fast decisions and decisions made without much thought are sometimes more prosocial than slower, carefully considered choices (Rand, 2016). See the Research Case box below for more details.

RESEARCH CASE

SPONTANEOUS GIVING AND
CALCULATED GREED

The idea that people have prosocial impulses draws on a few lines of theory and research (e.g. evolution, early development, brain imaging). A particularly provocative set of studies sought to observe these tendencies in the moment – literally over seconds – using a public goods game (Rand, Greene, & Nowak, 2012). As a participant in this task, you are paired with three other people (four in total). Each person gets 40 cents to play with, and they may keep it or donate some or all of it to a common pool. All the money in the common pool is doubled, and then split equally among the four players (regardless of each's contribution). Note how this game has the key features of public goods: contributing is optional, and all benefit equally from what is created. What do you do? Let us consider the potential consequences. If everyone contributes their 40 cents to the common pool, it is doubled and each person ends up with 80 cents when it is allocated back to players. This seems good and fair; however, contributing to the common pool is not necessarily the best way to make money. Imagine that everyone else contributes their money to the common pool, but that you keep yours. In this case, you would walk away with 100 cents (your 40 + 60 from common pool), while others get only 60 each. To say things in a slightly different way, you get only 1 of every 2 cents that you contribute [(1 x 2)/4] – getting more from the common pool requires that others contribute too. Does that insight change your decision?

Researchers used this public goods game in three types of experiments to test whether people's impulses were more selfish (keep all 40 cents) or cooperative (contribute to the common pool) (Rand et al., 2012). First, they measured how fast participants made their decisions about whether to keep or donate, and they found that faster decisions were associated with higher contributions to the common pool (see Figure 7.2). This suggests that the quick impulse was to give, whereas the more deliberative (slower) choices yielded less giving to the common pool. A second approach forced people to make decisions either in less than 10 seconds, or only after 10 seconds had elapsed. This differs from the first approach by randomly assigning people to be fast or slow, as opposed to just measuring what they did naturally. Results were similar: fast decisions were more cooperative than slow decisions. In a third approach, participants were randomly assigned to four groups and asked to write a paragraph about a time when instinct led to a good or bad decision, or how careful reasoning

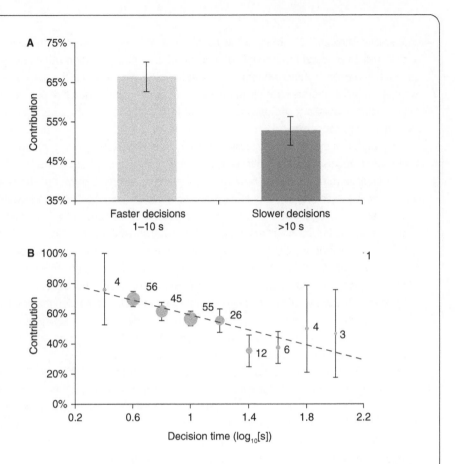

Figure 7.2 Faster decisions are more cooperative. Subjects who reach their decisions more quickly contribute more in a one-shot public goods game (n = 212). This suggests that the intuitive response is to be cooperative. A) Using a median split on decision time, the contribution levels are compared across the faster half versus slower half of decisions. The average contribution is substantially higher for the faster decisions. B) Plotting contribution as a function of $\log_{10}$-transformed decision time shows a negative relationship between decision time and contribution. Dot size is proportional to the number of observations, listed next to each dot.

lead to a good or bad outcome. The idea was that writing these paragraphs would prime people to think about the relative value of following first instincts versus careful reasoning. The results were that priming the benefits of instinct produced more

(Continued)

cooperative choices (i.e. giving to the common pool), whereas priming the benefits of deliberation produced more selfish choices. In sum, the collection of studies suggested that prosocial choices happen fast – intuitively – whereas selfish choices seem to require more deliberate strategizing. This runs counter to the notion that people must resist selfish impulses to do prosocial things. In this public goods game, it seemed more natural to cooperate.

This set of studies was provocative, both in its implications and in the number of subsequent studies it inspired. Although the general conclusion that prosocial choices can be intuitive remains viable, new studies have also revealed some questions and complexity. For example, two very large replication studies (i.e. where other researchers conduct the study again to see whether they get the same results) did not find the same differences between fast and slow choices (Bouwmeester et al., 2017), or primed choices (Camerer et al., 2018). Across studies where response time is manipulated, participants often fail to meet the short 10-second deadline, leading to ambiguity about whether or not to include those data in analyses. In addition, subsequent research suggests that the speed of responses is not the clear indicator of intuition that the initial studies assumed. Slow responses probably connote indecision or a sense of conflict more than strategic thinking (A. M. Evans, Dillon, & Rand, 2015). In essence, the timing in these studies turns out to be trickier than initially appreciated.

In addition, mixed results may depend in part on individual differences. First, it is worth noting that this particular situation – a public goods game, played once, with strangers – is somewhat unusual. Here, non-cooperation can produce greater profits (i.e. if you keep money and others contribute). However, the selfish approach can only work well in the short term. If you treated 'friends' in this way, they would not be your friends for long; people would not do business with you if you took but never gave. As such, many people display the typically useful impulse to cooperate (i.e. because cooperation often pays off, even if that is less true in this specific task). It is only with some strategic thinking that people see the opportunity (and no cost) in free riding on others' common pool contributions in this particular task (Rand, 2018; Rand et al., 2012). This is where individual differences become important. Some people have more experience with economic games. Indeed, many participants in these studies come from the same online pool (where they are paid), and some have participated in dozens of similar studies. It seems they have learned to maximize economic gains, rather than responding how most people would initially. Said another way, as people become 'expert' in these one-time economic games, they can see the potential for selfish paths to profit more easily – time and priming do not add much. If most participants in a study have experience with economic games, the study might produce null results. In a similar vein, spontaneous giving may be limited to people who score as 'prosocial' on the social value orientation measure (see the following Try It box; Mischkowski & Glöckner, 2016), or to people who feel like they typically have cooperative interactions in day-to-day life (Rand et al., 2012). Moreover, the impulse to cooperate in this public goods game seems less common in some cultures. For example, a study conducted in India found less cooperation and faster decisions to keep money, compared to an American sample (Nishi, Christakis, & Rand, 2017).

In sum, Rand et al. (2012) provided a compelling demonstration of intuitive prosociality 'in the moment', as well as spurring an active area of research and debate. With so much interest in these findings, the science is progressing rapidly, revealing when and where we find spontaneous giving. For example, a recent study found it in chimpanzees (Rosati, DiNicola, & Buckholtz, 2018)!

Neuroscience, developmental, and emotion research provide additional arguments for intuitive prosociality (Zaki & Mitchell, 2013). The neuroscience research draws on links between brain activation patterns and various behaviours. Putting prosociality aside for a moment, some parts of the brain, such as the prefrontal cortex and anterior cingulate cortex, are associated with self-control. Other parts of the brain are more associated with reward seeking, such as the ventral striatum and ventromedial prefrontal cortex. These brain correlates are found even in non-social tasks (e.g. delaying gratification versus obtaining money). With these general associations between brain regions and self-control versus reward seeking, we can examine activation during prosocial acts to see which regions are more active. Across a variety of tasks – such as donating money, seeing other people receive rewards, and cooperating with other people – brain-imaging studies find greater activation in the reward-associated areas (E. Fehr & Camerer, 2007; Zaki & Mitchell, 2013). Moreover, activation in the self-control areas is typically not associated with prosocial behaviours. Based on these brain activation patterns, we can infer that these prosocial acts have more to do with reward seeking (similar to instinctive responding) than with self-control. The prosocial acts appear more intuitive.

In a similar way, we can use assumptions about brain development to make inferences about self-control (or lack thereof) when we observe prosocial behaviour in young children. Very young children (e.g. less than two years) have not yet developed the cognitive capacity for self-control or delay of gratification. Thus, it is hard to argue that any of their behaviour requires much control. Nonetheless, researchers (and many parents) have observed prosocial acts in young children, such as spontaneously offering helpful information (e.g. saying where something is hidden), or picking up accidentally dropped objects (Warneken & Tomasello,

2009; Zaki & Mitchell, 2013). Young children also prefer helpful others, and they prefer to distribute resources equitably. Moreover, young children seem to enjoy acting in prosocial ways. For example, one study coded the facial expressions of children just under two years old. These children participated in a study where they were introduced to a puppet, received some treats, ate some treats, and asked to share some treats with the puppet (who seemed to eat the treat in a false bottom bowl). (For a video of the study, see: https://cic.psych.ubc.ca/research-materials-videos/example-stimuli/, 'sharing study'.) The children displayed the most happiness when giving one of their treats to the puppet – even more than when receiving or eating treats themselves (Aknin, Hamlin, & Dunn, 2012)! For young children in this study, it truly seemed better to give than to receive. This enjoyment might also help explain how prosociality occurs without deliberative reflection or self-control. It just feels good (at least some of the time – parents can also tell you about instances when their children were decidedly antisocial). Experiments and short intervention studies with adults similarly suggest positive emotions as a consequence of prosocial behaviours (Curry et al., 2018; see also the Try It box).

Pleasant emotions can also be a cause, rather than a consequence, of prosocial behaviour (DeSteno, 2009). This is yet another reason to think that some prosocial behaviours are less about reflective deliberation, and more about impulse; the emotional impulse can be prosocial. For example, the emotion of **awe** is elicited by perceiving things that are unexpected, profound, or amazing (e.g. extraordinary nature, childbirth, great music or art). Although these triggers are not social per se, awe seems to diminish petty individual concerns, and prompts people to see themselves as part of something bigger, an almost spiritual experience. Prosocial behaviours can come along with this recognition (Prade & Saroglou, 2016). In one example, participants were more likely to help an experimenter pick up dropped pencils if they had just spent a few minutes staring up at a grove of giant eucalyptus trees (which induced awe), compared to participants who looked at a more mundane tall building (Piff, Dietze, Feinberg, Stancato, & Keltner, 2015). It seems that awe provided a nudge towards helpful behaviour. Similarly, more clearly social emotions like elevation, gratitude, and compassion can drive prosocial acts. Witnessing others' morally good or prosocial acts can inspire people to behave similarly (with gratitude and elevation; Algoe & Haidt, 2009), as can an awareness of undeserved suffering in another person (with compassion; Goetz, Keltner, & Simon-Thomas, 2010).

TRY IT

Random Acts of Kindness

This chapter has discussed some arguments for intuitive prosociality to better understand the psychological processes that generate prosocial behaviours. However, the links with pleasant emotions and reward-related parts of the brain suggest potential for another important goal in positive psychology: happiness. Psychologists have harnessed these mood boosts in experiments and positive psychology exercises, and typically find a modestly sized increase following prosocial behaviours (Curry et al., 2018). Why not give it a try?

You have many options for implementing kindness in your life. One approach is simply to count and record your kind acts, for example every day for a week. Even with plans to merely count, you might find yourself doing more kind acts. Alternatively, set a goal to do a specific number of kind acts each day (maybe three or five). These can be small, like holding a door, complimenting someone, providing directions, or larger, like helping someone study or providing a meal. It can be helpful to record these planned acts at the end of the day, and to reflect on how others responded. Another approach is to spend money in prosocial ways – on other people. Recall Chapter 1's review of prosocial spending studies that suggest spending on others improves happiness more than spending on oneself.

With so many different ways to be kind, research continues on determining the best ways to implement acts of kindness. One guiding idea is to choose activities that help meet important psychological needs, such as those posited by self-determination theory (Dunn, Aknin, & Norton, 2014; Lyubomirsky & Layous, 2013; Weinstein & Ryan, 2010). That is, consider choosing kind acts that will also help you feel autonomous (so only do this if you want to!), related to others, and competent.

PHYSICAL ENVIRONMENTS: NATURAL AND BUILT

Other people have a near constant influence on us; yet even in those fleeting moments when we escape the social environment, we are still present in a physical place. As a recent review of environmental psychology began, "Wherever you go, there you are – and it matters" (R. D. Gifford, 2014, p. 543). The remainder of this chapter explores how the physical spaces that people inhabit play a role in behaviour and well-being. We will see similar themes and explicit links with the social environment, such as appeals to evolutionary theory and hints about solving the collective challenges needed to protect natural environments. More specifically, we begin with a bridge between physical environments and social environments: the reasonable person model.

The **reasonable person model** asserts that reasonableness – described as being sensible, fair, moderate, and cooperative – is encouraged by environments that meet people's informational needs (Basu & Kaplan, 2015; S. Kaplan & Kaplan, 2009). Said another way, irritability, selfishness, impatience, and so on often stem from the fatiguing circumstances people are in, and thus they can be remedied by changing those circumstances. The model focuses on physical environments and how these fit (or not) with individuals' needs, particularly in terms of information flow. This cognitive approach assumes that people constantly seek out information; they then use it to build, test, and revise mental models of how the world works. Moreover, the amount and flow of information from the environment are key to effective mental functioning. Boredom connotes too little information, whereas multitasking, random interruptions, or intense focus (e.g. on a textbook?) might provide too much information, particularly over longer periods of time. Effortful controlling of attention exacts a cost that accumulates until there is a break. When people become mentally fatigued, they perform poorly and behave less reasonably. In essence, aspects of the physical environment play an important role in how we navigate our social environments – reasonably, or not.

The reasonable person model is abstract, and the particular circumstances for optimal functioning will depend on people's experience, goals, traits, and many other factors. Sometimes people will need or want to push their cognitive limits in the service of meaningful pursuits. This can be useful; however, a change of pace or scenery is then needed to restore healthy functioning (S. Kaplan & Berman, 2010; Sullivan, 2015). The model also suggests that complete sensory deprivation is not optimal for recovery. Instead, environments that provide some stimulation, while allowing attention to wander freely, are restorative. Natural environments – trees, water, critters, etc. – typically provide excellent contexts to restore cognitive fatigue. For most people, natural environments represent a psychological break from fatiguing activities; they also provide a moderate degree of stimulation. For example, a waterfall, flock of birds, or garden has elements that engage people's attention, but in a way that does not require intense focus; it is a 'soft fascination' (S. Kaplan, 1995). Of course there are exceptions. Fleeing a predator or climbing a difficult rock-face involves intense focus in a natural environment; yet these circumstances are uncommon or then followed by some less demanding recovery time in a restorative environment.

Built spaces can also include elements conducive to recovery (Scopelliti & Giuliani, 2004), but most research in this domain has focused on nature and how it relates to cognitive tasks. For example, in one study Michigan students were given a series of demanding cognitive tests, and then they were asked to take a 50-minute walk, either through a nearby but secluded arboretum or along a busy city street (Berman, Jonides, & Kaplan, 2008). Following the walks, their attention was tested with a backwards digit span test. That is, participants were presented with a series of three- to nine-digit numbers, and they tried to repeat each number back in reverse order. The students performed better on this task following the arboretum walk, compared to the city walk. The implication is that time in nature helped restore cognitive resources, whereas the city walk did not. Navigating among other pedestrians, cars, signs, and so on was more cognitively demanding than walking among trees and wildlife. Other studies have found similar results with the digit span test – nature is associated with better performance – though results are somewhat mixed when considering cognitive tasks broadly (e.g. proof reading or distractibility; Ohly et al., 2016). Nonetheless, nature seems to be a physical environment with many benefits (Bowler, Buyung-Ali,

Knight, & Pullin, 2010; Capaldi, Passmore, Nisbet, Zelenski, & Dopko, 2015; Hartig, Mitchell, de Vries, & Frumkin, 2014).

Natural Environments

The reasonable person model grew from cognitive research on nature to suggesting broader benefits of having a clear head: reasonableness. Other approaches similarly suggest benefits of spending time in nature. The notion of **biophilia** posits that humans have an innate emotional attraction to other forms of life, to nature (Wilson, 1993). That is, humans evolved in natural environments, and our evolutionary history favoured people who developed strong bonds with and understanding of nature. Being attracted to lush greenery and the density of life around water, for example, meant that early humans were drawn to resource-rich places – good for survival.

A fascination with unpleasant or dangerous aspects of nature fits with this idea too; the emotional bond is not always positive. For example, it is easier to condition a fear of snakes in people (and monkeys), compared to other objects, presumably because fear of snakes has been adaptive over mammals' evolutionary history (Öhman & Mineka, 2003). Snakes also hold prominent places in art, religion, dreams, and so on; this fascination may connote the value of learning and teaching about environmental threats, driven by an evolutionarily shaped emotional link (Wilson, 1993). Snake fear is a clear and well-supported example of evolved preferences in the natural world; yet most aspects of nature are pleasing. We see this theme in other areas (e.g. emotions, close relationships): the negative features grab attention, but the positive ones are far more common. As such, connecting with nature is typically associated with well-being. Healthy natural environments signal important resources, and, similar to other adaptive things (like prosocial behaviour), people respond with the evolved reward of pleasant feelings (Buss, 2000).

Hundreds of years ago, most people spent most of their time in what we think of as nature. However, in modern times, more people live in cities than in rural areas, and time-use studies suggest that people spend over 90 per cent of their time indoors (Leech, Nelson, Burnett, Aaron, & Raizenne, 2002; MacKerron & Mourato, 2013). Additionally, modern culture seems to portray nature less and less. An analysis of English fiction books, films, and song lyrics found sharp decreases in nature references since 1950 (Kesebir & Kesebir, 2017). As such, there is now substantial variation in how much nature exposure people get, along with an average decrease over time. It is possible for some urban dwellers to avoid nature almost completely; yet others manage to still get a substantial dose. Defining nature is a thorny issue in modern times, but much of the studied nature is near or embedded in urban environments, such as parks, waterways, gardens, and so on. Nature is not restricted to remote or protected areas when studied by psychologists.

This variation in nature exposure allows researchers to study the correlation with well-being in day-to-day life. At the broadest level, people who live near green space tend to report more happiness. For example, in representative samples with 400,000 surveys, rural Canadians report being happier than urban Canadians (Helliwell, Shiplett, & Barrington-Leigh, 2018). Similarly, in a sample of 10,000 UK residents, living near green space was associated with higher life satisfaction and lower distress (White, Alcock, Wheeler, & Depledge, 2013). A large study in Denmark found that living near green space as a child was associated with better mental health later in adulthood (Engemann et al., 2019). These examples are based on 'objective' environments, but people who report subjective connections with nature also tend to be happier, for example when correlating questionnaire measures of nature relatedness and subjective well-being (Capaldi, Dopko, & Zelenski, 2014). Similarly, among 22,000 New Zealanders, reports of good access to green space were associated with higher life satisfaction (Fleming, Manning, & Ambrey, 2016). Although the Gallup World Poll (see Chapter 3) does not ask about nature per se, this representative sample of planet Earth finds that reports of environmental quality and protection are associated with higher life satisfaction and enjoyment (Diener & Tay, 2015).

Individual moments in nature are also associated with positive moods and decreased stress. For example, a UK smartphone app tracked momentary happiness and physical locations across more than a million observations. Although time in nature was infrequent (about 4 per cent of reports), it was also the happiest, on average (MacKerron & Mourato, 2013). Another recent study tracked 150 American children with GPS, and then used Google Street View and a computer program to literally count the green pixels representing the spaces children encountered in their daily travels (Li, Deal, Zhou, Slavenas, & Sullivan, 2018). More green space was again associated with better moods.

Moments in nature also allow for experimental (vs purely correlational) studies. This approach allows for stronger tests of whether nature is actually causing well-being. The results of experimental studies generally support the idea that nature can cause pleasant states and reduce stress. For example, the cognitive study where Michigan students walked through the city versus an arboretum also found that the arboretum walks produced more positive emotions (Berman et al., 2008). Similar walking studies have been conducted in many locations, with nature typically producing more positive, and less negative, feelings. Moreover, the mood boost from nature is often bigger than people expected beforehand (Nisbet & Zelenski, 2011). For example, you might be surprised to hear that students in Regina, Canada reported better moods walking through a park in winter conditions down to −20° C, compared to an otherwise similar walk indoors through connected buildings (Brooks, Ottley, Arbuthnott, & Sevigny, 2017). Other studies manipulate nature exposure in lab environments, for example by showing videos or photos of natural versus built scenes. These techniques typically improve positive moods and reduce stress too, but to a lesser degree than actual nature exposure (McMahan & Estes, 2015). Even unremarkable nature images are usually rated as more pleasant than typical built images or neutral objects (Dopko, Zelenski, & Nisbet, 2014; Joye & Bolderdijk, 2015). However, it is certainly possible to reverse the preference for nature, for example, with those snakes or other clearly hostile or disgusting contexts (van den Berg & ter Heijne, 2005). The main idea here is that it is easy to find nature that makes people feel good.

Positive psychologists have even created exercises that ask people to find and savour nature over the course of a couple weeks. Results are promising for increasing well-being when testing nature activities against control groups or over time (Passmore & Holder, 2017; Passmore & Howell, 2014; Richardson, Cormack, McRobert, & Underhill, 2016). In Japan, special nature areas are designated for the practice of *shinrin yoku*, or **forest bathing**, which involves mindfully interacting with a forest stroll. The term and activity were developed by government to promote the potential health benefits of nature, and research there has found calming effects in terms of subjective experience and some physiological indicators (Tsunetsugu, Park, & Miyazaki, 2010).

Nature exposure seems to promote physical health (Hartig et al., 2014). For example, a large UK study found that living near green space was associated with living longer (Mitchell & Popham, 2008). A study in Toronto, Canada estimated that having ten more trees on a city block was similar to being seven years younger in terms of people's overall subjective sense of health (Kardan et al., 2015). Although these examples are suggestive, it is difficult to find experimental studies that test nature's long-term health benefits compared to a control group. New drugs must be tested in this way (called randomized controlled trials), and similar research on nature would be valuable. However, it can be difficult to experimentally study the long-term effects of lifestyle factors, such as nature or the particular foods people eat, with true random assignment and control groups. As such, the current argument for nature's health benefits often draws on correlational studies and the short-term effects we can test with random assignment to natural spaces such as changes in stress, social activity, air quality, and physical activity – factors clearly linked to good physical health (Hartig et al., 2014).

This brings us back to the tenets of the reasonable person model. That is, nature seems to promote social and prosocial behaviours, which, in turn, can contribute to good health. For example, public housing projects in Chicago, USA provide a useful context in which to study nature and prosociality. Here, government assigns people to particular apartments, and the locations differ randomly in terms of the surrounding green space. Although all are in urban contexts, some apartments have grass and trees around them while others do not. Residents of the greener buildings were more likely to use outdoor common spaces and had stronger ties to their neighbours (Kuo, Sullivan, Coley, & Brunson, 1998; Sullivan, Kuo, & DePooter, 2004). In another set of public housing apartments, green space was associated with lower levels of crime (Kuo & Sullivan, 2001). Controlled laboratory-based experiments also suggest that nature can cause prosociality. For example, being exposed to nature (vs urban) images seemed to shift students' reports of life goals away from more selfish pursuits (e.g. fame and fortune) and towards more prosocial ends (e.g. closeness and betterment of society) (Weinstein, Przybylski, & Ryan, 2009). Similarly, in a laboratory-based commons dilemma, students who watched a brief nature video harvested (hypothetical) fish more sustainably that students who viewed an architecture video (Zelenski, Dopko, & Capaldi,

2015). Although none of these studies assessed cognitive fatigue per se (an important detail of the reasonable person model), they are all broadly consistent with the notion that nature can nudge people towards more prosocial behaviour.

The links between nature and prosocial behaviour suggest that spending time in nature might also be helpful in efforts to protect the natural environment. As the first half of this chapter described, environmental challenges are easily understood as social dilemmas. Nature seems like one more factor that promotes fairness and cooperation in these contexts. In addition, when people spend time in nature, they value it more and develop a sense of connection – views that are strongly linked to sustainable attitudes and behaviours (Mackay & Schmitt, 2019). For example, a longitudinal study found that children who spent more time in nature at age 6 grew up to engage in more pro-environmental behaviours at age 18 (G. W. Evans, Otto, & Kaiser, 2018). Even among highly nature-related people, spending 30 minutes in nature each day over the course of a month further increased their environmental concern by the end of this period, along with well-being and their sense of nature relatedness (Nisbet, 2015).

Over the past 15 years, a substantial part of my research has explored the potential of a 'happy path to sustainability' that goes through nature (Nisbet & Zelenski, 2011). That is, environmentally friendly attitudes, behaviours, and policies may become easier and more rewarding when people develop a closer connection with nature. Spending time in nature benefits human well-being (i.e. less stress, more happiness, better health), and seems to increase nature relatedness and environmental concern. This set of findings suggests that more time spent in nature would make for happier people and a healthier planet. I will not claim to be without bias on these issues, but the references in this section provide some receipts. Thus, I will close this section with a briefly described 'Try It': go outside and experience some nature!

Built Environments

Most people spend most of their time in built, indoor environments. Positive psychology is probably not the first thing that comes to mind when considering buildings; yet discovering the elements of built spaces that contribute to human flourishing has tremendous potential because they are omnipresent. In addition, a strong economic argument for healthy workplaces becomes clear when considering that companies typically spend much more on workers than on physical infrastructure (Veitch, 2018). Keeping those people happy and healthy promotes productivity. In addition, good design can reduce stress and improve recovery in hospitals. People spend most time in their residences, where the physical environment can support or hinder the basics of good health, such as restoration and sleep.

Most of the research on built spaces has focused on removing noxious elements (see Allen, 2016 for a broad review). For example, air that has pollutants, mould, or dust will be unpleasant and is associated with poor cognitive functioning and illness. Having good ventilation, along with reasonable levels of moisture, temperature, noise, and light, is associated with better outcomes. Many buildings have room to improve in providing these basics; yet such adjustments would still fall short of the optimal environments and flourishing that a positive psychology approach aspires to.

Further complicating matters, it is not always clear how to create optimal conditions. Removing pollutants is obvious, but people have different preferences when it comes to levels of light, temperature, and even noise (though in most workplaces, less noise is usually better). Moreover, the optimal levels shift with varying tasks and functions (Veitch, 2012). As a stark example, the bright light that helps you read fine print is much less desirable during a romantic dinner (and vice versa). Therefore, experts recommend giving people some control and choice, as opposed to a universal prescription for good design. The advice is based on field studies and elaborate experiments. For example, environmental psychologists set up a simulated office setting with cubicles and desks, recruited mid-level office workers for a day, and then systematically adjusted the lighting in a true experiment (Boyce, Veitch, Newsham, Jones, Heerwagen, Myer, & Hunter, 2006). This involved adding or subtracting desk lamps, and even changing the ceiling fixtures as participants performed various cognitive tasks. They found that some lighting types, such as adding indirect hanging fixtures, improved satisfaction broadly. Yet giving workers individual lights and control via dimmer switches further improved satisfaction and motivation. When people have control over lighting, they can adjust it to meet their preferences and particular task demands. The key idea is to provide good fit among three things: the individual person, the particular task, and the built space (with lighting, and other elements). To accomplish this, buildings must be designed with some flexibility. Single-use spaces can be honed to optimize a particular activity (e.g. an efficient assembly line), yet still allow adjustments for personal differences in comfort.

When adjusting lighting, it is wise to consider the time of day, in addition to immediate concerns. Light provides cues to the body and brain about time of day, and these cues help regulate sleep and other circadian rhythms. Human evolution occurred without electric lights, and their addition creates novel conditions. This is compounded when people spend much time indoors, particularly in winter and in northern regions. Windows that provide natural light help, but artificial lighting plays a role in well-being too. High levels of blue (i.e. short wavelength) light are helpful early in the day, improving alertness. In the evening, avoiding blue light improves sleep quality (Chellappa, Steiner, Oelhafen, Lang, Götz, Krebs, & Cajochen, 2013). The intensity and colour of light (i.e. blue vs yellow) depends on the bulbs; most schools and workplaces are occupied in the day, and blue-enriched light may be a good choice. Modern adjustable LED bulbs can shift between a variety of colours using the same bulb, and these fit well with the notion of individual control (or time-of-day programing). Computer, television, and phone screens also produce considerable blue light, suggesting benefits to reducing use in the hours before bedtime. Maintaining a regular sleep–wake cycle has broad implications for psychological and physical health (e.g. mood, hormones, sleep) and light is a key signal in these rhythms (Cho, Ryu, Lee, Kim, Lee, & Choi, 2015). Said another way, lightbulbs can contribute to well-being!

Workplaces increasingly value creativity as jobs become more about information and technology and less about repetitive routines. Designers try to facilitate this with physical spaces. Although the physical environment can prompt some behaviours and psychological states, optimizing space for particular outcomes is very complicated. Recall the reasonable person model, which suggests that variations in information flow and distractions can fatigue or restore people. This might imply that optimal work spaces are isolated, so that people can focus exclusively on their work. On the other hand, social contact can boost moods (potentially improving creativity), and some work requires frequent communication and collaboration. These competing effects and goals become clear when considering researchers', workers', designers', and employers' divided views about the desirability of open-plan offices (Davis, Leach, & Clegg, 2011; R. D. Gifford, 2014; Veitch, 2018). A primary benefit of open-plan offices is that they require less space and are then less expensive. They also provide some flexibility – it is easier to move furniture than walls. Yet regardless of furnishings, workers are closer together, which increases noise and potential for distraction. Social contact increases in open-plans, though it is not clear that productive collaborations increase along with it. Barriers (e.g. cubicles) provide some visual and noise privacy, but also block natural light and window views. Workers often report lower satisfaction and more stress in open-plan offices (compared to closed offices), unless the work requires frequent and immediate access to co-workers, which open-plans facilitate. Individual differences in distractibility and sensitivity to stimulation further complicate the effects of open-plan offices. As above, workplaces face a challenge in providing a good fit among the space, individuals, and their tasks.

Optimizing built spaces is very complicated. This contrasts with the previous section, which described some relatively straightforward benefits of (pleasant) nature exposure. Is there a way to harness nature's positive effects in built spaces? This question drives work in the area of biophilic design. An extension of biophilia more generally, **biophilic design** incorporates natural elements into built spaces to improve the aesthetic appeal and human well-being by creating a sense of connection with nature (Joye, 2007; Kellert, 2018). This includes direct use of nature, for example by incorporating plants, moving water, and more natural building materials like raw wood and rock. Views of nature from indoors can connect a built space with the surrounding environment. With these nature additions come the psychological benefits associated with nature. More dramatically, micro forests can grow indoors and nearby outdoor space (e.g. courtyards) can blend nature with desirable workspaces. One study asked workers to rate various spaces (typical office rooms and nature spaces with seating) on how good they would be for different work tasks (Mangone, Capaldi, van Allen, & Luscuere, 2017). The nature spaces were popular choices for many things (e.g. brainstorming, informal meetings, presentations, and breaks), though less so for focused work.

Beyond actual nature additions, biophilic design also mimics natural forms. Spanish architect Antoni Gaudí was explicit in his desire to mimic nature, such as in the tree-like pillars that support the canopy-like ceiling in Barcelona's Sagrada Familia church. Decorations on and in buildings often include representations of ivy, flowers, and animals. Natural forms tend to have fewer straight lines than the boxy and sterile buildings typical of modern construction. From a mathematical perspective, forms in nature tend to follow **fractal geometry** – to have repeating patterns of self-similarity at different scales (Joye, 2007). For example, think of the repeated branching of a tree (and then trees in a forest), a spiralling nautilus shell, and spider webs. These forms are complex, but they also have order (which can be represented in equations). Fractal forms can also be incorporated into built spaces. For example, consider the repeating geometric patterns of Islamic architecture; Western Gothic architecture often repeats arches across scales from grand to tiny; Asian temples repeat curves, pagodas, and shapes from small to large. Architects may not always be thinking of nature when designing, but the idea behind biophilia is that aesthetically pleasing forms will typically recapitulate nature.

Another principle of biophilic design involves creating spaces with a pleasing mix of prospect and refuge; that is, long views with a sense of expansiveness (prospect), as well as small, safe, and secure areas (refuge) from which to view them (Joye, 2007; Kellert, 2018). Rooms with exterior windows, porches, and balconies offer this. Even within buildings, a mix of open spaces and more obscured nooks, hallways with curves, or lighting that obscures or connects spaces can be adjusted to achieve a pleasing mix. There are many other principles, but the essence of biophilic design is to use and mimic natural forms to produce pleasing built spaces that facilitate evolved natural connections. Given the many benefits of nature, the approach has great potential to optimize built spaces for human flourishing.

In Focus

Virtual Environments

Increasingly, people's physical environments include phones and computers that provide portals to virtual environments. Television, video games, and virtual reality simulate distant physical spaces, and might even prompt a change of actual place (e.g. Pokémon Go). Although you may be home 'alone', social media offers a steady stream of information, putting you in contact with people around the globe.

(Continued)

Electronic devices make the experience of true solitude scarce (Coplan, Zelenski, & Bowker, 2017) and raise questions about how people respond to these novel virtual environments. For example, are screen time and social media making people unhappy, unhealthy, or unreasonable?

Unfortunately, social science has been slow to understand virtual environments, in part because it faces the challenge of rapidly changing technology and platforms (e.g. remember My Space, MSN messenger, or perhaps even Facebook by the time you read this?). Data often come from large surveys with outdated, vague, or broad questions such as "How many hours a week do you use a computer or television?", without regard to whether this is for chatting, photo editing, shopping, news, pornography, and so on. Moreover, researchers have taken different conclusions from the data that does exist. Early research noted troubling links between screen time, sedentary behaviour, and physical health, but more recent work is exploring how technology might encourage healthy behaviours (LeBlanc, Gunnell, Prince, Saunders, Barnes, & Chaput, 2017). Some observe that the rise of smartphones coincides with dramatic decreases in the well-being of US adolescents (Twenge, Martin, & Campbel, 2018). Others argue (with data) that a moderate amount of digital engagement seems most healthy (Przybylski & Weinstein, 2017), or that the average negative effect of technology use is very small compared to things like drug use, bullying, or eating and sleeping poorly (Orben & Przybylski, 2019). In large survey data, technology can be linked to many different outcomes; individual reports might focus on aspects that seem particularly dramatic (or not). Ultimately, the lack of specificity in these studies is a substantial problem. The question of whether or not technology is good or bad is just too broad.

One approach to these complexities is to treat virtual environments as just like other social environments. That is, rather than worrying about the details of particular platforms (e.g. Instagram vs Twitch), we can use familiar ideas from social psychology (Clark, Algoe, & Green, 2018). For example, people desire connection with others, to feel like they belong and that they are cared for. Internet behaviours can facilitate this when they actively engage friends and family. Sharing good news and constructively responding to others' disclosures enhances social bonds and fosters good feelings (see Chapter 8). In contrast, passively browsing others' online lives does little to foster connection and can lead to unfavourable and unpleasant social comparisons – there are always people out there who seem more attractive, skilled, or accomplished in some way. In a similar vein, online platforms can facilitate collaboration, socializing, and exposure to new ideas; they can also compete with important offline social relationships (Waytz & Gray, 2018). Some games and channels devour time and attention to an extent that people later regret (this non-valued absorption is sometimes called 'junk flow').

Smartphones make accessing information easy, and this brings costs and benefits. For example, an experiment randomly assigned students to find an unfamiliar building across campus either with or without using smartphones (Kushlev, Proulx, & Dunn, 2017). The phones helped accomplish the task quickly; yet students who could not use them had to ask other people for directions. At the end of the study, people without phones felt more socially connected; however, this did not translate to better moods than the phone group – phones made the task easier, which was also conducive to good moods. In another study, groups of friends were invited to have a meal together (Dwyer, Kushlev, & Dunn, 2018). Groups were randomly assigned to have their phones out on the table (and told that questions would be sent to phones), or off and in a box (and told that paper measures would be coming). After the meal, groups with phones out reported more distraction and less enjoyment during the meal. Although the differences were not large, the visual presence of a phone seemed to undermine the pleasantness of a meal shared with friends.

In sum, psychologists make some sense of virtual environments by focusing on particular behaviours that either promote or interfere with social connection. These behaviours probably have something to do with people's personalities too. Indeed, people's big five traits (extraversion, agreeableness, etc.) are accurately represented in the language they use online (Yarkoni, 2010). Moreover, Facebook profiles largely portray people as they truly are, rather than how they would ideally like to be, at least in terms of big five traits (perhaps mostly on good hair days though) (Back et al., 2010). It stands to reason that other online behaviours, such as actively socializing, also mirror dispositions; for example, extraverts have more friends on Facebook (Lönnqvist & Itkonen, 2014). That said, online environments may also allow some people (e.g. those with autism or severe anxiety) greater social opportunities than life offline does (Kim, 2017; Waytz & Gray, 2018).

Finally, academic psychologists have largely sidestepped the particular features of technology and design that might help facilitate or hinder healthy interactions with it. Companies are motivated to maximize engagement with their products, and they generate copious (unpublished) research to that end. Users attempt some control too; for example, by turning phones to greyscale to thwart the dazzling glitz of ensnaring design. Strong, independent research on design features and adjustments will help users make good choices in managing the ways they engage with virtual environments.

SUMMING UP

We considered two important sets of contexts that people navigate in day-to-day life: social and physical environments. Humans are extraordinarily interconnected. We must coordinate and exchange with others, and many of these 'partners' are people who we do not know well, or even at all. For positive psychology, an important subset of social interactions involves doing things that benefit other people (prosocial behaviour). Evolutionary theory points to reasons why helping others can also be good for the helper; for example, when it is directed towards family members or others who will return favours in the future, or to boost reputation and status. Evolutionary theory also argues for the benefits of nature and the inclusion of natural elements in built spaces.

Many social decisions take the form of dilemmas, where short-term self-interest comes in conflict with the collective interest or longer-term benefits. Environmental issues are clear examples. In these social dilemmas, cooperation provides the best outcome for all, but individual temptations can threaten collective well-being. Trust is helpful in facilitating cooperation, as are communication, clarity, social pressure, and many other contextual features of the dilemma.

In addition, people seem to have a natural impulse to cooperate in some situations. In support of this notion, very young children provide help, prosociality is associated with reward-linked parts of the brain, and pleasant emotions like awe and gratitude nudge people towards prosocial behaviours. Positive psychologists have examined emotions as an outcome of helping too, finding that acts of kindness and prosocial spending can produce happiness.

The influence of built environments on psychological and health outcomes is complex; there are few features that are universally good or bad. As such, designers seek to balance the fit among the space's features, functions, and the particular people who use them. Although the nuances of optimal natural spaces can also become complex (e.g. trees vs water vs sand), research is more consistent in suggesting that pleasant nature restores people's cognitive and emotional health. Most people spend most of their time in cities and buildings, suggesting value in increasing natural elements in these spaces (e.g. house plants, parks, urban trees), as well as taking more time to visit nearby nature. Moreover, increasing people's connection with nature may help resolve the social dilemmas underlying environmental threats.

TEST YOURSELF

1. How can evolutionary theory explain prosocial behaviour?

2. Give one example of each: A common resource dilemma and a public goods dilemma.

3. Name three factors that predict successful resolutions of social dilemmas.

4. Describe two pieces of evidence that support the idea of intuitive prosociality.

5. What does the reasonable person model suggest about the links between physical environments and psychological well-being?

6. What is biophilic design, and what does it assume about human nature?

WEB LINKS

An episode of the Radiolab podcast that describes a novel solution to a difficult social dilemma:

www.wnycstudios.org/story/golden-rule

An episode of the Planet Money podcast on optimal strategies in the classic prisoner's dilemma:

www.npr.org/sections/money/2018/05/30/615622421/episode-844-nice-game

The Behavioural Insights Team, or 'Nudge Unit', using psychology to prosocial ends:

www.bi.team

The International Well Building Institute, certifying healthy built spaces:

www.wellcertified.com/en

FURTHER READING

This brief article discusses some strategies for solving the social dilemma of climate change:

Van Lange, P. A. M., Joireman, J., & Milinski, M. (2018). Climate change: What psychology can offer in terms of insights and solutions. *Current Directions in Psychological Science, 27*(4), 269–274.

This open access chapter succinctly reviews the classic social psychology on helping:

Poepsel, D. L. & Schroeder, D. A. (2019). Helping and prosocial behavior. In R. Biswas-Diener & E. Diener (eds), *Noba textbook series: Psychology.* Champaign, IL: DEF publishers. doi:nobaproject.com

This article reviews research suggesting that nature can be used to promote human flourishing:

Capaldi, C. A., Passmore, H.-A., Nisbet, E., Zelenski, J. M., & Dopko, R. (2015). Flourishing in nature: A review of the benefits of connecting with nature and its application as a wellbeing intervention. *International Journal of Wellbeing, 5*(4), 1–16.

This report provides a broad and accessible review of research on healthy buildings:

Allen, J. G. (2016). *The 9 Foundations of a Healthy Building.* Retrieved from https://9founda tions.forhealth.org

---

REFERENCES

Aknin, L. B., Hamlin, J. K., & Dunn, E. W. (2012). Giving leads to happiness in young children. *PLOS ONE, 7*(6), e39211. https://doi.org/10.1371/journal.pone.0039211

Algoe, S. B., & Haidt, J. (2009). Witnessing excellence in action: The "other-praising" emotions of elevation, gratitude, and admiration. *The Journal of Positive Psychology, 4*(2), 105–127. https://doi.org/10.1080/17439760802650519

Allen, J. G. (2016). *The 9 foundations of a healthy building.* Retrieved from https://9foundations. forhealth.org

Arnocky, S., Piché, T., Albert, G., Ouellette, D., & Barclay, P. (2017). Altruism predicts mating success in humans. *British Journal of Psychology, 108*(2), 416–435. https://doi.org/10.1111/bjop.12208

Back, M. D., Stopfer, J. M., Vazire, S., Gaddis, S., Schmukle, S. C., Egloff, B., & Gosling, S. D. (2010). Facebook profiles reflect actual personality, not self-idealization. *Psychological Science, 21*(3), 372–374. https://doi.org/10.1177/0956797609360756

Balliet, D., Mulder, L. B., & Van Lange, P. A. M. (2011). Reward, punishment, and cooperation: A meta-analysis. *Psychological Bulletin, 137*(4), 594–615. https://doi.org/10.1037/a0023489

Balliet, D., Parks, C., & Joireman, J. (2009). Social value orientation and cooperation in social dilemmas: A meta-analysis. *Group Processes & Intergroup Relations, 12*(4), 533–547. https://doi.org/10.1177/1368430209105040

Balliet, D., & Van Lange, P. A. M. (2013). Trust, conflict, and cooperation: A meta-analysis. *Psychological Bulletin, 139*(5), 1090–1112. https://doi.org/10.1037/a0030939

Basu, A., & Kaplan, R. (2015). The reasonable person model: Introducing the framework and the chapters. In R. Kaplan & A. Basu (eds), *Fostering Reasonableness: Supportive Environments for Bringing Out Our Best*. Ann Arbor, MI: Maize Books. https://doi.org/10.3998/maize.13545970.0001.001

Batson, C. D., Ahmad, N., & Lishner, D. A. (2009). Empathy and altruism. In S. J. Lopez & C. R. Snyder (eds), *The Oxford Handbook of Positive Psychology* (pp. 417–426). New York: Oxford University Press.

Berman, M. G., Jonides, J., & Kaplan, S. (2008). The cognitive benefits of interacting with nature. *Psychological Science*, *19*(12), 1207–1212. https://doi.org/10.1111/j.1467-9280.2008.02225.x

Bouwmeester, S., Verkoeijen, P. P. J. L., Aczel, B., Barbosa, F., Bègue, L., Brañas-Garza, P., … Wollbrant, C. E. (2017). Registered replication report: Rand, Greene, and Nowak (2012). *Perspectives on Psychological Science*, *12*(3), 527–542. https://doi.org/10.1177/1745691617693624

Bowler, D. E., Buyung-Ali, L. M., Knight, T. M., & Pullin, A. S. (2010). A systematic review of evidence for the added benefits to health of exposure to natural environments. *BMC Public Health*, *10*(1), 456. https://doi.org/10.1186/1471-2458-10-456

Boyce, P. R., Veitch, J. A., Newsham, G. R., Jones, C. C., Heerwagen, J., Myer, M., & Hunter, C. M. (2006). Lighting quality and office work: Two field simulation experiments. *Lighting Research and Technology*, *38*(3), 191–223. https://doi.org/10.1191/1365782806lrt161oa

Brooks, A. M., Ottley, K. M., Arbuthnott, K. D., & Sevigny, P. (2017). Nature-related mood effects: Season and type of nature contact. *Journal of Environmental Psychology*, *54*, 91–102. https://doi.org/10.1016/J.JENVP.2017.10.004

Burnstein, E., Crandall, C., & Kitayama, S. (1994). Some neo-Darwinian decision rules for altruism: Weighing cues for inclusive fitness as a function of the biological importance of the decision. *Journal of Personality and Social Psychology*, *67*(5), 773–789.

Buss, D. M. (2000). The evolution of happiness. *American Psychologist*, *55*(1), 15–23.

Camerer, C. F., Dreber, A., Holzmeister, F., Ho, T.-H., Huber, J., Johannesson, M., … Wu, H. (2018). Evaluating the replicability of social science experiments in *Nature* and *Science* between 2010 and 2015. *Nature Human Behaviour*, *2*, 637–644. https://doi.org/10.1038/s41562-018-0399-z

Capaldi, C. A., Dopko, R. L., & Zelenski, J. M. (2014). The relationship between nature connectedness and happiness: A meta-analysis. *Frontiers in Psychology*, *5*(976), 976. https://doi.org/10.3389/fpsyg.2014.00976

Capaldi, C. A., Passmore, H.-A., Nisbet, E., Zelenski, J. M., & Dopko, R. (2015). Flourishing in nature: A review of the benefits of connecting with nature and its application as a well-being intervention. *International Journal of Wellbeing*, *5*(4), 1–16. https://doi.org/10.5502/ijw.v5i4.449

Chellappa, S. L., Steiner, R., Oelhafen, P., Lang, D., Götz, T., Krebs, J., & Cajochen, C. (2013). Acute exposure to evening blue-enriched light impacts on human sleep. *Journal of Sleep Research*, *22*(5), 573–580. https://doi.org/10.1111/jsr.12050

Cho, Y., Ryu, S.-H., Lee, B. R., Kim, K. H., Lee, E., & Choi, J. (2015). Effects of artificial light at night on human health: A literature review of observational and experimental studies applied to exposure assessment. *Chronobiology International, 32*(9), 1294–1310. https://doi.org/10.3109/07420528.2015.1073158

Clark, J. L., Algoe, S. B., & Green, M. C. (2018). Social network sites and well-being: The role of social connection. *Current Directions in Psychological Science, 27*(1), 32–37. https://doi.org/10.1177/0963721417730833

Clayton, S., & Opotow, S. (2003). Justice and identity: Changing perspectives on what is fair. *Personality and Social Psychology Review, 7*(4), 298–310. https://doi.org/10.1207/S15327957PSPR0704_03

Coplan, R. J., Zelenski, J. M., & Bowker, J. C. (2017). Leave well enough alone? The costs and benefits of solitude. In J. Maddox (ed.), *Social Psychological Foundations of Well-Being* (pp. 129–147). New York: Psychology Press. https://doi.org/10.4324/9781351231879

Curry, O. S., Rowland, L. A., Van Lissa, C. J., Zlotowitz, S., McAlaney, J., & Whitehouse, H. (2018). Happy to help? A systematic review and meta-analysis of the effects of performing acts of kindness on the well-being of the actor. *Journal of Experimental Social Psychology, 76*, 320–329. https://doi.org/10.1016/j.jesp.2018.02.014

Davis, M. C., Leach, D. J., & Clegg, C. W. (2011). The physical environment of the office: Contemporary and emerging issues. In G. P. Hodgkinson & J. K. Ford (eds), *International Review of Industrial and Organizational Psychology* (pp. 193–237). Hoboken, NJ: John Wiley & Sons.

De Dreu, C. K. W., & McCusker, C. (1997). Gain-loss frames and cooperation in two-person social dilemmas: A transformational analysis. *Journal of Personality and Social Psychology, 72*(5), 1093–1106. https://doi.org/10.1037/0022-3514.72.5.1093

de Waal, F. B. M. (2008). Putting the altruism back into altruism: The evolution of empathy. *Annual Review of Psychology, 59*(1), 279–300. https://doi.org/10.1146/annurev.psych.59.103006.093625

Deci, E. L., & Ryan, R. M. (2000). The "what" and "why" of goal pursuits: Human needs and the self-determination of behavior. *Psychological Inquiry, 11*(4), 227–268. https://doi.org/10.1207/S15327965PLI1104

DeSteno, D. (2009). Social emotions and intertemporal choice. *Current Directions in Psychological Science, 18*(5), 280–284. https://doi.org/10.1111/j.1467-8721.2009.01652.x

Diener, E., & Tay, L. (2015). Subjective well-being and human welfare around the world as reflected in the Gallup World Poll. *International Journal of Psychology, 50*(2), 135–149. https://doi.org/10.1002/ijop.12136

Dopko, R. L., Zelenski, J. M., & Nisbet, E. K. (2014). Nature salience increases judgments of environmental satisfaction. *Ecopsychology, 6*(4), 207–217. https://doi.org/10.1089/eco.2014.0042

Dunn, E. W., Aknin, L. B., & Norton, M. I. (2014). Prosocial spending and happiness: Using money to benefit others pays off. *Current Directions in Psychological Science, 23*(1), 41–47. https://doi.org/10.1177/0963721413512503

Dwyer, R. J., Kushlev, K., & Dunn, E. W. (2018). Smartphone use undermines enjoyment of face-to-face social interactions. *Journal of Experimental Social Psychology*, *78*, 233–239. https://doi.org/10.1016/j.jesp.2017.10.007

Engemann, K., Pedersen, C. B., Arge, L., Tsirogiannis, C., Mortensen, P. B., & Svenning, J.-C. (2019). Residential green space in childhood is associated with lower risk of psychiatric disorders from adolescence into adulthood. *Proceedings of the National Academy of Sciences*, 201807504. https://doi.org/10.1073/pnas.1807504116

Eriksson, K., Vartanova, I., Strimling, P., & Simpson, B. (2018). Generosity pays: Selfish people have fewer children and earn less money. *Journal of Personality and Social Psychology*. https://doi.org/10.1037/pspp0000213

Evans, A. M., Dillon, K. D., & Rand, D. G. (2015). Fast but not intuitive, slow but not reflective: Decision conflict drives reaction times in social dilemmas, *Journal of Experimental Psychology: General*, *144*(5), 951–966.

Evans, G. W., Otto, S., & Kaiser, F. G. (2018). Childhood origins of young adult environmental behavior. *Psychological Science*, *29*(5), 679-687. 095679761774189. https://doi.org/10.1177/0956797617741894

Fehr, E., & Camerer, C. F. (2007). Social neuroeconomics: The neural circuitry of social preferences. *Trends in Cognitive Sciences*, *11*(10), 419–427. https://doi.org/10.1016/j.tics.2007.09.002

Fehr, R., Gelfand, M. J., & Nag, M. (2010). The road to forgiveness: A meta-analytic synthesis of its situational and dispositional correlates. *Psychological Bulletin*, *136*(5), 894–914. https://doi.org/10.1037/a0019993

Fleming, C. M., Manning, M., & Ambrey, C. L. (2016). Crime, greenspace and life satisfaction: An evaluation of the New Zealand experience. *Landscape and Urban Planning*, *149*, 1–10. https://doi.org/10.1016/J.LANDURBPLAN.2015.12.014

Foddy, M., Platow, M. J., & Yamagishi, T. (2009). Group-based trust in strangers: The role of stereotypes and expectations: Research Report. *Psychological Science*, *20*(4), 419–422. https://doi.org/10.1111/j.1467-9280.2009.02312.x

Gifford, J., & Gifford, R. D. (2000). FISH 3: A microworld for studying social dilemmas and resource management. *Behavior Research Methods, Instruments, & Computers*, *32*(3), 417– 422. https://doi.org/10.3758/BF03200810

Gifford, R. D. (2014). Environmental psychology matters. *Annual Review of Psychology*, *65*, 541–579. https://doi.org/10.1146/annurev-psych-010213-115048

Gintis, H., Smith, E. A., & Bowles, S. (2001). Costly signaling and cooperation. *Journal of Theoretical Biology*, *213*(1), 103–119. https://doi.org/10.1006/jtbi.2001.2406

Gneezy, U., & Rustichini, A. (2000). A fine is a price. *The Journal of Legal Studies*, *29*(1), 1–17.

Goetz, J. L., Keltner, D., & Simon-Thomas, E. (2010). Compassion: An evolutionary analysis and empirical review. *Psychological Bulletin*, *136*(3), 351–374. https://doi.org/10.1037/a0018807

Hardin, G. (1968). The tragedy of the commons. *Science*, *162*(3859), 1243–1248. https://doi.org/10.1126/SCIENCE.162.3859.1243

Hartig, T., Mitchell, R., de Vries, S., & Frumkin, H. (2014). Nature and health. *Annual Review of Public Health, 35*, 207–228. https://doi.org/10.1146/annurev-publhealth-032013-182443

Helliwell, J., Shiplett, H., & Barrington-Leigh, C. (2018). How happy are your neighbours? Variation in life satisfaction among 1200 Canadian neighbourhoods and communities (Working Paper No. 24592). Cambridge, MA. https://doi.org/10.3386/w24592

Joye, Y. (2007). Architectural lessons from environmental psychology: The case of biophilic architecture. *Review of General Psychology, 11*(4), 305–328. https://doi.org/10.1037/1089-2680.11.4.305

Joye, Y., & Bolderdijk, J. W. (2015). An exploratory study into the effects of extraordinary nature on emotions, mood, and prosociality. *Frontiers in Psychology, 5*. https://doi.org/10.3389/fpsyg.2014.01577

Kaplan, S. (1995). The restorative benefits of nature: Toward an integrative framework. *Journal of Environmental Psychology, 15*(3), 169–182. https://doi.org/10.1016/0272-4944(95)90001-2

Kaplan, S., & Berman, M. G. (2010). Directed attention as a common resource for executive functioning and self-regulation. *Perspectives on Psychological Science, 5*(1), 43–57. https://doi.org/10.1177/1745691609356784

Kaplan, S., & Kaplan, R. (2009). Creating a larger role for environmental psychology: The Reasonable Person Model as an integrative framework. *Journal of Environmental Psychology, 29*(3), 329–339. https://doi.org/10.1016/j.jenvp.2008.10.005

Kardan, O., Gozdyra, P., Misic, B., Moola, F., Palmer, L. J., Paus, T., & Berman, M. G. (2015). Neighborhood greenspace and health in a large urban center. *Scientific Reports, 5*(1), 11610. https://doi.org/10.1038/srep11610

Kellert, S. R. (2018). *Nature by Design: The Practice of Biophilic Design.* New Haven, CT: Yale University Press.

Keltner, D. (2009). *Born to be Good.* New York: W. W. Norton & Company.

Kesebir, S., & Kesebir, P. (2017). A growing disconnection from nature is evident in cultural products. *Perspectives on Psychological Science, 12*(2), 258–269. https://doi.org/10.1177/1745691616662473

Kim, J.-H. (2017). Social media use and well-being. In J. E. Maddux (ed.), *Subjective Well-Being and Life Satisfaction* (pp. 253–271). London: Taylor & Francis.

Klapwijk, A., & Van Lange, P. A. M. (2009). Promoting cooperation and trust in "noisy" situations: The power of generosity. *Journal of Personality and Social Psychology, 96*(1), 83–103. https://doi.org/10.1037/a0012823

Kortenkamp, K. V., & Moore, C. F. (2006). Time, uncertainty, and individual differences in decisions to cooperate in resource dilemmas. *Personality and Social Psychology Bulletin, 32*(5), 603–615. https://doi.org/10.1177/0146167205284006

Kuo, F. E., & Sullivan, W. C. (2001). Environment and crime in the inner city: Does vegetation reduce crime? *Environment and Behavior, 33*, 343–367. https://doi.org/10.1177/0013916501333002

Kuo, F. E., Sullivan, W. C., Coley, R. L., & Brunson, L. (1998). Fertile ground for community: Inner-city neighborhood common spaces. *American Journal of Community Psychology, 26*(6), 823–851. https://doi.org/10.1023/A:1022294028903

Kushlev, K., Proulx, J. D. E., & Dunn, E. W. (2017). Digitally connected, socially disconnected: The effects of relying on technology rather than other people. *Computers in Human Behavior, 76*, 68–74. https://doi.org/10.1016/j.chb.2017.07.001

LeBlanc, A. G., Gunnell, K. E., Prince, S. A., Saunders, T. J., Barnes, J. D., & Chaput, J.-P. (2017). The ubiquity of the screen: An overview of the risks and benefits of screen time in our modern world. *Translational Journal of the American College of Sports Medicine, 2*(17), 104–113. https://doi.org/10.1249/TJX.0000000000000039

Leech, J. A., Nelson, W. C., Burnett, R. T., Aaron, S., & Raizenne, M. E. (2002). It's about time: A comparison of Canadian and American time-activity patterns. *Journal of Exposure Analysis and Environmental Epidemiology, 12*(6), 427–432. https://doi.org/10.1038/sj.jea.7500244

Li, D., Deal, B., Zhou, X., Slavenas, M., & Sullivan, W. C. (2018). Moving beyond the neighborhood: Daily exposure to nature and adolescents' mood. *Landscape and Urban Planning, 173*, 33–43. https://doi.org/10.1016/J.LANDURBPLAN.2018.01.009

Lönnqvist, J.-E., & Itkonen, J. V. A. (2014). It's all about extraversion: Why Facebook friend count doesn't count towards well-being. *Journal of Research in Personality, 53*, 64–67. https://doi.org/10.1016/J.JRP.2014.08.009

Lyubomirsky, S., & Layous, K. (2013). How do simple positive activities increase well-being? *Current Directions in Psychological Science, 22*(1), 57–62. https://doi.org/10.1177/0963721412469809

Mackay, C. M., & Schmitt, M. T. (2019). Do people who feel connected to nature do more to protect it? A meta-analysis. *Journal of Environmental Psychology, 65*. https://doi.org/10.1016/j.jenvp.2019.101323

MacKerron, G., & Mourato, S. (2013). Happiness is greater in natural environments. *Global Environmental Change, 23*(5), 992–1000. https://doi.org/10.1016/j.gloenvcha.2013.03.010

Mangone, G., Capaldi, C. A., van Allen, Z. M., & Luscuere, P. G. (2017). Bringing nature to work: Preferences and perceptions of constructed indoor and natural outdoor workspaces. *Urban Forestry and Urban Greening, 23*, 1–12. https://doi.org/10.1016/j.ufug.2017.02.009

McMahan, E. A., & Estes, D. (2015). The effect of contact with natural environments on positive and negative affect: A meta-analysis. *The Journal of Positive Psychology, 10*(6), 507–519. https://doi.org/10.1080/17439760.2014.994224

Mischkowski, D., & Glöckner, A. (2016). Spontaneous cooperation for prosocials, but not for proselfs: Social value orientation moderates spontaneous cooperation behavior. *Scientific Reports, 6*(21555), 1–5. https://doi.org/10.1038/srep21555

Mitchell, R., & Popham, F. (2008). Effect of exposure to natural environment on health inequalities: An observational population study. *The Lancet, 372*(9650), 1655–1660. https://doi.org/10.1016/S0140-6736(08)61689-X

Murphy, R., Ackermann, K., & Handgraaf, M. (2011). Measuring social value orientation. *Judgment and Decision Making, 6*(8), 771–781.

Nisbet, E. K. (2015). *Answering nature's call: Results of the 2015 David Suzuki Foundation's 30x30 nature challenge.* Retrieved from https://davidsuzuki.org/wp-content/uploads/2017/09/results-2015-david-suzuki-foundation-30x30-nature-challenge.pdf

Nisbet, E. K., & Zelenski, J. M. (2011). Underestimating nearby nature: Affective forecasting errors obscure the happy path to sustainability. *Psychological Science, 22*(9), 1101–1106. https://doi.org/10.1177/0956797611418527

Nishi, A., Christakis, N. A., & Rand, D. G. (2017). Cooperation, decision time, and culture: Online experiments with American and Indian participants. *PLOS ONE, 12*(2), e0171252. https://doi.org/10.1371/journal.pone.0171252

Ohly, H., White, M. P., Wheeler, B. W., Bethel, A., Ukoumunne, O. C., Nikolaou, V., & Garside, R. (2016). Attention Restoration Theory: A systematic review of the attention restoration potential of exposure to natural environments. *Journal of Toxicology and Environmental Health – Part B: Critical Reviews, 19*(7), 305–343. https://doi.org/10.1080/10937404.2016.1196155

Öhman, A., & Mineka, S. (2003). The malicious serpent. *Current Directions in Psychological Science, 12*(1), 5–9. https://doi.org/10.1111/1467-8721.01211

Orben, A., & Przybylski, A. K. (2019). The association between adolescent well-being and digital technology use. *Nature Human Behaviour.* https://doi.org/10.1038/s41562-018-0506-1

Ostrom, E. (2009). A general framework for analyzing sustainability of social-ecological systems. *Science, 325*(July), 419–422. https://doi.org/10.1126/science.1172133

Parks, C. D., Joireman, J., & Van Lange, P. A. M. (2013). Cooperation, trust, and antagonism: How public goods are promoted. *Psychological Science in the Public Interest, 14*(3), 119– 165. https://doi.org/10.1177/1529100612474436

Passmore, H. A., & Holder, M. D. (2017). Noticing nature: Individual and social benefits of a two-week intervention. *Journal of Positive Psychology, 12*(6), 537–546. https://doi.org/10.1080/17439760.2016.1221126

Passmore, H. A., & Howell, A. J. (2014). Nature involvement increases hedonic and eudaimonic well-being: A two-week experimental study. *Ecopsychology, 6,* 148–154. https://doi.org/10.1089/eco.2014.0023

Piff, P. K., Dietze, P., Feinberg, M., Stancato, D. M., & Keltner, D. (2015). Awe, the small self, and prosocial behavior. *Journal of Personality and Social Psychology, 108*(6), 883–899. https://doi.org/10.1037/pspi0000018

Prade, C., & Saroglou, V. (2016). Awe's effects on generosity and helping. *The Journal of Positive Psychology, 11*(5), 522–530. https://doi.org/10.1080/17439760.2015.1127992

Przybylski, A. K., & Weinstein, N. (2017). A large-scale test of the Goldilocks Hypothesis. *Psychological Science, 28*(2), 204–215. https://doi.org/10.1177/0956797616678438

Rand, D. G. (2016). Cooperation, fast and slow: Meta-analytic evidence for a theory of social heuristics and self-interested deliberation. *Psychological Science, 27*(9), 1192–1206. https://doi.org/10.1177/0956797616654455

Rand, D. G. (2018). Non-naïvety may reduce the effect of intuition manipulations. *Nature Human Behaviour, 2*(9), 602. https://doi.org/10.1038/s41562-018-0404-

Rand, D. G., & Epstein, Z. G. (2014). Risking your life without a second thought: Intuitive decision-making and extreme altruism. *PLOS ONE, 9*(10), e109687. https://doi.org/10.1371/journal.pone.0109687

Rand, D. G., Greene, J. D., & Nowak, M. A. (2012). Spontaneous giving and calculated greed. *Nature, 489*(7416), 427–430. https://doi.org/10.1038/nature11467

Richardson, M., Cormack, A., McRobert, L., & Underhill, R. (2016). 30 days wild: Development and evaluation of a large-scale nature engagement campaign to improve well-being. *PLOS ONE, 11*(2), e0149777. https://doi.org/10.1371/journal.pone.0149777

Rosati, A. G., DiNicola, L. M., & Buckholtz, J. W. (2018). Chimpanzee cooperation is fast and independent from self-control. *Psychological Science, 29*(11), 1832–1845. https://doi.org/10.1177/0956797618800042

Scopelliti, M., & Giuliani, V. M. (2004). Choosing restorative environments across the lifespan: A matter of place experience. *Journal of Environmental Psychology, 24*(4), 423–437. https://doi.org/10.1016/J.JENVP.2004.11.002

Service, O., Hallsworth, M., Halpern, D., Algate, F., Gallagher, R., Nguyen, S., … Kirkman, E. (2014). EAST: Four simple ways to apply behavioural insights. *Nesta, 53.* https://doi.org/http://behaviouralinsights.co.uk/publications/east-four-simple-ways-apply-behavioural-insights

Sullivan, W. C. (2015). In search of a clear head. In R. Kaplan & A. Basu (eds), *Fostering Reasonableness: Supportive Environments for Bringing Out Our Best.* Ann Arbor, MI: Maize Books. Retrieved from https://quod.lib.umich.edu/m/maize/13545970.0001.001/1:7/--fostering-reasonableness-supportive-environments-for?rgn=div1;view=fulltext

Sullivan, W. C., Kuo, F. E., & DePooter, S. F. (2004). The fruit of urban nature: Vital neighborhood spaces. *Environment and Behavior, 36*(5), 678–700. https://doi.org/10.1177/0193841X04264945

Trivers, R. L. (1971). The evolution of reciprocal altruism. *The Quarterly Review of Biology, 46*(1), 35–57. https://doi.org/10.1086/406755

Tsunetsugu, Y., Park, B.-J., & Miyazaki, Y. (2010). Trends in research related to "Shinrin-yoku" (taking in the forest atmosphere or forest bathing) in Japan. *Environmental Health and Preventive Medicine, 15*(1), 27–37. https://doi.org/10.1007/s12199-009-0091-z

Twenge, J., Martin, G., & Campbel, W. (2018). Decreases in psychological well-being among American adolescents. *Emotion, 18*(6), 765–780. https://doi.org/10.1037/emo0000403

van den Berg, A. E., & ter Heijne, M. (2005). Fear versus fascination: An exploration of emotional responses to natural threats. *Journal of Environmental Psychology, 25*(3), 261–272. https://doi.org/10.1016/J.JENVP.2005.08.004

Van Doesum, N. J., Van Lange, D. A. W., & Van Lange, P. A. M. (2013). Social mindfulness: Skill and will to navigate the social world. *Journal of Personality and Social Psychology, 105*(1), 86–103. https://doi.org/10.1037/a0032540

Van Lange, P. A. M., Joireman, J., & Milinski, M. (2018). Climate change: What psychology can offer in terms of insights and solutions. *Current Directions in Psychological Science, 27*(4), 269–274. https://doi.org/10.1177/0963721417753945

Van Lange, P. A. M., Joireman, J., Parks, C. D., & Van Dijk, E. (2013). The psychology of social dilemmas: A review. *Organizational Behavior and Human Decision Processes, 120*(2), 125–141. https://doi.org/10.1016/j.obhdp.2012.11.003

Veitch, J. A. (2012). Work environments. In S. D. Clayton (ed.), *The Oxford Handbook of Environmental and Conservation Psychology* (pp. 1–84). New York: Oxford University Press. https://doi.org/10.1093/oxfordhb/9780199733026.001.0001

Veitch, J. A. (2018). How and why to assess workplace design: Facilities management supports human resources. *Organizational Dynamics, 47*(2), 78–87. https://doi.org/10.1016/j.orgdyn.2018.01.002

Warneken, F., & Tomasello, M. (2009). Varieties of altruism in children and chimpanzees. *Trends in Cognitive Sciences, 13*(9), 397–402. https://doi.org/10.1016/j.tics.2009.06.008

Waytz, A., & Gray, K. (2018). Does online technology make us more or less sociable? A preliminary review and call for research. *Perspectives on Psychological Science, 13*(4), 473–491. https://doi.org/10.1177/1745691617746509

Weinstein, N., Przybylski, A. K., & Ryan, R. M. (2009). Can nature make us more caring? Effects of immersion in nature on intrinsic aspirations and generosity. *Personality & Social Psychology Bulletin, 35*(10), 1315–1329. https://doi.org/10.1177/0146167209341649

Weinstein, N., & Ryan, R. M. (2010). When helping helps: Autonomous motivation for prosocial behavior and its influence on well-being for the helper and recipient. *Journal of Personality and Social Psychology, 98*(2), 222–244. https://doi.org/10.1037/a0016984

White, M. P., Alcock, I., Wheeler, B. W., & Depledge, M. H. (2013). Would you be happier living in a greener urban area? A fixed-effects analysis of panel data. *Psychological Science, 24*(6), 920–928. https://doi.org/10.1177/0956797612464659

Wilson, E. O. (1993). Biophilia and the conservation ethic. In S. R. Kellert & E. O. Wilson (eds), *The Biophilia Hypothesis* (pp. 31–41). Washington, DC: Island Press. https://doi.org/citeulike-article-id:6451153

Wu, J., & Axelrod, R. (1995). How to cope with noise in the iterated prisoner's dilemma. *Journal of Conflict Resolution, 39*(1), 183–189.

Yarkoni, T. (2010). Personality in 100,000 Words: A large-scale analysis of personality and word use among bloggers. *Journal of Research in Personality, 44*(3), 363–373. https://doi.org/10.1016/J.JRP.2010.04.001

Zaki, J., & Mitchell, J. P. (2013). Intuitive prosociality. *Current Directions in Psychological Science, 22*(6), 466–470. https://doi.org/10.1177/0963721413492764

Zelenski, J. M., Dopko, R. L., & Capaldi, C. A. (2015). Cooperation is in our nature: Nature exposure may promote cooperative and environmentally sustainable behavior. *Journal of Environmental Psychology, 42*, 24–31. https://doi.org/10.1016/j.jenvp.2015.01.005

8

Close Relationships

INTRODUCTION

It took baby monkeys to convince psychologists that love was important – and not (only) because monkeys are adorable. In the first half of the twentieth century, many leading psychologists saw affection and expressions of love as problematic, especially for children. Behaviourist John Watson warned parents not to pet their children because "mother love is a dangerous instrument", and that there would be "serious rocks ahead for the over-kissed child" (quoted in Blum, 2002, p. 37). Watson's ideas were not the clear conclusion of research – love was seen as too mushy for serious scientific study. With widespread views like this, the biblical aphorism 'spare the rod, spoil the child' became professional advice from psychologists. Physicians in this period were concerned with the spread of germs and thus similarly urged parents not to hold or play with their babies too much. Freud offered an alternative perspective on parent–child relationships, but it was bizarrely sexual and also warned against babies' over-indulgence in physical contact. The study of love was off to a rocky start.

What do baby monkeys have to do with any of this? Their behaviour provoked an accidental discovery by Harry Harlow, an animal cognition researcher who, curiously, was often quite cold and severe himself. Harlow's team kept a colony of macaques for research, and this involved much human intervention in raising the babies. Babies were kept separately from mothers and hand fed with little bottles. Their keepers noticed that baby monkeys clung tightly to the cloth pads in their cages, and had tantrums when the pads were replaced for sanitary reasons. Babies kept in cages without these cloths failed to thrive (Harlow, 1958).

These casual observations provoked a systematic experiment, one that would eventually change psychology's view on love.

The affectionate bond between mothers and babies may seem obvious; yet at the time behaviourists explained it away as the result of simple conditioning. Essentially, babies loved their mothers because mothers fed them and food was rewarding – not a lot of warmth in that explanation! In the new study, baby macaques were housed with two 'surrogate mothers'. The surrogates were not actual monkeys, but models. One was made of wire mesh and included a bottle; food was regularly available. The other surrogate had no food, but was made of warm, comfortable cloth. Given the choice between these two mothers, baby macaques overwhelmingly preferred the warm, cuddly mother (Harlow, 1958). They would leave it briefly to feed on the wire mother, but they spent most of their time in what looked like an affectionate bond with the soft mother. This finding was the exact opposite of what the behaviourists predicted – food was not the key to bonding, physical affection was. As the researcher, Harry Harlow, put it, "The wire mother is biologically adequate but psychologically inept" (Harlow, 1958, p. 677). The cloth mothers were used as a source of soothing when stressed, and the baby monkeys became agitated when separated from them. This study suggested that affection is as basic a need as food (see Figure 8.1).

Figure 8.1 One of Harlow's (1958) monkeys with the soft surrogate mother

A cloth mother, warm and cuddly as she might be, is still not a perfect parent. Additional studies showed that having good social relationships with others was important to young macaques' healthy development. Harlow noted, "It takes more than a baby and a box to make a normal monkey" (1958, p. 675). These ideas dovetailed with British psychiatrist John Bowlby's observations of human children (see van der Horst, LeRoy, & van der Veer, 2008). His **attachment theory** describes how separation from caregivers often produced problems, and how children who enjoy secure bonds with parents grow up to expect stable close relationships as adults (Ainsworth & Bowlby, 1991). Indeed, since the 1960s, research has consistently echoed the importance of close bonds, and the need for love is near universal in contemporary thinking. For example, some hospitals have begun 'volunteer cuddler' programmes to ensure the young children can receive physical affection even when parents are unavailable. And as an example at the other end life, having a high-quality marriage is associated with longer survival after congestive heart failure (Coyne, Rohrbaugh, Shoham, Sonnega, Nicklas, & Cranford, 2001). Social support is broadly associated with better health and well-being across ages and in many domains (Uchino, 2009). Humans are a social species, and close relationships are essential to our survival and our thriving. Indeed, a study of the very happiest people found that good social relationships stood out as the one characteristic they all had (Diener & Seligman, 2002).

In this chapter we consider close relationships from a positive psychology perspective. Even as the importance of close relationships became apparent, psychology still focused on what went wrong in relationships, or how people were damaged when they lacked good relationships. These are important insights, but with the arrival of positive psychology, more attention is being paid to behaviours that promote highly satisfying relationships, and how strong relationships help promote thriving in other areas of life. We begin with the core of close relationships: love.

WHAT IS LOVE?

Before reading further, take a minute to jot down an answer to the question "What is love?". What words or short phrases describe the important features of love? Next, consider whether there are there different kinds of love in different relationships; if so, write those down too. (We will come back to your lists later.)

Love is at the centre of close relationships. People have many relationships, and some of these are quite casual. For example, you have a 'relationship' with your hairdresser, a distant cousin, and even a person you see on the bus every day. The interactions that come from these relationships can provide substantial benefits and enjoyment – or not. Either way, they lack key features of close relationships. In this chapter, we consider relationships where intimacy and interdependence, that is closeness and mutual needs, are much stronger.

This includes romantic bonds, but also close friendships and some family relationships. Love seems a common link among these bonds. Yet defining love, its exact boundaries, and its types can still be tricky.

In the moment, love is an emotion. As with other emotions, people have a unique subjective experience of love – we know what it feels like. Love includes physiological changes (e.g. feeling warm, a strong heartbeat), and people feel motivated to express affection and connect with another. As positive psychologists articulate new lists of basic positive emotions (see Chapter 2), love has been a common addition (e.g. Shiota, Neufeld, Danvers, Osborne, Sng, & Yee, 2014). In this way, love is a momentary emotional experience.

Love is also unique, compared to other emotions, in implying something more long term. Of course we can speak of other 'trait emotions'; for example, a joyous person experiences frequent episodes of joy. Yet each moment of joy can be separate, about different things. When we experience or express love for someone, it implies a relationship that persists over time. Imagine the cad who feels and expresses intense 'love' one night, only to have it fade away the next morning. Do we believe that his moment was truly love, quickly aroused and then quickly gone? No, we expect love to move more slowly (notwithstanding the romantic notion of love at first sight). It develops over time and transcends momentary experience into the future. As another example, you have probably had the experience of loving a family member even while also intensely disappointed or angry with that person. In this way, love is more than a momentary experience; we use the word love to describe relationships.

At the beginning of this section, I asked you to write down some phrases that describe love. There is a good chance your list included something like trust, honesty, caring, friendship, happiness, warm feelings, intimacy, respect, or commitment. These are the kinds of answers that Canadian students generated when Fehr (1988) asked them about love in a series of studies. Rather than using experts and theories, she was asking lay people how they thought about love. Very similar to what you did earlier, participants were asked to list features of love. This method, known as the prototype approach, is a useful way to understand ideas with fuzzy boundaries and without clear rules.

As discussed in Chapter 1, defining positive psychology itself is like this; its topics have a family resemblance, but without hard rules for deciding what is and what is not positive psychology. In the **prototype approach**, people first list features (e.g. of love); then, in a second step, others rate how typical those features are. Knowing the most prototypical features helps us to better understand the concept. For example, in positive psychology, happiness is a central, prototypical topic. Self-control also fits in positive psychology (as a strength that helps people thrive), but seems less central than happiness; it is not the first example that comes to mind. Topics similar to happiness are more likely to be part of positive psychology.

When people are asked about love, the most prototypical features (i.e. the best examples) tend to be things like trust, caring, and honesty (Fehr, 1988; Fehr & Russell, 1991). Aspects of sexual attraction, such as passion, gazing at each other, and touching, are rated as less typical. Importantly, this even applies when people are asked to list features of romantic love specifically (Regan, Kocan, & Whitlock, 1998). To be clear, sexual desire and longing are seen as important parts of romantic love, but still slightly less central than trust, caring, and acceptance. It seems that love – at least as understood by lay people – has a common core. Said another way, love typically includes trust, caring, and honesty. The subset of romantic love relationships also includes sexual desire and longing, yet these features are not relevant to other love relationships (e.g. very close friends). Of course, it is also possible to have sexual desire without love, but we can distinguish that as lust.

In Focus

What Do People Think About Love?

Table 8.1 lists some common aspects of love, with the most prototypical near the top. The middle column gives the percentage of people (Canadian students) who identified the characteristic when asked to list all the features of love they could think of in three minutes. The right column is from a different study where another group of students rated how central the features were to the concept of love, using a scale that ranged from 1 (extremely poor feature) to 8 (extremely good feature). Note that dozens more features were listed and rated; this is only a subset.

Table 8.1   Ranking the prototypical features of love

Feature	% of Lists Present	Mean Centrality Rating (1–8)
Trust	15	7.5
Caring	44	7.3
Honesty	11	7.2
Friendship	23	7.1
Respect	11	7.0
Commitment	14	6.8
Accept other as is	16	6.8
Supportiveness	9	6.8
Intimacy	5	6.5

(Continued)

Table 8.1 (Continued)

Feature	% of Lists Present	Mean Centrality Rating (1–8)
Responsibility	4	6.0
Sexual passion	9	5.8
Sacrifice	13	5.4
Excitement	4	5.0
Security	6	5.0
Dependency	4	2.8
Scary	3	2.3

Source: Adapted from Fehr (1988)

These descriptions of love, drawn from people's lists and ratings, have been corroborated by studies that ask about love in less direct ways. When people think about love, features that are rated as most typical stand out. In one example, research participants were asked to rate statements about a loving couple for how natural the statements sounded (Fehr, 1988). Many of these statements included hedges, such as 'sort of' or 'somewhat'. Statements that hedged typical features of love were judged to be less natural, compared to when less typical features were hedged. For example, it seems more natural to say "Pat sort of admires Chris", compared to "Pat sort of trusts Chris". Trust is a central feature of love, so we expect it to be true of a love relationship – there should be no 'sort of' about it! People are also faster to identify the more typical features of love when response times are carefully measured. In other studies using statements, participants are more likely to remember prototypical features of love relationships, compared to more peripheral features. This finding even extends to falsely remembering typical statements (e.g. "Casey trusts Jordan") that were not actually presented (Fehr, 1988; Regan et al., 1998). In sum, research shows that the typical features of love stand out in ratings, hedges, memory, and response times – they come to mind more easily. This makes us more confident in the love prototype. Love is commonly understood as being about trust, caring, and honesty, with other aspects applying to some love relationships more than others.

Kinds of Love

Lay people's lists and ratings can tell us much about how people think about love, but those views may not correspond closely to how the brain is actually processing things. It may be that there is not one physiological or psychological process common to all love experiences, even with much agreement on the central features of love. In addition, many of us have the sense that there is more than one kind of love (Fehr & Russell, 1991). For example, a boy's love for his mother seems different than the mother's love for his father. Psychologists have proposed various ways to carve up the potential sub-types of love (Berscheid, 2010; Graham, 2011; Hendrick & Hendrick, 1989; Shiota et al., 2014; Sternberg, 1986). These efforts often take a more theoretical approach. Rather than creatively listing examples of love types, there is an effort to identify underlying causes of differences in loves. For example, evolutionary approaches suggest that sexual love serves a very different purpose than nurturing love (i.e. mating versus protecting, respectively). These differences are mirrored in behaviour. Whereas people take risks to pursue sexual interests, they tend to avoid risk when caretaking. As such, it seems useful to distinguish these two loves as separate emotions (Shiota et al., 2014).

Despite some disagreement on the details, most theories include at least two kinds of love: passionate love and companionate love, sometimes referred to by the Greek names *eros* and *storge* (Berscheid, 2010). **Passionate love** occurs in the context of romantic relationships, and is primarily about intense attraction. It typically begins with liking, physical desire, and exciting uncertainty, and it promotes (motivates) sexual relationships. **Companionate love** is more like a strong friendship. It begins with familiarity, similarity, and seeing positive qualities in another person, and it promotes (motivates) spending more time together and other expressions of liking. Although described as 'friendship love', companionate love is also important in romantic relationships. Companionate love is more about the caring, whereas passionate love is more about the physical attraction. Companionate love may also exist outside romantic relationships, such as between close friends and other family members. See the Try It box for example questionnaire items that assess passionate love (eros) and companionate love (storge).

TRY IT

Measuring Love

Here are part of the instructions and sample items from commonly used scales that measure passionate love and companionate love in romantic relationships. Respondents are asked to think of a particular person they love(d), and to judge how much the statements apply on a scale:

1-------2-------3-------4-------5-------6-------7-------8-------9

Not at all true of me   Extremely true of me

(Continued)

Passionate Love

"We would like to know how you feel (or once felt) about the person you love, or have loved, most passionately. Some common terms for passionate love are romantic love, infatuation, love sickness, or obsessive love."

I would rather be with _____ than anyone else.

I want _____ physically, emotionally, mentally.

For me _____ is the perfect romantic partner.

I possess a powerful attraction for _____.

Companionate Love

"We would also like to know how you feel (or once felt) about the person you love, or have loved, most companionately. Some common terms for companionate love are affectionate love, tender love, true love, or marital love."

I strongly desire to promote the well-being of _____.

I feel emotionally close to _____.

_____ is able to count on me in times of need.

I expect my love for _____to last for the rest of my life.

Source: Adapted from Hatfield & Rapson (2013)

With questionnaire measures of companionate love and passionate love, researchers have studied individual differences in the experience of love. Gender easily comes to mind, spurred by notions represented in John Gray's bestselling book title *Men are from Mars, Women are from Venus*. Are men and women's views of love so different that they seem to come from different planets? Researchers have rejected such dramatic claims of stark gender differences, seeing much more similarity and overlap between men and women in their data (Reis & Carothers, 2014). Yet in her review of many studies, Fehr (2015) concluded that women often score somewhat higher on measures of companionate love, whereas gender differences are rarely found on measures of passionate love.

In addition, when differences emerge they sometimes contradict stereotypes. Going beyond the love types per se, there are indications that men may be the more romantic gender. For example, a series of studies found that men were more likely to say 'I love you' first in relationships, and also think about getting serious earlier than women (Ackerman, Griskevicius, & Li, 2011). On the other hand, men are also more interested in casual sex and having many partners (Schmitt et al., 2003; Schützwohl, Fuchs, McKibbin, & Shackelford, 2009). Even when such differences are found, it is important to keep in mind that they describe averages, with many individual men and women bucking the overall trends. Fortunately, it seems that men and women are both from Earth when it comes to love.

In one study, researchers questioned men and women from two sides of planet Earth about love; they compared people from China and North America (Sprecher & Toro-Morn, 2002). Overall, there were more cultural differences than gender differences. Said another way, the average Chinese person and American person differed more than the average man and woman. Across cultures, we see some vast differences in romantic and family relationships. Whereas some cultures see an individual's romantic feelings as the best reason for marriage, other cultures pay more attention to pragmatic or economic concerns. The entire family's assessment may be important, with parents even arranging marriages for their children. For a time, such differences led psychologists to believe that the notion of romantic love may not apply in non-Western cultures. However, these views evolved, and both passionate and companionate loves are now viewed as largely universal (Berscheid, 2010; Hatfield, Bensman, & Rapson, 2012).

Although the data are preliminary, studies suggest that people in Asian cultures report more companionate love and less passionate love, compared to people in Western cultures (Fehr, 2015). Limited data are not the only reason to be cautious about cultural differences in love, however. Cultures also change over time, and the last 50 years have seen dramatic changes in marriage trends across many countries (Western and Asian). Cultural differences in love are a moving target. Despite some cultural differences, there is also substantial similarity. For example, people almost everywhere agree that the most important feature in a marriage partner is mutual love or attraction (Buss et al., 1990). Some arranged marriages may begin with uncertainty about love, but this does not diminish love's value as they develop.

Unsurprisingly, having more love in relationships is associated with higher satisfaction (Acevedo & Aron, 2009). People who report more love also tend to stay in their relationships longer, especially if they are unmarried (Le, Dove, Agnew, Korn, & Mutso, 2010). Views about passionate love and companionate love can differ on how relationships unfold. People who see love as largely about passion tend to be more satisfied. On the other hand, a loss of companionate love is viewed as a better reason to end a relationship (Fehr, 2015). It seems we can imagine relationships persisting (unhappily) without passion, but less so when respect and caring are gone. Thus, the happiest, lasting relationships have high levels of both passionate and companionate love.

Perhaps more surprising is how love tends to change over time in relationships. Both passionate love and companionate love tend to be high early in relationships; yet both tend to decline with time, as does average relationship satisfaction (VanLaningham, Johnson, & Amato, 2001). To be clear, love is typically still strong after many years, but the trend is for it to be a bit less strong than in the early stages of the relationship (Hatfield, Pillemer, O'Brien, & Le, 2008). There is no good evidence for the idea that initial passion normally fades to friendship in long-term relationships. Both are important early, and both fluctuate over the course of long relationships. The average is a small decline in both, but individual couples travel in both directions, and may reverse course multiple times. Despite the gloomy average, there is good news here: long relationships can still have passion, if not the outright obsession of young love (Acevedo & Aron, 2009). Yet there remains plenty of room for positive psychologists to learn more about and to promote behaviours that keep romantic relationships thriving!

In Focus

Is Oxytocin Really the 'Hug Hormone'?

The hormone oxytocin gets a lot of good press. People have called it the love hormone, the cuddle chemical, the moral molecule, and a handful of other adorable, alliterative monikers. It turns up in studies of breast-feeding, trust, childbirth, and empathy (Bartz, 2016; A. Campbell, 2010; Carter, 1998). Could it be the physiological basis of love? In a popular TED Talk, Paul Zak (2011) prods his audience, "your prescription from Dr. Love: eight hugs a day", explaining that hugs release oxytocin, which in turn strengthens relationships and increases happiness for all. This love hormone sounds like good stuff; yet many scientists have become dismayed by bold claims in the popular press. They are urging people to take a second look at the research on oxytocin (Bartz, Zaki, Bolger, & Ochsner, 2011; Graustella & MacLeod, 2012; Nave, Camerer, & McCullough, 2015).

Some of this scepticism comes from concerns about the basic science. The enthusiasm for oxytocin as a love hormone began before it was studied in humans at all. For example, the hormone seems important to maternal attachment in sheep. As scientists mapped oxytocin's effects in sheep brains, they learned it influenced mothers' sense of smell. If oxytocin is important to human bonding, it will almost certainly act in a different way – smell is not how humans bond (Bartz et al., 2011). There is always a gap between animal research and human outcomes, and that gap has yet to be closed for oxytocin. In humans, much of the research with oxytocin is correlational. Such studies tell us where we are likely to see oxytocin, but less about cause and effect. A clever solution to this problem came in the form of a nasal spray. There are now studies that experimentally manipulate oxytocin, comparing it to placebos, by shooting them into participants' noses. Although intriguing, it is not clear whether nasally sprayed oxytocin makes it across the blood–brain barrier consistently – the oxytocin might not even get to the brain in these studies (Leng & Ludwig, 2016)! This might help explain another issue: some of the key oxytocin results have been difficult to reproduce (Lane, Luminet, Nave, & Mikolajczak, 2016). In sum, researchers are still working out the basic science of oxytocin in humans; conclusions about what it does are premature.

Even setting aside the technical issues about research methods, results of human studies are painting a much more complex picture than we see in the popular press. Oxytocin has been associated with so many different things, it seems incorrect to focus on love as its primary function. As an analogy, we do not call legs the 'football limbs' – legs are involved in playing football, but they do so much more, and many other body parts are also needed to play. Studies of oxytocin have linked it to increased trust, cooperation, empathy, facial recognition, positive communication, and memories of maternal care (Bartz et al., 2011). The studies tend to link oxytocin to the more positive sides of these outcomes, but results can depend on gender, personality, and circumstances – the findings are not clear and consistent. The list of outcomes also extends to some less lovey things, such as envy and in-group bias. Should we conclude that the love hormone is also the racism hormone?

In essence, we are still figuring out how best to study oxytocin in humans, and still in the early stages of gathering reliable correlates. As we learn more, it seems likely that oxytocin will play some role in the physiology of human social relationships. However, that role is unlikely to cleanly map onto a tricky psychological concept like love. This illustrates a general truism at the intersection of neuroscience and psychology. The way our brains do things is often distinct from our notions about psychologically important concepts. Just as looking for the football limb is a fool's errand, there is probably no single hormone for love. Moreover, finding physiological correlates rarely explains psychological ideas in easy or clear ways. Identifying hormones does not make love any more or less real.

(Continued)

We can still learn more about how the brain does love, and the specific functions of oxytocin. For example, a more nuanced hypothesis is that oxytocin helps high-light social information, making us more aware in a way that could have prosocial or antisocial consequences, depending on the circumstances (Bartz et al., 2011). Also, none of this means that Dr Love is wrong to prescribe hugs. Hugs are nice, and we do not need a clear path through oxytocin to see their psychological bene-fits. Indeed, one recent study found that people experimentally exposed to the cold virus became less ill over the following weeks if they got more hugs (Cohen, Janicki-Deverts, Turner, & Doyle, 2015). Hugs seemed to convey social support, which also helps protect against illness. So, hooray for hugs, but it is an open question whether or not oxytocin has much to do with them.

HOW DO PEOPLE CREATE SATISFYING RELATIONSHIPS?

Love is at the centre of close relationships; yet psychologists want to understand the details beyond this single concept. In this section, we consider some of the personal characteristics and day-to-day processes that seem to facilitate strong relationships. Keep in mind that the majority of findings in this area have been gleaned from romantic relationships. Still, there is a sense among researchers that many of these things will operate similarly in platonic close relationships – the sex stuff is an obvious exception though. Also, keep in mind the caveat that participants generally come from heterosexual relationships and wealthy English-speaking countries. It is not clear whether how one responds to sharing good news should be much different in Italian same-sex relationships, for example, but we simply do not have the data to know one way or the other with certainty.

In the Beginning…

Social psychologists have studied the early stages of relationships. They have identified some of the circumstances and the interpersonal behaviours that promote new relationships. Early on, social psychologists learned that simple proximity and exposure to other people predicted liking them (Bornstein, 1989). Of all the people in the world with whom you might develop close relationships, it is most often the people who are physically near and who you see frequently. Deeper relationships develop when people mutually share things. This applies to physical gestures; we tend to mimic people around us, and this mimicry indicates positive interactions (Lakin, Jefferis, Cheng, & Chartrand, 2003). For example, you might see a first date at a café, and, curiously, both people are leaning in, both with legs crossed, both with fingers resting lightly on their cheeks. This would be a good sign.

Through conversations, deeper relationships develop as people disclose increasingly personal information. Indeed, the power of this process has been harnessed in the 'fast friends' lab procedure where strangers can become quite close after about 45 minutes (Aron, Melinat, Aron, Vallone, & Bator, 1997). The trick to this is asking and answering questions carefully selected by the researcher. The questions are designed to be innocuous at first (e.g. would you like to be famous?), and then incrementally progress towards more intimate personal details (e.g. how do you feel about your relationship with your mother?). People build intimacy and feel closer as they disclose progressively more important things about themselves and learn more about their partners.

In the early stages of romantic relationships, similarity in background, interests, values, and personality is also conducive to liking (Botwin, Buss, & Shackelford, 1997; Montoya, Horton, & Kirchner, 2008). The adage 'opposites attract' is generally not supported by research. Physical attractiveness is, perhaps obviously, attractive. However, similarity is less important when it comes to looks. People mostly agree on attractive features, and beauty is desirable in a potential partner (Lee, Loewenstein, Ariely, Hong, & Young, 2008) – yet it is not at the top of most people's lists (Buss et al., 1990).

Personality Features

Similarity can be attractive when it comes to personality, but it becomes less important as people get to know each other better (Montoya et al., 2008). Indeed, some traits are simply more or less desirable. For example, most people would agree that a friendly, hard-working, and calm person is nicer to be around – or to be married to – than a mean, lazy grouch. Thus, when it comes to the big five personality traits – agreeableness, conscientiousness, and emotional stability in this example – are features that most people find attractive, regardless of similarity (Botwin et al., 1997). As another example, narcissists love themselves, but they are usually not looking for more vanity, entitlement, and self-centredness in their mates.

Beyond initial attraction, traits also predict how satisfied people are in their relationships. When it comes to happiness in relationships, having similar traits in couples is not particularly important. Being, or having a partner, high in desirable traits predicts happier and longer lasting relationships – especially for conscientiousness and emotional stability (Malouff, Thorsteinsson, Schutte, Bhullar, & Rooke, 2010). Of course, all is not lost if you have some undesirable traits. Most of us do, and they are but one of many components in relationships. For example, one study found that newlyweds high in neuroticism (i.e. low emotional stability) were just as happy with their relationships if they were having lots of sex (Russell &

271

McNulty, 2011). Moreover, all traits involve trade-offs, and even undesirable characteristics have advantages in some circumstances (Ein-Dor & Hirschberger, 2016; Nettle, 2006).

When it comes to close relationships, broad traits like the big five are not as directly relevant as the more relational idea of attachment styles (Noftle & Shaver, 2006; Simpson & Rholes, 2012). Coming from Bowlby's attachment theory, **attachment styles** refer to the mental models or expectations that people have about close relationships. For example, you may strongly believe that a partner will be there for you in a time of need, or perhaps be somewhat less certain of that responsiveness. Attachment styles are habitual over time in that earlier experiences in close relationships, beginning with primary caregivers in infancy, create ideas about what to expect in future relationships. The theoretical focus is often on these early experiences, but expectations about relationships continue to adjust with new experiences.

Attachment theory assumes that people naturally seek out social support when threatened, and that this is rooted in our evolution as a social species. If early caregivers were seen as available and responsive when threats emerged, a secure attachment style would develop. People with **secure attachment** styles have confidence that support will be available when needed. This, in turn, makes them less dependent on actual support – believing that support is easily available means not having to worry about minor threats. Secure attachment brings confidence in relationships, and is associated with many of the positive relationship behaviours discussed in this chapter. Secure relationships also help people navigate the world more generally, allowing them to explore new things and thus to grow (Feeney & Thrush, 2010; Mikulincer & Shaver, 2007).

In contrast, poor relationships with inconsistent support contribute to anxious or avoidant attachments. **Anxious attachment** is associated with low self-esteem, doubt, and concerns that others will not be available when needed. These insecure beliefs drive frequent attempts to get reassurance from others, which, ironically, can drive people away. The anxiously attached come across as needy and annoying. **Avoidant attachment** is also thought to result from inconsistent support, but the response takes the opposite strategy: shunning others when threats emerge. Avoidant attachment is characterized by lack of trust and extreme self-reliance. It is thus hard for avoidantly attached people to develop deep intimacy.

Unsurprisingly, secure attachments are associated with higher-quality and happier relationships (Noftle & Shaver, 2006; Simpson & Rholes, 2012). However, this does not mean that the first few years of life shape our destiny. Attachment styles are characteristics of individuals, but they do change somewhat over time (Fraley, 2002; Fraley, Roisman, Booth-LaForce, Owen, & Holland, 2013). Just as anxious attachment can lead to problems in relationships, good relationships with responsive partners can foster more secure attachments. In addition, different relationships can have different attachments (Mikulincer & Shaver, 2007). One may have avoidant attachments with an ex-boyfriend and an insensitive mother, while enjoying a secure attachment with a responsive husband. Finally, people's sense of attachment can even vary day to day (Pierce & Lydon, 2001); there are some circumstances that feel secure, and others that are more uncertain.

DISTINGUISHING POSITIVE PROCESSES IN RELATIONSHIPS

Positive psychologists have been particularly interested in the day-to-day thoughts, feelings, and behaviours of flourishing relationships. Some researchers suggest the analogy of a bank account for relationships (Lambert, Fincham, Gwinn, & Ajayi, 2011). Positive behaviours (e.g. doing a favour, expressing affection, listening carefully) are like making deposits, whereas negative behaviours (e.g. annoying or selfish acts) are like withdrawals. Relationships, like bank accounts, can only survive when the deposits exceed withdrawals. Moreover, healthy relationships will have built some 'savings' that provide a buffer for when inevitable difficulties arise. (This analogy may aid understanding, but it is probably unwise to keep an actual tally in your relationships!)

In the currency of relationships, positive and negative actions are not equal. Although positive behaviours are typically much more common in close relationships, the occasional bad behaviours are more costly. An equal balance of bad and good behaviour will bring a quick end to relationships. Indeed, one relationship expert estimates that people in healthy relationships have about five positive interactions for every negative one (Gottman, 1994). You may recall a similar pattern with emotions in Chapter 2. The idea is the same; bad is stronger than good – it gets our attention and has more severe consequences – yet good is much more frequent than bad, thankfully.

Thus, one reason to focus on the positive in relationships is that there is simply more of it to understand. In addition, the positive approach raises new questions. As with positive psychology more generally, we begin to think beyond how to alleviate suffering and conflict, and more about how to promote thriving. Ironically, the positive approach also suggests new ways in which things can go wrong. For example, it seems obvious that avoiding conflict is useful, but there might also be less obvious problems – such as boredom – when relationships lack intensely positive interactions (Harasymchuk, Cloutier, Peetz, & Lebreton, 2017). Research increasingly suggests that relationship goals aimed at doing good things for one's relationship are distinct from goals to avoid conflict. Positive psychologists are particularly interested in behaviours grounded in a desire to approach potential benefits (Knee & Reis, 2016).

Capitalization and Support

The process of **capitalization** occurs when people share good news with their partners. Beyond the news itself, there is potential to bolster a positive experience by sharing it. Indeed, studies using the experience sampling method (where participants report on events and emotions repeatedly while going about their day-to-day lives) have found that shared positive events are associated with larger boosts in moods, compared to unshared events

(Gable, Reis, Impett, & Asher, 2004; Lambert, Gwimm, Baumeister, Strachman, Washburn, Gable, & Fincham, 2013). Moreover, it is not just that bigger events are more likely to be shared; the association remains even after statistically adjusting for the events' importance.

Sharing good news has potential to boost moods, but the benefits also depend on how partners respond to the news. Research has focused on two dimensions of difference in those responses: how active versus passive and how constructive versus destructive the responses are. Active responses involve enthusiastically engaging with follow-up questions and conversation, whereas passive responses are muted acknowledgements. Constructive responses are positive, echoing the view of the person who is capitalizing; destructive responses take the opposite tact, finding potential negatives in what seemed like good news or dismissing it altogether. The combination of these two dimensions sets up four kinds of responses (think of a 2 × 2 box of highs and lows). The best response is usually active and constructive.

To illustrate, imagine Jesse has just received news that she was accepted for a PhD programme at a prestigious university. When Jesse shares the news with her partner, an active-constructive response would be something like "That is wonderful! Do you know who your mentor will be? It sounds like you will be able to do some really exciting research there; tell me more!". The **active-constructive response** shows interest and savours the good news. In contrast, a passive-constructive response would be much less enthusiastic; for example, a warm smile and "Good job, sweetie". It is still positive, but does not engage deeply or prompt additional conversation. Destructive responses are more obviously negative. For example, in an active-destructive response, Jesse's partner might say "Oh jeez, I guess that means you will have to move away from all your friends. And the heavy work-load there – it's not like you'll have time for friends anyway. Are you sure you can keep up?". This response is active, but in taking good news and finding problems with it. Even when there are valid concerns, rushing to them first is unlikely to benefit the relationship. Finally, a passive-destructive response does not engage with the good news and mostly ignores it, for example, "Hmm, I guess you got lucky. Hey, can you pick up my laundry on your way home from school tomorrow?".

Again, the biggest and most consistent benefits come with active-constructive responses to capitalization attempts. This has been found with self-reports in experience sampling studies, when couples are brought into the lab and their conversations are coded by observers, and when 'responses' are randomly assigned in experiments (Gable, Gonzaga, & Strachman, 2006; Lambert, Gwinn, Baumeister, Strachman, Washburn, Gable, & Fincham, 2013; Monfort et al., 2014). For example, one study had romantic couples come to a lab where they were then put in separate rooms. One person worked on a mental skills task, allowing the experimenter to create a good news event by giving positive feedback about task performance. Couples communicated with each other via electronic messages, but the key responses were actually determined by the experimenter (unbeknownst to participants). When participants received active-constructive responses to good news, they experienced twice as much positive emotion, compared to other kinds of responses (Lambert et al., 2013). Capitalizing was most beneficial with an actively constructive partner. Indeed, people who generally view their partners as likely to provide active-constructive responses are also more satisfied in their relationships (Gable et al., 2004).

It is perhaps easy to see why destructive responses are problematic, but why should it be so important that constructive responses also be active? The importance of an active approach suggests that the process is not just about the mood, but also about what the response can communicate about one's partner and the relationship. Although passive-constructive responses can be perfectly pleasant, they do not indicate the same level of interest or caring, compared to more active responses. Feeling like partners understand, care, and engage with our concerns – known as perceived partner **responsiveness** – is a hallmark of healthy relationships (Reis, Clark, & Holmes, 2004). Active-constructive responses indicate this kind of engagement. They communicate that your partner cares about things that are important to you.

This is similar to how gratitude works in close relationships. We tend to be grateful when receiving something that is particularly valued, not just merely positive. These well-chosen favours provide the additional benefit of communicating an understanding of individuals' needs – they show responsiveness (Algoe, 2012).

As with gratitude, capitalization attempts occur with something positive. This makes them especially useful times to assess a partner's responsiveness. Good news situations have less risk for a truly bad outcome, even if partners are not at their best. Even so, the way partners respond to good news can indicate how they would deal with less pleasant situations. Thus, capitalization attempts can help establish a broader sense of support (Shorey & Lakey, 2011); they include subtle communication about the relationship and what to expect from a partner. The analogy of a smoke detector can be helpful: it is best to test it when there is no fire. In a fire, a faulty detector is much more problematic. Even if it does work then, you are too busy dealing with the stress of the fire to appreciate the detector's good work (Gable, Gosnell, Maisel, & Strachman, 2012). Similarly, sharing good news provides an opportunity for partners to demonstrate their care and concern in a low-risk context. An excited and interested reaction to another's good news suggests that you would also be there for them if something went wrong. Of course, it also helps savour the good news itself, creating a shared positive experience.

These ideas have parallels with how psychologists understand social support more generally (Gable et al., 2012; Shorey & Lakey, 2011). **Social support** refers to all the ways other people can provide assistance. For example, it can include advice, money, listening, hugs, favours, influencing others, and so on – anything that might be seen as helpful. The notion that social support is important to successful coping is widespread, and there are clear links between support and well-being. However, there are also ways for social support to create problems. For example, the giver might not be very skilled in knowing what, exactly, is needed, and provide something that is not actually helpful. Imagine a man who is stressed because his controlling wife stifles his efforts to pursue things independently. He might not appreciate his mother visiting to 'take care of him' while his wife is away on business. In addition, social support can create a sense of obligation to repay it in the future, or make someone feel bad that they could not cope with their problems alone. After observing some problems with social support, psychologists made a distinction between received support and perceived support. **Perceived support** is the belief that support would be forthcoming if it was needed; **received support** refers to tangible things that have been done or given (see review by Uchino, 2009).

Perceived social support is more consistently associated with well-being and physical health, compared to received support. The idea is similar to secure attachments described a few paragraphs back. Simply believing that support is available makes people less likely to need it, thereby avoiding some of the potential problems that can come with actual support attempts. In this way, merely communicating that support is available – or even secretly providing assistance – is often better for the recipient than showy gestures (Bolger, Zuckerman, & Kessler, 2000). Perceived social support is a resource that helps buffer stressful situations. In addition, positive psychologists are finding that a sense of security in relationships, and the perception of support it brings, allows people to flourish by exploring new things and expanding their positive experiences (Feeney & Collins, 2014). In sum, positive experiences can be used to communicate support (with capitalization), and those perceptions of support are useful in dealing with both stress and more positive opportunities in the future.

TRY IT

Using Active-Constructive Responding in Your Relationships

There are now many studies suggesting that relationships benefit from active-constructive responses to good news. Although most of these studies have included people who are romantically involved, similar processes are likely at work in other close relationships. For this exercise, choose someone who is relatively close to you (family, friend, romantic partner) and who you communicate with frequently. During the next few days, try to be more aware of opportunities to provide active-constructive responses as you interact with this person. The 'news' you respond to does not have to be big, just something positive that the person shares. You can also construe 'news' broadly. For example, "Ha, look at how silly that squirrel is acting" is, in a way, sharing good news, and it is an opportunity for active-constructive responding by taking an interest.

Of course, use common sense too; for example, do not respond enthusiastically to a truly bad or potentially destructive idea or plan. Also, try to be authentic in your response and avoid glee that is overly forced. Do try to see the positive and engage more enthusiastically; find an interesting facet to follow up with. After all, you care about this person and thus probably care about the things that are important to them.

After a few days, reflect on your experiences. When were you able to provide active-constructive responses? What followed from them? How did if feel for you? How did the other person respond? Has it influenced the way you see your relationship?

Exciting and Self-Expanding Activities

Another way to make deposits in your relationship bank account is by engaging in fun, novel, and challenging activities with a partner. According to self-expansion theory, one of the great things about being in a new relationship is that you have new and exciting experiences; these, in turn, help broaden your sense of self. Beyond the enjoyable dates per se, new partners bring abilities, interests, and habits that are novel. For example, ballet, billiards, bird watching, or bowling might not be things you have paid much attention to, but because one is a favourite of your paramour, you suddenly learn much more about it. People find these new activities fun and instructive, and they feel happier about their relationships when doing them (Graham, 2008). Over longer periods of time, couples that engage in more novel, exciting, and challenging activities also report higher levels of satisfaction (Aron, Norman, Aron, McKenna, & Heyman, 2000).

More formally, **self-expansion theory** makes two key assumptions (Aron et al., 2000; Xu, Lewandowski, & Aron, 2016). First, people have a deep motivation to grow, learn, explore, and become competent, and thus experience enjoyment from these things – a notion with a long history in psychology (e.g. White, 1959). These growth activities expand the sense of self. Second, people can also expand the self through their romantic relationships because they take on aspects of their partners; individuals' sense of self merges with intimate others. For example, you might have known newlyweds who suddenly seem to have no preferences, opinions, or desires of their own. Instead, you hear "*We* can't get enough *Game of Thrones; we* think the conservatives will win the next election; *we* don't care for pepperoni on *our* pizza". Even if slightly annoying for outsiders, this merging is enjoyable for the couple, and some of the bliss may be due to the individuals' self-expansion. They have each been able to take on attractive characteristics of the other.

TRY IT

Measuring Intimacy as Overlap in Selves

The notion that selves merge and expand in romantic relationships is captured by a popular and simple assessment tool, the **Inclusion of Other in Self measure**. People indicate the degree of overlap between the self and a partner, each represented by circles (see Figure 8.2). Indicating greater overlap correlates with other measures of closeness, intimacy, and even whether or not couples break up in the future (Aron, Aron, & Smollan, 1992).

Please circle the picture below which best describes your relationship

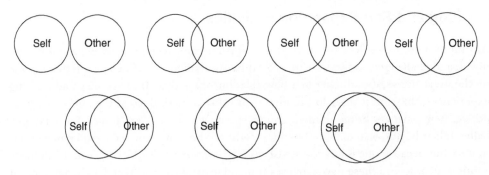

Figure 8.2 The inclusion of self in other measure from Aron et al. (1992)

At the beginning of relationships, self-expansion happens easily and quickly; everything is new, and people are eager to merge (Slotter & Gardner, 2009). With more time, the rate of self-expansion typically slows as people have learned and experienced more with their partners. This may help explain why feelings of relationship satisfaction and love tend to decrease over time too. A potential antidote is engaging in more novel activities together, thus ensuring new ways to grow individuals' sense of selves as a couple. For example, one study surveyed US couples that ranged from newlyweds to those married more than 30 years. As in other studies, couples that were married longer were somewhat less likely to say they were "very intensely in love", though it was still about 40 per cent of couples married more than ten years. Those couples that were still intensely in love were also more likely to report engaging in more frequent novel and challenging activities (O'Leary, Acevedo, Aron, Huddy, & Mashek, 2012). They also had more positive thoughts about their partners, even when apart, and more sexual interest and behaviour towards their partners.

In a lab experiment, couples who engaged in a novel, challenging task reported feeling better about their relationships immediately after it (Aron et al., 2000). More specifically, some couples were literally tied together and told to traverse a large gym mat with an obstacle in the middle. They were to do this in less than one minute, while holding a pillow between them and without using hands or mouths to hold it. Couples who performed this novel, challenging, and somewhat silly task felt momentarily more satisfied in their relationships, compared to others in a control group.

These ideas have also been applied outside the laboratory, with encouraging results. For example, Australian couples were recruited for an online intervention study (Coulter & Malouff, 2013). Half were randomly assigned to a waitlist control group; they agreed to participate, but were not asked to do anything besides complete measures. The other half were asked to engage in novel and exciting activities for at least 90 minutes each week for a month. Both groups filled out questionnaires at the beginning and the end of that four-week period. Unsurprisingly, scores remained similar for the control group over time, but the couples that engaged in exciting activities reported an increase in positive emotions and relationship satisfaction. Notably, those increases were still present when they were asked again four months after the intervention – at least among the 68 per cent of couples that were still available to complete questionnaires. Perhaps those couples gained some appreciation for the benefits of exciting activities and continued doing them after the instructions ended. What do you think accounts for the continued boost even months later?

In another study, Canadian couples were randomly assigned to a weekend of either self-expanding novel activities, or to a control group instructed to engage in more familiar and comfortable activities (Muise, Harasymchuk, Day, Bacev-Giles, Gere, & Impett, 2019). The researchers were particularly interested in sex as an outcome, as this is another thing that often fades over time in relationships (McNulty, Wenner, & Fisher, 2016). Interestingly, couples that were assigned the self-expanding activities reported more sexual desire, along with more relationship satisfaction, at the end of the weekend. An experience sampling study of long-term couples also suggested a link between exciting activities and sex: on days when couples reported more self-expanding activities, they also reported more and better sex (Muise et al., 2019).

Sex is exciting, and perhaps even novel and challenging at times. Thus, it seems like it could be a way to increase relationship satisfaction. Can couples really fornicate their way to happiness? Research has found a correlation between sexual activity and relationship satisfaction, as well as subjective well-being more generally. However, it seems that more sex is not always better. Large surveys of Americans suggest that the happiness benefits of more frequent sex peak at about once per week (Muise, Schimmack, & Impett, 2015) – more is better, but only to a point. Of course, surveys reflect broad averages, so we should not take once a week as the optimal number for every individual. The surveys are also correlational, so we do not know whether sex is causing happiness or whether happiness is stimulating more sex. See the Research Case to learn how some researchers tried to address this problem – resulting in mixed success.

RESEARCH CASE

JUST DO IT MORE?

Most research on the link between happiness and sexual frequency is correlational. You might think that it would be impossible to do a true experiment, where people are randomly assigned to have sex, but that is exactly what one research group attempted (Loewenstein, Krishnamurti, Kopsic, & Mcdonald, 2015). They focused on married couples recruited via newspaper adverts and flyers – there was no random assignment of sex partners. In addition, the experimental manipulation was not an all-or-none proposition. Rather, some couples were randomly assigned to double their sexual frequency, and they were compared to a control group with no such instructions. To be included in the study, couples needed to be heterosexual, age 35–65, free from significant issues around sex (pain or conflict), and currently having sex between once a month and three times a week. (This range captures many couples, and researchers speculated that this range would make a doubling noticeable, yet also not pass an upper limit for diminishing returns.) The participants were then tracked daily over the next three months with a short online questionnaire that assessed moods (e.g. cheerful, tense, peppy, sad) and sexual experiences. They were paid for participation, and earned bonuses for completing the questionnaires regularly.

Over the course of the study, couples in the experimental group did not quite double their sexual activity, but they were successful in having more sex than the control group: about eight times per month compared to about six times for the controls (see Figure 8.3). Did having more sex make couples happier? Surprisingly, no; in fact, the couples assigned to have more sex reported significantly less positive affect and less sexual desire and enjoyment from sex. The results were opposite of what the researchers predicted. We might make sense of this by considering a different, qualitative study that interviewed both people who self-identified as having great sex, and sex therapists. The interviews suggested that the best sex is less about accomplishing specific behaviours (e.g. orgasm), and more about being fully present in the moment, authenticity, and good communication (Kleinplatz et al., 2009). Perhaps the requirement to have more sex interfered with these things. The researchers speculated that sex may still cause happiness 'in the wild' (despite their contradictory results), but that trying too hard can shift the focus from intimacy and enjoyment to merely doing it. They concluded that their study "answers a different question from the one it set out to address; it addresses how requesting a couple to have more sex affects happiness, wanting, and enjoyment, but not whether the naturalistically occurring relationship between sexual frequency and these variables is causal" (Loewenstein et al., 2015, p. 217). This is one reason why you will not see a "Try It: Have More Sex" box in this book. Instead, the better advice is probably a bit sneakier – recommending novel and exciting activities in general may end up improving sexual and relationship satisfaction.

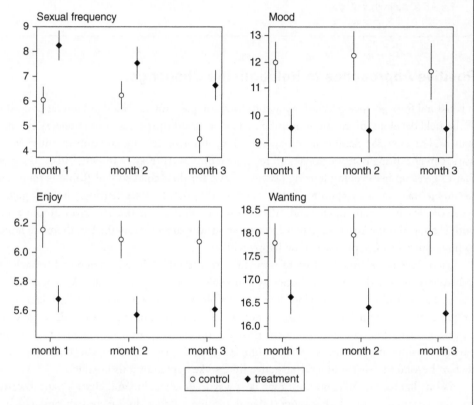

Figure 8.3 Sexual frequency, enjoyment, wanting, and mood

Source: Loewenstein et al. (2015)

This study highlights important lessons beyond sex. Although experimental methods have the advantage of stronger causal inferences (compared to correlational methods), the approach can also make circumstances so unnatural that they change the psychological processes. Correlational studies typically observe associations as they occur,

(Continued)

avoiding this issue, and are thus sometimes more informative. Nonetheless, caution is still warranted in translating correlational observations into practice. Even when thoughts or behaviours correlate with positive outcomes under naturalistic conditions (e.g. sex and happiness), we cannot assume that promoting those thoughts or behaviours with interventions will produce the same benefits – the intervention procedures need to be tested and refined. It is possible for well-intentioned interventions to backfire, as in this study.

Positive Approaches to Relationship Challenges

It is natural for a positive psychology text to focus on pleasant activities and interactions, but as the field develops, more attention is being paid to healthy processes in less cheery circumstances. For example, sacrificing for a close other, although difficult and unpleasant in some ways, can also bring both personal and relationship rewards (Day & Impett, 2016). Imagine that Li gives up her evening fencing classes to care for their child so that Robin is then free to pursue training in competitive figure skating. Although Li loses fencing, she may gain a sense of closeness, authenticity, and satisfaction for helping someone she loves. Robin gains both skating and the knowledge that Li is a responsive partner. Nonetheless, there are limits to how much sacrifice people can be happy with.

Just as love is endemic to close relationships, so is conflict. Even barring bad behaviour, individuals' needs, desires, and hopes will not align perfectly, for example when Robin wants skating and Li wants fencing. The way people work through such conflicts can serve to strengthen relationships by demonstrating care and commitment (Overall, Grime, & Simpson, 2016). Difficult circumstances provide contexts to prove one's mettle to self and partner. Positive psychologists are beginning to unpack productive approaches to conflict that go beyond merely avoiding destructive things like contemptuous hostility.

As one lighter example, humour may be a way to ease tension and chart a path towards common ground. Initial studies suggest that deploying humour during conflict can help, but that it requires some nuance to be successful. The kind of humour is important. Aggressive humour that includes (subtle) insults may escalate conflict, whereas more affiliative inside jokes that draw on shared experiences work better (L. Campbell, Martin, & Ward, 2008). Even so, differences in attachment styles can influence how a joke is perceived, and not always in helpful ways (Winterheld, Simpson, & Oriña, 2013). Conflict is a difficult situation for insecurely attached people; this makes it hard to practise or appreciate the nuanced art of comedy. Indeed, productive resolution of conflicts needs to be sensitive to individual differences in attachment concerns. Whereas anxious people require a sense of their partner's commitment to the relationship, avoidant people are more sensitive to feeling valued as autonomous individuals (Overall et al., 2016). How to best communicate love, support, respect, and commitment – in the face of conflict – is a topic ripe for additional study by positive psychologists.

Given that there will be some hurtful conflict in all close relationships – everyone has bad days – it is also important that there is forgiveness. **Forgiveness** involves a shift in motivation, putting aside a transgression and wishing the offender well. In close relationships, having made some earlier positive deposits that built trust and intimacy helps. The process of forgiveness itself may also ultimately provide a benefit too, for example by signalling the importance of the relationship and the value of the transgressor. Forgiveness is associated with relationship satisfaction and commitment, and it seems likely that each can cause the others at times (McCullough, Rachal, Sandage, Worthington, Brown, & Hight, 1998). Failing to forgive in close relationships is almost not an option. Some core features of love – such as trust and caring – are simply at odds with prolonged ill will towards a partner. Longitudinal studies suggest that a lack of forgiveness can impair future conflict resolution too (Fincham, Beach, & Davila, 2007). Without forgiveness, close relationships cannot thrive.

SUMMING UP

This chapter has considered the tricky concept of love, and a few of the characteristics and processes found in flourishing close relationships. Most people agree that the key elements of love include trust, caring, and honesty, and these features are most important in both romantic and non-romantic close relationships. Psychologists also distinguish among different types of love, and here a consensus exists that the sexual, exciting, and passionate elements of love can be split off as unique to romatic relationships. There is less consensus around additional sub-types of love, but nurturing and familial love are commonly suggested. Despite gender stereotypes and cultural differences in marriage arrangements, researchers have found much similarity in people's ideas and experiences of love across these categories. With that said, friendship-like love may be somewhat more important to women and Asians, on average.

Close relationships often begin when people are physically close to one another, share similar traits, attitudes, and values, and engage in mutual disclosure of personal information. With time, personality similarity appears less important to satisfying relationships. Instead, individual differences like secure attachment style, emotional stability, conscientiousness, and agreeableness are positively associated with relationship outcomes, whether or not partners share them. Positive psychologists also study the more momentary processes that are associated with good relationships such as signalling security, sharing good news, and engaging in exciting activities. Sharing good news boosts its positive emotional impact, especially when a parter responds in an active and constructive way. Similarly, engaging in exciting activities avoids boredom and promotes a sense of satisfying growth in relationships. Finally, processes such as humour, forgiveness, and sacrifice expand the scope of positive psychology to conflict and its successful resolution.

This text frequently revisits the thorny issue of defining positive psychology. Chris Peterson, a key founder of the movement, cut through the brush with a pithy three-word summary of its main message: other people matter. The scope of his statement is broader, yet clearly includes the notion that close relationships are central to our well-being. He, and most positive psychologists, would point to close relationships as one of the most potent places to target when building a happier life. We are tuned in and tied to the people we love. The day to day of close relationships is not utopian; conflict, insecurity, or boredom are also normal. Fortunately, we are learning that some of the tools to cope with these challenges are quite pleasant. Increasing and improving the good times seem to offer some protection from the bad – and this approach to protection is fun!

TEST YOURSELF

1. How has the prototype approach identified key features of love?

2. Compare and contrast companionate love and passionate love, including where you are likely to find them.

3. Why are some neuroscientists uncomfortable with calling oxytocin the hug hormone?

4. How are gratitude and active constructive responses similar in close relationships?

5. What are the two key assumptions of self-expansion theory?

WEB LINKS

International Association for Relationship Research: www.iarr.org

Science of Relationships Blog: www.scienceofrelationships.com

Paul Zak's popular TED Talk on oxytocin: www.ted.com/talks/paul_zak_trust_morality_and_oxytocin

Caution about oxytocin and more in Molly Crockett's TED Talk on neuro-bunk: www.ted.com/talks/molly_crockett_beware_neuro_bunk

FURTHER READING

This classic article on love is unexpectedly entertaining:

Harlow, H. F. (1958). The nature of love. *American Psychologist, 13*(12), 673–685.

This article proposes a new taxonomy of four love types:

Berscheid, E. (2010). Love in the fourth dimension. *Annual Review of Psychology, 61*, 1–25.

This book collects various chapters themed around optimal relationships:

Knee, C. R., & Reis, H. T. (2016). *Positive Approaches to Optimal Relationship Development.* Cambridge: Cambridge University Press.

To explore gratitude in close relationships more deeply, see:

Algoe, S. B. (2012). Find, remind, and bind: The functions of gratitude in everyday relationships. *Social and Personality Psychology Compass, 6*(6), 455–469.

To learn more about exciting activities in the face of relational boredom, see:

Harasymchuk, C., Cloutier, A., Peetz, J., & Lebreton, J. (2017). Spicing up the relationship? The effects of relational boredom on shared activities. *Journal of Social and Personal Relationships, 34*(6), 833–854.

REFERENCES

Acevedo, B. P., & Aron, A. (2009). Does a long-term relationship kill romantic love? *Review of General Psychology, 13*(1), 59–65. http://doi.org/10.1037/a0014226

Ackerman, J. M., Griskevicius, V., & Li, N. P. (2011). Let's get serious: Communicating commitment in romantic relationships. *Journal of Personality and Social Psychology, 100*(6), 1079–1094. http://doi.org/10.1037/a0022412

Ainsworth, M. D. S., & Bowlby, J. (1991). An ethological approach to personality development. *American Psychologist, 46*(4), 333–341. http://doi.org/10.1037/0003-066X.46.4.333

Algoe, S. B. (2012). Find, remind, and bind: The functions of gratitude in everyday relationships. *Social and Personality Psychology Compass, 6*(6), 455–469. http://doi.org/10.1111/j.1751-9004.2012.00439.x

Aron, A., Aron, E. N., & Smollan, D. (1992). Inclusion of other in the self scale and the structure of interpersonal closeness. *Journal of Personality and Social Psychology, 63*(4), 596–612. http://doi.org/10.1037/0022-3514.63.4.596

Aron, A., Melinat, E., Aron, E. N., Vallone, R. D., & Bator, R. J. (1997). The experimental generation of interpersonal closeness: A procedure and some preliminary findings. *Personality and Social Psychology Bulletin, 23*(4), 363–377. http://doi.org/10.1177/0146167297234003

Aron, A., Norman, C. C., Aron, E. N., McKenna, C., & Heyman, R. E. (2000). Couples' shared participation in novel and arousing activities and experienced relationship quality. *Journal of Personality and Social Psychology, 78*(2), 273–284. http://doi.org/10.1037//0022-3514.78.2.273

Bartz, J. A. (2016). Oxytocin and the pharmacological dissection of affiliation. *Current Directions in Psychological Science, 25*(2), 104–110. http://doi.org/10.1177/0963721415626678

Bartz, J. A., Zaki, J., Bolger, N., & Ochsner, K. N. (2011). Social effects of oxytocin in humans: Context and person matter. *Trends in Cognitive Sciences, 15*(7), 301–309. http://doi.org/10.1016/j.tics.2011.05.002

Berscheid, E. (2010). Love in the fourth dimension. *Annual Review of Psychology, 61*, 1–25. http://doi.org/10.1146/annurev.psych.093008.100318

Blum, D. (2002). *Love at Goon Park: Harry Harlow and the Science of Affection.* New York: Basic Books.

Bolger, N., Zuckerman, A., & Kessler, R. C. (2000). Invisible support and adjustment to stress. *Journal of Personality and Social Psychology, 79*(6), 953–961. http://doi.org/10.1037/0022-3514.79.6.953

Bornstein, R. F. (1989). Exposure and affect: Overview and meta-analysis of research, 1968–1987. *Psychological Bulletin, 106*(2), 265–289. http://doi.org/10.1037/0033-2909.106.2.265

Botwin, M. D., Buss, D. M., & Shackelford, T. K. (1997). Personality and mate preferences: Five factors in mate selection and marital satisfaction. *Journal of Personality, 65*(1), 107–136. http://doi.org/10.1111/j.1467-6494.1997.tb00531.x

Buss, D. M., Abbott, M., Angleitner, A., Asherian, A., Biaggio, A., Blanco-Villasenor, A., … Yang, K.-S. (1990). International preferences in selecting mates: A study of 37 cultures. *Journal of Cross-Cultural Psychology, 21*(1), 5–47. http://doi.org/10.1177/0022022190211001

Campbell, A. (2010). Oxytocin and human social behavior. *Personality & Social Psychology Review, 14*(3), 281–295. http://doi.org/10.1177/1088868310363594

Campbell, L., Martin, R., & Ward, J. (2008). An observational study of humor use during a conflict discussion. *Personal Relationships*, *15*, 41–55.

Carter, C. S. (1998). Neuroendocrine perspectives on social attachment and love. *Psychoneuroendocrinology*, *23*(8), 779–818. http://doi.org/10.1016/S0306-4530(98)00055-9

Cohen, S., Janicki-Deverts, D., Turner, R. B., & Doyle, W. J. (2015). Does hugging provide stress-buffering social support? A study of susceptibility to upper respiratory infection and illness. *Psychological Science*, *26*(2), 135–147. http://doi.org/10.1177/0956797614559284

Coulter, K., & Malouff, J. M. (2013). Effects of an intervention designed to enhance romantic relationship excitement. *Couple and Family Psychology: Research and Practice*, *2*(1), 34–44. http://doi.org/10.1037/a0031719

Coyne, J. C., Rohrbaugh, M. J., Shoham, V., Sonnega, J. S., Nicklas, J. M., & Cranford, J. A. (2001). Prognostic importance of marital quality for survival of congestive heart failure. *The American Journal of Cardiology*, *88*(5), 526–529. http://doi.org/10.1016/S0002-9149(01)01731-3

Day, L. C., & Impett, E. A. (2016). For it is in giving that we receive: The benefits of sacrifice in relationships. In C. R. Knee & H. T. Reis (eds), *Positive Approaches to Optimal Relationships* (pp. 211–231). Cambridge: Cambridge University Press.

Diener, E., & Seligman, M. E. P. (2002). Very happy people. *Psychological Science*, *13*, 413–438.

Ein-Dor, T., & Hirschberger, G. (2016). Rethinking attachment theory: From a theory of relationships to a theory of individual and group survival. *Current Directions in Psychological Science*, *25*(4), 223–227. http://doi.org/10.1177/0963721416650684

Feeney, B. C., & Collins, N. L. (2014). A new look at social support: A theoretical perspective on thriving through relationships. *Personality and Social Psychology Review*, *19*(2), 113–147. http://doi.org/10.1177/1088868314544222

Feeney, B. C., & Thrush, R. L. (2010). Relationship influences on exploration in adulthood: The characteristics and function of a secure base. *Journal of Personality and Social Psychology*, *98*(1), 57–76. http://doi.org/10.1037/a0016961

Fehr, B. (1988). Prototype analysis of the concepts of love and commitment. *Journal of Personality and Social Psychology*, *55*(4), 557–579. http://doi.org/10.1037/0022-3514.55.4.557

Fehr, B. (2015). Love: Conceptualization and experience. In *APA Handbook of Personality and Social Psychology, Volume 3: Interpersonal Relations* (vol. 3, pp. 495–522). Washington, DC: American Psychological Association.

Fehr, B., & Russell, J. A. (1991). Concept of love viewed from a prototype perspective. *Journal of Personality and Social Psychology*, *60*, 425–438. http://doi.org/10.1037/0096-3445.113.3.464

Fincham, F. D., Beach, S. R. H., & Davila, J. (2007). Longitudinal relations between forgiveness and conflict resolution in marriage. *Journal of Family Psychology*, *21*(3), 542–545. http://doi.org/10.1037/0893-3200.21.3.542

Fraley, R. C. (2002). Attachment stability from infancy to adulthood: Meta-analysis and dynamic modeling of developmental mechanisms. *Personality and Social Psychology Review*, *6*(2), 123–151. http://doi.org/10.1207/S15327957PSPR0602_03

Fraley, R. C., Roisman, G. I., Booth-LaForce, C., Owen, M. T., & Holland, A. S. (2013). Interpersonal and genetic origins of adult attachment styles: A longitudinal study from infancy to early adulthood. *Journal of Personality and Social Psychology*, *104*(5), 817–838. http://doi.org/10.1037/a0031435

Gable, S. L., Gonzaga, G. C., & Strachman, A. (2006). Will you be there for me when things go right? Supportive responses to positive event disclosures. *Journal of Personality and Social Psychology*, *91*(5), 904–917. http://doi.org/10.1037/0022-3514.91.5.904

Gable, S. L., Gosnell, C. L., Maisel, N. C., & Strachman, A. (2012). Safely testing the alarm: Close others' responses to personal positive events. *Journal of Personality and Social Psychology*, *103*(6), 963–981. http://doi.org/10.1037/a0029488

Gable, S. L., Reis, H. T., Impett, E. A., & Asher, E. R. (2004). What do you do when things go right? The intrapersonal and interpersonal benefits of sharing positive events. *Journal of Personality and Social Psychology*, *87*(2), 228–245. http://doi.org/10.1037/0022-3514.87.2.228

Gottman, J. (1994). *What Predicts Divorce? The Relationship between Marital Processes and Marital Outcomes*. New York: Simon & Schuster.

Graham, J. M. (2008). Self-expansion and flow in couples' momentary experiences: An experience sampling study. *Journal of Personality and Social Psychology*, *95*, 679–694. http://doi.org/10.1037/0022-3514.95.3.679

Graham, J. M. (2011). Measuring love in romantic relationships: A meta-analysis. *Journal of Social and Personal Relationships*, *28*(6), 748–771. http://doi.org/10.1177/0265407510389126

Graustella, A. J., & MacLeod, C. (2012). A critical review of the influence of oxytocin nasal spray on social cognition in humans: Evidence and future directions. *Hormones and Behavior*, *61*(3), 410–418. http://doi.org/10.1016/j.yhbeh.2012.01.002

Harasymchuk, C., Cloutier, A., Peetz, J., & Lebreton, J. (2017). Spicing up the relationship? The effects of relational boredom on shared activities. *Journal of Social and Personal Relationships*, *34*(6), 833–854. http://doi.org/10.1177/0265407516660216

Harlow, H. F. (1958). The nature of love. *American Psychologist*, *13*(12), 673–685. http://doi.org/10.1037/h0047884

Hatfield, E., Bensman, L., & Rapson, R. L. (2012). A brief history of social scientists' attempts to measure passionate love. *Journal of Social and Personal Relationships*, *29*(2), 143–164. http://doi.org/10.1177/0265407511431055

Hatfield, E., Pillemer, J. T., O'Brien, M. U., & Le, Y.-C. L. (2008). The endurance of love: Passionate and companionate love in newlywed and long-term marriages. *Interpersona: An International Journal on Personal Relationships*, *2*(1), 35–64. http://doi.org/10.5964/ijpr.v2i1.17

Hatfield, E., & Rapson, R. (2013). Companionate love scale. Retrieved 23 December 2016, from www.midss.ie

Hendrick, C., & Hendrick, S. S. (1989). Research on love: Does it measure up? *Journal of Personality and Social Psychology*, *56*(5), 784–794. http://doi.org/10.1037/0022-3514.56.5.784

Kleinplatz, P. J., Ménard, A. D., Paquet, M.-P., Paradis, N., Campbell, M., Zuccarino, D., & Mehak, L. (2009). The components of optimal sexuality: A portrait of "great sex." *The Canadian Journal of Human Sexuality, 18*(1–2), 1–13.

Knee, C. R., & Reis, H. T. (2016). *Positive Approaches to Optimal Relationship Development.* Cambridge: Cambridge University Press.

Lakin, J. L., Jefferis, V. E., Cheng, C. M., & Chartrand, T. L. (2003). The chameleon effect as social glue: Evidence for the evolutionary significance of nonconscious mimicry. *Journal of Nonverbal Behavior, 27*(3), 145–161. http://doi.org/10.1023/A:1025389814290

Lambert, N. M., Fincham, F. D., Gwinn, A. M., & Ajayi, C. A. (2011). Positive relationship science: A new frontier for positive psychology? In K. M. Sheldon, T. B. Kashdan, & M. F. Steger (eds), *Designing Positive Psychology* (pp. 280–292). New York: Oxford University Press.

Lambert, N. M., Gwinn, A. M., Baumeister, R. F., Strachman, A., Washburn, I. J., Gable, S. L., & Fincham, F. D. (2013). A boost of positive affect: The perks of sharing positive experiences. *Journal of Social and Personal Relationships, 30*(1), 24–43. http://doi.org/10.1177/0265407512449400

Lane, A., Luminet, O., Nave, G., & Mikolajczak, M. (2016). Is there a publication bias in behavioral intranasal oxytocin research on humans? Opening the file drawer of one lab. *Journal of Neuroendocrinology, 28*(4). http://doi.org/10.1111/jne.12384

Le, B., Dove, N. L., Agnew, C. R., Korn, M. S., & Mutso, A. A. (2010). Predicting nonmarital romantic relationship dissolution: A meta-analytic synthesis. *Personal Relationships, 17*(3), 377–390. http://doi.org/10.1111/j.1475-6811.2010.01285.x

Lee, L., Loewenstein, G., Ariely, D., Hong, J., & Young, J. (2008). If I'm not hot, are you hot or not? Physical-attractiveness evaluations and dating preferences as a function of one's own attractiveness. *Psychological Science, 19*(7), 669–677. http://doi.org/10.1111/j.1467-9280.2008.02141.x

Leng, G., & Ludwig, M. (2016). Intranasal oxytocin: Myths and delusions. *Biological Psychiatry, 79*(3), 243–250. http://doi.org/10.1016/j.biopsych.2015.05.003

Loewenstein, G., Krishnamurti, T., Kopsic, J., & Mcdonald, D. (2015). Does increased sexual frequency enhance happiness? *Journal of Economic Behavior and Organization, 116*, 206–218. http://doi.org/10.1016/j.jebo.2015.04.021

Malouff, J. M., Thorsteinsson, E. B., Schutte, N. S., Bhullar, N., & Rooke, S. E. (2010). The Five-Factor Model of personality and relationship satisfaction of intimate partners: A meta-analysis. *Journal of Research in Personality, 44*(1), 124–127. http://doi.org/10.1016/j.jrp.2009.09.004

McCullough, M. E., Rachal, K. C., Sandage, S. J., Worthington, E. L., Brown, S. W., & Hight, T. L. (1998). Interpersonal forgiving in close relationships II: Theoretical elaboration and measurement. *Journal of Personality and Social Psychology, 75*, 1586–1603.

McNulty, J. K., Wenner, C. A., & Fisher, T. D. (2016). Longitudinal associations among relationship satisfaction, sexual satisfaction, and frequency of sex in early marriage. *Archives of Sexual Behavior, 45*(1), 85–97. http://doi.org/10.1007/s10508-014-0444-6

Mikulincer, M., & Shaver, P. R. (2007). Boosting attachment security to promote mental health, prosocial values, and inter-group tolerance. *Psychological Inquiry*, *18*(3), 139–156. http://doi.org/10.1080/10478400701512646

Monfort, S. S., Kaczmarek, L. D., Kashdan, T. B., Drazkowski, D., Kosakowski, M., Guzik, P., … Gracanin, A. (2014). Capitalizing on the success of romantic partners: A laboratory investigation on subjective, facial, and physiological emotional processing. *Personality and Individual Differences*, *68*(2014), 149–153. http://doi.org/10.1016/j.paid.2014.04.028

Montoya, R. M., Horton, R. S., & Kirchner, J. (2008). Is actual similarity necessary for attraction? A meta-analysis of actual and perceived similarity. *Journal of Social and Personal Relationships*, *25*(6), 889–922. http://doi.org/10.1177/0265407508096700

Muise, A., Harasymchuk, C., Day, L. C., Bacev-Giles, C., Gere, J., & Impett, E. A. (2019). Broadening your horizons: Self-expanding activities promote desire and satisfaction in established romantic relationships. *Journal of Personality and Social Psychology*, *116*(2), 237–258.

Muise, A., Schimmack, U., & Impett, E. A. (2015). Sexual frequency predicts greater well-being, but more is not always better. *Social Psychological and Personality Science*, *7*(4), 295–302. http://doi.org/10.1177/1948550615616462

Nave, G., Camerer, C., & McCullough, M. (2015). Does oxytocin increase trust in humans? A critical review of research. *Perspectives on Psychological Science*, *10*(6), 772–789. http://doi.org/10.1177/1745691615600138

Nettle, D. (2006). The evolution of personality variation in humans and other animals. *American Psychologist*, *61*(6), 622–631. http://doi.org/10.1037/0003-066X.61.6.622

Noftle, E. E., & Shaver, P. R. (2006). Attachment dimensions and the big five personality traits: Associations and comparative ability to predict relationship quality. *Journal of Research in Personality*, *40*(2), 179–208. http://doi.org/10.1016/j.jrp.2004.11.003

O'Leary, K. D., Acevedo, B. P., Aron, A., Huddy, L., & Mashek, D. (2012). Is long-term love more than a rare phenomenon? If so, what are its correlates? *Social Psychological and Personality Science*, *3*(2), 241–249. http://doi.org/10.1177/1948550611417015

Overall, N. C., Grime, Y. U., & Simpson, J. A. (2016). The power of diagnostic situations: How support and conflict can foster growth and security. In C. R. Knee & H. T. Reis (eds), *Positive Approaches to Optimal Relationships* (pp. 148–170). Cambridge: Cambridge University Press.

Pierce, T., & Lydon, J. E. (2001). Global and specific relational models in the experience of social interactions. *Journal of Personality and Social Psychology*, *80*(4), 613–631. http://doi.org/10.1037/0022-3514.80.4.613

Regan, P. C., Kocan, E. R., & Whitlock, T. (1998). Ain't love grand! A prototype analysis of the concept of romantic love. *Journal of Social and Personal Relationships*, *15*(3), 411–420. http://doi.org/10.1177/0265407598153006

Reis, H. T., & Carothers, B. J. (2014). Black and white or shades of gray: Are gender differences categorical or dimensional? *Current Directions in Psychological Science*, *23*(1), 19–26. http://doi.org/10.1177/0963721413504105

Reis, H. T., Clark, M. S., & Holmes, J. G. (2004). Perceived partner responsiveness as an organizing construct in the study of intimacy and closeness in D. J. Mashek & A. Aron (eds), *Handbook of Closeness and Intimacy* (pp. 201–255). New York: Psychology Press.

Russell, V. M., & McNulty, J. K. (2011). Frequent sex protects intimates from the negative implications of their neuroticism. *Social Psychological and Personality Science, 2*, 220–227. http://doi.org/10.1177/1948550610387162

Schmitt, D. P., Alcalay, L., Allik, J., Ault, L., Austers, I., Bennett, K. L., … Zupanèiè, A. (2003). Universal sex differences in the desire for sexual variety: Tests from 52 nations, 6 continents, and 13 islands. *Journal of Personality and Social Psychology, 85*(1), 85–104. http://doi.org/10.1037/0022-3514.85.1.85

Schützwohl, A., Fuchs, A., McKibbin, W. F., & Shackelford, T. K. (2009). How willing are you to accept sexual requests from slightly unattractive to exceptionally attractive imagined requestors? *Human Nature, 20*(3), 282–293. http://doi.org/10.1007/s12110-009-9067-3

Shiota, M. N., Neufeld, S. L., Danvers, A. F., Osborne, E. A., Sng, O., & Yee, C. I. (2014). Positive emotion differentiation: A functional approach. *Social and Personality Psychology Compass, 8*(3), 104–117. http://doi.org/10.1111/spc3.12092

Shorey, R. C., & Lakey, B. (2011). Perceived and capitalization support are substantially similar: Implications for social support theory. *Personality & Social Psychology Bulletin, 37*(8), 1068–1079. http://doi.org/10.1177/0146167211406507

Simpson, J. A., & Rholes, W. S. (2012). Adult attachment orientations, stress, and romantic relationships. *Advances in Experimental Social Psychology, 45*, 279–328. http://doi.org/10.1016/B978-0-12-394286-9.00006-8

Slotter, E. B., & Gardner, W. L. (2009). Where do you end and I begin? Evidence for anticipatory, motivated self–other integration between relationship partners. *Journal of Personality and Social Psychology, 96*(6), 1137–1151. http://doi.org/10.1037/a0013882

Sprecher, S., & Toro-Morn, M. (2002). A study of men and women from different sides of Earth to determine if men are from Mars and women are from Venus in their beliefs about love and romantic relationships. *Sex Roles, 46*(5–6), 131–147. http://doi.org/10.1023/A:1019780801500

Sternberg, R. (1986). A triangular theory of love. *Psychological Review, 93*(2), 119–135. http://doi.org/10.1037/0033-295X.93.2.119

Uchino, B. N. (2009). Understanding the links between social support and physical health. *Perspectives on Psychological Science, 4*(3), 236–255.

van der Horst, F. C. P., LeRoy, H. A., & van der Veer, R. (2008). "When strangers meet": John Bowlby and Harry Harlow on attachment behavior. *Integrative Psychological and Behavioral Science, 42*(4), 370–388. http://doi.org/10.1007/s12124-008-9079-2

VanLaningham, J., Johnson, D. R., & Amato, P. (2001). Marital happiness, marital duration, and the u-shaped curve: Evidence from a five-wave panel study. *Social Forces, 79*(4), 1313–1341. http://doi.org/10.1353/sof.2001.0055

White, R. W. (1959). Motivation reconsidered: The concept of competence. *Psychological Review, 66,* 297–333. http://doi.org/10.1037/h0040934

Winterheld, H. A., Simpson, J. A., & Oriña, M. M. (2013). It's in the way that you use it: Attachment and the dyadic nature of humor during conflict negotiation in romantic couples. *Personality & Social Psychology Bulletin, 39*(4), 496–508. http://doi.org/10.1177/0146167213479133

Xu, X., Lewandowski, G. W., & Aron, A. (2016). The self-expansion model and optimal relationship development. In C. R. Knee & H. T. Reis (eds), *Positive Approaches to Optimal Relationships* (pp. 79–100). Cambridge: Cambridge University Press.

Zak, P. (2011). Paul Zak: Trust, morality—and oxytocin? [Video file]. Retrieved from www.ted.com/talks/paul_zak_trust_morality_and_oxytocin.

Part V

Towards Increasing Positivity

9

Stability and Change

INTRODUCTION

In the summer of 1995 I was a university student in Chicago, USA when a heat wave killed over 700 people. As might be expected, the deaths were disproportionately high among the elderly, especially in poor and minority neighbourhoods. However, when looking more closely at the neighbourhood data, sociologist Eric Klinenberg noticed that broad demographic statistics did not fully explain the pattern of deaths. Surprisingly, some poor neighbourhoods had the lowest death rates in the city – ten times fewer deaths than nearby neighbourhoods separated by a single street, and similar to the most affluent neighbourhoods. These islands of positive outcomes denote a major topic of this chapter: resilience. Positive psychologists (and sociologists, apparently) are keenly interested in finding the people and communities that do well even in the face of significant adversity. Why were some poor neighbourhoods so successful in protecting their elderly residents from the deadly heat? In this case, Klinenberg explored the question by talking with people in their neighbourhoods, but he solved the mystery by being physically present there, rather than by what he heard. He noticed that the resilient places had clean sidewalks, many businesses, and parks. In contrast, the neighbourhoods with high death rates were semi-abandoned, with few stores or public places, and cracked and cluttered sidewalks. These differences in physical spaces seemed to underlie differences in the ways the communities functioned, either promoting or hindering social contact. This 'social infrastructure' translated into people knowing which neighbours might need help during the heat crisis, thus preventing deaths. Social infrastructure is thus a predictor of resilience. In this chapter, we will explore many others. (Podcast episode #346 at 99percentinvisible.org tells this story and more.)

Earlier this year, my home city, Ottawa, Canada, was again hit by a natural disaster. It was less dramatic (and thankfully much less deadly) than the heat wave of 1995, but tornados wreaked havoc on Ottawa in 2018. In the aftermath, I learned about a new charitable organization, Team Rubicon, that came to help with the clean-up. I am sure that there are stories of great resilience among members of the tornado-affected neighbourhoods, but even more interestingly, the Team Rubicon volunteers demonstrate significant reslience. The organization is composed primarily of military veterans who have transitioned their service into disaster relief. The charity thereby serves a dual function: to help reintegrate former soldiers to civilian life, and to do this by helping people in need. I hope it does not detract from the veterans' admirable service to point out that these positive acts provide a path to their personal well-being too.

This brings us to the other central theme of this chapter: how positive activities – often prosocial ones – can be harnessed to improve well-being. Our focus is more prosaic than veterans performing disaster relief, but this has the advantage of being more accessible to all people. Team Rubicon brings together the topics of resilience and personal efforts to improve well-being. At another level, these topics mirror positive psychology's attempts to encourage both stability and change. When we encounter adversity, maintaining well-being – stability – connotes flourishing. However, for less challenging circumstances, positive psychology suggests some techniques that can increase well-being – positive change.

RESILIENCE

Natural disasters, death, racism, and poverty are probably not the first things that come to mind when thinking about positive psychology. Indeed, a reasonable way to understand the focus of positive psychology is as positive topics (see Chapter 1); however, this notion must be qualified to allow room for resilience. **Resilience** refers to well-being despite difficult circumstances, and it has been a key part of positive psychology from the beginning. We find resilience (or not) when people face significant challenges. These include acute events like accidents, assaults, and loss of loved ones, as well as chronic adversity such as poverty, prolonged illness, or discrimination. Some degree of challenge is required to know whether a person is truly resilient or not. Personality characteristics can help predict resilient responses, but it is the responses – over time – that define resilience (Masten, 2001; Meredith et al., 2011; Rutter, 2012; Ryff et al., 2012). For positive psychologists, the focus on studying what goes right still applies in difficult circumstances.

Resilient responses are defined in relation to some challenge, but they do not require actual change. For example, if a person's home and cherished possessions were destroyed in an earthquake, maintaining good psychological health (not changing) is considered resilience. If a poor community has longevity that is similar to wealthier neighbourhoods nearby, it is a resilient community. Resilient responses can even include relatively brief periods of poor functioning; those who bounce back quickly are resilient. With time, some people even report personal growth and improved well-being following adversity, and this too demonstrates resilience. In sum, resilience is found in various patterns of stability and change through adversity; the common element is good outcomes given the degree of challenge.

Even setting aside the complexity of stability and change in resilience, some tricky issues remain in fully describing it. The first is how to calibrate what counts as a good outcome. We might ask, for example, how much distress can occur in the face of adversity and still be resilient? There are no easy answers here. One (non-ideal) approach might be to define resilient responses as those which are better than average. We would first need to decide who is included in the relevant group (e.g. all widows, young widows, widows who were primary caregivers), then assess them, and then define the least distressed half as resilient. However, this arbitrarily assumes that 50 per cent of people are resilient. Beyond arbitrary, you might also be surprised to learn that the 50 per cent resilience rate is actually lower than research estimates using other approaches (Galatzer-Levy, Huang, & Bonanno, 2018). For example, a study surveyed residents of New York City for symptoms of post-traumatic stress disorder (PTSD) six months after the 2001 terrorist attack (Bonanno, Galea, Bucciarelli, & Vlahov, 2006). Overall, about 65 per cent of people reported zero or one symptom, and the researchers considered them resilient. About 6 per cent reported high symptom levels, suggesting continued PTSD stemming from the attack, with the remaining 29 per cent showing moderate or recovering levels. Although this study documents substantial suffering, it also suggests that the most common response was resilience in the face of a potentially traumatic event.

The New York PTSD study used the criterion of no or one symptom to define resilience; this is still somewhat arbitrary, but it seems a reasonable way to define good functioning under the circumstances. Another way to find resilience is to track people over time, ideally with a measurement taken before the potentially traumatic event. This approach presents a challenge to researchers, yet dozens of studies have been able to measure people before and after adverse events. Many of these are studies of predictable events (e.g. military deployment, bereavement following illness), but others rely on luck, clever adjustments, or good records. For example, comprehensive medical records in the Netherlands were used to examine children's mental health before and after a major fireworks factory accident (more on that later) (Dirkzwager, Kerssens, & Yzermans, 2006). As another example, in 2004–2005 researchers began a study about scholarships for low-income women in New Orleans which included some measures of distress and social support. After Hurricane Katrina hit the city, they located most of the participants for a follow-up, and could track distress from before to after this major disaster (Lowe & Rhodes, 2013). In pre- and post-event studies like this, changes over time can be used to sort people into groups. Understandably, some people respond with a significant increase in distress. Others, however, are quite stable, with low levels of distress before the event which remain similar through it and after it. These people are considered resilient due to maintaining psychological heath despite difficult circumstances. Other people have significant distress even before the event, and still others undergo a period of distress and then recover, and so on – there are wide individual differences. Nonetheless, studies typically find that resilience is the most common pattern. For example, in a review of 54 longitudinal studies, the average rate of resilience was around 65 per cent (i.e. low distress before and after an event), with the next largest group, about 20 per cent, showing substantial recovery during the studies' periods (Galatzer-Levy et al., 2018). Although some quibble with the statistical details (Infurna & Luthar, 2016), the results across these traumatic event studies are striking: resilience is common.

This conclusion accords with observations from chronic adversity too. For example, developmental researcher Ann Masten (2001) characterized resilience in children as "ordinary magic". This idea has two parts: first, research shows that children from difficult circumstances (e.g. poverty, mental illness in parents) often grow up to become productive and well-adjusted adults; and second, overcoming early adversity does not seem to require any super powers – normal human coping responses usually suffice. As another example, African Americans report high levels of psychological well-being despite racial discrimination and social inequalities in the USA (Keyes, 2009). None of this means that adversity carries no risk, but instead suggests that many people successfully overcome challenges. As with so many other areas, threats and negative outcomes understandably grab attention – we should help remedy them – yet their power can also obscure the ordinariness of positive resolutions.

Another challenge in characterizing resilience is deciding what, exactly, must go right to qualify. For example, if a chronically ill person has pervasive uncertainty about her purpose in life, but generally experiences pleasant moods, is she resilient? For practical reasons, individual studies typically consider only a small set of potentially relevant factors. Returning to the study of 2001 New Yorkers, many people seemed resilient on measures of PTSD, but perhaps they were still depressed or had substantially reduced life satisfaction – we simply do not know. Some critics argue that we cannot trust the high resilience rate estimates because there could always be unmeasured variables that would display problems (e.g. Infurna & Luthar, 2016). It is hard to dismiss this idea, and caution is warranted to avoid making too much of exact estimates for resilience rates. However, it also seems unlikely that research consistently measures the wrong things, and that substantial ill-being is hiding in those unmeasured factors. Most individual studies are too limited to make confident conclusions about psychological health broadly (complete resilience), but critiques become unfalsifiable if they appeal to an endless list of hidden or unmeasured possibilities.

With so many definitional ambiguities in the details of resilience, knowing the exact rate seems impossible or arbitrary. Yet debate continues on the issue, probably because it has implications for treatment and interventions. To the extent that resilience is common, it suggests that most people will not require special attention following potentially traumatic events; instead, treatments might be reserved for the few who would otherwise suffer (Bonanno, Brewin, Kaniasty, & La Greca, 2010). On the other hand, if problems are common then broad-based interventions seem more appropriate. At the risk of being cynical, the people who provide psychological services hardly seem unbiased in seeing need for their services (Maddux, 2008); however, positive psychologists have a different perspective. Even if resilience is common, positive psychologists have a role in promoting greater flourishing – their work does not depend on things going wrong. Even so, it is abundantly clear that some people do suffer, and also that some circumstances and personal characteristics are more conducive to resilience than others. Whether to hone interventions, identify people at risk, or study what goes right, there is broad interest in learning more about where we find resilience.

Finding Resilience

The clearest predictor of difficulty following potentially traumatic events is the degree of exposure. For example, in disasters some people are physically injured, lose property, or see the horrific suffering of others, whereas other people are less directly affected. The more exposure, the less resilience, on average (Bonanno et al., 2010). Returning once again to the New York 2001 study, an average of only 6 per cent of the New Yorkers surveyed indicated probable PTSD overall, but the rates were higher for people who were physically or symbolically closer to the attack: 11 per cent if a friend or relative was killed, 25 per cent for those present in the World Trade Center, or 12 per cent if they were involved in the rescue. Additionally, about 30–40 per cent more people reported moderate symptoms across these groups (Bonanno et al., 2006). Similar patterns emerge in most studies of natural disasters where more direct involvement produces more problems. In addition, the objective challenge of discrete events sometimes plays out over longer periods of time, such as when people are displaced, lose employment, and so on. Lower rates of resilience come with continuing challenges.

Broad reviews of resilience research point to many features of personality and the social context that also predict better outcomes when facing adversity (Bonanno et al., 2010; Masten, 2001; Meredith et al., 2011; Rutter, 2012; Ryff et al., 2012). Rather than pointing to one key strength, research suggests that broad collections of resources, or complex interactions among them, facilitate resilience. With that caveat, some personality features that seem helpful are emotional stability (vs neuroticism), positive emotionality, a general sense of control (mastery, internal locus of control, self-efficacy), and good self-regulation (part of trait conscientiousness). Religiosity seems to provide a buffer in stressful circumstances, likely because it fosters a sense of meaning and connects people to others (Diener, Tay, & Myers, 2011). In addition, adaptive coping styles include those that are problem focused, avoid rumination, and are prone to finding some benefit or seeing a challenge (vs defeat) in adversity. That said, even the best coping strategies will not apply to every situation; there is value in having flexibility. By analogy, it is better to have more tools in the box, along with the knowledge about when to use each (Bonanno & Burton, 2013). Positive thinking and optimism are helpful, but within reason; self-enhancement complemented by a realistic sense of what can and cannot be controlled may be best.

Measures of trait resilience also exist (other names include toughness or hardiness). However, these are at odds with the contemporary view of resilience as an outcome and as requiring challenge to be revealed. Moreover, trait resilience questionnaires often combine some of the more general personal characteristics already listed in the previous paragraph. For example, **mental toughness** includes aspects of self-efficacy, emotion regulation, attention regulation, optimism, and so on. It also predicts successful completion of stressful tasks like elite military training and performance in work and academic settings (Gucciardi, Hanton, Gordon, Mallett, & Temby, 2015).

It is worth noting that many of the personality characteristics that predict resilient responses also describe healthy functioning in general. That is, some of the things that positive psychology seeks to foster for their own sake, such as positive emotions or sense of mastery, also predict resilient responses over time in longitudinal studies (Ryff et al., 2012) – they seem helpful if present before adverse events. Similarly, intelligence, education, and wealth (socio-economic status) are personal resources that help people cope with adversity. Without a specific negative event, lacking them can be seen as a chronic challenge, and where good psychological health despite low socio-economic status indicates resilience. Still, high socio-economic status is also helpful in coping with potentially traumatic events when they do occur (Bonanno et al., 2010).

Social support is another commonly identified predictor of resilience. A recent issue of the journal *Child Development* solicited articles from experts who were tasked with describing a few concrete ways to foster resilience in children at risk (Luthar & Eisenberg, 2017). With remarkable consistency, the answers revolved around increasing the well-being of primary caregivers (typically mothers) via social support and improving their parenting techniques. The reasoning around these suggestions is like a set of Russian matryoshka dolls, with layer upon layer of healthy relationships needed to build resilient people. The risks themselves are often poor relationships; moreover, in the face of other difficulties (e.g. poverty, mental illness, abuse), parents do well when they have social support, children do well when they have close bonds with parents, and well children have positive, prosocial peer relationships. Strong social bonds are the treatment and the cure. At the other end of life, better social relationships predict remaining healthy in old age; similarly, decreases in social contact over time are associated with greater cognitive decline among older adults (Ryff et al., 2012). Throughout the lifespan, feeling a sense of connection with one's community, having secure attachments, and families with emotional warmth predict resilient responses (Meredith et al., 2011). Major events like accidents, disasters, births, and deaths often play out in positive or negative ways to the extent that they enhance or threaten social relationships (Bonanno et al., 2010). As Chapter 8 describes in more detail, our bonds with other people matter greatly. This is especially true when facing challenges.

The philosopher Friedrich Nietzsche famously quipped "Whatever does not kill me makes me stronger", and thereby offered a hypothesis about past negative experiences and future resilience. Psychologists have tested this idea, and the research suggests that Nietzsche was at least half right. Previous experience with adversity can be protective, but it can also put people at greater risk for future problems (Bonanno et al., 2010; Rutter, 2012). Fortunately, this apparent contradiction becomes understandable if we look more closely at the details. Having a history of mental illness, severe abuse, stress, and trauma are generally risk factors for poor outcomes in the future. Predispositions and unfortunate experiences can produce dysregulated coping systems; they are especially sensitive to stressors, and additional adversity compounds their problems. For these people, adversity does not add strength. For example, an impressive study used comprehensive medical records to track changes in children's well-being before and after a fireworks factory accident in Amsterdam, comparing victims to a control group over time (Dirkzwager et al., 2006). Children affected by the disaster experienced substantially more distress, sleep disturbance, and anxiety issues. The effects were greatest for children who were displaced to a new home (i.e. theirs was destroyed by the explosion). The next largest predictor of increased problems in the victim group was a history of psychological problems before the disaster. Keep in mind that the control group also included some people with a history of psychological problems. Nonetheless, the disaster exacerbated these challenges among victims. Said another way, past difficulties had not made them stronger.

On the other hand, small to moderate amounts of stress can build toughness. In experiments with baby squirrel monkeys, permanent separation from the mother creates long-term problems; however, babies who were periodically separated for only two hours at a time grew up to have better cognitive control and stress hormone profiles, compared to baby monkeys who were never separated from their mothers (Lyons & Parker, 2007). In the context of humans, a large longitudinal study of American adults produced conceptually similar results. It assessed people's cumulative lifetime adversity (i.e. from a list of 37 negative events like disaster, divorce, injury, etc.) and found that moderate levels were associated with the highest life satisfaction and the lowest distress, PTSD symptoms, and impairment in work and social life (Seery, Holman, & Silver, 2010). In other words, having some past adversity predicted better health over time, compared to having no adversity at all. Still, having a lot of lifetime adversity was most problematic. Other research with humans suggests that getting through past adversity might be helpful too. For example, older adults tend to be more resilient after disasters, particularly if they have experienced similar emergencies in the past (Bonanno et al., 2010). On the other hand, young children often take longer to recover from traumatic events. Again, it may be that some adverse experience helps people cope with new stressors, so long as that past experience has not left psychological scars.

POST-TRAUMATIC GROWTH

Positive psychologists have been keen to explore an even rosier form of resilience: when people experience benefits related to their challenges. For example, in a moving TED Talk, Stacey Kramer (2010) describes her brain tumour as 'the best gift I ever survived'. The negatives of brain cancer are obvious, but Stacy balances these against the way her illness brought family and friends together, recalibrated her priorities, redefined her spirituality, and provided new understanding of her body. (She notes that the bevy of flowers and good drugs were nice too.) Stacey, like some other survivors, has a sense that, although she does not wish cancer on other people, she would not change her own experience. **Post-traumatic growth** describes the process whereby people find benefits (e.g. meaning, personal strength, new possibilities) following a traumatic experience. This idea is also captured by similar jargon terms like benefit finding, meaning making, adversarial growth, or stress-related growth. Traumatic experiences are defined by the intense fear, helplessness, and horror that they cause, but many people also report some benefits. The estimates vary widely by event and the people being studied, but it is common to find that more than 50 per cent of people report some positives that came from their traumatic events – often along with substantial negatives (Jayawickreme & Blackie, 2014; Lechner, Tennen, & Affleck, 2009; Linley & Joseph, 2004).

The high rate of benefit finding does not imply that positives appear quickly or easily. Rather, the prevailing idea is that struggle becomes a catalyst for growth. For example, many traumatic events (e.g. assault, serious injury, bereavement) involve a dramatic change in life. These events challenge people's assumptions about the way the world works and their expectations for the future. The process of coping with these changes, developing new expectations and goals, or finding new forms of meaning can produce a sense of growth (Davis & Porter, 2018). Like Stacey Kramer, the people who experience post-traumatic growth describe a wide variety of benefits, such as a deeper spirituality, an enhanced sense of personal strength, new priorities in life, a new bodily awareness (with illness), and better social relationships (Hefferon, Grealy, & Mutrie, 2009; Helgeson, 2010; Tedeschi & Calhoun, 1996). Many of these positive perceptions are captured in the Post-Traumatic Growth Inventory (PTGI) – see specific examples in the Try It box.

TRY IT

The Post-Traumatic Growth Inventory

To be clear, this box does not suggest that you seek out a traumatic experience. Rather, it introduces the Post-Traumatic Growth Inventory (PTGI; Tedeschi & Calhoun, 1996), which is commonly used to assess the perceived benefits that come from a traumatic event. To take the inventory, people are asked to rate a series of 21 statements on the degree to which the change occurred in their lives as a result of a focal crisis or disaster. The rating scale ranges from 0 ("I did not experience this change as a result of my crisis") to 5 ("I experienced this change to a very great degree as a result of my crisis"). Here are some of the items:

1. I have a greater sense of closeness with others.

2. I better accept needing others.

3. I have a greater feeling of self-reliance.

4. I am better able to accept the way things work out.

5. I am able to do better things with my life.

6. I developed new interests.

7. I can better appreciate each day.

8. I changed my priorities about what is important in life.

9. I have a better understanding of spiritual matters.

10. I have a stronger religious faith.

These items can be summed to an overall score of post-traumatic growth, or divided into narrower subscales to indicate specific domains of growth: relating to others (1 and 2), personal strength (3 and 4), new possibilities (5 and 6), appreciation of life (7 and 8), and spiritual change (9 and 10). Higher scores indicate more perceived growth.

The number of people who eventually report benefits from their adversity is substantial; yet not everyone does, and it can take a long time for others. Some psychologists take this as an indication that psychotherapy and advice should encourage people to search for meaning and personal growth following traumatic events (e.g. Linley & Joseph, 2004). Others, however, find more reasons for caution in the research (e.g. Lechner et al., 2009). Reservations revolve around three issues: individual differences, whether or not people actually change following trauma, and whether or not growth – or potentially inaccurate perceptions of growth – is positively associated with well-being.

Regarding individual differences, some general caution is warranted in moving from the correlations observed in naturalistic settings to interventions that artificially try to increase a seemingly good thing. This can be a useful strategy, but recall the sobering examples of self-esteem (Chapter 5) and frequency of sex (Chapter 8). Despite the clear positive links with well-being, attempts to increase self-esteem or frequent sex have not turned out well. Perhaps forcing people to search for benefits in their adversity would have similarly poor consequences (Coyne & Tennen, 2010). Research suggests that the search for meaning in adversity is not always successful. For example, a study of people with recent spinal cord injury observed that those who searched for meaning – and found it – over the course of a year reported less depression and higher subjective well-being, compared to people who searched but did not find meaning (Davis & Novoa, 2013). Interestingly, a substantial minority of people did not report searching for meaning at all; their well-being was similar to those who found meaning, and it was higher than the people who searched without finding meaning. These results are correlational too, yet they indicate that some spinal cord patients adapt just fine without seeking meaning. Sending them on a search that might fail seems questionable. To be fair, the concern here remains mostly hypothetical. Strong clinical trials of benefit-finding interventions do not exist. On the other hand, some other psychological interventions for trauma (e.g. critical incident stress management) seem to do more harm than good (Bonanno et al., 2010; McNally, Bryant, & Ehlers, 2003). Testing the efficacy of new interventions is essential, as is consideration of individual differences when implementing them. Perhaps only some people will benefit from their meaning searches.

In addition, research has questioned whether or not self-reports of growth accurately capture positive changes (Frazier, Tennen, Gavian, Park, Tomich, & Tashiro, 2009; Jayawickreme & Blackie, 2014; Owenz & Fowers, 2018). To the extent that questionnaires do not measure actual growth, it warrants suspicion about the research suggesting a link between (self-reported) growth and other positive outcomes. Part of the critique against growth questionnaires is conceptual, arguing that they require people to report on things that are very difficult to know. For example, the PTGI (see Try It box) asks people to take many mental steps to answer its questions. You must know your current level on a dimension (e.g. how well you relate to others) and your level before the traumatic event; you must then compare them to assess how much you have changed; finally, you must determine how much of the change is due to the traumatic event. The last of these seems very difficult to ever know, even with an accurate memory. In addition, studies in similar domains suggest that people are not very accurate in assessing how much they have changed over time, such as on personality traits or relationship satisfaction (Frazier et al., 2009; Jayawickreme & Blackie, 2014).

Beyond the conceptual issues around difficult questionnaires, two longitudinal studies cast doubt on the accuracy of perceived post-traumatic growth (Frazier et al., 2009; Owenz & Fowers, 2018). These studies are especially informative because they measure people both before and after potentially traumatic events. They accomplished this by recruiting large numbers of students to complete questionnaires about their current standing on the dimensions of well-being assessed by the PTGI (e.g. personal strength, relationships, spirituality). They then waited a few months, and during that time some students experienced traumatic events. One study was focused on romantic relationship break-ups (Owenz & Fowers, 2018). The other asked about a wide variety of traumatic events (e.g. having a loved one suddenly die or become seriously ill/injured, personally life-threatening events, and unwanted sexual attention); 71 per cent of these were rated as causing intense fear, helplessness, or horror (Frazier et al., 2009). The subset of students who experienced a traumatic event was then asked to again rate their current (post-trauma) status on the same dimensions of well-being; critically, they also reported separately on their perceptions of growth – the standard PTGI, which asks people to rate how much they think they have changed as a result of their trauma. In other words, the studies had a more objective measure of change over time (subjective ratings, but both before and after trauma), and this was compared to the usual PTGI which is entirely retrospective. In both studies, the perceptions of growth (PTGI) were not strongly associated with measures of actual change. Some people did change over time (positive and negative); however, these were not the same people who reported changing on the retrospective questionnaire. Thus, the studies cast doubt on the notion that measures like the PTGI are assessing true change over time.

Of course the studies have limitations. For example, the timeframe of studies was short; perhaps the growth and perceptions were still in flux. The short timeframe, along with the all-student samples, might also limit the kinds of trauma that were captured. Still, studies with other clever methods have also raised concerns about the accuracy of growth self-reports. In one example, breast cancer survivors reported on their experiences of change (both positive and negative) ten years after their diagnoses (Helgeson, 2010). The researchers also asked close others (mostly spouses) how the patient had changed, and the agreement was not strong, especially for the positive changes. It is not clear which rating is more correct, but these results cast further doubt on the accuracy of retrospective growth reports. With findings like these accumulating, researchers now tend to think that questionnaires like the PTGI measure perceptions of growth, and that those perceptions often differ from reality. Still, it remains plausible that even illusory perceptions of growth are useful or healthy (cf. Taylor & Brown, 1988).

We will address the link between perceived growth and well-being shortly, but first it is important to ask whether actual growth occurs following trauma. Is there more to growth than illusory perceptions? A recent analysis of Twitter language around the November 2015 terrorist attacks in Paris is suggestive (Garcia & Rimé, 2019). Unsurprisingly, the use of negative emotion words spiked with the attack; however, words related to helping others and shared values (e.g. *liberté*, *egalité*, *fraternité*) also increased shortly after, and their use stayed elevated for much longer. Twitter language is an indirect indicator of psychological processes. Here, that divergence from reflective self-reports is a strength. The language changes over time suggest a genuinely increased sense of solidarity following the terrorist attack.

Additional evidence for actual post-traumatic growth comes from a recent meta-analysis that combined results from over 100 studies of major life events (Mangelsdorf, Eid, & Luhmann, 2018). The focus was on how well-being changes over time. To be included, studies did not have to assess perceptions of change (e.g. with retrospective questionnaires), but they did need to assess current well-being at multiple time points. Most of the major events were negative and potentially traumatic; however, about 25 per cent were positive (e.g. marriage, lottery win, new job, aesthetic surgery). This massive analysis concluded that actual growth does sometimes occur following major life events, but with some important caveats. First, the clear changes were limited to some aspects of well-being. For example, major events improved social relationships, self-esteem, and mastery – on average – but surprisingly, there was not much evidence for substantial change in spirituality or sense of meaning. Second, results were similar across positive and negative events. There were minor differences; for example, social relationships seemed especially likely to improve with negative events, and mastery more likely to improve with positive events. Still, the idea that positive events can improve relationships, mastery, and self-esteem suggests the reality of a newer idea: **post-ecstatic growth**, or positive change following a major good event (see Roepke, 2013; Taubman-Ben-Ari, Findler, & Sharon, 2011). Third, some of the studies considered in this analysis included control groups of people with no major life events, and these studies produced less support for the idea of event-related growth. Some studies found that event groups changed more, but others found that control groups changed more. Perhaps these mixed results connote real-world complexity where growth depends on the particular events or outcomes. They also raise the possibility that some of the growth found in studies without control groups is due to normal maturation, rather than unfolding from a major life event. Although this meta-analysis included many studies, its broad scope also means that the more nuanced issues remain ambiguous pending even more data (e.g. studies with control groups, more event types, additional measures of well-being). In sum, there does appear to be evidence for real growth following trauma, though it is not universal.

We now return to what may be the most important question around post-traumatic growth: does it promote good psychological health? Given that actual growth (change over time) does not correspond well with perceptions of growth (assessed with retrospective questionnaires), it is possible to ask the question twice. For objective change over time, the question seems to answer itself. Growth is defined by increases in desirable characteristics such as strong interpersonal relationships, self-esteem, and mastery; these are hallmarks of psychological health. Some studies also hint that actual growth is associated with less distress (Frazier et al., 2009). The primary limitation here is that actual growth may not extend across all potential areas of well-being simultaneously. Still, with little evidence of trade-offs across domains (e.g. mastery at the cost of spirituality), the actual growth seems like a real benefit.

Turning to perceptions of growth and well-being, the answer is frustratingly ambiguous. The perception of growth is comforting in and of itself, and it connotes a subjective sense of well-being, at least in those growth domains. In addition, many individual studies found that perceptions of growth were associated with less distress and other desirable outcomes (Lechner et al., 2009; Linley & Joseph, 2004). In addition, perceived growth is associated with positive coping strategies, and can be viewed as part of those coping efforts (Jayawickreme & Blackie, 2014; Lechner et al., 2009). On the other hand, some studies find that perceptions of growth are associated with higher levels of distress. For example, the two studies that tracked large groups of students from before to after traumatic events found that those

306

who experience more distress also reported the most growth (Frazier et al., 2009; Owenz & Fowers, 2018). It seems plausible that the experience of distress might prompt perceptions of growth. To the extent that distress is the catalyst, we should expect that the most distressed people will feel like they changed the most. On the other hand, if perceptions of growth are genuinely helpful, that distress should then fade with time. This seems to happen for some people (e.g. the spinal cord patients who found meaning and had less depression over time; Davis & Novoa, 2013), but results differ across studies. For example, a study of Dutch soldiers deployed to Iraq tracked perceptions of growth and PTSD symptoms over time (Engelhard, Lommen, & Sijbrandij, 2015). It found that soldiers who reported high levels of growth five months after returning home were more likely to develop PTSD symptoms over the following ten months – growth predicted increases in distress over time.

Resolving these contradictions is difficult. It may be that perceptions of growth bring both costs and benefits, or that the effects depend on the level of distress, individual differences, or the particular traumatic event (Lechner et al., 2009). Nonetheless, the current state of research suggests that trying to build actual strengths – rather than mere perceptions of increased strengths – has better potential to help people who have experienced trauma. Said another way, there is probably little value in trying to convince people that their lives are better because of traumatic experiences; yet fostering actual strengths is obviously beneficial.

INTENTIONAL POSITIVE CHANGE AND INTERVENTIONS

Research on major life events has shown that they can prompt changes in well-being. Moreover, although the events studied are often negative, newer research on post-ecstatic growth suggests the possibility of positive change from positive events. Still, such events are either hard to plan for or are not the kinds of things that can (or should) be repeated too often, such as getting married, a new job, or aesthetic surgery. Are there other things that people can do to improve their happiness? Positive psychology is premised on the idea that a focus on well-being can make lives happier and better. Still, it is worth considering a couple of challenges to this idea.

The first challenge is data that show that subjective well-being is typically very stable over long periods of time, has substantial heritability and lack of non-genetic parenting effects, and is prone to adaptation when major events do perturb levels (i.e. the hedonic treadmill; see Chapter 3 or Diener, Heintzelman, Tay, Wirtz, Lutes, & Oishi, 2017). Earlier in this chapter, we reviewed research showing that most people are resilient, but the researchers often defined resilience as people's well-being staying the same despite major life challenges. Here, happiness's resistance to change is good news. However, the tendency towards stability may also work against efforts to systematically improve well-being. These facts set up a challenge for efforts at positive change. Yet we have also seen that happiness levels are not immutable. Stability and heritability are not 100 per cent, and the hedonic treadmill can be slow to catch up. Moreover, the wide variations in happiness across cultures tell us that people's circumstances matter greatly. Collectively, then, research suggests that increasing well-being may not be easy, but it seems possible. Still, knowing that happiness can change (with extreme circumstances) is not the same as knowing how to improve the happiness of well-functioning people.

Positive psychologists have argued that people's choices are an important part of the happiness puzzle, in addition to genes and circumstances (Lyubomirsky, Sheldon, & Schkade, 2005). In other words, a desire to become happier can pay off when people invest effort in that goal. On the other hand, some folk wisdom suggests that pursuing happiness directly is a sure way to lose it (Fordyce, 1983). This idea is echoed in an empirical challenge that suggested that valuing happiness too much could be problematic. That is, researchers developed a questionnaire to assess how much people value happiness, and they found that high valuing was negatively correlated with actual happiness (Mauss, Tamir, Anderson, & Savino, 2011). Of course it is possible that low happiness might motivate valuing it more, rather than valuing reducing happiness. To address this, the researchers also performed an experiment where valuing happiness was induced by having participants read about the benefits of happiness; a few minutes later, these participants experienced worse moods, compared to a control group, when they watched a pleasant film (Mauss et al., 2011). These studies argue against the wisdom of actively working towards happiness. (They may even argue against reading a book about positive psychology, but how could that be true?)

Fortunately for positive psychology (and your happiness as a reader), many other studies suggest that a narrower interpretation of Mauss et al.'s (2011) studies is warranted. First, other experiments have shown that active efforts at momentary mood improvement do work (Quoidbach & Gross, 2015). For example, participants who listened to pleasant music after being asked to try to improve their mood (vs a control group told to act naturally) reported more positive emotions (Ferguson & Sheldon, 2013). You might be thinking that the participants were merely trying to please the experimenter, given the obvious instructions, but the same instructions had no influence when the music was ambiguous, rather than actually pleasant. This increases our confidence that efforts did matter and suggests that trying to feel good requires some actual pleasant stimuli too. Actively trying to boost moods is not exactly the same as valuing happiness, but it is reassuring to know that efforts to boost moods can succeed (compare this to savouring in Table 9.1).

In addition, there may be something idiosyncratic about parts of the valuing happiness questionnaire. When the individual items were examined in a German sample, only some were associated with lower happiness; for example, "I am concerned about my happiness, even when I am happy" predicted lower happiness (Luhmann, Necka, Schoenbrodt, & Hawkley, 2016). Yet other items, such as "Feeling happy is extremely important to me", had small positive correlations with happiness. Other researchers have crafted similar questionnaires, such as the prioritizing positivity scale (e.g. "I structure my day to maximize my happiness"), and found positive correlations with subjective well-being (Catalino, Algoe, & Fredrickson, 2014). It may be that valuing happiness excessively connotes problems for some people – worrying about happiness is still worrying. Nonetheless, slight variations on this theme, such as prioritizing happiness and making choices to bring it about, appear to be more helpful.

Finally, these links can also differ by culture. Valuing happiness has correlated with lower subjective well-being in the US, but not in Germany; moreover, the correlation seems to turn positive in Russia and East Asia (Ford et al., 2015). It may be that valuing happiness inspires different pursuits in different places, and some of these pursuits are more effective than others. Taking an even broader view, a study of 47 countries found that average life satisfaction was higher in the countries that valued positive emotions more (Bastian, Kuppens, De Roover, & Diener, 2014). Yet the individuals in those countries who experienced more non-valued (unpleasant) emotions were especially dissatisfied. In other words, the cultural norm of valuing positive emotions seems helpful overall, but with some extra happiness cost for people who do not experience them.

In sum, although there are some provocative findings in this area, we do not find a robust challenge to the notion that actively working towards a happy life will necessarily backfire. There are certainly some ineffective ways to pursue happiness and some unhelpful mindsets. However, these do not foreclose the possibility of better strategies that are effective in boosting happiness. Ultimately, the best way to answer the question of whether or not happiness can be increased intentionally is to test some boosting techniques directly. We turn to those efforts now.

Positive Psychology Interventions

Positive interventions are activities designed to foster a lasting improvement in well-being, and that are supported by empirical research (Parks & Biswas-Diener, 2013). For example, previous chapters' Try It boxes suggested that you engage in acts of kindness, use signature strengths in new ways, or savour a positive experience. These are all components of positive interventions, though at very low doses given the one-time invitations. Experiments have tested these activities and found that participants, on average, experience happiness boosts over time and compared to control groups (Bolier, Haverman, Westerhof, Riper, Smit, & Bohlmeijer, 2013; Sin & Lyubomirsky, 2009; Weiss, Westerhof, & Bohlmeijer, 2016; White, Uttl, & Holder, 2019). We will return to the details of empirical tests shortly, but for now note that this defining criterion – supportive research – distinguishes positive interventions from other forms of self-help, treatment, or advice that have not been subjected to such tests.

Positive intervention activities are often brief and self-guided, though additional structure and support might be offered online, via smartphone apps, or even by a live human coach or counsellor. The most intensive versions involve six to twelve weeks of psycho-therapy sessions and can be applied in clinical settings (Cheavens, Feldman, Gum, Michael, & Snyder, 2006; Fava, Rafanelli, Cazzaro, Conti, & Grandi, 1998; Rashid, 2015). Yet all positive interventions differ from other forms of assistance in that they focus on posi-tive processes and increasing well-being, rather than on reducing or eliminating negative thoughts or symptoms. Keep in mind that mental illness can co-occur with happiness, and that some people who are free from mental illness are not very happy. Positive interventions are designed to boost happiness, rather than treat dysfunction per se. Moreover, they focus on positive processes. For example, they do not target stress reduction, problematic inter-personal habits (e.g. hostility, avoidance), or self-critical thoughts. These are worthy targets with potential for beneficial treatments; however, positive interventions instead encourage positive behaviours, emotions, and thoughts. This is distinct from eliminating the negative. Reasonably happy and well-functioning people might benefit from positive interventions and further boost their well-being. Of course it is possible that increasing positive thoughts could reduce depression, or that reducing stress might ultimately promote happiness. The distinction here is about the focus and goals (positive interventions focus on positive); moreover, it highlights a core theme of the positive psychology movement: that flourishing is not merely the absence of distress.

As one final point of clarification, not all mood-boosting activities count as positive interventions. The benefits must outweigh the costs, for example by building some psy-chological resource for the future. Eating a giant bowl of ice cream might feel good, but the ultimate gains are unlikely to be valued. Perhaps you are reading this, but not really in the mood for studying. Putting the book down in favour of a video game might feel good, but the benefit would be short lived – 'books to games' is not a positive intervention if you would regret the choice later. To be clear, this is not an argument against all hedonism (i.e. pursuing good feelings), but the time horizon should extend beyond the current moment. Positive interventions must produce a net gain to well-being over time.

Dozens of activities have been studied as positive interventions, and Table 9.1 provides many examples. For the most part, these are individual activities that require only minimal instruction and that can be practised in self-guided ways. The inspiration for many of these activities came from observing the characteristics of happy people. For example, happy people tend to be sociable, kind, grateful, optimistic, and so on. These interventions ask people to emulate these characteristics with concrete actions, such as cultivating gratitude by counting positive life events, or expressing gratitude by sending letters of appreciation. Of course the personality-level correlations are ambiguous about causal direction (perhaps happiness causes gratitude instead), and there is always uncertainty that interventions will play out the same way as the naturalistically observed processes (again, recall the examples of self-esteem and sexual frequency). What does the research say about the efficacy of positive intervention activities?

Table 9.1 Positive intervention activities

Intervention Technique	Brief Description
Three good things	Typically done daily, people write down good things that occurred; sometimes they are further asked to reflect on why those good things happened.
Three funny things	A variation where people write the three funniest things that they did or experienced and why they happened.
Using signature strengths in new ways	People first assess their character strengths (see Chapter 4), choose those with the highest scores, and then commit to engaging in new ways of expressing them in daily life.
Gift of time	Variations include spending (more) time with a close other, or spending time in a way that helps another person.
Acts of kindness	Committing to doing nice things for other people can be much smaller than the gift of time; a variation involves merely counting your acts of kindness at the end of each day.
Gratitude journal (counting blessings):	This involves noticing kind acts done by others; this can be a daily exercise based on specific events, or more substantial writing about important people (e.g. a loving father or supportive mentor).
Gratitude letter	Writing a letter to express gratitude to a person who has helped you, but never been properly thanked. The letter may or may not be delivered.
One door closes, another opens	A writing exercise where people describe times in the past where a negative event turned out to have some unexpected positive consequences.
Best possible self	Visualizing or writing about an ideal future self; sometimes described as cultivating optimism and sometimes as a way to clarify what is most important and meaningful.
Loving kindness meditation	This involves some instruction and then the practice of focusing on feeling love and compassion towards and from other people during meditation.
Savouring positive experiences	This can involve focusing attention in the moment to fully experience pleasant sensations or activities; it can also include memory building such as taking photos; reminiscing about past positive experiences or describing them to others are additional forms of savouring (see Chapter 2).

(Continued)

Table 9.1 (Continued)

Intervention Technique	Brief Description
Active constructive responding	When other people share good news, try to respond in ways that are supportive and further engage with the person and news; for example, by asking enthusiastic questions (see Chapter 8).
Cultivating sacred moments	This involves some instruction about rituals and finding symbolic, meaningful objects; then spending time focusing and absorbing oneself with spiritual thoughts to foster transcendent experiences.
Engaging with nearby nature	Spend time in and appreciate nearby nature; for example, by taking photos of elements that provoke positive emotional reactions.
Goal setting and planning	This includes some instruction on how to set and pursue personal goals, along with assignments to implement with actual goals; goal progress can improve well-being over time.

Do Positive Interventions Increase Happiness?

Many studies have assessed the effects of positive interventions. Major reviews and meta-analyses (which average the results of many studies) consistently conclude that positive interventions can indeed cause increases in well-being (Bolier et al., 2013; Quoidbach & Gross, 2015; Sin & Lyubomirsky, 2009; Weiss et al., 2016). This conclusion applies when assessing changes in subjective well-being (life satisfaction and positive emotional balance), broader aspects of psychological well-being (purpose, positive relationships, autonomy, etc.), and depression symptoms (not positive per se, but often assessed in these studies). In addition, studies that focus on clinical populations (i.e. people with medical conditions such as cancer or psychological conditions like depression and anxiety) similarly find that patients experience well-being boosts, on average, after engaging in positive interventions (Chakhssi, Kraiss, Sommers-Spijkerman, & Bohlmeijer, 2018). This is good news for positive psychology – it validates core messages and applications. However, despite the positive headline conclusion, the broad reviews also point to gaps, ambiguities, and room for improvement. Because scientific evidence is also a core value of positive psychology, it is important to also understand the limitations of the evidence produced to this point, and what can be done to make it more robust. This is not merely an academic issue; better science makes for better applications.

The overall message is that positive interventions can work, but this does not mean that we have strong evidence for every individual tool in the collection. For example, the technique of using active-constructive responding is frequently mentioned in reviews (based on encouraging non-intervention research; see Chapter 8), but the only two studies that tested it as an intervention produced inconclusive results (Schueller, 2010; Woods, Lambert, Brown, Fincham, & May, 2015). Additionally, when the results of many intervention studies are averaged, the degree of well-being change is relatively small, compared to control conditions. The potential upsides of widespread use and the relatively low cost of these interventions mean that reliable but small effects could still produce tremendous benefits. Still, dramatic boosts in happiness are not the norm. Moreover, few studies track participants very long after the initial intervention, and when they do, the size of the happiness boosts gets smaller. For example, writing a gratitude letter today is unlikely to make you happy a year from now. This may seem obvious; yet the ultimate goal for positive interventions is to foster lasting gains in well-being. The more intensive interventions, such as those that involve direct contact with a counsellor and that involve weeks of (group) therapy, tend to produce larger and longer lasting results. Such interventions are not the prototypical positive activities, but they are usually included in the meta-analyses that conclude successful well-being increases. We must be careful to avoid ascribing the effects of intensive interventions to trivial activities.

There is also room for improvement among the studies that test positive interventions. The major reviews and meta-analyses exclude very poor-quality studies, but they still include studies with important limitations. Reviews have plainly stated that there is a need for additional high-quality studies (Hone, Jarden, & Schofield, 2015; Quoidbach & Gross, 2015). Moreover, when study quality was explicitly rated as part of some meta-analyses, there were more low- and moderate-, compared to high-, quality studies (Bolier et al., 2013; Chakhssi et al., 2018; Weiss et al., 2016). To be clear, this is not unusual – even for research on common health and well-being recommendations; however, it does point to important ambiguities in the research. As a dramatic example, the US government's updated *2015 Dietary Guidelines for Americans* removed the advice to use dental floss because its efficacy was not supported by research (CBC News, 2016). That is, when the press asked to see the scientific evidence for the recommendation, there was little to show. Most dentists still believe that flossing is a wise thing to do; the issue is primarily a lack of strong studies to make a clear, evidence-based determination. There is danger in letting the advice outpace the research in positive psychology too.

Research limitations in this domain include things like the particular people who are studied, the analyses used to draw conclusions, lack of transparent reporting on procedures, and suboptimal research designs. In fairness to researchers, some of these challenges are difficult to overcome, but they nonetheless limit confidence in conclusions. For example, studies are often smaller than ideal, and this contributes to lack of statistical precision and increased error in conclusions (White et al., 2019). Positive intervention research faces some unique challenges too. For example, in drug studies a pill can be given to participants without them, or the person giving it to them, knowing whether it is medicine or a placebo (i.e. a **double-blind study**). With positive interventions, this is much more difficult.

After all, positive interventions involve the participants' active participation. Furthermore, determining the best comparison or control conditions is tricky – there is nothing as similar as the placebo pill. Sometimes people who receive the positive intervention are compared to people who have done nothing at all, and so they differ in terms of the time and attention they have put into the study. More active comparison groups (e.g. writing about childhood memories) can help match efforts and expectations for change, but may introduce unintended differences between intervention and control groups, and thus add ambiguity about what is causing any observed differences. Because there is rarely a single best decision for these challenging issues, the solution is to conduct many studies with different specific limitations and then consider the results collectively. We need more of those studies.

A recent experiment reported a shocking result: people who jumped out of planes without parachutes were no more likely to be injured than people who wore them (Yeh et al., 2018). This was a real study, and people were invited to participate while they were in planes. In total, 92 people were invited, though only 23 agreed to jump. This makes it a small study, but this limitation seems insufficient to account for the parachute's null result. Instead, a difference between the people who agreed to participate (i.e. jump out of the plane) and those who did not might help. People who declined to participate were in planes at an average of 9146 m high, and travelling at 800 km/h; those who agreed were in planes at an average of 0.6 m high and 0 km/h. Said another way, being randomly assigned to wear a parachute had no effect when people jumped from small planes, but only people who were sitting still on the ground agreed to participate. The point of this study is to be ridiculous, but thereby to illustrate an important point. The people who end up in studies, or the people who complete them, can differ from those who do not participate or who drop out. The research on positive interventions has generally not done a good job of accounting for this in statistical analyses (Bolier et al., 2013; Hone et al., 2015). As such, it is plausible that the results are completely misleading (like the parachute study), but more likely that the positive effects will apply to only a subset of people in the general population. We only know about the people who complete the studies. If many people refuse invitations, it suggests that broad interventions will be less effective overall – an intervention will not work if people do not engage with it.

A final reason for scepticism – and again not unique to research on positive interventions – is publication bias. **Publication bias** occurs when studies' results influence whether or not they are communicated, for example via journal articles. Typically, the bias takes the form of favouring studies that indicate effective interventions. This tendency can severely distort the information available, for example when conducting a meta-analysis. If only supportive studies are published, then the average of those studies will support the efficacy of the intervention. But, if there were other, less supportive studies conducted, but never published, the meta-analysis will come to the wrong conclusion. The bias can operate at the level of researchers, when they only submit successes, or at the level of the journal editors, by only publishing successes. Publication bias is pervasive. For example, in psychology and psychiatry research, the results of published papers support researchers' hypotheses over 90 per cent of the time (Fanelli, 2012). Any experienced researcher will tell you that this rate does not match their experience when conducting, rather than publishing, studies. Publication bias clearly exists, but it is difficult to determine its extent in a particular domain – this involves guesses about what might exist hidden in researchers' file drawers. Nonetheless, statistical approaches can indicate, and attempt to correct for, bias. In the meta-analyses of positive interventions, the conclusions have been mixed; one found significant bias (Bolier et al., 2013), but another did not (Weiss et al., 2016). When statistically correcting for publication bias, the overall effect of positive interventions remained, but the average size shrank some more (see also White et al., 2019).

In sum, data clearly support the notion that positive interventions – in general – can increase well-being. Still, the positive activities they advocate are not magic; it takes substantial time and determination to reap meaningful benefits. In addition, given the relatively short history of positive intervention research, important gaps in knowledge remain. For example, research began by testing positive activities under controlled conditions, but less attention has been paid to the pragmatic details of implementing these tools more broadly (Hone et al., 2015). The science of positive interventions will always be complemented by the art and skill of practitioners who employ them. Counsellors and coaches know that different things work for different people. Still, researchers (and other implementation approaches, e.g. via apps) can assist them further by better understanding variation in results. Positive interventions can work, but questions remain about which ones, when, and for whom?

RESEARCH CASE

FORDYCE'S 14 FUNDAMENTALS

Long before the positive psychology movement, researcher and teacher Michael Fordyce showed how happiness could be increased through instruction and effort. This seminal work was published in two research articles (Fordyce, 1977, 1983). They received modest attention at the time and are arguably still under-appreciated. Nonetheless, Fordyce's work was pioneering and foreshadowed much of what was later developed with positive interventions. (He is one of many early but low-profile proponents of positive psychology's core messages.)

Fordyce began in the 1970s by reviewing the research on happiness. Back then there was considerably less to read, yet the basic conclusions hold up quite well

(Continued)

today. Fordyce set aside characteristics of happy people that would be difficult to change, such as income, family status, job satisfaction, and health, and instead focused on behaviours that he thought most people could enact in day-to-day life. Note that this strategy – trying to emulate the characteristics of happy people – is the inspiration for most contemporary positive interventions too. Fordyce distilled these characteristics down to 14 fundamentals and developed advice and activities to help people implement them. For example, to help develop a more outgoing personality, he suggests joining a club, smiling more, saying hello, practising meeting new people, and so on. Peppered into the advice are reminders that happy people do these things, and lots of encouragement. Although some of the fundamentals might not fit rigid views of positive interventions (e.g. stop worrying), collectively they clearly suggest a positive path to happiness. Indeed, the fundamentals "focus on happiness directly and explicitly, whereas other psychological effort focuses on topics that only indirectly and implicitly contribute to eventual happiness" (Fordyce, 1983, p. 497). The fundamentals are:

1. Keep busy and be more active.

2. Spend more time socializing.

3. Be productive at meaningful work.

4. Get better organized and plan things out.

5. Stop worrying.

6. Lower your expectations and aspirations.

7. Develop positive, optimistic thinking.

8. Become present oriented.

9. Work on a healthy personality.

10. Develop an outgoing, social personality.

11. Be yourself.

12. Eliminate negative feelings and problems.

13. Close relationships are the number one source of happiness.

14. Put happiness as your most important priority.

Offering happiness advice in the 1970s (or ever) is not especially unique, but Fordyce took the important next step of subjecting it to empirical research. Across seven studies he assigned some of his college classes to follow variations of the 14 fundamentals programme and others to control conditions. (Individuals were not randomly assigned, but classes were.) He would typically provide instruction during class, or, in the control groups, suggest that learning about psychology could improve happiness (to account for possible effects of this mere suggestion). Across these studies he found that students who learned about and implemented the fundamentals increased their happiness over time and compared to control groups. The implementation varied from two weeks to six weeks, and instructions varied from loose 'take it or leave it' to explicit requests to implement a fundamental each day. Although the more minimal versions provided some benefit, doing more and for longer generally worked better. In follow-up surveys, people who kept working on the fundamentals up to 18 months later reported lasting happiness increases. With more effort came more happiness. However, this pattern did not repeat when it came to the number of fundamentals. Receiving instruction in just four of the fundamentals produced happiness boosts that were very similar to receiving the full programme. Moreover, the partial programme seemed particularly effective when it was targeted at participants' individual weaknesses (e.g. poor organization, feeling phony, pessimism). This contrasts with the prominent theme of contemporary positive psychology that focuses on strengths. Nonetheless, the approach can still be understood as building positives (i.e. becoming organized, authentic, and optimistic).

Although Fordyce's research methods have some limitations, taken collectively his studies persuasively argue for the efficacy of positive interventions. With some knowledge, good advice, and effort, many of his students became meaningfully happier, and this is documented with good social science. Unfortunately, the broad approach of the 14 fundamentals makes it difficult to know why the programme worked, and whether there are parts that are more or less important. (His papers provide somepreliminary hints, but more research is needed on these nuances.) Contemporary research on positive interventions complements Fordyce's broad approach, often focusing on a single positive activity instead. This helps answer detailed research questions, but probably with some cost to overall effectiveness in boosting happiness. In both cases, the focus has been testing basics, rather than how to implement the interventions broadly.

How do Positive Interventions Increase Happiness?

Knowing that a variety of positive interventions can boost well-being, researchers have become more interested in understanding the reasons better. Not only will this contribute to the science of happiness, it is also clearly useful in implementing the positive interventions. There is much left to learn, but Figure 9.1 presents a useful road map to the detailed workings of positive interventions. This **positive-activity model** describes the important features of positive interventions (i.e. how they might be implemented), individual differences in how well they work, and the processes by which they increase well-being (see Lyubomirsky & Layous, 2013). The model is presented in a general way. It identifies important variations among applications, and provides a framework to integrate research on positive interventions.

In the model, 'between' activity features describe the important ways in which various exercises differ from one another. For example, the best possible self and memory-building activities are future-oriented, whereas the gratitude letter and the 'one door closes' activities are past-oriented. These dimensions might be useful in grouping or recommending a collection of activities to a particular kind of person. The 'across' activity features are elements that can be varied within a particular positive intervention. For example, social support can be added by including testimonials from others who have benefited from the activity. Positive interventions that include a variety of activities (e.g. multiple things from Table 9.1), or slight variations that keep an activity fresh (e.g. kindness towards family, then strangers, then co-workers), tend to be more effective. Variety helps prevent adaptation over time, thus maintaining well-being boosts longer, especially with continued practice. The dosage refers to the amount or frequency of an activity, for example performing two versus five acts of kindness, or doing this every day versus once a week. In general, doing more seems helpful, but there are some exceptions to this idea. When activities become tiresome, boring, or difficult, they will not produce happiness. For example, if I asked you to list 15 kind things that you did today, you might struggle to complete the list and decide that you are not a very kind person – not conducive to your well-being.

Considering differences in personality and circumstances is also important when implementing positive interventions. For example, putting more effort into positive activities, the motivation that supports this effort, and the beliefs that completing activities will be efficacious all contribute to positive results. Studies consistently show that people who actively seek out exercises and stick with activities get larger and longer lasting well-being increases (e.g. Lyubomirsky, Dickerhoof, Boehm, & Sheldon, 2011). Having social support helps too; imagine the difference, for example, between having a parent or partner tease you about your silly exercises and having them encourage your efforts at self-improvement. People's initial levels of well-being and their personality traits also predict their experience with positive interventions, but in potentially complex ways. A central, yet unresolved, question is whether less happy people gain more – because they have more room to improve – or whether already happy people benefit more because they are dispositionally prone to positive experiences.

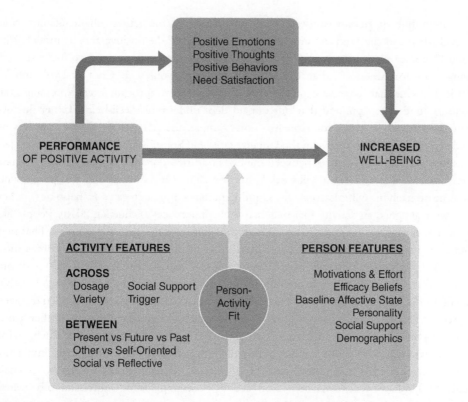

Figure 9.1 The positive activity model. The positive-activity model aims to explain how and why performing positive activities makes people happier. As illustrated at the top, positive activities increase positive emotions, positive thoughts, positive behaviours, and need satisfaction, all of which in turn enhance well-being. Features of positive activities (e.g. dosage and variety) and of the person (e.g. motivation and effort) influence the degree to which the activities improve well-being. An optimal person–activity fit (i.e. the overlap between activity and person features) further predicts increases in well-being.

Source: Lyubomirsky and Layous, 2013

Studies have pointed in both directions. For example, people high in trait neuroticism (characterized by negative emotionality) did not experience happiness increases after a week of writing down kind acts that they or others performed each day, but people scoring low on neuroticism did become happier (Ng, 2015). However, in a follow-up study, people high and low in neuroticism did not differ after three weeks of visualizing and writing about their best possible selves. These apparent contradictions might ultimately be resolved by considering the potentially complex interactions between individual differences and specific features of positive activities.

This notion of **person–activity fit**, or the match of the activity characteristics to an individual's personality and circumstances, is at the heart of the positive-activity model. With good fit comes more success. For example, expressing gratitude appears to increase well-being more for Americans than it does for Koreans (Layous, Lee, Choi, & Lyubomirsky, 2013). It seems that Koreans experience an obligation to reciprocate after expressing gratitude to another person, and that this unpaid debt undermines well-being. Other positive activities may work better for Koreans. For example, the same study found that acts of kindness were equally effective in the United States and South Korea; this activity seems less sensitive to cultural differences between the two countries. Fortunately, people seem to have some intuitive sense of what will work better for them. One study found that participants were more likely to complete exercises, and experienced greater gains in happiness, when they were assigned an activity that matched their preferences (Schueller, 2010). People like some activities more than others, and this seems important to their effectiveness. That said, there are also reasons to think that people should not just keep doing what comes most easily. Although doing more with signature strengths (i.e. based on highest scores) is an oft-used positive intervention, there are times when building on weakness or challenging habits can be useful. For example, when people were asked to use their lesser strengths (i.e. lowest scored) in new ways, their happiness improved as much as that of people in another group who used their highest-scored strengths more (Proyer, Gander, Wellenzohn, & Ruch, 2015). In a similar vein, people who are dispositionally introverted report increased positive emotions when they behave in extraverted ways, such as getting to know strangers (Zelenski et al., 2013). Many other forms of person–activity fit seem plausible but remain to be tested. For example, perhaps older people benefit more from reminiscing about past positive events, whereas younger people gain more from thinking about their best possible future selves.

The final aspect of the model, the path from activity to well-being, differs in its details based on activity features and personal characteristics. Different exercises target different processes, and people focus on different elements. For example, some activities or people might achieve increased well-being via closer social relationships, whereas others cultivate a largely internal positive outlook on life. Yet among this variation is a general sense that activities will work well when they feed forward to encourage additional positive thoughts, emotions, and behaviours. Said another way, an activity that only provides an immediate mood boost (e.g. watching a funny cat video) will not be enough to boost general well-being over the course of weeks or months. On the other hand, if that positive mood spurs additional positive processes, it might be enough. Perhaps you forward the cat-video link to an old friend, which prompts a nice conversation, or perhaps this little mood boost encouraged you to pay it forward by purchasing a coffee for a homeless person. I am not aware of a formalized cat-video exercise, but the thinking is similar for common positive interventions. Recall the **broaden and build** theory of positive emotions (Fredrickson, 2013), which suggests that they help build lasting resources. It is plausible that temporary mood boosts from positive activities begin upward spirals of additional positive thoughts, behaviours, and emotions. Perhaps there is a role for (moderately sized) bowls of ice cream in positive interventions after all (see Linley et al., 2013) – but only if they can build psychological resources. In a similar way, positive activities can satisfy basic needs, such as those proposed by **self-determination theory** (autonomy, competence, relatedness) (Ryan & Deci, 2000). Satisfying needs contributes to well-being directly (it is satisfying); moreover, satisfied people behave in psychologically healthy ways – this flourishing builds on itself.

In sum, the positive activity model provides a framework for describing positive interventions and how they work. Despite some remaining research gaps, it synthesizes many important findings. In essence, positive activities work better when there is a good fit between the person and the activity, when there is variety in the activities, and when the person and activity encourage more active engagement and effort. Finally, meaningful happiness change requires more than temporary mood boosts; activities should trigger additional positive thoughts, behaviours, and emotions. When all these factors are in place, positive interventions succeed in producing well-being improvements.

Broader Applications

The prototypical positive intervention uses activities like those in Table 9.1 and applies them to healthy people. However, a wider collection of activities that fall outside strict definitions of positive interventions are still part of the broader positive psychology family. These interventions are adapted to particular populations or settings (e.g. schools or workplaces), or they include things that are not as unambiguously positive, yet still with well-being as an ultimate goal. For example, as noted earlier, positive psychotherapy does seek to reduce dysfunction, even if dysfunction is not the focus of intervention. **Positive psychotherapy** mainly consists of working with some exercises shown in Table 9.1, and has been used with depression, anxiety, schizophrenia, and smoking cessation (Rashid, 2015; Seligman, Rashid, & Parks, 2006). In a similar vein, hope-based therapy was designed for people who are suffering, yet with a focus on strengths (Cheavens et al., 2006). It teaches **hope**, which is defined as setting goals, clear strategies for achieving those goals, and the motivation to carry them out. Drawing from other cognitive therapy approaches, it also encourages positive self-talk, such as "I am capable of this", and it includes regular monitoring of goal progress. Clarifying personally important goals and their successful pursuit are meant to decrease distress and improve well-being.

Acceptance and commitment therapy (ACT) differs from some traditional psychotherapy in that it does not seek to eliminate negative feelings; it is like positive psychology in promoting an authentic approach to life (Howell & Passmore, 2018). Still, the processes that ACT promotes differ in important ways from most positive interventions (Parks & Biswas-Diener, 2013). ACT teaches mindfulness techniques to take the sting out of unpleasant reactions, and it encourages an honest approach to current circumstances.

Mindfulness is an engaged, yet non-judgemental, mindset where attention is focused on the immediate moment; sensations and reactions are observed as being present, while self-relevant reactions (e.g. "this obstacle conflicts with my plans") are abandoned in favour of acceptance of the world the way it is (Brown & Holt, 2011). Some elements of mindfulness, such as focusing attention on the here and now, overlap with some positive intervention techniques. For example, appreciating nearby nature, cultivating sacred moments, and some savouring exercises involve directing attention to present, pleasant stimuli. However, there is also an important difference. Whereas these positive exercises are aimed at boosting momentary pleasant feelings, mindfulness is not. Just as a mindful frame detaches the self from the unpleasantness of difficult situations, it can work against full absorption and amplification of positives. Mindfulness may foster the conditions for well-being in the long term – these empirical links exist – but it does this with unique advice: to accept negatives and not focus on increasing positives (Brown & Holt, 2011; Parks & Biswas-Diener, 2013). Said another way, there is an inherent contradiction between the advice to be mindful and the advice to shift pursuits towards positive experiences. From the mindfulness perspective, the goal of happiness brings with it the worry that happiness is fleeting. This is not to say that a person or a practitioner cannot shift among positive intervention and mindfulness techniques. Yet this is best done with some awareness of an underlying tension between these forms of advice. Additional caution is warranted in assessing any particular mindfulness intervention. As the popularity of mindfulness training has exploded in recent years, so has proliferation of new versions – along with more scrutiny of their claims (Van Dam et al., 2018).

Most of the positive interventions in Table 9.1 focus on boosting subjective well-being even while their specific paths to happiness differ. Still, it is possible to expand boundaries of well-being to include additional valued characteristics. Although less prototypical as positive interventions, programmes that target other strengths often engage positive thoughts, feelings, and behaviours to promote mental health and prosociality. For example, there are promising programmes aimed at training empathy, forgiveness, self-compassion, self-control, self-efficacy, and so on (Friese, Frankenbach, Job, & Loschelder, 2017; Neff, 2011; Parks & Biswas-Diener, 2013). Although not reviewed in detail here, the general issues around assessing these programmes' effectiveness often mirror those of positive interventions. In addition, although these training targets are themselves valuable, they may ultimately facilitate happiness too, even if it is not their primary focus (similar to mindfulness training).

The **positive youth development** approach focuses on building these broader strengths in children, often in schools or via extra-curricular activities like sport (Catalano, Berglund, Ryan, Lonczak, & Hawkins, 2004; Larson, 2000; R. D. Taylor, Oberle, Durlak, & Weissberg, 2017). These efforts fit the ethos of positive psychology well by promoting skills and well-being (broadly), rather than targeting reductions in problematic behaviours like bullying, drug-use, or risky sexual practices. Nonetheless, promoting strengths may help protect against the problematic outcomes in youth too (R. D. Taylor et al., 2017). As with other interventions these approaches are not panaceas either, with small or inconsistent results across studies and many challenges when implementing programmes broadly.

Finally, at the outer branches of positive interventions' family tree we return to resilience. The variety of specific techniques and approaches under the umbrella of resilience training is vast, perhaps not surprising given the many ways in which resilience is assessed and defined (Chmitorz et al., 2017). To the extent that there is a common underlying idea, it is to teach strengths and skills to people, thus helping them cope effectively with future challenges. The particular content might focus on positive or negative content; yet resilience training is typically viewed as preventative mental health care. Interventions often occur before any particular problem is detected. For example, the UK Resilience Programme aimed to teach all children coping skills (regardless of individuals' risk) in an effort to prevent later depression (Challen, Machin, & Gillham, 2014). Similarly, employers are increasingly providing resilience training to keep workers well and productive (Vanhove, Herian, Perez, Harms, & Lester, 2016). Some lines of work bring special psychological risks and thus more need for resilience. For example, the Comprehensive Soldier Fitness programme in the US military is the largest application of positive psychology, where the training targets include physical, social, family, emotional, and spiritual fitness (Cornum, Matthews, & Seligman, 2011). In addition, when people experience a potentially traumatic event (e.g. natural disasters), other psychological first-aid programmes aim to prevent serious problems with things like practical assistance and fostering a sense of connection to community, self-efficacy, and hope (Bonanno et al., 2010; McNally et al., 2003).

Despite the diversity in resilience training programmes, they all share a less than robust record of empirical support. Often the lack of support is due to a lack of strong studies (like with dental floss), partially explained by challenging circumstances. For example, it is ethically questionable to randomly assign only some victims to receive psychological first aid, and organizations are often uninterested in providing programmes randomly to only half of their members. Still, such studies would go a long way to knowing how effective the treatments are, and then adding nuance about when and where. Some major reviews have taken pessimistic conclusions; for example:

> Although there are many programs available to the military and civilian communities, there is very little empirical evidence that these programs effectively build resilience. Similarly there are a number of factors related to resilience, but there is almost no evidence that resilience can be taught or produced. (Meredith et al., 2011, p. 75)

More optimistic conclusions exist too, though these are also tempered with caution (e.g. Bonanno et al., 2010; Vanhove et al., 2016). Nonetheless, the potential upside of such interventions is non-trivial, and some weaker forms of evidence are cautiously suggestive.

Rather than giving up on the potential, a strong argument exists for further research and development on resilience training programmes.

SUMMING UP

This chapter considered well-being, broadly defined, and how it changes or remains stable over time. In the context of major negative events or ongoing stressors, the stability of well-being is welcome and, fortunately, also common. Resilient responses can be understood as the maintenance of mental health through adversity, and as such are best measured by tracking people over time. Although resilience is easily found, predicting it requires a long list of personal characteristics and circumstances. As examples, people with a strong sense of control, self-regulation, positive emotionality, and an optimistic outlook tend to fare better, as do those who cope via problem solving, benefit finding, and seeing challenge in adversity. The greater the challenge, the less resilience, on average – hard things are hard; but social support, high socio-economic status, and religion can help buffer against poor outcomes. Previous experience with adversity can be helpful, but only to a point, and only if successfully resolved.

Although simply maintaining heath through adversity is impressive, some people experience benefits following traumatic events. These include things like improved social relationships, sense of meaning, personal strength, appreciation of life, and spirituality. Traumatic events disrupt habits and expectations, and this may prompt these perceptions of growth as people make sense of their post-trauma lives. Despite the intuitive appeal of such positive changes, considerable scepticism surrounds the idea that searching for growth should be encouraged. This is because perceptions of growth do not tend to match actual changes (growth) when they are both assessed over time. Moreover, perceptions of growth are associated with increased distress often enough to question whether or not they are truly healthy, or would be for most people.

This is not to say that well-being should not be pursued in general. Indeed, much of positive psychology rests on the assumption that it is possible – if not easy – to improve psychological well-being with intentional efforts. A wide variety of positive activities (e.g. gratitude journaling, savouring pleasant experiences, using strengths in new ways) can cause happiness boosts. However, effective positive interventions depend on a good fit between the activities' details and the personality and circumstances of the person who engages with them. In addition, substantial investment, effort, and variety are typically needed to produce meaningful and lasting increases in well-being. Finally, despite the clear possibility of interventions' benefits, substantially more research and development are needed to hone the details and widespread implementation of largely experimental techniques. There is plenty of work ahead for young positive psychologists to refine and apply work on positive interventions.

TEST YOURSELF

1. What personality features are associated with resilience, and why do contemporary views of resilience avoid defining it as those personality features?

2. Why is resilience sometimes described as 'ordinary magic'?

3. What are some of the domains in which people experience post-traumatic growth, and does it matter whether actual change versus perceptions of change are assessed?

4. Name two personal characteristics that are usually conducive to reaping benefits from positive interventions, and describe the notion of person–activity fit in general.

5. How might publication bias and the special characteristics of the people included in intervention studies distort conclusions?

WEB LINKS

Fordyce's happiness programme is preserved via his web page and Wayback Machine: https://web.archive.org/web/20070113073753/http://www.gethappy.net/

Internet-based exercises that draw from positive psychology and its extended family: www.happify.com

Ben Goldacre's TED Talk describing how publication bias severely distort our knowledge about treatment effectiveness: www.ted.com/talks/ben_goldacre_what_doctors_don_t_ know_about_the_drugs_they_prescribe

FURTHER READING

For an accessible review of many resilience findings in a large, longitudinal data set, see:

Ryff, C., Friedman, E., Fuller-Rowell, T., Love, G., Miyamoto, Y., Morozink, J., ... Tsenkova, V. (2012). Varieties of resilience in MIDUS. *Social and Personality Psychology Compass, 6*(11), 792–806.

This review article expands the scope of post-traumatic growth findings by focusing on qualitative studies:

Hefferon, K., Grealy, M., & Mutrie, N. (2009). Post-traumatic growth and life threatening physical illness: A systematic review of the qualitative literature. *British Journal of Health Psychology, 14*(2), 343–378.

Here is a recent review of happiness research with special attention to how findings can be applied in organizational and counselling psychology:

Diener, E., Heintzelman, S. J., Tay, L., Wirtz, D., Lutes, L., & Oishi, S. (2017). Findings all psychologists should know from the new science on subjective well-being. *Canadian Psychology, 58*, 87–104.

This article identifies some common features of questionable therapeutic claims:

Meichenbaum, D., & Lilienfeld, S. O. (2018). How to spot hype in the field of psychotherapy: A 19-item checklist. *Professional Psychology: Research and Practice*, 49(1), 22–30.

REFERENCES

Bastian, B., Kuppens, P., De Roover, K., & Diener, E. (2014). Is valuing positive emotion associated with life satisfaction? *Emotion, 14*(4), 639–645. https://doi.org/10.1037/a0036466

Bolier, L., Haverman, M., Westerhof, G. J., Riper, H., Smit, F., & Bohlmeijer, E. T. (2013). Positive psychology interventions: A meta-analysis of randomized controlled studies. *BMC Public Health, 13*(1), 119. https://doi.org/10.1186/1471-2458-13-119

Bonanno, G. A., Brewin, C. R., Kaniasty, K., & La Greca, A. M. (2010). Weighing the costs of disaster: Consequences, risks, and resilience in individuals, families, and communities. *Psychological Science in the Public Interest, 11*(1), 1–49. https://doi.org/10.1177/1529100610387086

Bonanno, G. A., & Burton, C. L. (2013). Regulatory flexibility. *Perspectives on Psychological Science, 8*(6), 591–612. https://doi.org/10.1177/1745691613504116

Bonanno, G. A., Galea, S., Bucciarelli, A., & Vlahov, D. (2006). Psychological resilience after disaster. *Psychological Science, 17*(3), 181–186. https://doi.org/10.1111/j.1467-9280.2006.01682.x

Brown, K. W., & Holt, M. (2011). Experiential processing and the integration of bright and dark sides of the human psyche. In K. M. Sheldon, T. B. Kashdan, & M. F. Steger (eds), *Designing Positive Psychology* (pp. 147–159). New York: Oxford University Press.

Catalano, R. F., Berglund, M. L., Ryan, J. A. M., Lonczak, H. S., & Hawkins, J. D. (2004). Positive youth development in the United States: Research findings on evaluations of positive youth development programs. *Annals of the American Academy of Political and Social Science, 591*, 98–124. https://doi.org/10.1177/0002716203260102

Catalino, L., Algoe, S. B., & Fredrickson, B. L. (2014). Prioritizing positivity: An effective approach to pursuing happiness? *Emotion, 14*(6), 1155–1161.

CBC News. (2016). No strong proof that flossing your teeth has medical benefit. Retrieved 26 April 2019 from https://www.cbc.ca/news/health/dental-floss-1.3703798

Chakhssi, F., Kraiss, J. T., Sommers-Spijkerman, M., & Bohlmeijer, E. T. (2018). The effect of positive psychology interventions on well-being and distress in clinical samples with psychiatric or somatic disorders: A systematic review and meta-analysis. *BMC Psychiatry, 18*(1), 211. https://doi.org/10.1186/s12888-018-1739-2

Challen, A. R., Machin, S. J., & Gillham, J. E. (2014). The UK resilience programme: A school-based universal nonrandomized pragmatic controlled trial. *Journal of Consulting and Clinical Psychology, 82*(1), 75–89. https://doi.org/10.1037/a0034854

Cheavens, J. S., Feldman, D. B., Gum, A., Michael, S. T., & Snyder, C. R. (2006). Hope therapy in a community sample: A pilot investigation. *Social Indicators Research, 77*(1), 61–78. https://doi.org/10.1007/s11205-005-5553-0

Chmitorz, A., Kunzler, A., Helmreich, I., Tüscher, O., Kalisch, R., Kubiak, T., … Lieb, K. (2017). Intervention studies to foster resilience – A systematic review and proposal for a resilience framework in future intervention studies. *Clinical Psychology Review, 59*, 78–100. https://doi.org/10.1016/j.cpr.2017.11.002

Cornum, R., Matthews, M. D., & Seligman, M. E. P. (2011). Comprehensive soldier fitness: Building resilience in a challenging institutional context. *American Psychologist, 66*(1), 4–9. https://doi.org/10.1037/a0021420

Coyne, J. C., & Tennen, H. (2010). Positive psychology in cancer care: Bad science, exaggerated claims, and unproven medicine. *Annals of Behavioral Medicine, 39*(1), 16–26. https://doi.org/10.1007/s12160-009-9154-z

Davis, C. G., & Novoa, D. C. (2013). Meaning-making following spinal cord injury: Individual differences and within-person change. *Rehabilitation Psychology, 58*(2), 166–177. https://doi.org/10.1037/a0031554

Davis, C. G., & Porter, J. (2018). Pathways to growth following trauma and loss. In C. R. Snyder, S. J. Lopez, L. M. Edwards, & S. C. Marques (eds), *The Oxford Handbook of Positive Psychology* (3rd edn, pp. 1–13). New York: Oxford University Press. https://doi.org/10.1093/oxfordhb/9780199396511.013.66

Diener, E., Heintzelman, S. J., Tay, L., Wirtz, D., Lutes, L., & Oishi, S. (2017). Findings all psychologists should know from the new science on subjective well-being. *Canadian Psychology, 58*, 87–104. https://doi.org/10.1017/CBO9781107415324.004

Diener, E., Tay, L., & Myers, D. G. (2011). The religion paradox: If religion makes people happy, why are so many dropping out? *Journal of Personality and Social Psychology, 101*(6), 1278–1290. https://doi.org/10.1037/a0024402

Dirkzwager, A. J. E., Kerssens, J. J., & Yzermans, C. J. (2006). Health problems in children and adolescents before and after a man-made disaster. *Journal of the American Academy of Child and Adolescent Psychiatry, 45*(1), 94–103. https://doi.org/10.1097/01.chi.0000186402.05465.f7

Engelhard, I. M., Lommen, M. J. J., & Sijbrandij, M. (2015). Changing for better or worse? Posttraumatic growth reported by soldiers deployed to Iraq. *Clinical Psychological Science, 3*, 789–796. https://doi.org/10.1177/2167702614549800

Fanelli, D. (2012). Negative results are disappearing from most disciplines and countries. *Scientometrics, 90*(3), 891–904. https://doi.org/10.1007/s11192-011-0494-7

Fava, G. A., Rafanelli, C., Cazzaro, M., Conti, S., & Grandi, S. (1998). Well-being therapy: A novel psychotherapeutic approach for residual symptoms of affective disorders. *Psychological Medicine, 28*(2), 475–480.

Ferguson, Y. L., & Sheldon, K. M. (2013). Trying to be happier really can work: Two experimental studies. *The Journal of Positive Psychology, 8*(1), 23–33. https://doi.org/10.1080/17439760.2012.747000

Ford, B. Q., Dmitrieva, J. O., Heller, D., Chentsova-Dutton, Y., Grossmann, I., Tamir, M., … Mauss, I. B. (2015). Culture shapes whether the pursuit of happiness predicts higher or lower well-being. *Journal of Experimental Psychology: General, 144*(6), 1053–1062. https://doi.org/10.1037/xge0000108

Fordyce, M. W. (1977). Development of a program to increase personal happiness. *Journal of Counseling Psychology, 24*(6), 511–521. https://doi.org/10.1037/0022-0167.24.6.511

Fordyce, M. W. (1983). A program to increase happiness: Further studies. *Journal of Counseling Psychology, 30*(4), 483–498.

Frazier, P., Tennen, H., Gavian, M., Park, C., Tomich, P., & Tashiro, T. (2009). Does self-reported posttraumatic growth reflect genuine positive change? *Psychological Science, 20*(7), 912–919. https://doi.org/10.1111/j.1467-9280.2009.02381.x

Fredrickson, B. L. (2013). Positive emotions broaden and build. *Advances in Experimental Social Psychology*, *47*, 1–53.

Friese, M., Frankenbach, J., Job, V., & Loschelder, D. D. (2017). Does self-control training improve self-control? A meta-analysis. *Perspectives on Psychological Science*, *12*(6), 1077–1099. https://doi.org/10.1177/1745691617697076

Galatzer-Levy, I. R., Huang, S. H., & Bonanno, G. A. (2018). Trajectories of resilience and dysfunction following potential trauma: A review and statistical evaluation. *Clinical Psychology Review*, *63*(June), 41–55. https://doi.org/10.1016/j.cpr.2018.05.008

Garcia, D., & Rimé, B. (2019). Collective emotions and social resilience in the digital traces after a terrorist attack. *Psychological Science*, *30*(4), 617–628. https://doi.org/10.1177/0956797619831964

Gucciardi, D. F., Hanton, S., Gordon, S., Mallett, C. J., & Temby, P. (2015). The concept of mental toughness: Tests of dimensionality, nomological network, and traitness. *Journal of Personality*, *83*(1), 26–44. https://doi.org/10.1111/jopy.12079

Hefferon, K., Grealy, M., & Mutrie, N. (2009). Post-traumatic growth and life threatening physical illness: A systematic review of the qualitative literature. *British Journal of Health Psychology*, *14*(2), 343–378. https://doi.org/10.1348/135910708X332936

Helgeson, V. S. (2010). Corroboration of growth following breast cancer: Ten years later. *Journal of Social and Clinical Psychology*, *29*(5), 546–574. https://doi.org/10.1521/jscp.2010.29.5.546

Hone, L. C., Jarden, A., & Schofield, G. M. (2015). An evaluation of positive psychology intervention effectiveness trials using the re-aim framework: A practice-friendly review. *The Journal of Positive Psychology*, *10*(4), 303–322. https://doi.org/10.1080/17439760.2014.965267

Howell, A. J., & Passmore, H. A. (2018). Acceptance and Commitment Training (ACT) as a positive psychological intervention: A systematic review and initial meta-analysis regarding ACT's role in well-being promotion among university students. *Journal of Happiness Studies*, 20(6), 1995–2010. https://doi.org/10.1007/s10902-018-0027-7

Infurna, F. J., & Luthar, S. S. (2016). Resilience to major life stressors is not as common as thought. *Perspectives on Psychological Science*, *11*, 175–194. https://doi.org/10.1177/1745691615621271

Jayawickreme, E., & Blackie, L. E. R. (2014). Post-traumatic growth as positive personality change: Evidence, controversies and future directions. *European Journal of Personality*, *28*(4), 312–331. https://doi.org/10.1002/per.1963

Keyes, C. L. M. (2009). The black–white paradox in health: Flourishing in the face of social inequality and discrimination. *Journal of Personality*, *77*(6), 1677–1706. https://doi.org/10.1111/j.1467-6494.2009.00597.x

Kramer, S. (2010). Stacey Kramer: The best gift I ever survived. Retrieved from www.ted.com/talks/stacey_kramer_the_best_gift_i_ever_survived

Larson, R. W. (2000). Toward a psychology of positive youth development. *American Psychologist*, *55*(1), 170–183. https://doi.org/10.1177/0164027586008001004

Layous, K., Lee, H., Choi, I., & Lyubomirsky, S. (2013). Culture matters when designing a successful happiness-increasing activity. *Journal of Cross-Cultural Psychology*, *44*(8), 1294–1303. https://doi.org/10.1177/0022022113487591

Lechner, S. C., Tennen, H., & Affleck, G. (2009). Benefit-finding and growth. In S. J. Lopez & C. R. Snyder (eds), *The Oxford Handbook of Positive Psychology* (2nd edn, pp. 633–640). New York: Oxford University Press.

Linley, P. A., Dovey, H., de Bruin, E., Transler, C., Wilkinson, J., Maltby, J., & Hurling, R. (2013). Two simple, brief, naturalistic activities and their impact on positive affect: Feeling grateful and eating ice cream. *Psychology of Well-Being: Theory, Research and Practice*, *3*(1), 6. https://doi.org/10.1186/2211-1522-3-6

Linley, P. A., & Joseph, S. (2004). Positive change following trauma and adversity: A review. *Journal of Traumatic Stress*, *17*(1), 11–21. https://doi.org/10.1023/B:-JOTS.0000014671.27856.7e

Lowe, S. R., & Rhodes, J. E. (2013). Trajectories of psychological distress among low-income, female survivors of Hurricane Katrina. *American Journal of Orthopsychiatry*, *83*(2 Part 3), 398–412. https://doi.org/10.1111/ajop.12019

Luhmann, M., Necka, E. A., Schoenbrodt, F. D., & Hawkley, L. C. (2016). Is valuing happiness associated with lower well-being? A factor-level analysis using the Valuing Happiness Scale. *Journal of Research in Personality*, *60*, 46–50. https://doi.org/10.1016/j.jrp.2015.11.003

Luthar, S. S., & Eisenberg, N. (2017). Resilient adaptation among at-risk children: Harnessing science toward maximizing salutary environments. *Child Development*, *88*(2), 337–349. https://doi.org/10.1111/cdev.12737

Lyons, D. M., & Parker, K. J. (2007). Stress inoculation-induced indications of resilience in monkeys. *Journal of Traumatic Stress*, *20*(4), 423–433. https://doi.org/10.1002/jts

Lyubomirsky, S., Dickerhoof, R., Boehm, J. K., & Sheldon, K. M. (2011). Becoming happier takes both a will and a proper way: An experimental longitudinal intervention to boost well-being. *Emotion*, *11*(2), 391–402. https://doi.org/10.1037/a0022575

Lyubomirsky, S., & Layous, K. (2013). How do simple positive activities increase well-being? *Current Directions in Psychological Science*, *22*(1), 57–62. https://doi.org/10.1177/0963721412469809

Lyubomirsky, S., Sheldon, K. M., & Schkade, D. (2005). Pursuing happiness: The architecture of sustainable change. *Review of General Psychology*, *9*(2), 111–131. https://doi.org/10.1037/1089-2680.9.2.111

Maddux, J. E. (2008). Positive psychology and the illness ideology: Toward a positive clinical psychology. *Applied Psychology*, *57*(S), 54–70. https://doi.org/10.1111/j.1464-0597.2008.00354.x

Mangelsdorf, J., Eid, M., & Luhmann, M. (2018). Does growth require suffering? A systematic review and meta-analysis on genuine posttraumatic and postecstatic growth. *Psychological Bulletin*, *145*(3), 302–338. https://doi.org/10.1037/bul0000173

Masten, A. S. (2001). Ordinary magic: Resilience processes in development. *American Psychologist, 56*(3), 227–238. https://doi.org/10.1037//0003-066X.56.3.227

Mauss, I. B., Tamir, M., Anderson, C. L., & Savino, N. S. (2011). Can seeking happiness make people unhappy? Paradoxical effects of valuing happiness. *Emotion, 11*(4), 807–815. https://doi.org/10.1037/a0022010

McNally, R. J., Bryant, R. A., & Ehlers, A. (2003). Does early psychological intervention promote recovery from posttraumatic stress? *Psychological Science in the Public Interest, 4*(2), 45–79. https://doi.org/10.1111/1529-1006.01421

Meredith, L. S., Sherbourne, C. D., Gaillot, S. J., Hansell, L., Ritschard, H. V., Parker, A. M., & Wrenn, G. (2011). *Promoting Psychological Resilience in the U.S. Military.* Santa Monica, CA: Rand Corporation.

Neff, K. D. (2011). Self-compassion, self-esteem, and well-being. *Social and Personality Psychology Compass, 5*(1), 1–12. https://doi.org/10.1111/j.1751-9004.2010.00330.x

Ng, W. (2015). Use of positive interventions: Does neuroticism moderate the sustainability of their effects on happiness? *The Journal of Positive Psychology 11*(1), 51–61. https://doi.org/10.1080/17439760.2015.1025419

Owenz, M., & Fowers, B. J. (2018). Perceived post-traumatic growth may not reflect actual positive change: A short-term prospective study of relationship dissolution. *Journal of Social and Personal Relationships,* 36(10). https://doi.org/10.1177/0265407518811662

Parks, A. C., & Biswas-Diener, R. (2013). Positive interventions: Past, present, and future. In T. B. Kashdan & J. Ciarrochi (eds), *Mindfulness, Acceptance, and Positive Psychology.* Oakland, CA: Context Press.

Proyer, R. T., Gander, F., Wellenzohn, S., & Ruch, W. (2015). Strengths-based positive psychology interventions: A randomized placebo-controlled online trial on long-term effects for a signature strengths- vs a lesser strengths-intervention. *Frontiers in Psychology, 6,* 1–14. https://doi.org/10.3389/fpsyg.2015.00456

Quoidbach, J., & Gross, J. J. (2015). Positive interventions: An emotion regulation perspective. *Psychological Bulletin, 141,* 655–693.

Rashid, T. (2015). Positive psychotherapy: A strength-based approach. *The Journal of Positive Psychology, 10*(1), 25–40. https://doi.org/10.1080/17439760.2014.920411

Roepke, A. M. (2013). Gains without pains? Growth after positive events. *Journal of Positive Psychology, 8*(4), 280–291. https://doi.org/10.1080/17439760.2013.791715

Rutter, M. (2012). Resilience as a dynamic concept. *Development and Psychopathology, 24*(2), 335–344. https://doi.org/10.1017/S0954579412000028

Ryan, R., & Deci, E. (2000). Self-determination theory and the facilitation of intrinsic motivation. *American Psychologist, 55*(1), 68–78. https://doi.org/10.1037/0003-066X.55.1.68

Ryff, C., Friedman, E., Fuller-Rowell, T., Love, G., Miyamoto, Y., Morozink, J., … Tsenkova, V. (2012). Varieties of resilience in MIDUS. *Social and Personality Psychology Compass, 6*(11), 792–806. https://doi.org/10.1111/j.1751-9004.2012.00462.x

Schueller, S. M. (2010). Preferences for positive psychology exercises. *The Journal of Positive Psychology*, *5*(3), 192–203. https://doi.org/10.1080/17439761003790948

Seery, M. D., Holman, E. A., & Silver, R. C. (2010). Whatever does not kill us: Cumulative lifetime adversity, vulnerability, and resilience. *Journal of Personality and Social Psychology*, *99*(6), 1025–1041. https://doi.org/10.1037/a0021344

Seligman, M. E. P., Rashid, T., & Parks, A. C. (2006). Positive psychotherapy. *American Psychologist*, *61*(8), 774–788.

Sin, N. L., & Lyubomirsky, S. (2009). Enhancing well-being and alleviating depressive symptoms with positive psychology interventions: A practice-friendly meta-analysis. *Journal of Clinical Psychology*, *65*(5), 467–487. https://doi.org/10.1002/jclp.20593

Taubman-Ben-Ari, O., Findler, L., & Sharon, N. (2011). Personal growth in mothers: Examination of the suitability of the posttraumatic growth inventory as a measurement tool. *Women and Health*, *51*(6), 604–622. https://doi.org/10.1080/03630242.2011.614324

Taylor, R. D., Oberle, E., Durlak, J. A., & Weissberg, R. P. (2017). Promoting positive youth development through school-based social and emotional learning interventions: A meta-analysis of follow-up effects. *Child Development*, *88*(4), 1156–1171. https://doi.org/10.1111/cdev.12864

Taylor, S. E., & Brown, J. D. (1988). Illusion and well-being: A social psychological perspective on mental health. *Psychological Bulletin*, *103*(2), 193–210. https://doi.org/10.1037/0033-2909.103.2.193

Tedeschi, R. G., & Calhoun, L. G. (1996). The posttraumatic growth inventory: Measuring the positive legacy of trauma. *Journal of Traumatic Stress*, *9*(3), 455–471. https://doi.org/10.1002/jts.2490090305

Van Dam, N. T., van Vugt, M. K., Vago, D. R., Schmalzl, L., Saron, C. D., Olendzki, A., … Meyer, D. E. (2018). Mind the hype: A critical evaluation and prescriptive agenda for research on mindfulness and meditation. *Perspectives on Psychological Science*, *13*(1), 36–61. https://doi.org/10.1177/1745691617709589

Vanhove, A. J., Herian, M. N., Perez, A. L. U., Harms, P. D., & Lester, P. B. (2016). Can resilience be developed at work? A meta-analytic review of resilience-building programme effectiveness. *Journal of Occupational and Organizational Psychology*, *89*(2), 278–307. https://doi.org/10.1111/joop.12123

Weiss, L. A., Westerhof, G. J., & Bohlmeijer, E. T. (2016). Can we increase psychological well-being? The effects of interventions on psychological well-being: A meta-analysis of randomized controlled trials. *PLOS ONE*, *11*(6), e0158092. https://doi.org/10.1371/journal.pone.0158092

White, C. A., Uttl, B., & Holder, M. D. (2019). Meta-analyses of positive psychology interventions: The effects are much smaller than previously reported. *PLOS ONE*, *14*(5), e0216588. https://doi.org/10.1371/journal.pone.0216588

Woods, S., Lambert, N., Brown, P., Fincham, F., & May, R. (2015). "I'm so excited for you!" How an enthusiastic responding intervention enhances close relationships. *Journal of Social and Personal Relationships*, *32*(1), 24–40. https://doi.org/10.1177/0265407514523545

Yeh, R. W., Valsdottir, L. R., Yeh, M. W., Shen, C., Kramer, D. B., Strom, J. B., … Nallamothu, B. K. (2018). Parachute use to prevent death and major trauma when jumping from aircraft: Randomized controlled trial. *BMJ, 363*, k5094. https://doi.org/10.1136/BMJ.k5094

Zelenski, J. M., Whelan, D. C., Nealis, L. J., Besner, C. M., Santoro, M. S., & Wynn, J. E. (2013). Personality and affective forecasting: Trait introverts underpredict the hedonic benefits of acting extraverted. *Journal of Personality and Social Psychology, 104*(6), 1092–1108. https://doi.org/10.1037/a0032281

10

Looking Forward

INTRODUCTION

We have now been through nine chapters of positive psychology. Therein we have seen that positive experience is common, from emotions to relationships to resilience, even while the negatives grab attention more easily. This is true of humans generally, including the humans who study psychology. About 20 years ago, some influential academics were struck by psychology's tendency to focus on the negative and they sought change. The positive psychology movement aims to correct an imbalance, to more fully explore the pleasures, strengths, and inspiring products of human thought and behaviour. In this final chapter, we take stock of positive psychology's contributions with an eye towards its future.

There are three parts to our look forward. At the broadest level, an even newer movement – the credibility revolution – has upended standard research practices in psychology and other fields. In doing so, it also raises new questions about the confidence we can have in the body of knowledge generated prior to it. This new awareness provides a context for interpreting research in positive psychology, and it suggests productive ways forward. In addition, positive psychology has developed and matured over the last 20 years. Defining the sub-discipline clearly has always been challenging, and its members continue to debate its identity going forward. For example, they question how long positive psychology should exist as a separate sub-discipline, and whether we need more negative in positive psychology. We will explore these 'meta' issues, around science and practice, but first let's turn to your future as an individual. I have saved a piece of positive psychology content for this last chapter – goals and how to accomplish them – and I hope this information will allow you to implement personally useful ideas that you have formed after engaging with this text. Learning about positive psychology provides a helpful basis for (re)considering personal goals, and the next section highlights relevant research and useful tips for successful goal pursuit.

GOALS: LOOKING AHEAD TO YOUR POSITIVE FUTURE

When you look forward, what you do you see? You might consider yourself years in the future (cf. the best possible self exercise in Chapter 9), yet thinking about the next days, weeks, and months is important too. What are you trying to accomplish? I hope that you will consider the topics addressed in this book. Some parts are more directly prescriptive than others, but there is information relevant to a full and satisfying life throughout. In addition, you surely have immediate goals, a to-do list, or moments when you suspect you could be using your time more wisely. Psychology has learned much about how people successfully pursue goals. Beyond getting important things done, successful goal pursuit can also boost well-being – think of the goal exercise and hope-based therapy mentioned in Chapter 9. As you think about personal goals, the positive activity model in Chapter 9 can be useful too. You may wish to adopt or adapt some of those specific activities, but I hope you will think beyond them. Regardless of the particular new activities you have in mind, the model highlights some key dimensions to consider (e.g. timing, social support, fit with personality) when initiating positive change.

Personality characteristics predict goal progress and accomplishment (e.g. McCabe & Fleeson, 2016; Sheldon, Jose, Kashdan, & Jarden, 2015), but they will not be our focus here. For example, **grit** describes individual differences in persistence through difficulty and is strongly associated with the big five trait of conscientiousness. Both predict accomplishment, as do things like trait self-control, self-esteem, achievement motivation, and so on. However, with our current focus on tactics for goal pursuit, personality is mostly useful only indirectly. First, although it seems possible to intentionally change broad traits, it requires sustained efforts (Hudson, Briley, Chopik, & Derringer, 2018) – traits are quite stable over time by definition. Moreover, unless trait change is your primary goal, it is an indirect way to accomplish what you want. For example, if your goal is to eat more fresh fruit, better to focus on that, specifically, than to first try to get there by increasing your general self-control.

Another reason to avoid emphasizing personality influences when discussing goals for change comes, ironically, from studies on another individual difference: mindsets. (I do not want to induce a fixed mindset here.) According to this line of research, people who believe that characteristics are malleable have **growth mindsets** (also known as incremental theories) and they often accomplish more than people with **fixed mindsets** (or entity theories), who believe characteristics are stable or inborn (Dweck, 2012; Dweck, Chiu,

Hong, & Inquiry, 1995). In academic contexts, growth mindsets are associated with higher performance because they promote more adaptive responses to setbacks. That is, when failures inevitably occur, people with fixed mindsets see it as diagnostic of their stable abilities (little can be done to change); those with growth mindsets can take it as feedback that more practice and learning is needed. In these circumstances, growth mindsets encourage persistence and effort.

Mindsets have been studied most in academic contexts, but can be applied in many domains, for example to morality (i.e. people's goodness is fixed or malleable) or happiness (i.e. about whether it can be changed; Dweck et al., 1995; Passmore, Howell, & Holder, 2018). The central idea is that believing that you can never change sets up a self-fulfilling prophecy, and this is a problem when things are not going well. Although mindsets are often studied as individual differences, their proponents also see them as malleable and have developed training programmes to encourage growth mindsets in students. So, what kind of mindsets do these proponents have then? As you consider self-relevant goals and positive personal changes, there may be value in adopting a growth mindset. Still, if you have already decided that you have a fixed mindset – and thereby do not see yourself being persuaded otherwise – not all hope is lost. A recent meta-analysis found that the links between mindset and academic achievement were quite small in most educational contexts – both as a correlation and when interventions tried to boost growth mindsets (Sisk, Burgoyne, Sun, Butler, & Macnamara, 2018). Growth mindsets may be helpful, but they are one of many factors.

Finally, by focusing on concrete goals, rather than broad changes, personality differences are genuinely less important. Recall from Chapter 4 that personality predicts long-term outcomes, such as occupational achievement, longevity, subjective well-being, and so on, but traits do not predict individual moments very well. Personality is typically revealed when averaging across many moments, over time or across situations. Recent studies corroborate this idea when it comes to goals by looking at what predicts goal progress over the course of weeks. That is, participants list a few goals at the beginning, and report on how much progress they have made later. These studies find that there is much more variation among the goals than between the people (Milyavskaya, Inzlicht, Hope, & Koestner, 2015; Werner & Milyavskaya, 2018). Said another way, some goals get accomplished and others do not, but it is not the case that some people accomplish all their goals while others do not – it depends more on the goal than the person.

Moreover, people are flexible in their momentary behaviours, for example very introverted people act in extraverted ways sometimes, just less often than extraverted people. Goals are key in directing these momentary behaviours (McCabe & Fleeson, 2016). When people have the goal to avoid wasting time, their behaviour becomes more conscientious to meet it. In addition, as we learn more about the reasons that traits predict goal accomplishment (on average, over time), we find that people with helpful traits typically use strategies that do not seem to depend on having particular traits (Locke & Latham, 2002). For example, people who score high on trait self-control often engage in adaptive behaviours because they have developed good habits (Galla & Duckworth, 2016). That is, high self-control people report using less effortful inhibition for things like healthy eating, sleeping, and homework – with strong habits, willpower is not needed. This implies that giving people good strategies for specific goals can override the unhelpful tendencies that come with some traits. In sum, a complete science of goal pursuit should include individual differences that predict success, but personality need not be a barrier to employing the useful strategies discussed next.

How to Pursue Your Goals

A key feature of successful goal pursuit is first choosing the right goal. Doing this requires thinking both about the broad domains of personal projects, and then in refining the details for maximum efficacy and satisfaction. At the broad level, we must revisit personality. A key element in pursing the right goals is knowing who you are. That is, goals that are consistent with your sense of true self, that are pursued for their own enjoyment, and that you pursue because you want to, are more likely to be accomplished and to produce well-being (Ryan & Deci, 2000; Sheldon, 2014). To connect these ideas to some jargon and elements of positive psychology already discussed, recall **self-determination theory** from Chapter 5. In this framework, flourishing comes from intrinsic pursuits that meet basic needs. Although the basic needs of autonomy, competence, and relatedness are assumed to be universal, they are also very broad. For example, a person could demonstrate competence by completing a marathon, raising a well-adjusted child, or coding a useful app. Individuals will differ in how they meet these key needs. In addition, self-determination theory warns that pursuing extrinsic goals – those forced on us by others, for pure financial gain, or to conform – are both more difficult to stick with over time and less rewarding. The main idea here is to consider, deeply, what goals you want to pursue and the reasons. Knowing oneself is helpful to successful goal pursuit as it guides good goal selection. Of course, there are things that we have to do, and some of the strategies below can help with those too, but when there is a choice, 'want to' goals portend success more than 'have to' goals (Milyavskaya et al., 2015). When choosing your pursuit of well-being, ensure that your core self is well represented in the path.

A complementary approach to understanding goals and performance comes from organizational psychology. **Goal-setting theory** describes the characteristics of goals that produce optimal performance, typically applied in domains where goals are not entirely intrinsic, such as workplaces or school (Locke & Latham, 1990, 2002, 2006). This is not to say that the principles cannot be useful for personal goals too, but the focus differs. According to goal-setting theory, goals are useful in four ways: they direct attention towards goal activities, energize behaviour (increase effort), induce persistence while unmet, and prompt people to engage strategies and their knowledge to help meet goals. In a workplace, these properties can help compensate for lack of intrinsic interest or enjoyment, for example in assembling gadgets. Goal-setting theory – and much supportive data – suggests that the goals most conducive to high performance are concrete, specific, and difficult (Epton, Currie, & Armitage, 2017). For example, 'make 248 bagels a day' is clear and easily measured, whereas 'produce more breakfast foods' is not. Goals to 'do your best' are vague and rarely produce results that are actually a person's best. Instead, concrete goals do. At bagel number 247, nearly anyone with a goal of 248 will find a way to produce another bagel, but without this concrete goal, 247 (or 221, or 100, or…) might seem like 'my best'.

The admonition to set difficult goals might seem less intuitive, but goal-setting theory is very clear on this point: "the highest or most difficult goals produced the highest levels of effort and performance" (Locke & Latham, 2002, p. 706). This applies when goals are set by oneself or others (e.g. boss or coach), so long as the person is committed to the goal – without commitment, goals lose their ability to motivate. Also, note that the positive effects of difficult goals are phrased not in terms of goal accomplishment, but rather in terms of performance. When performance can be assessed in clear ways (e.g. number of sales, products assembled, kilometres run), failing to meet a difficult goal (e.g. 229/248) can be superior to meeting an easier goal (e.g. 100/100). However, in novel situations or with more complex activities (e.g. establishing rapport with potential donors or choosing the best insurance plan), clear performance goals can be hard to set concretely. As such, learning goals – understood as trying to develop the best one can – can work better in these challenging contexts (Locke & Latham, 2002). Still, before deciding that a new task is too complex for concrete, specific goals, it is worth considering whether you can create narrower, incremental goals that have these qualities. For example, rather than 'complete a university degree', a more concrete goal would be 'submit all assignments on time this term'.

Setting good goals is an important first step, but perhaps even more important is developing wise plans to achieve them. Indeed, high-quality and specific plans are probably the most useful tool in successful goal pursuit. **Implementation intentions** are if–then plans which link specific circumstances with specific behaviours in service of a larger goal, and they work well (Gollwitzer, 1999; Gollwitzer & Sheeran, 2006). For example, imagine that your goal is to convince Blake to go to a formal dance with you, but you do not know Blake very well and the pursuit makes you nervous. A series of implementation intentions can help, such as: *if* I see Blake in the hall *then* I will smile; *if* Blake walks towards me *then* I will comment on the weather; *if* I feel myself getting nervous *then* I will remind myself that Blake initiated this interaction. As much as implementation intentions are clearly intentional at creation, their purpose is to remove the need for thought in key moments. These moments (i.e. the 'if') can be triggered by time, places, internal thoughts or feelings, or virtually any discrete signal. They provide a pre-commitment to goal-directed behaviour. This is useful in getting started, such as by setting a particular time (e.g. 8:00 is workout time), providing reminders (e.g. when waiting for the elevator, I will remind myself that taking the stairs is better), or identifying key opportunities (e.g. when I see my neighbour, I will ask about my missing flower pot).

Implementation intentions can also help protect goals from distraction or competing activities by developing specific plans for anticipated obstacles. It is wise to consider the things that could interfere with your plans before they occur. For example, if your fitness goals include walking 10,000 steps each day, develop a contingency plan for rainy days (perhaps a personal dance party in your room). To avoid having studying disrupted by social media, you might disconnect the internet or leave your phone in another room (i.e. if I study, then my phone goes away). On some days you will feel tired or anxious or busy; consider helpful little things you might say to yourself (e.g. I will feel better about myself later if I eat an apple rather than gummy bears), or making adjustments to planned behaviours (20 minutes of study is better than 0 minutes) to keep you on track with your goals. Of course strong implementation intentions will also help ensure that you get to your goals before you get weighed down with other things.

Research finds that implementation intentions predict successful goal pursuit among people who use them spontaneously; moreover, many experiments show that asking people to add implementation intentions to their goals improves success substantially (Gollwitzer & Sheeran, 2006). Fortunately, the strategy is easily conveyed – the previous paragraph should be enough to get you started. Implementation intentions take self-reflection out of goal pursuit in the immediate moment, but they still combine well with people's most important personal goals. For example, a study asked students to list their goals for the upcoming weekend and also rate these goals for how intrinsically motivated each goal was (Koestner, Lekes, Powers, & Chicoine, 2002). Half of the participants were randomly assigned to also develop implementation intentions for the weekend. On Sunday evening, students reported on their goal progress and their moods. Unsurprisingly, the students made more progress on intrinsic goals (i.e. the things they truly wanted to be doing), and goal progress was associated with better moods. Creating implementation intentions also fostered better goal progress overall, but especially for the intrinsic goals. Said another way, even with personally important intrinsic goals, progress (and happiness) depended on having good strategies for their pursuit.

Habits describe a process where a cue (e.g. an environmental context or internal feeling) produces an automatic behavioural response (Neal, Wood, & Quinn, 2006; Wood & Rünger, 2015). Habits share some characteristics with implementation intentions (e.g. the idea that contextual cues can trigger behaviours), but habits often lack clear intentions. That is, where implementation intentions are crafted to make desired behaviours easier in key moments, they still rely on carrying out those intentions. In contrast, habits are automatic. Understanding habits is important to goals because people often have goals to break undesirable habits or develop new habits. Indeed, creating a new habit can serve a goal well by making desirable behaviours occur without thought, after the new habit is established. Many of the useful strategies for goal pursuit reduce the need for willpower; habits are at the pinnacle of this principle.

Developing habits takes time and repetition, and during this period the cued behaviour is rewarded; however, once the habit is formed, the cue-induced behaviour can be rewarding on its own (Neal et al., 2006). For example, eating from a bowl of candy at the laundromat starts off as rewarding (yum!); yet once a habit of eating there is established, you might find yourself doing it even when full or with flavours you do not like much. The candy bowl is the cue; your eating has become automatic. Said another way, when habits exist, people's intentions are largely irrelevant (Webb & Sheeran, 2006). This can become a problem when intentions differ from habits (e.g. wanting to avoid sugar, stop smoking, check email less often). When trying to break a habit, it is useful to identify the cue for undesirable behaviour. This cue might then be avoided if possible or, alternatively, implementation intentions can help effortfully replace the response: *if* [habit cue] *then* [alternative behaviour]. Consider adding a reward to go along with the alternative behaviour and repeat regularly to foster a new habit (cf. Duhigg, 2012).

It is also possible to create a new habit, rather than merely replace a bad habit. The potential for new habits is greatest when you can identify a specific, regular cue that can signal the behaviour and that can be consistently rewarded (at least at first). In these circumstances the benefits of a desirable habit may even outweigh the motivational cost known as undermining intrinsic motivation. That is, motivation research shows that rewarding people for behaviours that they already want to do, for example by paying them, can reduce motivation once the external rewards stop (Deci, Koestner, & Ryan, 1999). In essence, their reasons for the behaviour shift from intrinsic to the extrinsic financial rewards. However, recent studies suggest that payments can be used strategically to develop new habits, and those new habits still foster the desired behaviour after payments stop – because they are habits. For example, researchers randomly assigned some people to be paid to exercise at the gym twice per week for a month, and compared them to people in a control group who were not paid for regular gym attendance (Charness & Gneezy, 2009). Perhaps obviously, the payments increased gym attendance while they were being doled out. More importantly, gym use was tracked for months after the payments stopped, and the formerly paid participants still continued to use the gym at higher rates than the control group. Said another way, for participants who did not go to the gym before this study, the payments seemed successful in generating a new and lasting habit. Of course this study does not directly compare intrinsic motivation to new habits, but it does suggest that bribery can be successful in inducing new habits. It may be difficult for you to find someone to pay you to reach your personal goals, but perhaps you can put your intrinsic motivation (and other strategies) to work in the service of developing a new habit. Payments are not the only rewards. Moreover, the repetition (vs financial incentive) is likely more important to habit formation. Another study found that people developed a gym habit without payments, but estimated that it took four visits per week for six weeks (Kaushal & Rhodes, 2015). In sum, if you have a goal that is amenable to habit formation, try committing to a regular schedule for a month to see whether this is enough to make it stick. You may also find that it is easier to get started with a one-month commitment, compared to a larger lifelong goal.

Again, the primary reason that implementation intentions and habits help people accomplish goals is that they reduce the need for effortful engagement in the moments that key behaviours are enacted. In other words, they reduce the need for willpower. Other techniques take this same general approach, and might be useful depending on your particular goal (see Duckworth, Gendler, & Gross, 2016; Duckworth, Milkman, & Laibson, 2018). **Commitment devices** draw on the good intentions people have before tempting moments, and they make later capitulation more difficult. For example, you might delete a distracting app during exam week, or subscribe to a service that accepts your money with instructions to not return it, or donate it to a repugnant organization, unless you meet some goal. Public commitments, even just to friends or families, also add some accountability and social pressure to follow through on goals. Some unwanted behaviours are not habitual (i.e. fully automatic) but are still prompted by cues in the environment. In these cases, changing the immediate situation can help, for example by filling the refrigerator with healthy foods or avoiding places that serve alcohol. Willpower is not needed for temptations that are out of sight and then out of mind. If the actual situation cannot be changed, psychological distancing or reframing can help. For example, imagining tempting chocolates as little pieces of poo might reduce their appeal, or deciding that your co-worker's taunts are more about his miserable marriage than about you, can help you to avoid screaming at him.

For activities that are onerous but do not require full attention (e.g. cleaning, exercise), **temptation bundling** might help. This involves combining an undesirable task with a (guilty) pleasure. For example, one study allowed people access to engaging audiobooks only at the gym, and found that this technique increased their exercise by about 50 per cent (Milkman, Minson, & Volpp, 2014). The key is to find two activities where bundling makes both activities better: less guilt from the pleasures and easier to do the difficult activity. In addition, the activities should be done simultaneously; giving in to temptation today with promises about all the good behaviours you will do tomorrow does not count!

Finally, most goal pursuit entails some setbacks and small failures. Self-compassion is helpful in these moments (see Chapter 5). Being rigid and self-critical is especially problematic when it becomes a path to abandoning goals after small failures. For example, after small stumbles it can be easy to think "Well, today is a lost cause", or "Forget it all then". Building some flexibility or buffers into goals can help. Also recall that self-compassionate people still try to be their best selves; they are kind to themselves during failure, and this helps them bounce back quickly.

POSITIVE PSYCHOLOGY: TAKING STOCK AND LOOKING FORWARD

A primary consequence of the positive psychology movement has been to make some topics more prominent. It found mainstream psychology's relative inattention to strengths, positive experiences, well-being, resilience, and so on problematic. In response, positive psychologists promoted research, communication, and applications in these areas. In the time that I have been writing this book (years!), another movement has become prominent in psychology and other sciences: the credibility revolution. Although some still debate the enduring impact of recent changes, the term revolution correctly implies that something big is happening (Nelson, Simmons, & Simonsohn, 2018; Spellman, 2015; Vazire, 2018). The **credibility revolution** describes dramatic changes in how (psychological) scientists conduct, report, and evaluate research, with reforms aimed at increasing the confidence of findings. It raises broad questions about how much we can trust the research record in positive psychology; yet I hope you will remain optimistic about our trajectory – better methods produce better science, which feeds forward to better applications. Many of the topics considered in this section transcend positive psychology; they may even seem tangential for people focused on a better understanding of the good life. Still, positive psychology holds its scientific basis as a core value, and science is a key element that distinguishes it from other similar approaches. Thus, I argue that the way positive psychology grapples with the credibiltiy challenges and opportunities will guide its future and impact more strongly than will debate about which topics should receive more attention. (That said, some speculation on future directions is coming too.) As we explore issues in the credibility revolution, think about how they colour the trustworthiness of individual studies, such as those that pepper this book when you read, "For example, one study found…".

Replication as a Key Feature of Science

The credibility revolution has also been referred to as a 'replication crisis'. This phrasing is somewhat pessimistic (with emerging solutions, the crisis has turned to opportunity), but the term has the strength of pointing to a key issue: replication. **Replication** is a hallmark of science, and it is demonstrated when a study is repeated. When findings are true, replication studies will usually produce the same results. The qualifier 'usually' acknowledges that sometimes individual findings are due to random chance or error, rather than regularities in the world. However, these exceptions, or failures to replicate, should be rare if a body of research is indeed revealing truths. The credibility revolution was sparked, in part, by increasing concerns that many findings in psychology were not successfully replicating. This is cause for concern, but understanding the implications requires that we distinguish between two forms of replication.

With **direct** (or exact) **replications** a new study attempts to repeat the procedures of an original study as closely as possible. The purpose of a direct replication is to determine whether or not specific procedures reliably produce the same results. For example, if you conducted a study that found that watching a ten-minute clip of BBC's *Blue Planet* produced an increase in self-reported awe, my direct replication study should use the same video clip (vs a different ten minutes or a different nature documentary) and the same questionnaire measure of awe. Furthermore, I might try to recruit participants of a similar age and cultural background, and I should conduct my study in a similar context (e.g. in a quiet lab room versus over the internet). If you conducted your study on Tuesdays and Thursdays only, perhaps I should do the same, and so on. As we begin to articulate the many specific details of an original study that could possibly change in a replication study, it becomes clear that no replication study is truly an exact repetition – it may be better to think of these as 'close replications'. Nonetheless, direct replications attempt to keep the important details the same. Moreover, if the original study's authors made a general conclusion about *Blue Planet* and awe, not mentioning anything about the day of the week, then it seems reasonable to gloss over these differences in a direct replication attempt. Surely chemists do not worry about the day of the week when replicating their studies. On the other hand, humans are quirky beings, and psychology is still trying to get a handle on which factors matter. Direct replications' successes and failures can help point to those factors and thus inform future theories.

Even when a set of procedures reliably and universally produces the same result (i.e. consistently successful direct replications), we need another type of replication – conceptual replication – to assess that result's meaning and interpretation (Crandall & Sherman, 2016). **Conceptual replications** re-test the basic idea of an original study, but intentionally change the procedures in some meaningful way. The purpose of the procedure change is to ensure that the original finding is not due to idiosyncratic features of the particular methods. In psychology, we are mostly interested in things that are intangible and nonmaterial, such as thoughts and emotions. Even when we are interested in physical things (e.g. room aesthetics or the presence of another person), they often have many possible exemplars and may still be psychologically important to the extent that they represent an idea, rather than a physical thing per se. As such, we can rarely manipulate or measure the things we care about directly. Chapter 1 discussed the problems of confounds and third variables – unmeasured things that might correlate with our manipulations and assessments, and that might actually account for the results. For example, although *Blue Planet* is a lovely documentary, psychologists are not particularly interested in how it, specifically, affects emotions. Rather, *Blue Planet* might get used in a study because it is one way to expose people to nature – one of many possible ways. The problem here is that even with 100 successful direct replications of the link between *Blue Planet* and awe, we still do not know that the concept 'nature' is responsible for the awe with much confidence. *Blue Planet* may instead produce awe because of narrator David Attenborough's charming voice, or the quality of an HD video, or the stunning musical score, and so on. This is one reason why any single study's results should be treated with caution. Even if the results are reliable (i.e. directly replicated), the individual finding's true meaning is often ambiguous. Conceptual replications focus on the underlying ideas and test these by employing new, complementary methods. So, for example, my conceptual replication of the *Blue Planet* study might use different nature videos, audio recordings of birds, or actual walks in a park to expose people to nature. Similarly, I might change the measurement of awe to a different self-report questionnaire or an observation of bodily expression or physiological arousal.

When a variety of conceptual replications produce similar results, we become more confident that the broader underlying idea is correct (e.g. nature exposure produces awe). On the other hand, when results differ across conceptual replications, interpretation is difficult. Moreover, when failed conceptual replications are at odds with a plausible or personally held idea, there is a temptation to attribute the failure to details of the new procedure, rather than the underlying idea. (Scientists strive for accuracy but are not immune from biases in interpretation.) In our running example, the failure to find an effect of nature on bodily expressions of awe might be attributed to a lack of agreement about what awe expressions look like. In addition, typical statistical approaches treat null results as ambiguous, and this provides another plausible rationale to avoid concluding a real failure. This statistical excuse applies to both conceptual and direct replications. Although reasonable in the abstract, the excuses combine poorly with the way science is communicated, which typically ignores ambiguous results.

As noted in Chapter 9, over 90 per cent of published studies report results that confirm hypotheses (Fanelli, 2012), though this rate is higher than for all the studies conducted (and not published). With this **publication bias**, replication failures go unnoticed, leaving a distorted record of mainly supportive research. Other forms of publication bias make it difficult to publish even successful replications. By their nature, successful replications confirm something that has already been found. In contrast, status and acclaim come to journals and scientists who produce new discoveries, rather than confirming 'old news'. As such, there have been few incentives for individual scientists to conduct replication studies, despite replication's importance to science in general (Nosek, Spies, & Motyl, 2012). (This can be understood as a social dilemma where individual incentives are at odds with the collective good; cf. Chapter 7.) Prior to the credibility revolution, little replication research was being conducted or reported. This created the conditions for zombie false findings to stay alive in print without the challenge of failed replication attempts. Also, true findings often lack the confidence that would come from systematic supportive replications. Without replication studies, it is hard to tell the zombies from the truths. Thus, lack of replication studies and publication bias were (are) big problems, but not the only ones.

From Challenge Comes Positive Change

The stories of a few focal events illustrate how psychology was drawn into the credibility revolution. For example, in 2011, an article in a prominent psychology journal reported nine studies that suggested that humans have ESP (extra sensory perception) or, more specifically, the ability to know the future before it has happened (Bem, 2011). Most people – including the journal editors – found these results highly implausible; however, they were published because the studies appeared free of obvious flaws and would be very exciting if true. Because the findings were so implausible, there was an unusual rush to replicate them by other researchers. Those direct replication studies did not produce the same results (e.g. Galak, LeBoeuf, Nelson, & Simmons, 2012), and the original ESP results now seem like **false positives** – a statistical term for when tests conclude that a finding is true when it is, in fact, false. Still, even with the record corrected on this particular finding – something that happened unusually fast in this case – researchers were perplexed at how their standard practices could produce conclusions that were so absurd (i.e. in the original paper). Their incredulity sparked deep reflection, a renewed interest in replication studies, and research about how research is conducted (meta-science), and ultimately helped drive the credibility revolution.

Another early and influential pair of studies showed that listening to the Beatles song "When I'm Sixty-Four" caused people to become younger (Simmons, Nelson, & Simonsohn, 2011). Even more than ESP, this finding is obviously impossible. That was the point of the paper, deliciously titled "False Positive Psychology…" (for the statistical term – not a dig at our sub-discipline). The researchers had collected real data from real people, but also used a series of questionable – but perhaps not uncommon – practices to arrive at impossible conclusions. They argued that other, more plausible findings in academic journals might arrive at similarly erroneous conclusions without anyone realizing it. To support this argument, they performed computer simulations that showed that using a few questionable practices together could generate completely false findings 60 per cent of the time! The questionable practices included things like adding statistical controls, omitting an experimental condition, reporting only some collected measures, and repeatedly checking results and adding more participants if they were not statistically significant. 'Statistically significant' is a term that should indicate that an effect is unlikely to be due to chance alone, often defined as '$p < .05$'. However, as the "When I'm Sixty-Four" demonstration shows, $p < .05$ can be very misleading. Indeed, misunderstanding and miscommunication around p-values likely plays an important role in false positive results and subsequent failures to replicate them.

To be clear, the questionable research practices (e.g. omitting variables, adding controls) sometimes have justifiable reasons (e.g. in very large studies, not everything can be reported in a single article). Indeed, researchers widely acknowledge their use and situational acceptability in surveys (John, Loewenstein, & Prelec, 2012). The problem arises, however, when researchers 'justify' only the choices that lead to $p < .05$ (statistical significance), ignoring other analyses that are less supportive. This search and biased reporting of statistically significant results is termed **p-hacking**. Indeed, simply conducting many different analyses increases the chances that a false positive result will be found. Statistical conventions rely on probability and chance, and when no effect actually exists, each new analysis is like spinning a false positive roulette wheel. In addition, the potential for error (i.e. false positives) is higher in small studies because they estimate things less precisely. In the 'bad old days' many were taught that statistically significant results in small samples meant that a result was very robust – this is wrong; small studies will only find true effects if they are very large, but small studies more typically find false positives that merely appear large.

Even relatively simple studies can include many choices or potential extra analyses. For example, researchers choose whether or not to exclude unusual cases, whether to look for gender, age, or ethnicity differences, which measures to focus on, combine, or split apart, and so on. Researchers' natural inclinations towards discovery can drive these explorations, and it is possible that thorough investigations can reveal important new insights. However, many researchers have failed to appreciate how much these explorations can increase the chances of false positives. Even the researchers who conducted the simulations showing that this flexibility can produce false positives 60 per cent of the time were astonished by their findings. They later reflected that questionable practices had seemed like jaywalking – wrong but probably harmless, but that after running the simulations, it became clear that they are more like robbing a bank (Simmons et al., 2018). The American Statistical Association weighed in with a similar conclusion: "Conducting multiple analyses of the data and reporting only those with certain p-values (typically those passing a significance threshold) renders the reported p-values essentially uninterpretable" (Wasserstein & Lazar, 2016, pp. 131–132). Until recently, many researchers were woefully unaware of the statistical dangers in common exploratory practices. In addition, researchers' curiosity was further tempted by journal editors and publication bias. When it came to publication, finding statistically significant analyses often meant the difference between a journal article and an unreported study. In this way, publication bias can also be understood as keeping some analyses – rather than entire studies – from being reported (Nelson et al., 2018). The distorting effect on recorded knowledge remains problematic nonetheless.

With renewed statistical concerns, the ESP article, and a few other high-profile failed replication attempts, researchers began to take a more systematic approach to replication in psychology. As a prominent example, the massive Reproducibility Project (OSC, 2015) selected 100 studies published in the year 2008 and set out to conduct direct replications. Research teams each took one study and replicated it. They often had the input of original authors to assist with procedural details, and they posted a record of those details and their analysis plans online before conducting the replication studies. The effort involved hundreds of researchers and thousands of participants. When all the results were collected, the project found that about one third to one half of the studies successfully replicated. (The range here acknowledges alternative criteria that could be used to decide success.) In addition, the average size of replication study effects was only half the size of those reported in the original studies – the important differences were often much smaller when replicated. These results were generally viewed as disappointing. Although perfect replication was not expected, or even desirable (we want researchers to take some risks), most would hope for a better than 50–50 chance that a randomly chosen study would replicate. Across a handful of similar large-scale replication projects now complete, the running average remains around 50 per cent.

The Reproducibility Project does not tell us why more studies did not replicate success-fully, but we have already considered some likely culprits. It is possible that original study findings were due to chance (error), and that publication bias contributed to a high rate of chance results in journals. Additionally, questionable research practices in the original studies might have produced biased statistics rather than revealing true effects. (It is unlikely that original results were completely fraudulent, as fabricated data are rare and not tolerated.) It is also possible that the replication research teams unwittingly made some errors or that some minor changes to procedures were more consequential than anticipated. Moreover, the characteristics of participants often differed between the original and replication studies; for example, they were conducted at different universities, often even in different countries, and all were conducted in different years.

Differences in the characteristics of participants are attractive explanations for failed replications – after all, an entire sub-discipline of cross-cultural psychology focuses on such differences. On the other hand, without direct evidence for a particular cultural difference, there are reasons to be suspicious of blanket disclaimers. Notably, another massive replica-tion project (Many Labs 2) replicated 28 classic studies, with each replication repeated by teams across many countries (Klein et al., 2018). Cultural and other demographic differ-ences across the samples did not explain whether or not studies replicated. Rather, about 50 per cent of results again replicated, and individual results either replicated everywhere or nowhere. There were few meaningful cultural differences in this collection of 28 studies. Still, the general approach of replicating studies across different cultures, age groups, and contexts remains an excellent tool to test how general a result is, and to discover potentially important patterns of difference.

Although the average replication success rates are disappointing, many view these proj-ects with considerable optimism. First, the approach to assessing replicability is itself very scientific. A key principle of science is that it is self-correcting, and identifying a problem is an important first step to solving it. In addition, psychology is a leader in assessing and addressing replication issues. Some fear that communicating failures will tarnish psychology, but the reverse seems to be true. In scenario studies, both scientists and lay people respect a commitment to getting things right – including admitting the failed replications – more than being correct in the first place (Ebersole et al., 2016; Fetterman & Sassenberg, 2015). More-over, other disciplines have since followed psychology's lead by coordinating large replica-tion projects of their own, for example in economics, experimental philosophy, and cancer biology. To be sure, publication bias and failed replications are not unique to psychology!

Positive psychologists will find both good and bad news with specific failed replication studies. For example, self-report measures of life satisfaction have been criticized as being too sensitive to momentary influences to be valid. Specifically, a 'classic' study showed that people rate their life satisfaction considerably higher on sunny days (Schwarz & Clore, 1983); however, newer and much improved studies show that the early result is untenable. Both direct and conceptual replications have not produced the weather effect (Yap,

Wortman, Anusic, Baker, Scherer, Donnellan, & Lucas, 2017), and weather is uncorrelated with life satisfaction ratings in very large studies (Lucas & Lawless, 2013) – the challenge to validity is unsupported. Of course not all corrections are so agreeable for positive psychology. For example, the classic facial feedback effect, which suggested that merely contracting smile muscles could elevate moods, was not supported in a large, multi-site replication attempt (Wagenmakers et al., 2016). Nonetheless, getting these things correct will pay off in the long run.

Correcting the record on individual findings is useful, but collectively, the failed replications also motivated a search for broader improvements. The credibility revolution is delivering these reforms. First, a change in mindset means that a single study's results must be interpreted more cautiously. With studies' replicability in doubt generally, we now expect more evidence. This is especially true for surprising findings. In addition, psychologists now recognize how questionable practices can drastically inflate the chances of a false positive finding. Researchers and journals are responding by reducing such practices and increasing the transparency of the research process. For example, this brief standard statement in journal articles helps assure readers that problematic practices have been avoided: 'We report how we determined our sample size, all data exclusions (if any), all manipulations, and all measures in the study' (Simmons et al., 2012). It is also increasingly common for researchers to make their raw data, measures, and very detailed procedures publicly available online (e.g. see https://cos.io). The internet makes sharing details easy, but it has taken the recent culture shift to nudge researchers into doing it. In addition to making choices more transparent, openly shared materials make both replication and follow-up studies much easier to conduct. Moreover, sharing raw data allows other researchers to re-analyse it in alternative ways, potentially allowing tests of hypotheses the original researcher never even considered.

Researchers are also making stronger distinctions between analyses that are confirmatory (i.e. for planned hypotheses) and those that are more exploratory. This is important in calibrating our confidence in the results. Recall that every new analysis increases the chances of false positives. Ideally, the results of exploratory analyses should be followed up with a new study for a strong confirmatory test. An ironclad technique to distinguish confirmatory and exploratory analyses is **pre-registration**. That is, before data are collected, the study's procedure and planned analyses are recorded online. In addition to reducing flexibility in analyses, public pre-registration makes it more difficult to hide a study with unsupportive results. Such registrations are legally required for new drug trials and would strengthen research in many other areas.

With increased awareness and scrutiny of problematic analysis practices, researchers are improving their methods to ensure that unbiased statistical approaches can reveal true effects. Most commonly, studies are including many more participants. In recent years it has become more obvious how ridiculously small, and thus error-prone, typical psychology studies have been. For example, to detect that men weigh more than women, on average, a study should have about 100 people (Simmons et al., 2013); many psychology studies are smaller than this even though they study differences that seem much more subtle. Psychologists are also combining efforts to conduct very large studies across many locations and thus arrive at high confidence answers while exploring the possibility that results depend on culture or location (e.g. see https://psysciacc.org/). Having definitive answers early in the research process is very valuable. As an example, recall the intuitive prosociality studies from Chapter 7; a massive multi-site replication study revealed some problems with key procedures very early in this line of research. Although a setback, new methods are being developed quickly in response to the clear concerns. The science of intuitive prosociality is correcting itself at a rapid pace in our current credibility revolution. In contrast, researchers plodded forward with other classic paradigms for decades before their issues became clear through recent massive replication studies (e.g. Hagger et al., 2016); this seems incredibly wasteful. Improved research practices may reduce the frequency of surprising or dramatic articles, but building scientific knowledge requires solid findings.

To summarize, recent years have been tumultuous yet productive for psychological science. New research underscores the longstanding, but oft ignored, warning to approach individual published findings with caution. Large, systematic replication projects find that some findings are very robust, but that a non-trivial set (perhaps half, on average) will not replicate consistently. Without a large replication study on the specific topic, it is hard to know which any particular finding is. Moving forward, better research methods, increased transparency, and broad collaborations are providing higher confidence results. This provides a strong basis for optimism about the future of positive psychology. Yet at the end of a textbook that summarizes past research, you may reasonably wonder whether you have wasted time learning about false positives. Undoubtedly, new research will challenge some old ideas and findings; this is just how science works. Still, whereas individual findings are easily questioned (i.e. the 'for example, one study found…'), they sometimes represent one of many possible examples. I will confess that ignoring a single study with a fascinating finding is difficult, and some of those examples remain. However, I have also tried to signal places where the evidence is stronger (e.g. the correlates of happiness) or weaker (often phrased as 'hints', e.g. that multicultural experiences increase creativity) or in substantial debate (e.g. oxytocin as the hug hormone). In sum, as with science more generally, I have tried to provide the best answers available in positive psychology right now. They will be better tomorrow, even better next year, and so on far into the future.

The Ongoing Contributions of Positive Psychology

In this final section of the book, let us take a look back at some highlights of positive psychology. I think you will find that, even through the lens of the credibility revolution, there is much to appreciate and some important contributions. In addition, we will consider some of the future directions, beyond methodological reforms, in which positive psychology is likely to travel.

In my view, positive psychology's most useful contribution has been to focus more attention on positive topics. At the time the movement began, people's typical (pleasant) experience was largely neglected by mainstream psychology. This is most evident when it comes to emotions. The classic theories were developed to explain unpleasant emotions, and an early focus on facial expressions meant that pleasant emotions were mostly ignored. Today, the list of positive emotions roughly equals that of negative emotions. Moreover, considering positive emotions more deeply has challenged old theories and definitions of emotion. The broaden and build model has provided space to study the varieties and purposes of positive emotions. Although some work related to the model has required revision (see Fredrickson, 2013), the core idea that positive emotions broaden cognition and build resources has been exceptionally generative. Going forward, research will continue to articulate more nuances about which particular positive emotions build which specific resources and how. As we learn more about positive and negative emotions, perhaps a new, comprehensive model will be able to explain both in similar ways.

Although early positive psychology sought to avoid the impression of being 'happiology', happiness is at the core of the sub-discipline. After debates about whether to define happiness as largely eudaimonic (meaning, authenticity, etc.) or as the components of subjective well-being (satisfaction and positive emotional balance), we seem to have settled into the more productive compromise of using specific terms to communicate clearly. (Still, 'happiness' is sometimes a useful catch-all to describe the good life.) More importantly, our knowledge about subjective well-being has exploded since the positive psychology movement began, and it had a pretty good head start even then. In particular, the Gallup World Poll has provided amazing data – representative samples of planet Earth across many years – and thereby provided useful information about the societal characteristics that contribute to well-being. Governments are increasingly interested in tracking national well-being, and in crafting policy to promote it. Mixing positive psychology with politics carries some risk, but findings seem to support policies that can appeal across ideologies. Happiness tracks freedom, clean environments, wealth, and social supports. In addition, positive psychology has made a strong start in developing techniques (interventions) that can meaningfully boost well-being over time. That said, plenty of work remains for researchers and practitioners to further hone our knowledge of what works best and for whom.

Positive psychology's founders began a project to create a new taxonomy of strengths and virtues. They succeeded in creating a list of valued personal characteristics that researchers and practitioners have found useful for communicating with one another and for highlighting the ways in which people can express their positive potential. Still, the details of the model (i.e. organization of strengths) remains a work in progress; moreover, creating the new model of positive individual differences may have overlooked some of the knowledge already generated by personality psychology. Going forward, there is value in learning to translate characteristics and research findings between the big five and the VIA strengths model.

Work on self-determination theory began before the positive psychology movement, but the two have grown together and enriched each other. Whereas much of positive psychology relies on 'micro-theories' (i.e. relatively narrow models to explain a few things), self-determination theory has an attractive breadth and integrative quality. From universal basic needs to an explanation for why people pursue various goals and the consequences for well-being, much of what positive psychology has learned can be tied to the framework. For example, authenticity, or behaving in accordance with one's sense of true self, is a hallmark of eudaimonia and a key to well-being in self-determination theory. Other aspects of the self-concept, such as self-efficacy, are malleable and useful in promoting effective goal pursuit. As a newer addition, self-compassion appears to be a useful self-view, while remaining a target for further research to confirm initial promising results.

This book devoted a chapter to the thinking parts of the mind, parts that are not as obviously linked to happiness, such as creativity, wisdom, and cognitive abilities. Still, as valued personal characteristics, it would be wise for positive psychology to continue working towards ways to further develop these strengths. Research on intelligence has a long history, well-established measures, and often includes massive data sets. As such, findings tend to be reliable, even while exciting new work emerges from research begun many years earlier, such as the exceptional accomplishments of the intelligence top 1 per cent. More relevant to happiness, we also reviewed research on affective forecasting errors. Learning about these may improve its pursuit (i.e. by making better choices about what will actually make you happier); however, correcting forecasting errors is tricky and future research might discover new techniques to make people better forecasters.

Another key finding of positive psychology is the astonishing importance of other people to our well-being and behaviour. This is especially true of close relationships, but also apparent with casual acquaintances and even strangers. Positive psychologists have helped rebalance views of human nature in this domain. That is, humans' evolutionary niche seems to be a knack for cooperation, even with a complementary tendency for competition. That people frequently help one another, and that this behaviour produces so much good feeling, is undeniable. Nonetheless, grand societal challenges (e.g. climate change or world peace) depend on strong strategies that engage cooperative tendencies. We have learned much about how people resolve social dilemmas, but much of this work has not had a strong connection with positive psychology. I suspect that the positive perspective has much to offer in this domain, and with potentially important consequences. In particular, protecting the natural environment will require broad cooperation. From my personal research perspective, fostering connections between people and nature will be good for both, and I hope more positive psychologists will lend their efforts to this pursuit.

In exploring love, we have found much similarity across kinds of loving relationships, genders, and cultures with a common core of trust, warmth, and respect. Yet because love was not seen as an important topic of study until relatively recently, we have limited long-term longitudinal data about love relationships across the lifespan – an important gap when loving bonds often last that long. The hints we have suggest that while love is largely maintained, it tends to decline over time, on average, along with relationship satisfaction. This presents an opportunity for positive psychologists. Research on positive processes in relationships – as opposed to conflict – is relatively recent. Newer areas typically have great potential for rapid advancement. With a better understanding of things like capitalization (sharing good news) and exciting activities, useful advice for thriving relationships will follow.

Finally, the ordinary magic of resilience through adversity is inspiring, if also the least pleasant aspect of positive psychology. We have found that resilience is relatively common and have identified many predictors of resilience. Still, without a clear route to improving resilience, efforts at fostering it remain works in progress. Some people seem to respond to traumatic events with perceptions of growth. Still, ambiguity around whether these perceptions actually connote positive mental health makes promoting them with interventions a risky proposition.

Interestingly, some positive psychologists have called for more appreciation and consideration of negatives in the sub-discipline (e.g. Ivtzan, Lomas, Hefferon, & Worth, 2016; Kashdan & Biswas-Diener, 2014; McNulty & Fincham, 2012; Pawelski, 2016; Wong, 2011). On the one hand, this seems at odds with an area defined by positivity. Yet with resilience as a core topic within positive psychology, a tension with narrow views of 'positive' has existed from the beginning of the movement. The invitation to consider more negative aspects takes a few different forms. For example, one view is that life has a lot of suffering, and that acceptance of this fact is ultimately part of the path forward towards well-being. Also quite dark is the notion that many people find deep meaning in very difficult events (e.g. death), and that because meaning is so important, positive psychology must focus more on these things. Other versions see value in being flexible in order to care for hurt or dysfunction when needed, while also offering paths towards flourishing when crises have passed. Still others object to the notion that much of anything can be usefully categorized as completely positive or negative; the tradeoffs and context are important. For example, being too happy might interfere with productivity, or forgiving an abusive partner might ultimately cause more problems. As noted in Chapter 1, determining where and how to apply the 'positive' in positive psychology remains a philosophical struggle.

Collectively, these calls for more integration of positive and negative psychology echo a prediction from very early in the movement: that once positive psychology brought about some balance, it would no longer be needed. There is appeal to the notion that a complete view of human psychology will necessarily need to be as broad as possible, both positive and negative. Still, positive psychology does not seem to be fading away or reabsorbed in a way that threatens its unique identity. Many other sub-disciplines exist within psychology (e.g. developmental, health, social, cognitive). Each of these, alone, has a somewhat incomplete view of human nature. Still, those who work in these sub-disciplines find it useful to associate with others who are working on similar issues without pressure to account for everything. It seems that a distinct – though not entirely isolated – positive psychology may well persist for a long time in a similar way. Indeed, there is still plenty more to learn about positive topics.

SUMMING UP

This chapter began by considering goals and their successful pursuit. Although individual differences like grit, self-control, and growth mindsets predict accomplishment, it is useful to focus on strategies that are available to everyone, regardless of personality. Motivation and fulfilment are typically higher when pursuing personally valued goals rather than responding to external pressures. Still, many strategies are helpful for both types. For example, setting detailed plans using an *if–then* approach makes it easier to follow through on good intentions. Planning to develop new habits takes time and repetition, but once established, desireable habits remove the need for conscious thought and effort. Other successful strategies similarly reduce the need for momentary willpower, such as by avoiding or changing problematic environments, making public commitments, or pairing onerous tasks with something fun.

The remainder of this chapter considered recent developments in positive psychology and briefly speculated about its future. Most notably, the credibility of findings in psychology have come under scruitiny following some dramatic examples of improbable results (e.g. on ESP) and failures to replicate classic findings in large projects. Recent events underscore the wisdom of treating individual findings with caution, especially when they come from small studies with potential for flexibility in analyses. As a positive response to credibility challenges, researchers and journals are seeking larger samples of participants, providing key information more openly (e.g. raw data, method details, analysis plans – often in web archives), improving statistical interpretations, and paying more attention to 'failed' studies and analyses where hypotheses were not supported. These efforts have increased the confidence of many true findings and identified problems (false findings) in both the classics and exciting new areas of research. Ultimately, these reforms are producing a substantially more solid base of research on which positive psychologists can develop useful applications. The future of positive psychology looks bright.

TEST YOURSELF

1. According to goal-setting theory, what kinds of goals are most effective?

2. What are implementation intentions?

3. What is the difference between a direct replication and a conceptual replication?

4. Describe three reasons why psychology studies' results might not replicate.

5. Describe two recent developments that will likely improve the replicability of psychological science.

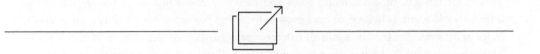

WEB LINKS

This podcast, hosted by researcher and teacher Tim Pychyl, explores the reasons for procrastination, including many tips on how to pursue goals more successfully:
http://iprocrastinate.libsyn.com

The Society for the Improvement of Psychological Science (SIPS) is a scholarly society that emerged with the credibility revolution:
https://improvingpsych.org

This video 'Dance of p-values' demonstrates some limitations of relying on $p < .05$ to decide what is a true finding or what is not:
www.youtube.com/watch?v=ez4DgdurRPg

FURTHER READING

For a broad review of self-regulation techniques, including some policy nudges, see:

Duckworth, A. L., Milkman, K. L., & Laibson, D. (2018). Beyond willpower: Strategies for reducing failures of self-control. *Psychological Science in the Public Interest, 19*(3), 102–129.

If you are contemplating broad personality trait change, rather than narrower goals, this article's appendix lists many activities that might help:

Hudson, N. W., Briley, D. A., Chopik, W. J., & Derringer, J. (2018). You have to follow through: Attaining behavioral change goals predicts volitional personality change. *Journal of Personality and Social Psychology*.

This article reviews key issues in the credibility revolution (or renaissance):

Nelson, L. D., Simmons, J. P ., & Simonsohn, U. (2018). Psychology's renaissance. Psychological Inquiry, 69, 511–534.

This brief and accessible article provides a discussion of difficulties with statistical inferences:

Nuzzo, R. (2014). Statistical errors: P values, the "gold standard" of statistical validity, are not as reliable as many scientists assume. *Nature, 506*(7487), 150–152.

This article challenges the notion that core topics can be universally positive, and argues for an integration of positive and mainstream psychology:

McNulty, J. K., & Fincham, F. D. (2012). Beyond positive psychology? Toward a contextual view of psychological processes and well-being. *The American Psychologist, 67*(2), 101–110.

REFERENCES

Bem, D. J. (2011). Feeling the future: Experimental evidence for anomalous retroactive influences on cognition and affect. *Journal of Personality and Social Psychology, 100*(3), 407–425. https://doi.org/10.1037/a0021524

Charness, G., & Gneezy, U. (2009). Incentives to exercise. *Econometrica, 77*(3), 909–931. https://doi.org/10.2139/ssrn.905026

Crandall, C. S., & Sherman, J. W. (2016). On the scientific superiority of conceptual replications for scientific progress. *Journal of Experimental Social Psychology, 66*, 93–99. https://doi.org/10.1016/j.jesp.2015.10.002

Deci, E. L., Koestner, R., & Ryan, R. M. (1999). A meta-analytic review of experiments examining the effects of extrinsic rewards on intrinsic motivation. *Psychological Bulletin, 125*(6), 627–668. https://doi.org/0033-2909/99S3.00

Duckworth, A. L., Gendler, T. S., & Gross, J. J. (2016). Situational strategies for self-control. *Perspectives on Psychological Science, 11*(1), 35–55. https://doi.org/10.1177/1745691615623247

Duckworth, A. L., Milkman, K. L., & Laibson, D. (2018). Beyond willpower: Strategies for reducing failures of self-control. *Psychological Science in the Public Interest, 19*(3), 102–129. https://doi.org/10.1177/1529100618821893

Duhigg, C. (2012). *The Power of Habit: Why We Do What We Do in Life and Business.* London: Random House.

Dweck, C. S. (2012). Mindsets and human nature: Promoting change in the Middle East, the schoolyard, the racial divide, and willpower. *American Psychologist, 67*(8), 614–622. https://doi.org/10.1037/a0029783

Dweck, C. S., Chiu, C., Hong, Y., & Inquiry, S. P. (1995). Implicit theories and their role in judgments and reactions: A world from two perspectives. *Psychological Inquiry, 6*(4), 267–285.

Ebersole, C. R., Axt, J. R., Nosek, B. A., Nosek, B., Alter, G., Banks, G. C., … Jinha, A. (2016). Scientists' reputations are based on getting it right, not being right. *PLOS Biology, 14*(5), e1002460. https://doi.org/10.1371/journal.pbio.1002460

Epton, T., Currie, S., & Armitage, C. J. (2017). Unique effects of setting goals on behavior change: Systematic review and meta-analysis. *Journal of Consulting and Clinical Psychology, 85*(12), 1182–1198. https://doi.org/10.1037/ccp0000260

Fanelli, D. (2012). Negative results are disappearing from most disciplines and countries. *Scientometrics, 90*(3), 891–904. https://doi.org/10.1007/s11192-011-0494-7

Fetterman, A. K., & Sassenberg, K. (2015). The reputational consequences of failed replications and wrongness admission among scientists. *PLOS ONE, 10*(12), e0143723. https://doi.org/10.1371/journal.pone.0143723

Fredrickson, B. L. (2013). Updated thinking on positivity ratios. *The American Psychologist, 68*(9), 814–822. https://doi.org/10.1037/a0033584

Galak, J., LeBoeuf, R. A., Nelson, L. D., & Simmons, J. P. (2012). Correcting the past: Failures to replicate psi. *Journal of Personality and Social Psychology, 103*(6), 933–948. https://doi.org/10.1037/a0029709

Galla, B. M., & Duckworth, A. L. (2016). More than resisting temptation: Beneficial habits mediate the relationship between self-control and positive life outcomes. *Journal of Personality and Social Psychology, 109*(3), 508–525. https://doi.org/10.1037/pspp0000026.More

Gollwitzer, P. M. (1999). Implementation intentions: Strong effects of simple plans. *American Psychologist, 54*(7), 493–503.

Gollwitzer, P. M., & Sheeran, P. (2006). Implementation intentions and goal achievement: A meta-analysis of effects and processes. *Advances in Experimental Social Psychology, 38*(06), 69–119. https://doi.org/10.1016/S0065-2601(06)38002-1

Hagger, M. S., Chatzisarantis, N. L. D., Alberts, H., Anggono, C. O., Batailler, C., Birt, A. R., … Zwienenberg, M. (2016). A multilab preregistered replication of the ego-depletion effect. *Perspectives on Psychological Science, 11*(4), 546–573. https://doi.org/10.1177/1745691616652873

Hudson, N. W., Briley, D. A., Chopik, W. J., & Derringer, J. (2018). You have to follow through: Attaining behavioral change goals predicts volitional personality change. *Journal of Personality and Social Psychology.* https://doi.org/10.1037/pspp0000221

Ivtzan, I., Lomas, T., Hefferon, K., & Worth, P. (2016). *Second Wave Positive Psychology: Embracing the Dark Side of Life.* Abingdon: Routledge.

John, L. K., Loewenstein, G., & Prelec, D. (2012). Measuring the prevalence of questionable research practices with incentives for truth telling. *Psychological Science, 23*(5), 524–532. https://doi.org/10.1177/0956797611430953

Kashdan, T. B., & Biswas-Diener, R. (2014). *The Upside of Your Dark Side*. New York: Hudson Street Press.

Kaushal, N., & Rhodes, R. E. (2015). Exercise habit formation in new gym members: A longitudinal study. *Journal of Behavioral Medicine*, *38*(4), 652–663. https://doi.org/10.1007/s10865-015-9640-7

Klein, R. A., Vianello, M., Hasselman, F., Adams, B. G., Adams, R. B., Alper, S., ... Nosek, B. (2018). Many Labs 2: Investigating variation in replicability across samples and settings. *Advances in Methods and Practices in Psychological Science*, *1*(4), 443–490. https://doi.org/10.1177/2515245918810225

Koestner, R., Lekes, N., Powers, T. A., & Chicoine, E. (2002). Attaining personal goals: Self-concordance plus implementation intentions equals success. *Journal of Personality and Social Psychology*, *83*(1), 231–244. https://doi.org/10.1037/0022-3514.83.*1*.231

Locke, E. A., & Latham, G. P. (1990). Work motivation and satisfaction: Light at the end of the tunnel. *Psychological Science*, *1*(4), 240–246. https://doi.org/10.1111/j.1467-9280.1990.tb00207.x

Locke, E. A., & Latham, G. P. (2002). Building a practically useful theory of goal setting and task motivation: A 35-year odyssey. *American Psychologist*, *57*(9), 705–717. https://doi.org/10.1037/0003-066X.57.9.705

Locke, E. A., & Latham, G. P. (2006). New directions in goal-setting theory. *Current Directions in Psychological Science*, *15*(5), 265–268. https://doi.org/10.1111/j.1467-8721.2006.00449.x

Lucas, R. E., & Lawless, N. M. (2013). Does life seem better on a sunny day? Examining the association between daily weather conditions and life satisfaction judgments. *Journal of Personality and Social Psychology*, *104*(5), 872–884. https://doi.org/10.1037/a0032124

McCabe, K. O., & Fleeson, W. (2016). Are traits useful? Explaining trait manifestations as tools in the pursuit of goals. *Journal of Personality and Social Psychology*, *110*(2), 287–301. https://doi.org/10.1037/a0039490

McNulty, J. K., & Fincham, F. D. (2012). Beyond positive psychology? Toward a contextual view of psychological processes and well-being. *The American Psychologist*, *67*(2), 101–110. https://doi.org/10.1037/a0024572

Milkman, K. L., Minson, J. A., & Volpp, K. G. M. (2014). Holding the Hunger Games hostage at the gym: An evaluation of temptation bundling. *Management Science*, *60*(2), 283–299. https://doi.org/10.1287/mnsc.2013.1784

Milyavskaya, M., Inzlicht, M., Hope, N., & Koestner, R. (2015). Saying "no" to temptation: Want-to motivation improves self-regulation by reducing temptation rather than by increasing self-control. *Journal of Personality and Social Psychology*, *109*(4), 677–693. https://doi.org/10.1037/pspp0000045

Neal, D. T., Wood, W., & Quinn, J. M. (2006). Habits—A repeat performance. *Current Directions in Psychological Science*, *15*(4), 198–202. https://doi.org/10.1111/j.1467-8721.2006.00435.x

Nelson, L. D., Simmons, J. P., & Simonsohn, U. (2018). Psychology's renaissance. *Psychological Inquiry*, *69*, 511–534.

Nosek, B. A., Spies, J. R., & Motyl, M. (2012). Scientific utopia: II. Restructuring incentives and practices to promote truth over publishability. *Perspectives on Psychological Science, 7*(6), 615–631. https://doi.org/10.1177/1745691612459058

OSC. (2015). Estimating the reproducibility of psychological science. *Science, 349*(6251), aac4716-aac4716. https://doi.org/10.1126/science.aac4716

Passmore, H.-A., Howell, A. J., & Holder, M. D. (2018). Positioning implicit theories of well-being within a positivity framework. *Journal of Happiness Studies, 19*(8), 2445–2463. https://doi.org/10.1007/s10902-017-9934-2

Pawelski, J. O. (2016). Defining the 'positive' in positive psychology: Part II. A normative analysis. *The Journal of Positive Psychology, 11*(4), 357–365. https://doi.org/10.1080/17439 760.2015.1137628

Ryan, R., & Deci, E. (2000). Self-determination theory and the facilitation of intrinsic motivation. *American Psychologist, 55*(1), 68–78. https://doi.org/10.1037/0003-066X.55.1.68

Schwarz, N., & Clore, G. L. (1983). Mood, misattribution, and judgments of well-being: Informative and directive functions of affective states. *Journal of Personality and Social Psychology, 45*(3), 513–523.

Sheldon, K. M. (2014). Becoming oneself: The central role of self-concordant goal selection. *Personality and Social Psychology Review, 18*(4), 349–365. https://doi.org/10.1177/1088868314538549

Sheldon, K. M., Jose, P. E., Kashdan, T. B., & Jarden, A. (2015). Personality, effective goal-striving, and enhanced well-being: Comparing 10 candidate personality strengths. *Personality and Social Psychology Bulletin, 41*(4), 575–585. https://doi.org/10.1177/0146167215573211

Simmons, J. P., Nelson, L. D., & Simonsohn, U. (2011). False-positive psychology: Undisclosed flexibility in data collection and analysis allows presenting anything as significant. *Psychological Science, 22*(11), 1359–1366. https://doi.org/10.1177/0956797611417632

Simmons, J. P., Nelson, L. D., & Simonsohn, U. (2012). A 21 word solution. *SSRN Electronic Journal.* https://doi.org/10.2139/ssrn.2160588

Simmons, J. P., Nelson, L. D., & Simonsohn, U. (2013). Life after p-hacking. *SSRN Electronic Journal.* https://doi.org/10.2139/ssrn.2205186

Simmons, J. P., Nelson, L. D., & Simonsohn, U. (2018). False-positive citations. *Perspectives on Psychological Science, 13*(2), 255–259. https://doi.org/10.1177/1745691617698146

Sisk, V., Burgoyne, A., Sun, J., Butler, J., & Macnamara, B. N. (2018). To what extent and under which circumstances are growth mindsets important to academic achievement? Two meta-analyses. *Psychological Science, 29*(4), 549–571. https://doi.org/10.1177/0956797617739704

Spellman, B. A. (2015). A short (personal) future history of revolution 2.0. *Perspectives on Psychological Science, 10*(6), 886–899. https://doi.org/10.1177/1745691615609918

Vazire, S. (2018). Implications of the credibility revolution for productivity, creativity, and progress. *Perspectives on Psychological Science, 13*(4), 411–417. https://doi.org/10.1177/174569 1617751884

Wagenmakers, E.-J., Beek, T., Dijkhoff, L., Gronau, Q. F., Acosta, A., Adams, R. B., … Zwaan, R. A. (2016). Registered replication report. *Perspectives on Psychological Science*, *11*(6), 917–928. https://doi.org/10.1177/1745691616674458

Wasserstein, R. L., & Lazar, N. A. (2016). The ASA's statement on p -values: Context, process, and purpose. *The American Statistician*, *70*(2), 129–133. https://doi.org/10.1080/000 31305.2016.1154108

Webb, T. L., & Sheeran, P. (2006). Does changing behavioral intentions engender behavior change? A meta-analysis of the experimental evidence. *Psychological Bulletin*, *132*(2), 249–268. https://doi.org/10.1037/0033-2909.132.2.249

Werner, K. M., & Milyavskaya, M. (2018). We may not know what we want, but do we know what we need? Examining the ability to forecast need satisfaction in goal pursuit. *Social Psychological and Personality Science*, *9*(6), 656–663. https://doi.org/10.1177/1948550617720274

Wong, P. (2011). Positive psychology 2.0: Towards a balanced interactive model of the good life. *Canadian Psychology*, *52*, 69–81.

Wood, W., & Rünger, D. (2015). Psychology of habit. *Annual Review of Psychology*, *67*(1), 289–314. https://doi.org/10.1146/annurev-psych-122414-033417

Yap, S. C., Wortman, J., Anusic, I., Baker, S. G., Scherer, L. D., Donnellan, M. B., & Lucas, R. E. (2017). The effect of mood on judgments of subjective well-being: Nine tests of the judgment model. *Journal of Personality and Social Psychology*, *113*(6), 939–961. https://doi.org/10.1037/pspp0000115

Glossary

Action tendencies   A component of emotions that refers to the motivation to do some things rather than others (e.g. flee or explore).

Active-constructive response   Following a capitalization attempt (i.e. sharing good news), this reaction involves showing interest and engagement and is associated with positive relationships.

Adaptation   Similar to the idea of the hedonic treadmill, it refers to the tendency for people to adjust to new circumstances; for example, it occurs when happiness returns to a baseline level following a major life event.

Affect (as a noun)   This term describes emotion-like phenomena, yet is generic, referring to feelings that differ in pleasantness, but without implying all aspects of an emotion

Affective forecasts   Mental assessments of future emotions or happiness; they help guide decisions, for example, when a person chooses an option that they believe will make them feel better than an alternative.

Agreeableness   One of the big five trait dimensions that includes trust, pro-sociality, cooperation, and modestly.

Altruism   This describes actions that benefit someone else, without clear personal benefit, or even at a potential cost to the actor; a subset of prosocial behaviours that are performed without conscious regard to potential personal benefits (though many accept a definition of altruism where some benefit may eventually accrue).

Anxious attachment   An attachment style (mental model) rooted in doubt and concerns that others will not be available when needed, and that produces excessive reassurance seeking and stifled exploration.

Appraisals   A component of emotions, the mental assessments of circumstances or interpreting things.

Attachment styles   Individual differences that are based in the mental models or expectations that people have about close relationships; commonly articulated as secure, anxious, and avoidant attachment styles.

Attachment theory   A set of propositions that describe how people develop mental models of close interpersonal relationships, and how these influence expectations and responses to new relationships, novelty, and threat; core ideas include three attachment styles: secure, anxious, and avoidant.

Authentic (authenticity)   Describes mental states or behaviours that are consistent with or expressions of a person's true self, as opposed to faked or coerced.

Autonomy   In self-determination theory, a basic need to pursue individual, intrinsic desires freely (vs pursuits influenced more by others).

Avoidant attachment   An attachment style (mental model) rooted in the belief that other people are unlikely to provide support when it is needed, and that produces extreme self-reliance and hampers intimacy.

Awe   An emotion that is elicited by perceiving things that are unexpected, profound, or amazing (e.g. extraordinary nature, childbirth, great music or art); it appears to generate cognitive change to accommodate this new information, prompts people to see themselves as part of something bigger, and promotes prosocial behaviours.

Basic emotion   One of a discrete set of feeling states; basic emotions meet specific criteria, such as having distinct physiology, expressions, experience, and so on which distinguish them from other affective states like moods.

Big five   A model or taxonomy of personality traits; 'big' refers to the breadth of each trait – they include many narrower facets; the big five traits are: extraversion, neuroticism, agreeableness, conscientiousness, and openness.

Biophilia   The notion that humans have an innate emotional attraction to other forms of life or healthy elements of nature, due to a long evolutionary history in natural environments.

Biophilic design   An approach to architecture that incorporates natural elements into built spaces to improve the aesthetic appeal and human well-being by creating a sense of connection with nature.

Broaden and build model   A theory about positive emotions which contends that they expand the scope of mental processes in the short term, which then facilitates accumulation of skills and resources in the future. This contrasts with the idea of specific action tendencies for negative emotions that narrow the scope of responses (e.g. flee, fight, or spit).

Capitalization   A jargon term that describes people sharing good news with others; it tends to enhance good feelings; psychologists also study how relational partners respond to capitalization attempts.

Commitment device   This is a goal pursuit strategy that draws on the good intentions people have before tempting moments to implement a change that makes later capitulation more difficult (e.g. deleting an overused app).

Common pool resource dilemmas   A type of social dilemma where some good (e.g. a natural resource) already exists, people can draw from that good and there is risk of depleting the good with overuse; also known 'take some' dilemmas or social traps.

Companionate love   A subtype of love that occurs in close relationships (i.e. in and beyond romantic), characterized by strong liking, respect, trust, and care; similar to the love-type *storge*.

Competence   In self-determination theory, a basic need to be capable and master new things.

Competitive altruism   This describes prosocial or generous acts where benefits to the actor are indirect, accruing via improvements to one's reputation; it occurs where reciprocity is unlikely (cf. reciprocal altruism) but is still considered an evolutionary adaptation due to the indirect benefits; also known as 'costly signalling'.

Conceptual replication   A type of study that re-tests the basic idea of another original study, but that intentionally changes the procedures in some way; the purpose of the procedure change is to ensure that the original finding is not due to idiosyncratic features of the particular method; often contrasted with direct replications.

Confounds   Similar to 'third variables' in the correlational approach, these are things that may be unintentionally manipulated beyond the focal independent variable in experimental studies.

Conscientiousness   One of the big five trait dimensions that includes achievement striving, self-control, orderliness, and dutifulness.

Convergent thinking   Often contrasted with divergent thinking, this is a mental process that solves problems in a linear or logical way with straightforward or single best answers.

Correlation coefficient   Abbreviated as r, it describes the strength and direction of association between two variables. The values of r can range from -1.0 to $+1.0$, with 0 indicating no association.

Correlational approach   A research or statistical method that focuses on determining whether, and how strongly, two things are linked.

Courage   In the VIA classification system, the broader virtue that includes emotional strengths that involve the exercise of will to accomplish goals in the face of opposition, external or internal.

Creativity   A characteristic involving novel ideas and products that have both uniqueness and usefulness.

Credibility revolution   A recent movement that includes changes in how (psychological) scientists conduct, report, and evaluate research, with reforms aimed at increasing the confidence of findings; it raises questions about how much we can trust past research in (positive) psychology.

Crystalized intelligence   Cognitive ability with the kinds of things taught explicitly in school, such as general knowledge and vocabulary; often contrasted with fluid intelligence.

Dependent variable   In the experimental approach, the outcome or thing that is (possibly) effected by the manipulation.

Dimensional perspective (on emotions)   A view that sees more subtle variations and fuzzy boundaries among affective states, compared to the distinct categories of the basic emotions view; it arranges emotional experiences in a conceptual space based on their similarities and differences.

Direct replications   A type of study that attempts to repeat the procedures of another original study as closely as possible; the purpose is to determine whether or not specific procedures reliably produce the same results. Also known as exact replications and contrasted with conceptual replications.

Dispositional authenticity A trait-like individual difference that refers to understanding and feeling and behaving like one's true self.

Divergent thinking A mental process that takes many paths to solutions, as opposed to a single logical path to one best solution; it is a key feature of creativity and often contrasted with convergent thinking.

Double-blind study A type of experiment where both the participant and the person administering the treatment (or experimental stimuli) do not know whether the participant is in an active or a control condition (e.g. drug or placebo); this reduces the possibility of bias and expectations influencing results.

Duchenne smiles A facial expression where both cheek and eye muscles contract, and that connotes genuine pleasant subjective experience; Duchenne smiles are contrasted with 'cheek only' smiles, which are easier to display voluntarily without actual positive feeling.

Duration neglect A phenomena where recollections of emotional experiences are insensitive to how long the experience lasted. Rather than all moments affecting memory evenly, the most intense and most recent moments exert more influence on memories.

Emotion traits Relatively stable individual differences in average emotional experiences over time (e.g. some people tend to experience more awe than others).

Emotional intelligence The abilities to perceive, understand, and regulate emotions adaptively; individual differences in emotional intelligence are less directly about the content of typical emotional experiences and more about the ability to recognize and use emotions well.

Emotions Feeling states that involve our physiology, thoughts, subjective feelings, motivation, expressions, and behaviour. During an emotion, (some of) these facets of bodily and mental activity seem to operate in concert.

Empathy–altruism model A set of propositions that posits that people sometimes help without regard to personal costs and benefits, and that this happens when they have empathetic concern for a person in need; most associated with psychologist Daniel Batson.

Essentialist view (of true self) A perspective that each person contains an immutable core (essence), a set of necessary defining features, or a singular true self.

Eudaimonia Synonymous with 'flourishing', a term that describes living a good life or psychological well-being; it can include things like living a virtuous life, authenticity, meaning, and personal growth; often contrasted with hedonia.

Experience sampling method A way of collecting data that includes many repetitions; normally used to track the ebb and flow of experiences/events in people's daily lives.

Experiencing self The subjective sense of self that feels things in the moment (often contrasted with the remembering self).

Experimental approach Typically contrasted with the correlational approach, it manipulates a variable and observes the manipulation's effect on a dependent variable, rather than merely observing the co-occurrence of two variables.

Experimental manipulation In the experimental approach, the way that one variable is changed for different participants; for example, instructing some participants to engage in prosocial spending, and others to spend on themselves.

Expressions A component of emotions referring to changes in the face (e.g. a smile), as well as in posture, tone of voice, and touch, and that has a communicative purpose.

Extraversion One of the big five trait dimensions, which includes sociability, high activity level, assertiveness, and cheerfulness; the opposite pole is commonly labelled introversion.

Extrinsic motivation A drive where there is some external pressure; often contrasted with intrinsic motivation, it covers a wide range from modest to extreme external influences, but is not completely self-determined.

Facets Relatively narrow personality traits. For example, the each of the broad big five traits contains narrower facets, such as trust, altruism, and sympathy as facets of agreeableness.

False positive A statistical term for when a test concludes that a finding/difference is true when it is, in fact, false.

Fixed mindset A subjective perspective where one believes that characteristics (e.g. ability, skill) are stable or inborn; also referred to as having entity theories, and contrasted with growth mindsets.

Flow A state of total absorption that occurs when a task's challenges are optimally fit to an individual's skill; a concept popularized by Mihaly Csikszentmihalyi.

Fluid intelligence Basic and abstract cognitive abilities, for example, processing speed and memory; often contrasted with crystalized intelligence.

Focusing illusion A reason for affective forecasting errors that occurs when people consider how much a future event or set of circumstances will influence their overall happiness and they weight that particular thing too much, ignoring other potentially important circumstances; also known as focalism.

Forest bathing A practice that involves mindfully interacting with a forest stroll and thought to promote health and relaxation; also known as *shinrin yoku* (in Japan).

Forgiveness In the context of a past transgression, it involves a shift in motivation, putting aside the transgression and wishing the offender well.

Fractal geometry A kind of mathematics that describes repeating patterns of self-similarity at different scales; these forms are common in nature and in attractive architecture.

Gallup World Poll (GWP) An annual survey begun by the Gallup organization in 2005 that samples the entire world and includes measures of well-being, among other things.

Goal-setting theory A set of propositions that describes which characteristics of goals produce optimal performance and why; it is typically applied in domains where goals are not entirely intrinsic, such as workplaces or schools.

Grit An individual difference related to persistence through difficulty; it is strongly associated with the big-five trait of conscientiousness.

Growth mindset A subjective perspective where one believes that characteristics (e.g. ability, skill) are malleable; also referred to as having incremental theories, and contrasted with fixed mindsets.

Habit A psychological and behavioural process where a cue (e.g. an environmental context or internal feeling) produces an automatic behavioural response.

Hedonia   An approach to defining happiness or well-being that focuses on pleasant feelings; often contrasted with eudaimonia.

Hedonic treadmill   Also known as adaptation, the idea that people's happiness tends to be stable, or will return to a baseline, even following major life events. Hedonic refers to the pleasantness of experience, and the treadmill implies that we are not really going anywhere.

Heritability   A numeric estimate of how much of a characteristic's variation in a group is due to differences in genes; it is inversely proportional to the amount of variation explained by differences in the environment.

Hope   Having or setting goals with clear strategies for achieving those goals, and the motivation to carry them out.

Humanity   In the VIA classification system, the broader virtue that includes interpersonal strengths that involve "tending and befriending" others.

Immune neglect   A reason for affective forecasting errors that occurs when people consider the impact of a negative event and fail to fully consider all the things they will do to successfully cope with it; the result is overestimation of the event's emotional impact.

Impact bias   A type of affective forecasting error that describes people's tendency to overestimate the intensity or duration of how much future events will change happiness.

Implementation intentions   These are concrete if–then plans that link specific circumstances with specific behaviours in service of a larger goal; they are an effective strategy for successful goal pursuit.

Inclusion of Other in Self (IOS) measure   A questionnaire used to assess intimacy where people indicate the degree of overlap between the self and a partner, each represented by a circle.

Independence   In relation to the self-concept, this is about seeing the self as unique and pursuing personal goals autonomously; North Americans and Western Europeans tend to have more independent self-concepts; often contrasted with interdependence.

Independent variable   In the experimental approach, the thing that is being manipulated.

Intelligence   An individual difference connoting cognitive ability or cleverness.

Interdependence   In relation to the self-concept, it is about seeing the self via social bonds, fitting into groups, and thereby considering others' wishes and social norms before acting. East Asians tend have more interdependent self-concepts; often contrasted with independence.

Intrinsic motivation   A drive where things are done for enjoyment, that are prompted by fully internal reasons, and that are endorsed by the true self; often contrasted with extrinsic motivation.

Intuitive prosociality   The idea or circumstances where humans' first impulses (i.e. easy or automatic) are generous, rather than selfish.

Jangle fallacy   This error occurs when thinking that two nearly identical things are different because they have different names (cf. the jingle fallacy).

Jingle fallacy   This error occurs when thinking that two actually different things are the same because they share a name (cf. the jangle fallacy).

Justice   In the VIA classification system, the broader virtue that includes civic strengths that underlie healthy community life.

Kin altruism   A form of prosocial behaviour where actions (benefits) are directed towards genetic relatives which, in turn, helps the actor propagate shared genes.

Latent inhibition   An automatic cognitive process whereby irrelevant information is blocked from consciousness or ignored.

Life satisfaction   An individual's subjective evaluation that things have gone well and that conditions are good.

Life stories   An element of personality that is unique to each individual, it is a personal narrative about the experiences and events that define the person.

Longitudinal studies   Studies that are conducted across at least two different points (days) in time, typically long-term studies over months and years.

Maximizing   A decision-making strategy where the very best choice is sought out with the cost of a lengthy search; often contrasted with satisficing.

Mental toughness   An individual difference related to resilience which includes aspects of self-efficacy, emotion regulation, attention regulation, and optimism.

Meta-analysis   A statistical approach to aggregating the results of many studies on the same topic; the goal is to average across the idiosyncrasies (or weaknesses) of individual studies and produce a reasonable estimate of the size of an effect.

Mindfulness   A mental state characterized by an engaged, yet non-judgemental, mindset where attention is focused on the immediate moment; sensations and reactions are observed as being present while self-relevant reactions (e.g. "this obstacle conflicts with my plans") are abandoned in favour of acceptance of the world the way it is.

Moods   Feeling states that are typically longer lasting (hours) and lack a clear subject or source, compared to emotions, which are shorter and usually more concretely about a particular thing.

Need for achievement   An individual difference in motivation for success; people high in need for achievement are driven by a deep desire to obtain excellence, and they tend to do well in business.

Neuroticism   One of the big five trait dimensions that includes tendencies to experience unpleasant emotions, self-consciousness, and vulnerability; the opposite pole is commonly labelled emotional stability.

Openness   One of the big five trait dimensions that includes imagination, liberalism, and interests in artistic, intellectual, and novel pursuits. Sometimes also called openness to experience, intellect, or culture.

p-hacking   A problematic practice in statistical analysis where researchers report only the choices/analyses that lead to $p < .05$ (statistical significance), ignoring other analyses that are less supportive of hypotheses.

Passionate love   A subtype of love that occurs in the context of romantic relationships and is primarily about intense (sexual) attraction; similar to the love type *eros*.

Perceived support   A subjective sense that social support (assistance) is or will be available if needed; this perception is contrasted with tangible received support.

PERMA   An acronym defined by Positive emotions, Engagement, Relationships, Meaning, and Accomplishment; positive psychology founder Seligman proposed these as the five key aspects of well-being, or ways of being happy.

Person–activity fit   In the positive-activity model, this is the degree of match between the intervention activity and the characteristics of an individual's personality and circumstances; in the model, more success comes from good fit.

Personal projects   These are the individual goals that people are working towards (both short and long term); they are unique to individuals, but are often assessed with ratings along common dimensions such as difficulty or support.

Personality   This refers to the individual, internal characteristics that produce regularities in thoughts, feelings, and actions, such as traits, values, and strengths.

Physiological changes   A component of emotions that occurs in the body (e.g. sweaty palms and racing hearts) and brain.

Positive interventions   Activities designed to foster a lasting improvement in well-being, and that are supported by empirical research; they focus on boosting happiness, rather than treat dysfunction per se.

Positive psychology   The parts of psychology that deal with (positive) experiences, dispositions, contexts, and processes, in individuals and groups, that facilitate well-being, achievement, and harmony.

Positive psychotherapy   Forms of psychological treatment that focus on personal strengths and positive activities, yet that use positive approaches to ultimately reduce dysfunction; typically, the approach adapts positive interventions designed for the general public to clinical populations.

Positive youth development   An intervention approach that focuses on building broad strengths in children, often in schools or via extra-curricular activities like sport; the focus is on building positives, rather than focusing on problematic behaviours.

Positive-activity model   A set of propositions that describes the important features of positive interventions (i.e. how they might be implemented), individual differences in how well they work, and the processes by which they increase well-being.

Positivity offset   This refers to people's tendency to approach the world with a somewhat pleasant affective state, optimism, and tendency towards positive evaluation (until contradicted by new information).

Post-ecstatic growth   Positive change following a major good event (cf. post-traumatic growth).

Post-traumatic growth   This describes the process whereby people find benefits (e.g. meaning, personal strength, new possibilities) following a traumatic experience. Also referred to by similar jargon terms like benefit finding, meaning making, adversarial growth, or stress-related growth.

Pre-registration   A step in research that involves recording a study's procedure and planned analyses online before data are collected (or analyzed); this record is made public and thus helps to reduce flexibility in analyses, clarifies the distinction between confirmatory and exploratory analyses, and makes it more difficult to hide a study with unsupportive results.

Press   This refers to the external influences on a person, and how those influences are perceived; press can trigger motivations or behaviours.

Prosocial behaviour   This refers to any actions that increase another's well-being, such as helping, sharing, or cooperation, even if such behaviours also clearly increase the actor's well-being; compare to altruism.

Prototype approach   A method for articulating the meaning of a concept or contents of a category; typically, research participants are first asked to list features (e.g. of love); then, in a second step, others rate how typical those features are.

Psychological well-being   This can refer specifically to the features of positive mental health listed by Carol Ryff (i.e. self-acceptance, positive relations with others, autonomy, environmental mastery, purpose in life, personal growth), or more generally to good mental health.

Psychophysiology   This involves the measurement of bodily functions like heart rate, electrodermal activity, finger temperature, and so on, to infer psychological processes such as emotions.

Public goods dilemmas   A type of social dilemma about creating a benefit that does not yet exist, where some people contribute resources to create a good, and if successful the good benefits everyone, regardless of individuals' contribution levels; also known as 'give some' dilemmas or social fences.

Publication bias   A phenomenon where studies' results influence whether or not they are communicated, for example via journal articles. Typically, the bias takes the form of favouring studies that indicate effective interventions or hypothesis-confirming results.

Qualitative methods   Typically contrasted with quantitative methods, they are less about putting numbers on phenomenon and broadly generalized findings and more about gathering rich, detailed, open-ended information from individuals.

Quantitative research (methods)   Typically contrasted with qualitative research, this is more about measuring in a way that allows for numeric comparisons and seeks to establish generalizable truths. These studies frequently compare large groups of people on dimensions that have been defined by the researchers (e.g. scores on a questionnaire) and draw conclusions from statistical tests.

Random assignment   The process whereby participants are sorted into the different groups of an experimental manipulation, such that each participant has an equal chance of being in each group. This helps ensure that the two groups are roughly equal in terms of the participants' average backgrounds, personalities, and so on.

Reasonable person model A set of propositions that asserts that reasonableness – described as being sensible, fair, moderate, and cooperative – is encouraged by environments that meet people's informational needs; in contrast, irritability, selfishness, impatience, and so on often stem from fatiguing circumstances and environments.

Received support In contrast to the belief of perceived support, this refers to actual tangible things that have been done or given by another person to assist someone in need.

Reciprocal altruism A form of prosocial behaviour where genetically unrelated people will help one another over time; it is considered an evolutionary adaptation because people who exchange favours and cooperate succeed more than those who do not.

Relatedness In self-determination theory, a basic need to feel connected and have good interpersonal relationships with close others.

Remembering self The mental object that recalls past experience, such as when completing a retrospective questionnaire about past emotions (often contrasted with the experiencing self).

Replication A hallmark of science, this is demonstrated when a study is repeated; when findings are true, replication studies will usually produce the same results.

Resilience This refers to people maintaining well-being despite difficult circumstances; some challenge must be present, and the extent of the well-being needed is proportional to the challenge; e.g. a small well-being reduction or a speedy recovery could still demonstrate resilience.

Responsiveness A behaviour or characteristic of a relationship partner that demonstrates understanding, care, and engagement with the partner's concerns; it is a hallmark of healthy relationships.

Satisficing A decision-making strategy where a reasonably good (but not perfect) option is chosen sooner rather than later; often contrasted with maximizing.

Secure attachment An attachment style (mental model) rooted in confidence that support will be available from close others when needed.

Self-compassion A self-view defined by three components: kindness towards the self, an awareness of common humanity, and a mindful approach to negative parts of the self.

Self-concept People's subjective sense of who they are, more about perceptions of reality than about objective reality per se; for example, individuals' beliefs about competence and worth define self-esteem, a part of the self-concept.

Self-determination theory This broad theory assumes that all humans are motivated by three basic growth needs: **competence**, **autonomy**, and **relatedness.** Pursuing these intrinsic needs produces more enduring motivation and satisfaction (cf. externally motivated pursuits).

Self-efficacy This is the personal belief that one can successfully enact behaviours that will lead to desirable outcomes. People have many different efficacy beliefs; they are typically separated for the particular domain or task at hand.

Self-enhancement The tendency to see oneself in a positive way, potentially even including distorting experience to maintain a positive view.

Self-esteem   A positive evaluation of the self; it is having a subjective sense of worth, competence, and personal satisfaction in valued domains.

Self-expansion theory   A set of propositions that describe an area of positive relationship behaviours; it suggests that people have a deep motivation to grow, that they experience enjoyment from these things, and that novel experiences in relationships promote satisfaction via this self-expansion.

Self-reference effect   This refers to people's ability to remember things better when they are associated with the self-concept; whether true of the self or not, simply considering things in relation to the self improves memory.

Signature strengths   The small handful of character strengths (i.e. positive traits) that are a particularly deep and intrinsic part of people; the strengths that feel strongest and most authentic.

Social dilemmas   Situations where individuals must choose between maximizing immediate personal benefit or contributing to collective well-being, and where the system breaks down unless enough people cooperate.

Social support   This refers to all the ways other people can provide assistance to another person in need, such as with advice, money, listening, hugs, favours, or influencing others.

Social Value Orientation (SVO)   An individual difference in the tendency to behave prosocially; three orientations are typically distinguished: prosocial, individualist, and competitive, and measures of these predict how people respond in social dilemmas.

State authenticity   The perception or feeling that one is currently behaving in accordance with the true self; it varies from moment to moment.

States   In contrast to the more enduring traits, these are the temporary variations in thoughts, feelings, and behaviours; they are short-term units that are more sensitive to the immediate context.

Strengths   Also known as character strengths, these are trait-like individual differences that are positive and widely valued. A list of strengths is articulated in the VIA classification of character strengths.

Subjective experience   A component of emotions that refers to one's personal, first-person, phenomenological feeling.

Subjective well-being   A jargon term for happiness; it is defined by three components: high life satisfaction, experiencing many pleasant emotions, and experiencing few unpleasant emotions.

Temperance   In the VIA classification system, the broader virtue that includes strengths that protect against excess.

Temptation bundling   This is a goal-pursuit strategy that involves combining an undesirable task with a (guilty) pleasure (e.g. listening to a favourite song only while cleaning dishes).

Third variable problem   In correlational research, this is one reason why the two correlated variables may not cause one another, i.e. because a 'third variable' is a common cause of both. (For example, ice cream sales and the number of people wearing short trousers are positively correlated, but both are caused by the 'third variable' of hot weather.)

Traits These are descriptive labels that refer to regularities in thoughts, behaviours, and feelings, and that differentiate among people. They are dimensions of difference such that one's score on a trait indicates similarity with some other people (who share the score) and difference from others (who do not). Traits can also be viewed as average tendencies over time.

Transcendence In the VIA classification system, this is the broader virtue that includes strengths that forge connections to the larger universe and provide meaning.

Trust The belief that another or others will respond in cooperative or mutually beneficial ways.

Validity A characteristic of measurement tools (e.g. questionnaires) that is present when the tool accurately assesses the intended construct; for example, it returns higher scores when more of that thing is present in the person being assessed.

VIA classification of character strengths A model that lists and organizes 24 strengths (i.e. positive trait-like individual differences) according to six broader virtues. VIA stands for 'values in action', but is rarely articulated in contemporary uses.

Virtues In the VIA model, six virtues are the higher order characteristics that encompass groups of the narrower 24 strengths (similar to how narrower facets make up broad big five traits).

WEIRD An acronym used to convey the idea that much research in psychology has focused on Western, Educated, Industrialized, Rich, and Democratic societies.

Wisdom (VIA version) In the VIA classification system, this refers to the broader virtue that includes cognitive strengths that entail the acquisition and use of knowledge. (See also the more general definition.)

Wisdom: A characteristic or tendency towards thinking in ways that include multiple perspectives and that recognize uncertainty; it includes knowledge about the pragmatics of life and a motivation to apply this beyond narrow self-interest; it is also the name for one of the VIA virtues.

Index